G. Michael Schneider

Macalester College, St. Paul, MN

Co-authors of the first edition:

Steven W. Weingart

Data General Corporation

David M. Perlman

Cray Research

Second Edition

AN INTRODUCTION TO PROGRAMMING AND PROBLEM SOLVING WITH PASCAL

John Wiley & Sons

New York   Chichester   Brisbane   Toronto   Singapore

To my wife, *Ruthann*, and my children, *Benjamin* and *Rebecca*

Library of Congress Cataloging in Publication Data

Schneider, G. Michael.
    An introduction to programming and problem
solving with PASCAL.

    Bibliography: p.
    Includes indexes.
    1. PASCAL (Computer program language)   2. Electron-
ic digital computers – Programming.   I. Weingart,
Steven W.   II. Perlman, David M.   III. Title.

QA76.73.P2S36   1982   001.64'24   82-2809
ISBN 0-471-08216-3   AACR2
ISBN 0-471-80447-9 pbk.

Printed in the United States of America

10 9

FOREWORD

The maturation of programming into an art or a science is characterized by our ability to abstract essential principles from particular cases. As fundamental concepts emerge, a notation is needed to express them. We have become accustomed to calling such a formal notation a "language." The better it is tailored toward expressing the essential abstractions, the better it is suited to introduce the subject of programming, because the more it can recede into the background. Ideally, the language presents itself as the natural notation to express the basic concepts of programming, and it should hardly need further attention and explanation.

Yet, in the design and analysis of algorithms, we are forced to express ourselves unusually exactly. This implies that we need a thorough mastery and precision in understanding our language. Is it therefore surprising that its details still consume a considerable amount of time in teaching the art of programming?

The language Pascal was developed in the late 1960s in recognition of the fact that the language used is of paramount importance in programming. The authors of this book have chosen Pascal as a vehicle, and they are able to concentrate on the fundamental principles of programming and problem solving. Nevertheless, the details of the language are given due attention, and they are clearly motivated. Consequently, they appear as rules that can be understood instead of merely being memorized. The book explains the style of programming that was the guiding idea in the design of Pascal. By explicitly motivating the principles of structured programming and the corresponding features of Pascal, it provides insight instead of merely coverage.

N. Wirth
Zürich, Switzerland August 1977

PREFACE

This textbook represents the culmination of my efforts to develop an introductory programming course that would reflect the growing concern for teaching the design and development of high-quality, reliable software. It follows closely the outline of the course entitled CS1, Computer Programming I, as described in ACM Curriculum '78. (*Communications of the ACM,* March, 1979.) Too often a student's introduction to programming has been through a service course where the major concern is the syntax of some elementary programming language, and the programs are graded solely on the basis of whether or not they produce correct results. Unfortunately, these service courses often instill and reinforce bad programming habits, and later attempts to "unlearn" them are usually futile. (In this respect it is interesting to note that the students who encounter some difficulty in the course are *not* the ones without prior programming experience, but those who have already had a low-level exposure to FORTRAN or BASIC. These students are forced into rethinking their approach to programming.)

It is incorrect to assume that beginning programming students are unable to handle "higher-level" concepts. I have found it both reasonable and worthwhile to present the topics of problem specifications and algorithm development, top-down modular programming, structured coding, and program testing along with details of a particular language. When these topics are introduced during the *initial* stages of learning, they instill good programming habits immediately. The results are solutions that are well thought out, programs that are well structured, and documentation of high quality. This is simply because our students have not been taught any other way. To them, it is the normal way of doing things.

This book has three goals; in order of importance, they are:

1. Introducing *all* aspects of the programming and problem-solving process, including problem specification and organization, algorithms, coding, debugging, testing, documentation, and maintenance.
2. Introducing what constitutes *good* programming style and how to produce a high-quality finished product. These points are brought out in numerous Style Clinics throughout the text.
3. Teaching the syntax of the Pascal programming language.

I have chosen to use Pascal as the programming language because it is an excellent language for introducing these concepts. However, I did not wish merely to replace a FORTRAN-based service course with a Pascal service course. Instead, I wanted to develop a textbook that uses Pascal as a *vehicle* to introduce a range of programming concepts. Although a large portion of this book is directed, of necessity, toward our third goal, this should be viewed in its proper perspective.

Chapters 1 and 2 introduce the student to the preparatory work that must be done prior to the coding phase—problem specification and algorithm development. Chapters 3, 4, and 5 introduce the basic elements of the Pascal language. In class I treat the syntactic details to these chapters quickly and prefer to concentrate on the stylistic aspects discussed in the text and in the style clinics. Chapter 6 discusses debugging, program testing, documentation, and maintenance. Chapters 7 to 10 introduce the remaining features of Pascal, including subprograms and advanced data structures. Again, in class the syntactic rules are covered quickly, and the conceptual and stylistic details are considered at greater length. Chapter 11, one of the most important chapters in the book, discusses techniques for developing and managing large ''real-world'' problems and writing quality programs. Sufficient time should be allowed to ensure that the material in that chapter is treated adequately.

This text is currently being used in a one-quarter introductory undergraduate computer science course at the University of Minnesoty and Macalester College. The students include both computer science and noncomputer science majors. This textbook assumes no prior programming experience or extensive mathematical background on the part of the student. The programming examples have been chosen to span a wide range of numeric and nonnumeric applications. In addition, I have avoided aspects of Pascal that might be specific to a particular computer system. Where machine-dependent details are required (e.g., control cards), I have referred the student to his or her instructor for the necessary information.

I would like to thank my coauthors on the first edition, Steven Weingart and David Perlman. Although they were unable to assist in the preparation of the second edition, I have borrowed freely from their original ideas and writings.

I also thank two people whose names do not appear on the front cover but who contributed significantly to the production of the book: Rajiv Kane, who helped to test the numerous programming examples in the book, and Sandy Whelan, who typed and proofread the final manuscript. I am grateful to the many referees whose excellent suggestions were so liberally used. Special thanks must go to Andy Mickel of the University of Minnesota Computer Center who reviewed the manuscript and initiated and encouraged my interest in Pascal as a language tool for teaching programming. Without the help of these people, this project would still be only an idea.

I sincerely hope that this book will contribute to an improvement in the quality of programming instruction and to the view of computer programming as a rational and organized discipline.

G. Michael Schneider

CONTENTS

STYLE CLINICS

Chapter 1

AN INTRODUCTION TO COMPUTER PROGRAMMING

1.1 INTRODUCTION

This book is about programming. However, that statement is not as simple as it may first seem. What we mean when we use that term, and what others mean, may be quite different. What we imply by the term *computer programming* is "the entire series of steps involved in solving a problem on a computer." Too often, however, the word *programming* has been used as a synonym for the word *coding*—the process of writing statements in some existing computer language. Classes that have purported to teach computer programming have frequently been nothing more than long litanies of syntactic do's and dont's for some specific language. The worst part of this approach is that it tends to reinforce the mistaken idea that the best technique for solving problems on a computer is to take a pencil and a piece of paper, begin writing a program, and keep writing until you are done. You then hope that you have produced a valid solution. Nothing could be further from the truth. An enormous amount of preparatory work must precede the actual coding of any potential solution. This preparation involves steps such as defining exactly what is wanted, clearing up any ambiguities or uncertainties in the statement of the problem, deciding how to solve it, and roughing out the outline of the solution in some convenient notation. In fact, if this preparatory work has been done well, the coding phase, which seems the most important to many people, becomes relatively straightforward and uncreative. It becomes simply the mechanical translation of the solution for a problem into grammatically correct statements of some particular language.

In addition, just as we must spend much time and effort before we code, we still have much to do after we have finished coding. We must then grapple with the problems of detecting and correcting errors, polishing the documentation, and testing, validating, and maintaining the program.

1

The point we are trying to make is that computer programming is an extremely complex task made up of many individual phases, all of which are important and all of which contribute to the solution of a problem. Do not confuse the concept of programming with any single phase (e.g., coding) to the exclusion of all others. We hope this explains why the first complete Pascal[1] program does not appear until the end of Chapter 4. When constructing your own programs, the Pascal coding should be preceded by a great deal of preparatory work clarifying, organizing, structuring, and representing your solution. Failing to understand this principle is the first and greatest mistake you can make when learning computer programming.

1.2   THE STEPS INVOLVED IN COMPUTER PROGRAMMING

In the introduction to this chapter we stressed that programming involves many steps. Let us be a little more specific and describe the actual steps involved.

1.   *Defining the Problem*. The inclusion of this step seems trivial. It is obvious that we must know exactly what we want to do before we can begin to do it. But this ''obvious'' phase is too often overlooked or omitted by programmers who begin their work on problems fraught with ambiguities and uncertainties. A clear understanding of exactly what is needed is absolutely necessary for creating a workable solution. The task of defining the problem will be discussed in the remaining sections of this chapter.

2.   *Outlining the Solution*. Except for the simplest of problems, a program will not be composed of a single task but of many interrelated tasks. For example, a computerized payroll system would most certainly not be viewed as a single program. Instead, it will probably contain several program units that validate input data, sort and merge files, compute and print paychecks, print output reports and error logs, and keep year-to-date information. On large projects that involve a number of programs and programmers, it becomes extremely important to specify both the responsibilities of each task and how these individual tasks interrelate and interact. This is to ensure that the pieces being developed separately are designed in the context of the whole.

   Of necessity, the early programs in this textbook are short and simple and composed of single tasks. For these programs the outlining phase can probably be neglected without severe complications. However, they should be viewed as ''toys'' being used for teaching purposes only. In later chapters we will be devoting a great deal of time to program development, program structure, and the management of large, real-world programming projects composed of many separate modules.

---

[1]Pascal is *not* an acronym and is therefore not written out in capital letters. The language was named in honor of the French mathematician and religious fanatic Blaise Pascal (1623–1667).

3. *Selecting and Representing Algorithms.* We have now specified the various tasks and subtasks required to solve our problem. For each task we know what information we will provide and what results we want to produce. But we have not yet specified *how* the program is to accomplish its stated purpose. An *algorithm* is the specific method used to solve a problem. The algorithm may be one already developed and published in the literature or one of our own creation and design. For reasons that we will discuss later, it is not a good idea to begin immediately coding the informal specifications of an algorithm directly into some existing programming language. Instead, it is advantageous to describe the details of the proposed solution in an algorithmic representation that is independent of any computer language or machine. In Chapter 2 we will discuss algorithms and their development. In addition, we will describe in detail one specific method of representing algorithms.

4. *Coding.* Only after unambiguously defining the problem, organizing a solution, and sketching out the step-by-step details of the algorithm can we consider beginning to code.

Your choice of which computer language to use will probably be dictated by three considerations.

1. The nature of the problem.
2. The programming languages available on your computer.
3. The dictates and limitations of your particular computer installation.

Some programming languages are general purpose; others are very specific for certain classes of problems. Some languages are very widely available; others can be run only on a very few computers. Figure 1-1 lists a few of the more common programming languages that you may encounter.

In this textbook we will employ the language called Pascal. It is a very elegant language, complex enough to introduce important concepts in computer programming but simple enough to be a good teaching tool in a course in computer programming. Chapters 3 to 5 and 7 to 10 will describe the correct use of the Pascal language. However, our concern is not merely to teach you how to use Pascal correctly but how to use it well. We will devote a great deal of effort to developing a set of guidelines to aid you in writing "good" programs. These guidelines, taken together, constitute a *programming style* and will be presented both in the text and in numerous *Style Clinics* throughout the book.

5. *Debugging.* The novice programmer quickly learns that a problem is far from solved once the program has been coded and run. We must still locate and correct all the inevitable errors. This is a time-consuming and often agonizing task. Section 6.3 provides some tips and guidelines to make debugging more manageable and less painful.

Language	Approximate Date of Introduction	General Application Areas
FORTRAN	1957	Numerically oriented language. Most applicable to scientific, mathematical, and statistical problem areas. Very widely used and very widely available.
ALGOL	1960	Also a numerically oriented language but with new language features. Widely used in Europe.
COBOL	1960	The most widely used business-oriented computer language.
LISP	1961	Special-purpose language developed primarily for list processing and symbolic manipulation. Widely used in the area of artificial intelligence.
SNOBOL	1962	Special-purpose language used primarily for character string processing. This includes applications such as text editors, language processors, and bibliographic work.
BASIC	1965	A simple interactive programming language widely used to teach programming in high schools and colleges.
PL/1	1965	An extremely complex, general-purpose language designed to incorporate the numeric capabilities of FORTRAN, the business capabilities of COBOL, and many other features into a single language.
APL	1967	An operator-oriented interactive language that introduced a wide range of new mathematical operations that are built directly into the language.
Pascal	1971	A general-purpose language designed specifically to teach the concepts of computer programming and allow the efficient implementation of large programs.
Ada	1980	A new systems implementation language designed and built for the Department of Defense.

Figure 1-1. Survey of some widely used computer languages.

6. *Testing and Validation.* Getting results from a program is not enough. We must guarantee that they are the correct results. Furthermore, we must try to convince ourselves that the program will, indeed, produce correct results in

all cases, even those that have not been explicitly tested. Section 6.4 discusses the testing and validating of computer programs.

7. *Documenting*. The documentation of a program is a continual process. The program specifications from step 1, the algorithmic representation from step 3, and the program itself from step 4 can all be considered part of the documentation of a program. However, after successfully completing the program, we must ensure that our documentation is complete and in a finished, usable form. This includes both *technical documentation* for the programmers who may be working with and modifying the completed program and *user-level documentation* for the users of the program. Section 6.5 contains guidelines and standards for both levels of documentation.

8. *Program Maintenance*. As you will be discovering, this textbook is concerned with effective communication between persons, not just communication between a person and a computer. This will be evident from our treatment of topics such as program clarity, program readability, and documentation. This concern is caused by the fact that programs are not static entities. They frequently become outdated as errors are discovered, new problems need to be solved, or new equipment becomes available. Programs written weeks, months, or even years ago will frequently need to be reviewed, understood, and then modified by someone else. Unless we are careful to document what we have done and write our programs clearly, systematically, and legibly, this step can be frustrating or even impossible. Even if we always maintain our own programs we may find that time has dimmed our memories and that we require the same high-quality documentation as anyone else. Because the best possible documentation is simply a clearly written, well-organized, and well-structured program, we can in a sense say that this entire textbook is devoted to facilitating the continuing task of program maintenance.

Finally, we should stress that the programming process just described is not as linear as these eight steps may lead you to believe. Most of these steps overlap each other; for example, documentation will be written continually during program development. Many of these steps will have to be repeated; for example, as debugging uncovers errors, we will go back to recode portions of our program or to rethink the solution. The point of this discussion was simply to show that programming is a complex job. It is easy to become a good *coder;* reading this textbook and learning the rules of Pascal should accomplish that. Your goal should be a higher one: to become a good *programmer*, someone who understands and can manage the entire spectrum of programming responsibilities. However, in this fuller sense of the word, programming cannot be passively taught but must be actively learned through practice and experience. When accomplished, however, it is a much more creative and rewarding experience.

1.3   THE PROBLEM DEFINITION PHASE

The *problem definition phase* involves developing and clarifying the exact specifications of the problem. In short, we must find out exactly what we are supposed to do. Because this is such an obvious step, many programmers skip it entirely and neglect to think about and understand the problem they are attempting to solve. As a result, they frequently begin to develop a program with an ill-defined and ill-conceived statement of the problem. This can lead to confusion, uncertainty and, worst of all, an incorrect solution.

Another reason that the problem definition phase is often handled poorly by programmers is that this topic tends to be slighted both in programming textbooks and in classroom instruction. This slighting becomes obvious when we view the way in which programming assignments are usually presented in a learning environment. The problem definition phase is done independently of the student, either by the teacher or the author. A well-defined problem is neatly typed onto a sheet of paper, copied, and presented to the student. It states explicitly something such as the following: "You are to input values for A, B, and C, perform operations I, J, and K, and produce results X, Y, and Z." The student is rarely bothered by or concerned with nagging questions such as "Where did we get the values A, B, and C?" "Why did I pick operations I, J, and K over the alternatives L, M, and N?" "What if it should become impossible for me to successfully complete operation I?" "Don't you think we should also present the user with the value of W?" If these questions are important, they will have already been addressed and answered by others. Students do not get to treat them as part of the programming assignment. They do only what the handout specifies.

Of course, in "real life" (a term we will use frequently to refer to the way things happen outside a classroom environment), problems are rarely so well defined and unambiguous. On the contrary, it is not at all uncommon for people to describe problems in terms that are ill defined, ambiguous, and virtually useless in their initial form. Often the originator of the problem is not a programmer and has had little or no experience working with computers and understanding their capabilities and limitations. From that point of view it would be perfectly natural and understandable for a person in the business world to pose problems in the following loose forms.

Can your computer help us with our inventory control problem?

I sure would like to automate our payroll and accounting system. We have six secretaries who do nothing all day but type paychecks and produce federal and state tax reports.

Can we put computer terminals in all our warehouses so that order processing can be automated?

Likewise, the scientist might suggest the following problems.

> *Can your computer reduce this mountain of experimental data to something I can manage?*
>
> *Could we write a program to look at X-rays and automatically locate malignancies?*
>
> *I would like to create a simulation model of the ecosystem of a freshwater Minnesota lake.*

To the experienced programmer, all of these represent valid application areas of computers, but all are much too vague to form the basis of potential solutions. How do we proceed?

We need a dialogue with the problem originator to work mutually toward a clearer understanding of exactly what is wanted. By thinking and rethinking the problem and discussing the capabilities of a computer, we will clarify the problem and make it take shape. Where options exist, the alternatives must be presented and a rational choice made.

What will ultimately result from these interactions is a set of written *problem specifications* that spell out in clear, unambiguous language the exact problem we are attempting to solve. These problem specifications will contain three important classes of information. Although these classes need not be itemized and discussed separately, all the following must be included.

1. *Input Specifications*. This section describes the input to the program. This should include answers to the following questions.
   (a) What specific values will be provided as input to the program?
   (b) What format will the values be in (order, spacing, accuracy, units)?
   (c) For each input item, what is the valid range of values that the input may assume?
   (d) What restrictions (if any) are placed on the use of these values? May we modify the input? May we discard the input when we are done?
   (e) How will we know when we have exhausted the input? Will there be a special symbol or will we have to determine that for ourselves?

2. *Output Specifications*. Just as we needed to specify the input provided to the program, we must describe in detail the output that will be produced. The output specifications must include answers to the following types of questions.
   (a) What values will be produced?
   (b) What is the format of these values (significant digits, decimal accuracy, units, and location on the page)?

(c) What specific annotation, headings, or titles are required in the finished report?

(d) Is there any indication as to the amount of output that will be produced? (This will guide us in making intelligent choices among alternative methods. A technique satisfactory for handling 10 items may be useless when used with 10 million items.)

Typically, one of the most effective ways to present output specifications is simply to show a detailed example of the output reports that the program will be producing.

3. *Special Processing.* If everything were to progress smoothly we probably would have all the information we need to go on to the next phase of programming. However, as you are probably aware, that rarely happens. As Murphy's Law states, "If something can go wrong, it will." In a problem specification document it is important that we itemize special conditions that must be checked and that we specify the recovery action to take if such a condition does occur. These special conditions could be considered as either unusual circumstances that require unique handling or as errors that require correction and recovery. In either case, any possible variations from the norm should be included in the written specifications of the problem. These special processing details are most frequently overlooked and omitted in problem specification documents.

The input, output, and special processing specifications represent the most important information collected during the problem definition phase. However, you may be wondering why we have omitted one of the most fundamental parts of any problem-solving process—the *method* of solution. We have been very careful to specify in detail what we have to start with and what we wish to end up with, but we have given no indication about *how* we are to accomplish this task.

This omission was done consciously. The detailed, step-by-step specification of the algorithms used to solve a problem is usually not part of the written specifications. There are good reasons for this. Most users do not care about how we obtain the answers as long as they are correct and we do not spend too much computer time. In addition, if we specify too early the low-level details of how an operation must be performed, we lock the programmer into the use of that specific technique. He or she now lacks the flexibility to pick and choose what may be the best technique for solving a particular problem within some particular environment. For example, some techniques work very well on large programs, while others do not. Some techniques may be very easy to implement but are inherently inefficient. The programmer should be relatively free to evaluate the needs of the user and choose the most appropriate technique.

This clear separation between problem definition and algorithms may not always exist in a classroom environment. There the problem definition will frequently contain both the problem specifications and a requirement of which algorithm must be used to solve the problem. Usually this choice has been made to teach the student a particular programming concept or because it is the only technique the instructor feels the student will be able to manage.

In real life this is rarely the case. The problem originator is concerned only with getting the desired results and not with how we achieve them, as long as the finished program is not grossly inefficient. Once we have produced a mutually satisfactory written problem specification, we are free to choose the algorithm that best solves the stated problem. Methods for choosing and representing computer algorithms and criteria for comparing their efficiency constitute the second phase of the problem-solving process and will be discussed in Chapter 2.

To give you some experience in program development, some of the later programming exercises in this book have intentionally been left incomplete. These exercises can be recognized by the parenthesized comments following the problem statement. These comments hint at important details purposely omitted. For these omissions there are no single right answers or correct approaches. You will have to list and evaluate whatever alternatives there seem to be and choose what you feel is the most reasonable solution.

Style Clinic 1-1 _____

Think First, Code Later

Henry Ledgard, in *Programming Proverbs* (Hayden Book Co. Inc., 1975), stated an interesting corollary to Murphy's Law that he called Murphy's Law of programming. Stated simply, it says: "The sooner you start coding your program, the longer it is going to take." Although the truth of this maxim has not been formally proved, personal experiences have more than borne out its correctness. Trying to write anything but the simplest of programs without a well-organized solution outline is like building a house with hammer, nails, and lumber but no blueprints. Chaos soon follows.

Think first, think second, think some more, and only then begin to write your program.

1.4 EXAMPLES

1.4.1 Table Look-Up

Let us use as our first example a very simple yet very important problem in computer programming—*table look-up*. This particular application does not usually occur as a separate and complete problem in its own right but as a single task within a much larger programming project. For example, in a payroll system we may need to look up an employee's pay rate in a pay rate table; in a language translation program we may need to look up a word in a dictionary list to find its equivalent in another language; finally, in a typical criminal justice application, we might need to look up a license plate in a list of stolen automobiles.

The problem is usually phrased in a form something like the following.

> *Given a list of values, along with one special value that we wish to find, look through the list and print out whether or not that special value occurs anywhere within the list.*

That simple problem statement might seem fairly clear. However, if we apply the criteria discussed in the preceding section, we find that it is actually an extremely poor and unacceptable description of the table look-up problem. All of the following questions have been left unanswered:

> *Given a list of values, along with one special value . . .*

1. What specific type(s) of values are contained in the list?
2. Do we know how many elements are in the list?
3. What type of value is the special value?
4. What is the range of values that the items in the list may assume?
5. Can there be duplicates in the list?

> *. . . print out whether or not that special value occurs anywhere within the list.*

6. Exactly what message do we want to produce if the value is found?
7. Exactly what message do we want to produce if the value is not found?
8. Do we want any other information printed in addition to one of the preceding two messages?

The answers to all of these questions will have to be provided.

If we use the stolen automobile problem as a specific example, we might find that discussions with knowledgeable authorities have led us to a problem statement of the type shown in Figure 1-2a.

This problem statement is considerably more formal than the previous one and represents a significant improvement. However, even this problem statement is far from complete. It is ambiguous about certain situations. Reread the specifications in Figure 1-2a and you will see that they neglect to specify what we should do in the following circumstances.

You will be given a variable length table of six-character license plate identifiers in the following form.

Characters 1, 2:   A-Z
Characters 3, 4, 5, 6:   0-9

The last license plate in the list will be the special value "AA0000" and is used solely to mark the end of the list.

You will also be given one single key value that will be in the same format as the table entries.

Develop a program that determines whether the key value occurs anywhere within the table. If it does occur, print the following message.

plate no. "ccnnnn" reported stolen

If it does not occur, produce the following message.

plate no. "ccnnnn" not reported stolen

Figure 1-2a. First refinement of the problem description.

1. The key value we are searching for is in an incorrect format. For example, the license plate ABC123.
2. The key value occurs more than once in the table. Do we find just the first occurrence or all occurrences?
3. Do we stop after processing a single key value or will there be a number of different keys?
4. Will the table be directly available or must we read it from some input device?

(There are numerous other questions we would have to address in an actual system. How are new numbers added to the list, how do we remove numbers once the automobiles are found, and what about the other information that we would need such as names, dates, and places? We will not bother with all these questions now.)

Valid answers to the preceding questions must be determined through discussions of the valid alternatives. For example, the problem of handling invalid data could be resolved simply by adding the following statement.

If the key value does not conform to the specified format for license plate entries, produce the following message.

cccccc
invalid format — please check and re-enter

Skip the remainder of the processing phase for this data case.

The second problem, that of multiple entries, has a greater number of alternatives.

The correct one would simply be the one that gives the police the information they wanted. One possibility would be to modify the previous specifications to read as follows.

Write a program to find every *occurrence of the key value within the list. If there has been at least one such occurrence, produce the following message.*

   plate no. "ccnnnn" reported stolen "nn" times

where "nn" is the total number of occurrences of the designated license plate in the list.

The complete specifications for this problem are shown in Figure 1-2*b*.

You will be given a data set in two distinct parts. The first part is a master list of license plate numbers of stolen automobiles. Each data item contains one six-character license plate identifier in the following format.

   Columns 1, 2:   A-Z
   Columns 3, 4, 5, 6:   0-9

The last license plate number in the list is the special value "AA0000" and is used solely to mark the end of the list. The entire list is currently stored on a magnetic tape file labeled PLATES.

The second part of the data set is on punched cards and contains license plates in the same format as the list just described. If this data set contains an entry in an improper format, produce the following message:

   cccccc
   improper format—please check and re-enter

and omit the processing of that item.

Develop a program that will input a license plate number from a punched card and locate *all* occurrences of that number in the master list. If the license plate never occurs in the master list, produce the following message.

   plate no. "ccnnnn" not reported stolen

If the number appears at least once in the master list, produce the following message:

   plate no. "ccnnnn" reported stolen "nn" times

where "nn" is the total number of occurrences of the license plate in the master list.

Repeat this process for every data card provided and then halt.

Figure 1-2b. Problem specifications for the table look-up program.

Contrast the final problem statement in Figure 1-2*b* with the initial one given on p. 10. What has resulted from this development is a clear, unambiguous statement of the problem that we will be solving. The input that is required and the output that will be produced are clearly stated. If the statement as written in Figure 1-2*b* is not acceptable, it is very easy to change at this stage. If the statement is acceptable, it will form the basis for the next stages of program design. In either case, it is extremely important to have such a complete specification.

The development of a computer algorithm for actually performing the table lookup operation described here will be shown in Chapter 2.

1.4.2 Statistical Comparisons

Assume that we were approached by an English instructor with the following problem. The instructor would like to know if the students who do well on the midterm examination always do well on the final exam, or are there a significant percentage of students who have learned significantly more (or less) and whose performance on the final differs markedly from the first exam. The scores on both exams are available in the instructor's record book but, because there are over 200 students in the class, it would be difficult to do the operations manually. The instructor would like some type of comparison between the performances on the two examinations to use as a guide to plan for the next semester. When we inquire further about this "measure" and what it should be, the instructor claims to be totally unfamiliar with and untrained in the area of statistics and cannot help us. If we are also not trained in statistics, we must seek out a third party—a competent statistician.

After we describe our problem, the statistician states that it sounds as though we want a *correlation*—a statistical measure of the relationship between pairs of values. Furthermore, the statistician states that we can either correlate the raw scores themselves, in which case we end up with what is called a *correlation coefficient,* or we can correlate the rankings of the scores (e.g., third best on the midterm, fifth best on the final) and get a *rank correlation coefficient*. In simple terms, the implications of using each measure are described to us.

We can now go back to the problem originator with a choice of techniques and the criteria needed to make an intelligent choice. Assume that, after listening to the alternatives, the instructor decides the rank correlation coefficient is what is really wanted. We explain that this coefficient is a numerical value that will range between -1 and $+1$. Values at the extremes represent a very high degree of relationship between the two sets of scores, and values near zero represent little or no relationship. For example, if every student's rank on the midterm examination were identical to his or her rank on the final, the rank correlation coefficient would be exactly $+1.0$. If every student's performance on the midterm were totally unrelated to his or her performance on the final (an unlikely situation), the rank correlation coefficient would be near 0.000. For a more formal interpretation of the significance of this numerical coefficient, the instructor will need to go to a handbook on statistics. We plan to provide only the numerical value.

This initially seems unacceptable to the instructor, who does not want to be bothered doing statistical interpretations. The instructor had originally thought that our program would produce a numerical measure and also interpret its meaning by producing one of the following messages.

extremely significant relationship
very significant relationship
significant relationship
little relationship
no relationship
cannot determine

Our own experience with computers and programming, however, warns us that this type of qualitative decision making will not be easy. It might require as much programming effort as all the rest of our work combined. If the interpretation of the results is performed manually, we can save a great deal of programming effort, and the instructor can maintain greater control over the interpretation process. After numerous discussions about this, the instructor agrees (reluctantly) to a program producing a single rank correlation coefficient, which the instructor will interpret.

At this point in the problem specification, we can also get the detailed formats of the examination scores in the instructor's grade book and begin writing the input specifications for the problem. After looking in the grade book, we realize that we have encountered another problem; some students were excused from taking one or both of the examinations. We cannot merely leave the score blank or enter a 0 because 0 represents a valid (although poor!) score and could ruin the computations. We could simply omit from the data any student not taking both exams. However, the instructor tells us that a listing of all students who did not take one or both examinations is also needed. We decide to use the special value -1 to indicate that a student did not take an examination. Since a -1 cannot possibly be a valid examination score, we can distinguish between a student taking or not taking an examination. This should allow us to produce correctly the information desired.

We now go back one last time to the statistician to say that we have chosen one of the suggested techniques. The statistician gives us a good formula for computing this value and, in addition, warns us about a potential pitfall—the problem of ties. We will be assigning ranks to scores. We will need a policy on how to assign ranks to tie scores. There are at least four ways to handle this.

Score	Rank	Score	Rank	Score	Rank	Score	Rank
100	1	100	1	100	1	100	1
95	2	95	2	95	2	95	2.5
95	3	95	2	95	2	95	2.5
85	4	85	3	85	4	85	4
(1)		(2)		(3)		(4)	

Our own experience with ties (primarily in sports, not statistics) would probably have led us to choose method (2) or (3), assigning the highest rank to all tie scores. However, the statistician warns us that to get the most accurate results we must use method (4), assigning the *average* of all tie rankings to the tie scores. We agree to do that.

We are finally in a position to draw up a formal set of written problem specifications that defines the problem we will be solving. They are shown in Figure 1-3 on the next page. (This problem is solved in Chapter 11.)

This example, much more so than the previous one, illustrates the time and effort involved in developing adequate problem specifications. In this example we used the services of three people: the problem originator and the programmer as before but, in addition, a specialist in a particular application area. We had numerous conferences and extracted compromises when difficult decisions had to be made. But, again, it was worth it because we ended up with a clear, concise, unambiguous problem specification statement that is acceptable to all parties concerned. How much better to spend the time now to make sure that we are doing what we are supposed to do than to find out after additional work has been done. It is easy to make changes now but much more difficult once the program has begun to be "cast."

1.5 CONCLUSION

In a learning environment, most problems will be presented in a well-defined form of the type shown in Figure 1-2b or Figure 1-3. This does not mean that the problem definition phase has been omitted or neglected. Instead it has been done for you. Someone (the instructor, the author) has had to carry out the operations described in this chapter. He or she has had to work from an initial ill-conceived and "rough" idea of the problem to the formalized, detailed, complete problem specification document given to you as a programming assignment. However, even though this step may often be done by someone else, problem specification is a critically important phase in the overall programming process and one that you should always be aware of. Get into the habit early of looking closely and critically at problem statements, even those that may appear to be thorough and complete. If there are any ambiguities or omissions, clear them up, through discussions with the problem originator, *before* you begin the next phase of programming described in the next chapter.

EXERCISES FOR CHAPTER 1

[An asterisk (*) means that the answer to this question is contained in the Selected Answers to Exercises at the end of the text.]

1. For each of the following general problem areas develop a thorough, complete, and unambiguous problem specification document. Assume that you are the problem originator and can select the proper alternatives for your needs.

Exercises continued on page 17

You will be given a series of data lines, each containing three values separated by one or more blank spaces. The first value is a student identification number. It will be a six-digit integer. The next two values are examination scores. They correspond to the scores of that student on the midterm and final examinations. Both values must be integers in the range 0 to 100. If a student did not take either examination, a value of −1 is entered in the proper place. If either (or both) of the scores is invalid or missing, discard both scores and do not use those values in the following computation. The end of the data will be denoted by a student identification number of 000000.

Develop a program to input the preceding values and compute a rank correlation coefficient among all valid scores. Ties will be handled by assigning to the tie scores the average of all tie rankings. The program will produce as output the following reports.

REPORT 1—CORRELATION REPORT
THE FOLLOWING STUDENTS HAD TWO LEGAL SCORES AND WERE INCLUDED IN THE COMPUTATION

STUDENT ID	MIDTERM SCORE	RANK	FINAL SCORE	RANK
nnnnnn	xxx	xx.x	xxx	xx.x
nnnnnn	xxx	xx.x	xxx	xx.x
.	.	.	.	.
.	.	.	.	.
.	.	.	.	.
nnnnnn	xxx	xx.x	xxx	xx.x

nnn   LEGAL SCORES
±n.nnn   RANK CORRELATION COEFFICIENT

The program will also produce an error report with the '*' character used to indicate a score that is missing or in error.

REPORT 2—ERROR LOG
THE FOLLOWING STUDENTS HAD ONE OR MORE SCORES MISSING OR IN ERROR AND INDICATED BY '*'; THEY WERE NOT USED IN THE PRECEDING COMPUTATION

STUDENT ID	MIDTERM SCORE	FINAL SCORE
nnnnnn	xxx *	xxx
nnnnnn	xxx	xxx *
.	.	.
.	.	.
.	.	.
nnnnnn	xxx *	xxx *

mm   IMPROPER SCORES
nn   STUDENTS OMITTED

Figure 1-3. Problem specifications for the statistical correlation program.

*(a) Compute the mean, standard deviation, and range on a set of test scores.

(b) Find the root of a function $f(x)$. The root is the point x such that $f(x) = 0$.

(c) Count the number of times the word ''Pascal'' appears in some English language text.

(d) Merge two lists a and b, sorted into descending order, into a single list c, also in descending order.

(e) Compute weekly take-home pay from daily time cards.

2. For each of the following general problem areas discuss some possible ''special processing'' circumstances. That is, describe the abnormal situations that should probably be included in the problem specification document and suggest a recovery mechanism to handle them.

*(a) Determine whether an integer value, k, is a prime number.

(b) Compare two text strings a and b to see if they are identical.

(c) Compute the roots of a quadratic equation using the quadratic formula:

$$r = \frac{-b \pm \sqrt{b^2 - 4ac}}{2a}$$

(d) Sort a list of N integer values into increasing numerical sequence.

(e) Multiply two matrices M_1 and M_2 to produce a result matrix M_3.

*3. Discuss the following problem statement in terms of what information is missing or inadequate in order for the problem to be fully defined. Make some assumptions about the missing information and rewrite the specification so it meets the standards described in this chapter.

Write a program to compute a weekly paycheck for an employee from a set of five time cards. Each time card contains two values—the time the worker arrived and the time he or she left. The five cards correspond to the five working days in the week. From these cards determine the total number of hours worked this week. The data set of each employee also includes an employee master card that contains the employee's name, social security number, and hourly pay rate. Compute this worker's gross pay by paying the regular hourly rate for the normal hours worked and time-and-a-half for overtime. When you have completed the computation, write out a pay-stub containing the name, social security number, and gross pay for the employee. Then go on to the next employee and continue until you are done.

Chapter 2

ALGORITHMS

2.1 INTRODUCTION

The most fundamental concept in computer science is the *algorithm*. Informally, we can view an algorithm as a way to solve a problem, as a set of directions, or as a recipe that tells us exactly how to go about getting desired results. We work with algorithms all the time, although we are not often so formal as to call them that. The set of instructions that tells us how to put a tricycle together from its component parts, the procedures for going through college registration, and the recipe for making an apple pie are all probably examples of valid algorithms. Even the following directions taken from a shampoo label could be called a "shampooing algorithm."

1. Wet hair.
2. Lather.
3. Rinse.
4. Repeat.

(However, because it does not conform in some respects to the definition of an algorithm, it is actually invalid.)

More formally, we will define an *algorithm* as an ordered sequence of well-defined and effective operations that, when executed, will always produce a result and terminate in a finite amount of time.

By "ordered sequence" we mean that after the completion of each step in the algorithm, the next step is unambiguously defined. We must always know exactly where to look for the next instruction. The ordering could, for example, be specified by numbering the steps with the positive integers and following the sequencing rule.

> *Unless told to do otherwise or unless we are at the last step, upon completion of step i go on to step (i + 1); i = 1, 2, . . .*

Alternatively, the ordering could be implied by position. Upon completing the operation on line i, we execute the operation written on the line just below—(i + 1). Since we will sometimes not wish to follow the assumed sequence of steps, some steps in our algorithms may say, in effect, "Do not go on to step (i + 1); instead, do step k." Regardless of how we phrase the instruction, our identification of the next step must be completely unambiguous. One problem with the "shampooing algorithm" is that step 4 defines the next step ambiguously. We cannot tell which of the preceding steps are to be repeated.

Inherent in the concept of a sequence of operations is the idea of a beginning and an end. An algorithm must always have one clearly understood starting point and one or more clearly understood ending points. The starting point can be implied—we usually assume that we are to start at step 1—or it can be stated explicitly (one step may be labeled START). More than one starting point would create ambiguity about where to start, violating the ordering condition just stated. However, it is perfectly acceptable to identify one or more of the steps in the algorithms as *terminators*—steps that, when executed, terminate execution of the entire algorithm. The reason for this is that frequently a problem can be divided into two or more disjoint sections, depending on the particular value being processed. However, regardless of which section we execute, we wish to stop after completing that section.

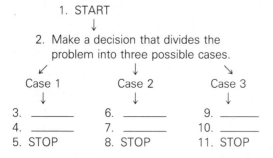

This outline contains a single clearly identified starting point (step 1) and three clearly defined terminators (steps 5, 8, and 11). The set of steps executed will always be either (1, 2, 3, 4, 5), (1, 2, 6, 7, 8), or (1, 2, 9, 10, 11).

The existence of one or more terminators, however, is insufficient to guarantee that execution will actually stop. This trivial (and, from a programming point of view, awful) set of operations

.

.

.

5. go to step 7
6. STOP
7. go to step 5

.

.

.

makes that fact quite obvious. To have a valid algorithm, we must guarantee that, regardless of the data we select, executing the algorithm from the beginning will eventually cause us to execute one of the terminators and thereby halt. We should not, however, confuse the term "eventually" with terms such as "quickly" or "efficiently." All we are saying is that the algorithm will always terminate after a finite number of steps. It is theoretically unimportant whether that number is 1 or 10^{10000}. Practically, of course, we may reject a valid algorithm that takes too much time because it is impractical or inefficient. For example, an exhaustive search algorithm of all chess games possible from a given board position can be formally specified, but it would take about 10^{40} years to work through a game at current machine speeds. Furthermore, the algorithm must terminate in a finite time for any arbitrary set of data, regardless of how pathological.

The last fundamental characteristic of algorithms is that each individual operation must be both "effective" and "well defined." By "effective" we mean that some formal method must exist for carrying out that operation and getting an answer. For example,

- Compute n + 1.
- Determine if x is odd.
- Wait 1 hour and 17 minutes.
- Take the square root of two to three decimal place accuracy.
- Proceed to Room 1234.

are all effective operations, and we could easily carry out all of them. However,

- Compute n ÷ 0.
- Determine the largest prime number.
- Write out the exact value for the square root of 2.
- Wait −1 hour.
- Find out if there is or is not a god.

are not effective. They either cannot be evaluated or we have no idea how to go about answering them.

Second, each individual operation must be "well defined"—clearly understandable and totally unambiguous to the person or machine executing the algorithm. A basic question about algorithms concerns the type of well-defined operations we are allowed to write at each step. That is, what are the building blocks from which we can compose an algorithm? These building blocks, usually referred to as *primitives,* will change with the level of sophistication displayed by that person or machine. For example, the following is a possible recipe for apple pie.

1. Make the crust.
2. Make the apple filling.
3. Place the filling inside the crust.
4. Bake at 375° F for 30 minutes.

This might be acceptable to a person familiar with pie making; however, steps 1 and 2 would probably be unclear and ambiguous for the majority of people with no baking experience. For these people those two steps would not be considered acceptable baking primitives. Operations such as

MIX x INTO y

MEASURE x units OF ingredient

STIR x

COOK x AT y° for z minutes

COOK x UNTIL condition

whose meaning is less ambiguous to most people would be more realistic examples of cooking primitives. However, even these simple statements may not be acceptable primitives if there is any ambiguity or uncertainty about their meaning. For example, does COOK mean bake, broil, fry, or grill?

We can now define *primitive operations* more formally. They are the most sophisticated and complex operations that the person or machine executing the algorithm is capable of directly understanding and performing and that do not have to be broken down into more basic steps. One of the major purposes of the next section will be to develop an acceptable and adequate set of primitive commands that we can use in developing computer algorithms.

In summary, an algorithm is a procedure for performing a particular task. The procedure must have the following characteristics.

1. Upon completing the execution of each step, we will always know the identity of the step to be executed next.
2. There is a single clearly defined starting point and one or more clearly defined stopping points.

3. In all cases, the algorithm will terminate after a finite number of steps.
4. The algorithm is composed of effective primitives whose meaning is clear and unambiguous to the person or machine executing it.

Looking back at the shampooing algorithm, we can now see that it is invalid for two reasons. First, the identity of the steps to be repeated at step 4 is ambiguous—do we go back to step 1, 2, or 3? Second, there is no provision to terminate this algorithm. It would repeat forever, or at least until we ran out of shampoo, hot water, or patience! In the next section we will provide the necessary tools for rewriting this algorithm to conform to the preceding requirements.

2.2   DEVELOPING ALGORITHMS

The process of developing an algorithm to solve a specific problem can be a trial-and-error process requiring numerous attempts, much the same as the process of developing the outline of a story. Programmers will make some initial attempt at a solution and review it to test its correctness. The errors they discover will usually lead to insertions, deletions, or modifications in the existing algorithm or possibly to scrapping that attempt and beginning anew. This refining continues until the author is satisfied that the algorithm is essentially correct and ready to be executed. The more experience we gain in developing algorithms, the closer our first attempt will be to a correct solution and the less revision will be required. However, under no circumstances should a beginning programmer view developing an algorithm as a single-step operation. This point needs to be stressed very early, since many of the algorithms contained in this textbook are presented simply as correct solutions. They represent, however, the final stage, either for the authors or others, in the development of suitable algorithms. That development is often complicated by false starts and dead ends and obstructed by innumerable errors—errors obvious to everyone except their creators. In fact, the final version of the algorithm itself may still contain errors that will not be discovered until the algorithm is actually run as a computer program.

2.2.1   Example One—Table Look-Up

The best way to introduce the algorithmic process is to work through an example. In Chapter 1 we developed the specifications for a very common programming problem called table look-up (see Figure 1-2b). Our problem now will be to develop an algorithm to solve that problem correctly. The technique we will use in this example will be the simplest and most obvious—*sequential search*. We will look at the first element, the second element, the third, and so on, until we either find the item we are looking for or we come to the end of the list. If the list is in no particular order (e.g., numerical or alphabetical) the sequential search is actually the best technique available. However, if the list has already been organized in some fashion, the sequential search, which does not take advantage of any such organization, is usually the most inefficient technique. This is an important point and one that we will develop more fully later.

For this example, assume that the list contains n items called $a_1, a_2, \ldots, a_n$, and the special value we are searching for is termed the ''key.''

First Attempt

Is a_1 equal to the key?

Is a_2 equal to the key?

.

.

.

Is a_n equal to the key?

This would seem to be the most straightforward and logical solution to the problem, but it is a totally unacceptable algorithm for several reasons. The number of steps it takes to write out the algorithm is directly proportional to the size of the problem. As the size of the list grows very large, the number of statements becomes intolerable. We are not using the power of the computer and are missing a fundamental concept in programming—*iteration* (the repetitive execution of a group of operations). Instead of writing a set of operations n distinct times, we should strive to write them only once and successively execute them as many times as needed. This way, the representation of the algorithm is relatively independent of the specific data set with which we are working.

In this problem, for example, we could use a variable i as a pointer or an index into the list in place of the constants $1, 2, \ldots, n$. As we change the value of i, the expression a_i would successively refer to each of the values $a_1, a_2, \ldots, a_n$. We would no longer have to write the same question n separate times as we did in the first attempt.

When looking at the initial attempt, you probably assumed that the first line was the starting point of the algorithm. This is the convention we always use in interpreting recipes or instructions. Since an unambiguous starting point is an absolute necessity, we will formally adopt this convention. In order to gain the maximum clarity when writing algorithms, we will assume that there is an algorithmic primitive called START that must appear exactly once as the first line of the algorithm. The first executable primitive is the one immediately following the START command. Since the algorithm must also eventually terminate, we will similarly adopt the convention that there is a primitive called stop that may appear one or more times anywhere within the algorithm. When we come to a stop, execution of the algorithm is terminated. In addition, we will include a primitive called END OF THE ALGORITHM that must physically be the last line. (Remember, a stop can appear anywhere within an algorithm, not just at the end.) The START and END primitives will always be capitalized to help us visually identify the beginning and end of the algorithm. Thus our algorithms will look like this.

$$\text{START}$$
$$\text{statement} - 1$$
$$\text{statement} - 2$$
$$.$$
$$.$$
$$\text{statement} - n$$
$$\text{END OF THE ALGORITHM}$$

Next let us look closely at each line of the initial attempt. They each say, ''Is a specific element of the list equal to the key?'' That is a troublesome statement. What are we supposed to do if they are equal? What do we do if they are not? It is not clear. What we need is a formal way to ask a question or test a condition, with the answer affecting what we do next. The most common way to implement this is by using the *if/then/else* primitive. This algorithmic primitive is written as follows.

$$\text{if condition then}$$
$$\text{operations}$$
$$\text{else}$$
$$\text{operations}$$

The condition specified in the if primitive represents any condition that can be understood and evaluated by the person or machine executing the algorithm and that produces a value of true or false. If the indicated condition is true the entire set of operations contained in the then clause is executed and the else clause is skipped. If the condition is false the operations contained in the then clause are skipped and the else clause is executed. Thus there will never be any ambiguity about exactly what operations are to be performed. If the set of operations in either clause is lengthy, to avoid confusion we may use a bracket, [, to identify visually all primitives belonging to the same clause.

$$\text{if condition then}$$
$$\left[\begin{array}{l} s_1 \\ . \\ . \\ . \\ s_n \end{array} \right.$$

else
$$
\begin{bmatrix}
s_1 \\
\cdot \\
\cdot \\
\cdot \\
s_m
\end{bmatrix}
$$

The following are examples of the use of this primitive.

if $x < 0$ then compute $\sqrt{-x}$

else compute $\sqrt{x}$

If the condition $x < 0$ is true we will execute the then clause and take the square root of $-x$ (since the negative of a negative value is positive). If the condition $x < 0$ is false (i.e., $x \geq 0$) we will skip the then clause and execute the else clause, which computes the square root of x.

if there is no more data to process then
    stop
else
    process the next data set

If the condition is true there are no more data and the algorithm will execute the stop primitive and halt. If the condition is false we will skip the stop primitive and execute the primitives in the else clause—effectively processing that data set. (Since the condition specified in the if/then/else primitive must be evaluated by the person or machine executing the algorithm, the preceding command is meaningful only if there is some effective way to determine if there are actually any more data.)

A useful variant of the if/then/else primitive is the if/then form.

if condition then operations

If the condition is false we do not execute any operations but simply go on to the next step in the algorithm. The if/then/else and the if/then constructs are the basic "question-asking" or "condition-testing" primitives used in constructing computer algorithms.

Another obvious primitive is needed: a way to print the results produced by our algorithm. Our output primitive will be simply

write values

We will adopt the convention that a value within double quotation marks, " ", is a message to be written out exactly as is. A letter or word not in quotation marks represents an item whose current value is to be printed. If x is the value of net pay that we wish to print, we could say

write "weekly net pay is", x

Finally, we will assume that our computer has all the arithmetic capabilities of any sophisticated electronic calculator. Therefore the commands

> add a to b (or a + b)
> subtract a from b (or b − a)
> multiply a times b (or a * b, a × b, a · b)
> divide a into b (or b/a, b ÷ a)
> take the square root of a (or $\sqrt{a}$)
> increment a by 1
> decrement a by 1
>
> .
>
> .
>
> .
>
>   etc.

or anything similar will all be considered valid algorithmic primitives that can be evaluated by our machine.

Let us now apply what we have discussed and rewrite our algorithm.

Second Attempt

> START
>   if a_i equals the key then
>   write "found at location", i
>   stop
>   else
>   increment i by 1
>   repeat
> END OF THE ALGORITHM

This begins to take on the form of a computer algorithm in that we are iterating—repeatedly executing a group of statements. However, the algorithm is not yet close to being correct.

If we look at the second line of the algorithm we will see that it refers to the ith element of the list a. However, neither the value of the index i nor the values in the list have been explicitly specified. We have committed an *initialization error*. We are trying to use an item (add with it, print it out, test it) before we have given it a value. Every algorithm must explicitly specify how a value will be assigned to an item before attempting to use that item. The two most common ways to assign values are by using internal and external data. *Internal data* means values created within the algorithm itself. *External data* means that the specific values reside on some external input device separate from the person or machine executing the algorithm. The values are made available to that person or machine by "reading in" the data from this device.

We will assume the existence of two algorithmic primitives for these two approaches.

1. *Internal Data.* Set variable to a value (or an expression); for example:

   set x to 1
   set index to the sum of a and b (of course, a and b must already be defined)
   set interest to (principal x balance)
   set z to a $+$ b $\div$ c $\times$ d $-$ e

2. *External Data.* Read values; for example:

   read the values of x, y, and z
   read the elements a_1, a_2, . . ., a_n

With the set primitive the variable takes on the value of the expression specified in the set statement. With the read primitive the variables take on the values that come in from the input device. In either case, we have assigned a value to a variable and can now use that variable throughout our algorithm. Remember this fundamental rule of programming: you must always assign a value to an object *before* you attempt to use it in any way.

Another problem with our algorithm as it currently stands has to do with our attempt to iterate. If we look at the next-to-last line of the algorithm we find that the command "repeat" is unacceptable. Like the shampooing algorithm, it states neither what to repeat nor how often to repeat it. One of the characteristics of algorithms that is starting to become obvious is the constant use of iteration. Every algorithm we write will have groups of statements repeated some large number of times. When developing algorithms, it would be nice to think specifically in terms of *looping primitives*—constructs that specify both a block of statements to be repetitively executed and criteria for determining exactly how many times it is to be executed. The most natural ways to think of iteration are as repetition some fixed number of times or repetition until some event occurs. For example, using our baking analogy mentioned at the beginning of this chapter, we can see these two classes of repetition:

· Repetition for a fixed count.

    Add 2 cups of flour

    Stir 20 times

    Separate the whites and yolks of 3 eggs

· Repetition until some condition occurs.

    Beat egg whites until stiff

    Cook until cake is 2 inches high

    Let cool until temperature is 105°

We will provide primitives for both types of repetition.

while condition do

s_1

s_2

.

.

.

s_n

end of the while loop

The while primitive allows us to repeat a group of algorithmic primitives $s_1, s_2, \ldots,$ s_n as long as some condition is true. The condition specified in the while clause is any effective condition that can be understood by the person or machine executing the algorithm and that evaluates to either true or false. The condition is checked initially and, if it is true, all statements $s_1, \ldots, s_n$ are performed. The condition is then evaluated again. This process is repeated continually until the condition becomes false. If the condition is false to begin with, none of the statements is executed.

repeat count times

s_1

s_2

.

.

.

s_n

end of the repeat loop

Count represents any constant or variable that has a nonnegative whole number as its value. The primitives $s_1, \ldots, s_n$ are executed as many times as specified by the value of count. If count is initially zero, the primitives $s_1, \ldots, s_n$ are not executed.

We can now begin to construct iterative algorithms using the preceding two primitives as building blocks.

Third Attempt

```
START
        read in the size of the list, n
        read in the list a₁, . . . , aₙ and the key
        set i to 1
        set found to false
        while found is false and (i < n) do
                if aᵢ equals the key then
                        set found to true
                else
                        increment i by 1
        end of the while loop
        if the key was found then
                write "the value was found at location", i
        else
                write "the value was not found"
        stop
END OF THE ALGORITHM
```

The algorithm now looks sufficiently correct to begin checking it by trying out sample cases. We must be very careful to check its performance both on simple, valid cases and on the following.

1. *The Boundary (or Extreme) Cases.* How does the algorithm perform at the extremes of the valid cases, for example, finding elements at the very beginning or end of a list or setting the list size to the smallest or largest allowable value?

2. *The Unusual Cases.* What happens when we input data that violate the normal conditions of the problem or represent an unusual condition? For example, what happens if the key cannot be found in the list or we are given a list of length 0?

3. *The Invalid Cases.* How does the algorithm react for data that are patently illegal or completely meaningless, such as a list of length − 1? Such meaningless data occur frequently in programming environments and can be caused, for example, by pressing the wrong key when creating the data. A cardinal rule of computer programming that we will follow throughout this book is that an algorithm should work correctly and produce meaningful results for any data whatsoever, regardless of how pathological or absurd. We call this *foolproof programming*.

Let us look at how the algorithm as it now stands works under this set of requirements. We will take as a sample data set the following values.

$$n = 4 \qquad a_1 = 13$$
$$a_2 = 5$$
$$a_3 = 21$$
$$a_4 = 22$$

For the sample cases of key = 13, 5, or 21, the algorithm works correctly. (Validate this and all other assertions by working through the algorithm with paper, pencil, and the designated data.) For the value key = 35 the algorithm also produces the expected result—the message, "The value was not found." However, for the value key = 22, the algorithm incorrectly produces the same message. The problem arises in the sixth line of the algorithm, which tests for termination. When we test the condition $i < n$, we are, in effect, asking if we have come to the end of the list. However, we are asking that question *before* we have actually tested the last item. The correct condition to test is actually $i \leq n$. This mistake is representative of a very common class of programming mistakes called *off-by-one errors*—performing an iteration either one time too few or one time too often. It is extremely important when developing algorithms to ensure that your iterations terminate at the correct step by testing and evaluating these boundary conditions.

```
START
        read in the size of the list, n
        if n ≤ 0 then
                write "invalid list size, cannot process"
        else
          ┌  read values for a₁, a₂, . . . , aₙ
          │  read in a value for key
          │  set i to 1
          │  set found to false
          │  while found is false and (i ≤ n) do
          │          if aᵢ equals the key then
          │                  set found to true
          │          else
          │                  increment i by 1
          │  end of the while loop
          │  if the key was found then
          │          write "the value was found at location", i
          │  else
          └          write "the value was not found"
        stop
END OF THE ALGORITHM
```

Figure 2-1. Table look-up algorithm using sequential search.

What if the value of n is equal to or less than 0? Of course, this is meaningless but, as we said before, you should be able to state that your algorithm still operates properly. In this case it does not. The third line of the algorithm on page 30 will attempt to read data that do not actually exist. One simple test will allow us to catch this invalid situation. The finished version of the algorithm is shown in Figure 2-1 on page 31.

We have spent a great deal of time developing this simple algorithm, probably more than it deserves. However, this problem has introduced some very important concepts that will recur throughout this book: iteration, the structure and organization of algorithms, and some common programming errors. Most important, we have developed a set of primitives to use in representing and writing algorithms. This set of primitives, which we will call an *algorithmic language,* is summarized in Figure 2-2.

```
START
stop
if condition then operations else operations
if condition then operations
set variable to a value (or expression)
read values
write values
add x to y
subtract x from y
multiply x times y
divide x into y
increment x
decrement x
while condition do
           .
           .
           .

end of the while loop

repeat count times
           .
           .
           .

end of the repeat loop
{ any message inside braces will be a comment to the
  reader and not part of the algorithm }
END OF THE ALGORITHM
```

Figure 2-2. Representative algorithmic primitives.

However, algorithmic languages are informal and contain few, if any, strict rules of grammar or syntax. The primitives we introduced are merely examples of statements that are typically used to design algorithms. Feel free to modify them or to add others that may seem more natural or convenient to you.

One question you are probably asking now is why we chose to develop and use an algorithmic language as the vehicle for presenting algorithms. Is this the only way to represent algorithms, or are there alternate, and better, techniques?

The answer is that we are using an algorithmic language because it represents an ideal compromise between the representational extremes of natural language (the language we speak and write) and the Pascal programming language. We could write algorithms directly in English text. For example, the table look-up algorithm in Figure 2-1 would start out something like the following.

Let's first read in the data. If there are no items in the list, we will want to write out an error message. Now we are going to start looking through the list by asking. . . .

This approach has some obvious limitations. It is very wordy. The sentences that we write are not limited to any particular form or vocabulary. They might be totally unrelated to the statements available in the programming language we will eventually use. This could make the actual coding phase very difficult. Finally, the sentences themselves would not give us any clues as to the relationship between parts of the algorithm or any indication of general organization. It would simply appear as a single, large, unstructured paragraph.

Given these arguments, a natural first reaction is to go to the opposite extreme: forget about any intermediate representations and develop the algorithms directly in a programming language that, in our case, is Pascal. A portion of the table look-up algorithm might now appear as follows.

```
program tablelookup (input, output);
var
    i, n           :integer;
    key            :real;
    a              :array [1..100] of real;
begin
    readln(n);
    if n <= 0 then
        writeln ('invalid list size, cannot process')
    else
    begin
        for i := 1 to n do
            readln(a[i]);
                    .
                    .
                    .
```

Again, the disadvantages become immediately apparent. By writing directly in Pascal, we necessarily become concerned with syntactic considerations that are not really part of the algorithmic development process—considerations such as the location of semicolons, the delimiting of reserved words, type declarations for variables, and the declaration of specific external files. These concerns have no place in this development phase and can, in fact, slow down this process by inundating us with extraneous detail. They should be relegated to the *coding phase,* where we are specifically concerned with translating algorithmic primitives into the syntax of some specific programming language.

Therefore an algorithmic language such as the one described in Figure 2-2 is a reasonable compromise for the following reasons.

1. By a judicious choice of algorithmic language primitives, we can ensure that our final algorithms will be closely related to our desired programming language, thus facilitating the next step of translation into that language. You will soon discover that the algorithmic language used in this textbook is very closely related to Pascal.

2. We will not, however, be bogged down in the restrictive syntax of a specific language. An algorithmic language should be viewed as a set of guidelines for building algorithms, not as a rigid set of rules. There will not be any rules for punctuation, spelling, vocabulary, or use of synonyms.

3. The representation of algorithms in our algorithmic language, along with a judicious use of indentation, will clearly indicate the relationships between various statements and allow us to gain a better picture of the overall organization and structure of our solution.

We should stress that not all programmers use algorithmic languages like the one in Figure 2-2. There are many other representational techniques, with one of particular importance. We will mention it for the sake of completeness but will not use it in this book. The other technique in widespread use is the *flowchart*. Essentially, a flowchart is a blueprint or a logical diagram of the solution to a problem. The algorithm is constructed out of boxes, with the shape of each box indicating the kind of operation being performed. Figure 2-3 shows some of the generally accepted flowcharting symbols. The actual operation to be performed is written inside the symbol. The arrow (or arrows) coming out of the symbol indicates which operation to perform next. The algorithm is executed by starting at the oval symbol labeled START, following the arrows and performing all indicated operations, and continuing until we reach the oval symbol labeled STOP. The table look-up algorithm that we first developed would probably look something like the flowchart in Figure 2-4.

A comparison of Figures 2-1 and 2-4, two representations of the same algorithm, shows quite clearly what we feel is the biggest drawback to flowcharts: they do not clearly indicate the hierarchical structure of the algorithm. Using boxes and arrows

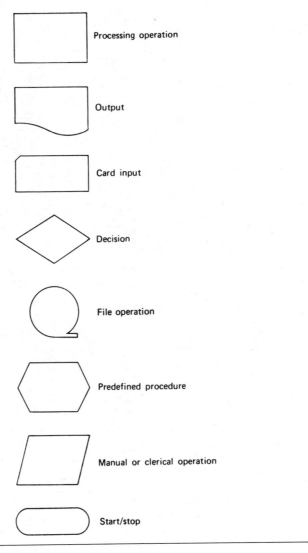

Figure 2-3. Some standard flowchart symbols.

instead of algorithmic primitives prevents certain structural aspects of the problem from becoming immediately apparent—aspects such as loops, nested tests, or disjoint clauses. The basic trouble with the flowchart is that it allows too much freedom. Arrows can be used to connect any one box to another, anywhere in the algorithm. This can result in a spaghettilike tangle of lines and boxes exemplified by Figure 2-4 and so typical of many flowcharts. These diagrams can be extremely difficult to

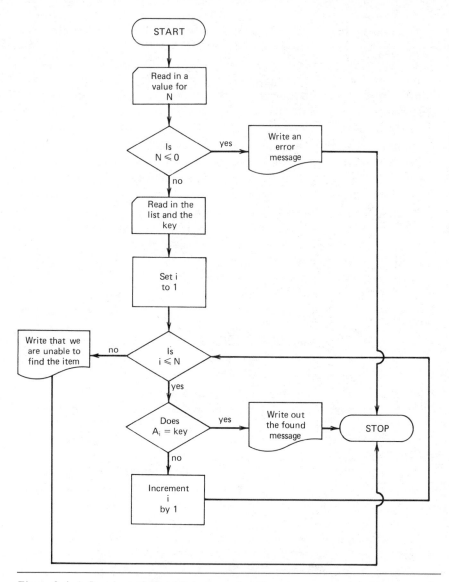

Figure 2-4. A flowchart of the table look-up algorithm.

untangle and comprehend. Because of this, it is difficult to determine if the algorithm is a correct solution to the problem. There are special types of flowcharts, called *structured flowcharts,* that restrict the types of allowable operations and interconnections in order to produce well-organized and readable diagrams. These structured flowcharts are a popular and reasonable alternative to algorithmic languages.

The flowcharting technique is useful primarily for macro-level or *system flow-charts* where we are concerned with the most general level of operations needed to solve a large problem. Each element of a system flowchart would typically represent a fairly large and complex manual, clerical, or computer procedure for which an algorithm must be developed and implemented. These individual procedures could be developed and represented using an algorithmic language similar to the one described in this chapter.

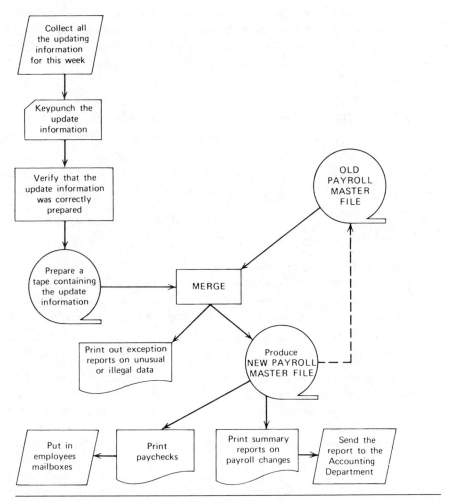

Figure 2-5. Example of a system-level flowchart.

Figure 2-5 is a system flowchart for the implementation of a file merge—combining an old master file with updating information to produce a new master file and other reports. This specific example shows a payroll file containing salary information on every employee. The update information could be the list of all employees who have been hired, fired, promoted, or demoted during the past week. The output may be both a new payroll file incorporating all the new information as well as the various reports required by the company. Most of the broad operations on that flowchart would become distinct computer problems that would have to be defined, developed, and solved individually and then combined into a single system.

After viewing the same algorithm represented in a number of different ways, you may have a strong opinion about which representation is "best" or most "natural." This brings us to an important conclusion about the representation of algorithms. It is not so important which particular technique you use as long as you use something that you can work with comfortably and that allows you to develop correct algorithms independent of and unencumbered by the syntactic limitations of any specific programming language.

2.2.2 Example Two—A Better Table Look-Up

In the first example we developed an algorithm for searching a list sequentially from beginning to end. However, if the list we are searching is already organized in some fashion (e.g., alphabetically), that technique is foolish. Imagine looking for SMITH, JOHN J. in the New York City telephone directory by beginning with AARD-VARK, ALAN A. and continuing sequentially! Instead, we quite naturally open the book somewhere in the middle and move rapidly toward the desired name. Let us develop an algorithm that efficiently searches an alphabetized list of names either to locate a particular name or to ascertain that it is not in the book. It is essentially the same problem as before, but the data are organized differently.

The main purpose of this example will not be to show how to represent the algorithm but to show how to find it. In the previous example we were primarily concerned with developing an algorithmic language. The algorithm itself, the actual sequence of steps, just "happened." However, what do we do when we have no idea of how to proceed in solving a problem? Is there any technique or guideline for aiding a programmer in this *algorithm discovery* or problem-solving process?

As in any creative process, there is no foolproof method for developing good or even correct algorithms. Just as with a poem, an essay, or the plot for a novel, nothing, other than experience, can guarantee results every time. But that does not mean that discovering an algorithm is a completely unstructured, trial-and-error process. There are techniques, guidelines, and aids to help a programmer develop reasonable solutions to complex problems.

Probably the single most important design aid is the technique called *top-down program design*; it is also known as *modular development* or *stepwise refinement*. In a top-down design we initially describe the problem we are working on at the highest, most general level. The description of the problem at this level will usually be concerned with what must be done—not with how it must be done. This description will usually not be in the algorithmic primitives that we developed in the previous section. Instead, it will be described in terms of complex, higher-level operations. We must take all of the operations at this level and individually break them down into simpler steps that begin to describe how to accomplish the tasks. If these simpler steps can be represented as acceptable algorithmic primitives, we need not refine them any further. If not, we refine each of these second-level operations individually into still simpler steps. This stepwise refinement continues until each of the original top-level operations has been described in terms of acceptable primitive statements.

This top-down approach to developing algorithms offers a number of significant advantages over trying to develop solutions in a random, unorganized fashion. First, and most important, it allows the programmer to keep "on top of" a problem and view the developing solution in context. The solution is always proceeding from the highest levels down. With other techniques we may find ourselves bogged down with very low-level decisions at a very early stage. It will be difficult to make these decisions if it is not clear how they may affect the remainder of the problem. For example, it would probably be difficult to decide what type of table look-up technique to choose before we know how the table will be used, what it will look like, or what values it will contain.

This top-down development process is virtually identical to the outlining process frequently used in the preparation of a critical essay, novel, or other large written work. This book, for example, was developed by first specifying the sequence of chapters it would contain. Then we began to detail the sections within each chapter. Only then did we begin to actually write the sections themselves. In this way, one can intellectually manage the development of a 400 page book without getting lost in a welter of details. The analogy to a computer program is apt. By specifying the highest-level operations first, we can develop our programs in an orderly, systematic fashion. We will not get lost in the vast syntactic details during the initial stages of program development.

Another advantage of top-down development is that it is a very good way to delay decisions on problems whose solution may not be readily apparent. At each stage in the development, the individual operation will be refined into a number of more elementary steps (Figure 2-6). If we are not sure how to proceed with step a_2 we can still work on step a_1. If the best methods to use with a_{11} and a_{12} are not obvious we could proceed with steps a_{13} and a_{14} and, later on, come back and finish the problem.

Finally, by dividing the problem into a number of subproblems, we have made it easier to share problem development and to work in teams. For example, one person could be responsible for step a_1, while another handles a_2. The person in charge of a_1 could either handle it personally or delegate steps a_{11}, a_{12}, a_{13}, and a_{14} to four other

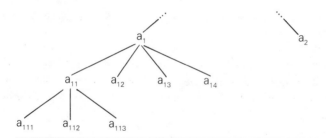

Figure 2-6. Example of stepwise refinement.

programmers and manage and coordinate their efforts. On large problems (certainly larger than the little problem we are developing here!) this latter advantage takes on extraordinary importance.

In school students are usually discouraged from trying to solve assigned problems together. Competition among individuals is much preferred, even encouraged. While realizing that you may be asked to solve programming problems alone for class, we want to emphasize that in the real world people are becoming more and more concerned with how to manage and use teams of programmers to solve problems more effectively. We will say more about team efforts in Chapter 11, where we discuss large, real-world problems.

We will now use the top-down technique just discussed to develop a better table look-up algorithm. The very highest level of the algorithm is shown in Figure 2-7 (the steps are numbered for reference in the text).

1. input the list
2. input the key we are searching for
3. search the list
4. if the key was found then
5.   write an appropriate message
6. else
7.   write some other appropriate message

Figure 2-7. Top-level description of the table look-up algorithm.

Figure 2-7 describes the problem only at the level of the highest and most general operations. Each step will have to be extensively refined until it is expressed in terms of algorithmic primitives. For example, we could initially concern ourselves with statement 1: How do we do the input operation and what checking is necessary? One possible refinement of statement 1 is shown in Figure 2-8.

If the steps shown in Figure 2-8 are all acceptable primitives, we are finished. If not, we can refine them even further. For example, in step 1.3, the appropriate recovery action could be described in more detail, as shown on the following page.

1.1 read in the length of the list, n
1.2 if n $\leqq$ 0 then
1.3   take the appropriate recovery action
1.4 else
1.5   read in the list elements $a_1, a_2, \ldots , a_n$

Figure 2-8. Refinement of the input section of the algorithm.

1.3 write "The list size was specified incorrectly.
      Processing will stop."

If, however, we were not sure what recovery procedures we would need to initiate, we would merely leave step 1.3 as it is and continue with another part of the algorithm. Eventually we would have to come back to this point and fill in the missing details. This is a good example of how top-down methods allow us to delay decisions on low-level implementation details.

We can now begin refining and describing the main part of the algorithm—step 3 of Figure 2-7. When we open a telephone directory to search for a name, we do not, as we did in Example 1, begin looking on page 1. We usually open the book somewhere in the middle and see whether we are too far or not far enough; that is, we see whether to continue our search in the first or second half. We can repeat the halving until we reach the desired page and name. This idea of looking somewhere in the middle and discarding the half that is not needed will form the basis for the first refinements of step 3. Figure 2-9 shows the refinement.

Figure 2-9 gives an excellent high-level view of this search technique but leaves a number of questions unanswered. For example, what is this "middle" item we are referring to? Obviously it will be the item halfway between the top and bottom of

3.1 set found to false
3.2 while we have not found what we are looking for and we have not exhausted the list do
3.3   locate the "middle" item of what remains of the list
3.4   if the middle item equals the key then
3.5   we have found the item, so set found to true
3.6   else
3.7   if the key is in the top half of the list then
3.8   discard the bottom half of the list
3.9   else
3.10   discard the top half of the list
3.11 end of the while loop

Figure 2-9. First refinement of the searching section of the algorithm.

whatever part of the list we are looking at. Therefore, somewhere in the algorithm, we must include a definition of the items at the top and bottom of the list.

> 2.01 initialize top to 1, the index of the first item in the list
> 2.02 initialize bottom to n, the index of the last item in the list

We can now refine step 3.3 as follows.

> 3.3 set middle to $\dfrac{\text{top } + \text{ bottom}}{2}$ (rounded to the nearest integer)

Now that we have defined the top and bottom of the list, we can explain what it means to "discard" half the list, as we directed in steps 3.8 and 3.10. We can discard a portion of the list merely by calling the middle item the new top or new bottom. That is, we reset "top" or "bottom" to "middle." Figure 2-10a shows the current situation. If we reset the top pointer to the value of middle, we discard the top half, as shown in Figure 2-10b, and if we reset the bottom pointer to the value of middle, we discard the bottom half, as in Figure 2-10c. We can represent this in our algorithm as follows.

> 3.7   if the value of the middle item > key then
> 3.8   set bottom to middle
> 3.9   else
> 3.10   set top to middle

This entire process will continue either until we find the desired item (the value of the middle item equals the key) or the list is exhausted (top and bottom have the same value).

The technique we have just developed is called the *binary search* algorithm. The complete algorithm is shown in Figure 2-11. Before coding it into Pascal, we should apply the testing criteria discussed earlier to see whether or not the algorithm as written

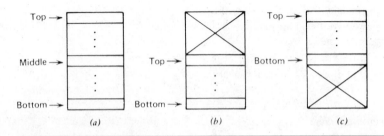

Figure 2-10. Discarding half the list.

START
    read in the size of the list, n
    if n ≦ 0 then
        write "The list size is incorrect. Processing cannot continue."
    else
        read in the list $a_1, \ldots, a_n$
        read in the key
        set top to 1
        set bottom to n
        set found to false
        while found is false and top ≦ bottom do
            set middle to $\dfrac{\text{top } + \text{ bottom}}{2}$ (rounded to the nearest integer)
            if a _middle equals the key then
                set found to true
            else
                if a _middle is greater than key then
                    set bottom to middle − 1
                else
                    set top to middle + 1
        end of the while loop
        if the item was found then
            write "found at position", middle
        else
            write "sorry the key was not found"
    stop
END OF THE ALGORITHM

Figure 2-11. The binary search algorithm.

operates correctly on all data cases and finds the desired name. We must be sure to include the boundary, unusual, and illegal cases, as well as valid data sets. (In fact, the operations shown in Figure 2-10 contain a classic boundary condition error caused by the resettings in steps 3.8 and 3.10 and the computation in step 3.3. As written, the algorithm would not locate the key if it occurred as the *first* item in the list. This is why it is so important to check your algorithm on these boundary and limiting cases. The algorithm given in Figure 2-11 corrects this flaw. We will have much more to say about program testing in Chapter 6.)

This example has introduced an important point concerning algorithms: the top-down approach is an excellent design aid for producing computer algorithms. Look back at Figure 2-11 and imagine trying to develop the finished algorithm in one step.

Even if that project does not seem too difficult, imagine trying to design algorithms that are 10, 100, or even 1000 times more complex. Without some strategy for organizing we would soon be lost. We will develop the large case studies presented in this text in a top-down fashion for clarity and experience with this design method.

2.2.3 Example Three—Averaging

An important point to notice in the previous examples is that we have developed two different algorithms for two different types of lists, one unordered, one ordered. A simple change in the way the data were organized allowed us to develop an improved method for searching. The purpose of an algorithm is to process data, and the way the data are represented will strongly influence the algorithm that finally results. Although they frequently may be discussed separately, you should always consider the topics of data organization and algorithm development as inextricably related. Although some lower-level decisions concerning the data may be postponed (e.g., Should values be integers or real numbers? Should names be limited to 20 characters?), the higher-level decisions (e.g., Should the data be stored in a list? Should they be sorted?) will usually need to be made at the time the algorithm is being developed.

As an example of this point, consider the problem of computing the average of a set of examination scores using the well-known formula

$$\text{Average} = \frac{\text{sum of all scores}}{\text{number of scores}}$$

Before we can even begin to design the algorithm, we must make an important decision about the organization of the data. Computing an average does not require us to read all the data values in advance. We could, if we wished, read one data item at a time. We would input a value, add it to a running total, keep track of how many scores we have processed, and then bring in the next value. This would require only a single storage location for all the scores. This strategy would probably result in an algorithm like that of Figure 2-12.

Alternately, we could decide to use a list and immediately input all examination scores into this list. We would now compute the average by working through the list, from beginning to end, summing up the scores as we go. We would now end up with something similar to Figure 2-13. We have produced two different algorithms, not because the problem is different but because the data have been organized differently. This is an important point to be aware of in computer programming. The solution to a problem is the result of a series of decisions on *both* data representation and algorithmic technique. Solutions will progress as a series of interrelated decisions on how the data will be represented and on how we can process data in that form. Also, like the top-down development of algorithms, the development of data structures also proceeds in a top-down fashion, from the most general concerns to the most specific.

START
>   set the running total to 0
>   set the score counter to 0
>   while there are still scores to process do
>   read a single score
>   add that score to the running total
>   increment score counter by 1
>   end of the while loop
>   if score counter is 0 then
>   write a message that there were no scores
>   else
>   set average to running total divided by score counter
>   write out the average
>   stop
END OF THE ALGORITHM

Figure 2-12. Averaging algorithm without lists.

For example, in Figure 2-13 we are concerned only about the structure of the data—it should be represented and stored as a list of values e_1, e_2, . . ., e_n. As yet, we do not care about the actual format of the examination scores—whether they are integers between 0 and 100 or decimal quantities in the range 200.0 to 800.0. That decision can be postponed until a later point.

We will have a great deal more to say about data representation throughout this text and specifically in Chapters 3, 7, 9, and 10.

2.2.4 Example Four—Words, Words, Words

This last example will not try to introduce any new concepts relating to algorithms but, instead, will try to tie together a number of concepts that have been introduced in the first two chapters. It will also introduce an important new application area called *text processing*. Too often we think of computers and computer programs as devices for manipulating numerical information and solving mathematical problems. Of course, this is an important area of application. However, equally as important is the processing of textual information—characters, words, lines, paragraphs, and chapters. This application is becoming extremely important in the areas of text analysis, word processing, office automation, and electronic mail.

This example is a simple problem to take a string of characters, isolate the separate words in the text, and keep count of the length of each word just found. The problem specification statement is given in Figure 2-14.

One of the first decisions we will need to make is how we will store the data—

START
    set the running total to 0
    read in the list size, n
    if $n \leqq 0$ then
        write ''sorry, no scores to process''
    else
        read in the entire list $e_1, e_2, \ldots, e_n$
        set i to 1
        repeat n times
            add e_i to the running total
            increment i by 1
        end of the repeat loop
        set average to running total divided by n
        write out the average
    stop
END OF THE ALGORITHM

Figure 2-13. Averaging algorithm using a list.

in this case the characters of the text. We could initially read them all in to some very large list, but since we do not know how many characters there will be, this may be impractical and inefficient. Alternately, we could read in a ''chunk'' of data at a time

---

You will be given an arbitrarily long sequence of characters as input. You are to isolate each separate **word** *in this text, where a word is defined as any sequence of nonblank characters bounded on either side by at least one blank character. You are then to classify that word into one of the following four categories.*

Short:	*1–3 characters*
Medium:	*4–6 characters*
Long:	*7–9 characters*
Extra long:	*10 or more characters*

Continue until the end of the text is encountered. The end is marked by the special symbol '\$' immediately following the last word. You are then to output the percentage (0.0 − 100.0) of words in the text that fell into each of the four categories and stop.

Figure 2-14. Specification for the word count problem.

(say 100 characters), store that chunk in a list, and process that chunk. The next chunk would then simply go on top of the previous one. This might be considered analogous to decomposing the text into lines or pages and processing one line or page at a time. Finally, the simplest way would be to store one character at a time. We would read one character, process it, and move on to the next. In a sense, we would have a one-character "window" into the text that moves sequentially left to right, one character at a time. We will adopt this latter approach for the algorithm we are about to develop.

Before we begin designing the algorithm, we should clear up any other ambiguities in the problem statement of Figure 2-14. For example, what about punctuation? Should the string 'end!' be considered as a three-character word followed by an exclamation point instead of as a four-character word? We will make the assumption that the only punctuation symbols appearing in the text are the period (.) and comma (,) and that whenever they appear they will always be considered as punctuation symbols and not as part of the word. In addition, we will assume that punctuation marks will immediately follow the last character of the word and will always be followed by at least one blank character (or the symbol $). There may be other ambiguities in the problem statement, and you should read it over carefully before proceeding. Always be satisfied that you understand exactly what the problem is asking for *before* attempting to solve it.

The problem, at its highest and most general level, is easy to specify. It is the operation of finding and classifying words until there is no more text left to process.

> START
> >   while there is still more text to process do
> >   >   find the next word
> >   >   classify that word
> >   end of the while loop
> >   compute the percentages in each classification
> >   write out the results
> >   stop
> END OF THE ALGORITHM

We must now refine these high-level operations down to our basic algorithmic primitives. The process of finding a word is easy to understand. We simply throw away blanks until we come to the first nonblank character that signifies the start of a word. Then we simply count the number of nonblank characters until we come to the first blank character or punctuation symbol that marks the end of the word.

> >   while the current character is a blank do
> >   >   read a character
> >   end of the while loop
> >   set length to 0

          while the current character is *not* a blank, '.', or ',' do
              read a character
              increment length by 1
          end of while loop

The process of classifying a word according to its length is simply a series of questions to determine which of the four categories it belongs to.

          if length ≦ 3 then
              increment short by 1
          else if length ≦ 6 then
              increment medium by 1
          else if length ≦ 9 then
              increment long by 1
          else
              increment extralong by 1

Finally, the output will be the computation of percentages.

          set total to short + medium + long + extralong
          if total = 0 then
              invoke the error-handling procedures
          else
              write "percentage of short words is," short/total * 100
              write "percentage of medium words is", medium/total * 100
              write "percentage of long words is", long/total * 100
              write "percentage of extra long words is,"
                            extra long/total * 100

Notice that we have checked to see that the total number of words is not zero because this would lead to division by zero—an undefined operation. (Remember our definition of foolproof programming.) If this situation occurs, obviously something is wrong because the user gave us nothing (or a string of blanks) to process. Our algorithm will specify that if this occurs, we are to invoke some nebulous "error-handling procedures" that are as yet unspecified. This is a good example of the idea of delayed decisions on lower-level implementation details. Of course, we will eventually have to specify what these error-handling procedures actually do, but we can postpone that specification until we have completed other tasks and are ready to address this one.

    The complete algorithm for this problem is shown in Figure 2-15. The reader should now review the algorithms that have been presented in this section—Figures 2-1, 2-11, 2-12, 2-13, and 2-15—and review the basic concepts of algorithms that they illustrate.

START
    set total to 0
    set short, medium, long, and extralong to 0
    read in the first character of the text
    while the current character ≠ '$' do
        while the current character is a blank do
            read the next character
        end of the while loop
        set word length to 0
        while the current character is not blank, ',', or '.' do
            read the next character
            increment word length by 1
        end of while loop
        if current character is ',' or '.' then read next character
    { This last operation discards the punctuation symbol if there
      was one. We will now be looking at a blank or a '$' }
        if word length ≦ 3 then
            increment short by 1
        else if length ≦ 6 then
            increment medium by 1
        else if length ≦ 9 then
            increment long by 1
        else
            increment extralong by 1
    end of the while loop
    set total to short + medium + long + extralong
    if total = 0 then
        invoke error-handling procedures
    else
        write "percentage of short words is", short/total * 100
        write "percentage of medium words is", medium/total * 100
        write "percentage of long words is", long/total * 100
        write "percentage of extra long words is", extralong/total * 100
    stop
END OF THE ALGORITHM

Figure 2-15. The word analysis algorithm.

1. The *definition* of an algorithm—an ordered sequence of well-defined and effective primitive operations that always terminates in a finite time.

2. The *representation* of algorithms in an algorithmic language of the type shown in Figure 2-2.

3. The *development* of algorithms using a top-down development approach.
4. The importance of the *data representation* to the final algorithm that is developed.
5. The *robustness* of algorithms so that they work properly on all cases—not just the regular or expected cases.

Style Clinic 2-1 _____

Don't Reinvent the Wheel

The preceding discussion may have given you the mistaken impression that all algorithms are designed by the programmer from scratch. That is completely false. In most cases, all or part of an algorithm needed to solve a problem can be found in the published literature of computer science or related disciplines. There is an almost limitless number of well-documented and well-analyzed algorithms for performing virtually any task. For certain common problems—sorting, searching, merging, root finding, matrix operations, simple statistics—there may be as many as a dozen different methods from which to choose. So before you begin your task, first see if someone has already done the work for you. It may save a lot of time and effort.

2.3 THE EFFICIENCY OF ALGORITHMS

(**Note.** *This section may be skipped without loss of continuity.*)

The previous sections have been concerned solely with techniques for finding and representing algorithms. However, as our discussion of the two methods of searching showed, some correct solutions are better than others. Pragmatic considerations require that the algorithms we design be both formally correct and reasonably efficient. That will require us to develop criteria for defining "efficiency" and procedures for comparing and evaluating alternative techniques.

The most obvious measure would be simply to take an algorithm, supply it with a specific set of data, and count either the number of steps or the amount of time it takes to produce the desired solution. What this would produce, however, is merely a measure of efficiency for a very specific case that may have no relationship to the performance of the algorithm for a completely different set of data. An algorithm for finding a name in a telephone book by sequentially searching all names from A to Z would probably provide acceptable performance for telephone books with less than 50 entries. Its performance on the Minneapolis directory would be totally unacceptable. What we need is a way to formulate a general guideline that says that for any arbitrary set of data, one particular algorithm will probably be better than another. Specifically, we would like to associate a value n, called the *size* of the problem, with a value t, the computer *time* needed to produce the answer. The association would be in the form of a formula, t = f(n), where the function, f, is usually called the *time complexity* of the algorithm.

What is the meaning of this value n? It is simply a measure of the size of the problem we are attempting to solve. For example, if we are sorting a list into alphabetic order, a natural measure of the size would be the number of elements in the list. If we are inverting a matrix, we would probably choose the dimensions (i.e., the number of rows and columns) of the matrix. Finally, if we are building a data base, the number of individual entries in the files could measure the size.

We will examine two examples we developed earlier—the table look-up algorithms shown in Figures 2-1 and 2-11. A natural choice for the size of this problem would be the size of the list we are searching. With the sequential search method we may, in the worst case, need to look at all n items in the list to find the desired one or determine that the value is not there. Thus the relationship between t and n would be given by

$$t = c * n \quad \text{(for the worst case)}$$

where c is some constant based on the internal speed of the machine we are working with and the number of machine instructions it takes to look at an item in the list. Formulas like this one are rarely used for computing exact timings because the constant c is frequently difficult to obtain. However, that was not what we wanted, anyway. What we really want from a formula is a general guideline to aid us in evaluating and comparing algorithms. We can get this information by using what is called *O-notation*.

$$t = O[f(n)]$$

Formally, the O-notation concept [which is read as ''t is on the order of f(n)''] says that there exist constants M and n* such that if t = O[f(n)], then t < Mf(n) for all n > n*.

This imposing-looking definition is not really that difficult to understand. Informally, the definition says that the computing time of the algorithm grows no faster than a constant times f(n) [i.e., time ≈ M · f(n)]. Thus, as n increases (i.e., the problem gets bigger), the time to solve it increases at a rate approximated by the function f(n).

For example, assuming that the order of an algorithm is $O(n^2)$ then, if n, the size of the problem, doubled, the time to solve the problem would increase about fourfold. If n tripled the new solution would take about nine times as long as the old one. The concept of the *order* of an algorithm is then an approximate measure of the amount of resources used when solving a problem. (In this section the only resource we will look at will be time, but one can do a similar analysis using *memory space* as the resource to be optimized.) Our goal obviously will be to design algorithms of the *smallest order possible*. An algorithm A is said to be of a lower order than algorithm B if there is a point N such that for all problems larger than N, method A always takes less time than method B. We cannot state exactly how much time the algorithm will require for a particular data set but, by choosing the lowest-order algorithm, we can say that as the size of the problem increases the time needed to compute a result will not increase as rapidly, and that at some point the lower-order algorithm will always take less total time than a higher-order algorithm. This is the general guideline we have been looking for, and this is why O-notation has become the fundamental technique for describing the efficiency properties of algorithms.

Looking again at the sequential search algorithm, we can clearly see that it is O(n) since, in the worst case, we would have to look at each of the n items in the list. If the list were to double in size, the time to search the entire list would also double. Let us now analyze the binary search algorithm of Figure 2-11.

With each comparison, we halve the size of the list still under consideration. Therefore the list will be 1/2, 1/4, 1/8, 1/16, . . .—its original size. In the worst possible case this process will continue until the list is empty. We can represent that by saying that the greatest possible number of comparisons will be k, where k is defined as the first integer value such that

$$2^k \geqq n \qquad \text{(the length of the list)}$$

If we now take the logarithm of both sides we get

$$k \geqq \log_2 n$$

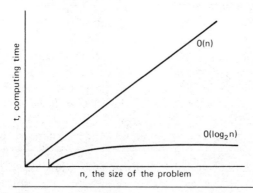

Figure 2-16. Comparison of 0(n) and 0(log₂n) algorithm.

and the order of the binary search algorithm can be written as $O(\log_2 n)$. This is a lower-order algorithm than the sequential search because it grows more slowly as n gets larger (see Figure 2-16). Thus the larger a list, the more time we save by using a binary search instead of a sequential search. For a list of 50,000 items the sequential search would, in the worst case, require 50,000 comparisons, while the binary search would never require more than $\log_2(50,000)$, or about 16. This represents an improvement factor of about 3000!

The statement that the binary search is more efficient than the sequential search is somewhat misleading, however. For the binary search to work correctly, the list we are searching must be sorted. The sequential search works for both sorted and unsorted lists. To compare the efficiency of each, we must add the time it takes to sort a list to the time required for the binary search. Many real-world problems that require searching also require sorting; in these cases the binary search will be more efficient than the sequential search once the sorting has been done.

Since sorting—putting a list into an ordered sequence—is such a common process, we now look at algorithms for sorting as a second example of finding time-efficient algorithms. One of the most common techniques for sorting is called the *exchange sort*. With this method we search the list to find the largest element. We interchange that element with the element currently in the first position. We now find the largest item remaining in the list, beginning our search at position 2. When we find it, we interchange it with the element currently in the second position of the list. After repeating this operation n − 1 times, where n is the size of the list, the entire list will be sorted. The exchange sort algorithm is shown in Figure 2-17.

To find the largest element the first time through the list will require us to look at all n values in the list. Finding the second-largest element, however, will require looking at only n − 1 values, and so forth. Therefore a measure of the total number of comparisons required to perform the exchange sort is:

$$n + (n - 1) + (n - 2) + \ldots + 2 = \sum_{i=2}^{n} i$$
$$= \frac{n(n + 1)}{2} - 1$$
$$= \frac{1}{2} n^2 + \frac{1}{2} n - 1$$

For large problems (i.e., for large values of n) the term containing the n^2 completely overwhelms the other terms. In general, when analyzing algorithms, we treat all lower-order terms as relatively unimportant and do not use them in the computations. Furthermore, the coefficient $1/2$ is also unimportant in comparison with n^2, and we can discard it. The complexity of the exchange sort can thus be written as $O(n^2)$.

There are dozens of other sorting algorithms. If, after actually writing and running

```
START
      read in the list size n
      if n ≤ 0 then
            write "illegal list size, cannot sort"
      else
            read in the entire list a₁, a₂, . . ., aₙ
            if n = 1 then
                  the list is already sorted so we are done
            else
                  set i to 1
                  repeat (n − 1) times
                        find the largest item in the list beginning at position i
                        interchange the largest item just found and the
                              item at position i in the list
                        increment i by 1
                  end of the repeat loop
            write out a₁, a₂ . . ., aₙ
      stop
END OF THE ALGORITHM
```

Figure 2-17. Algorithm for the exchange sort.

an exchange sort program, we are not satisfied with its performance, we could either attempt to improve that program or choose a different algorithm. A fundamental concept in the study of algorithms is the following.

> *The most significant gains in efficiency do not come from trying to speed up an inefficient algorithm but by finding a new and better algorithm of a lower order. The efficiency gains to be made by the latter can exceed the former by orders of magnitude.*

Thus we would gain most not by trying to improve the algorithm of Figure 2-17 but by choosing a new sorting algorithm with a lower order than the n^2 characteristic of the previous method.

Let us look at one more sorting procedure, which we will call the *merge sort,* to see if we can find one of a lower order. The merge sort is the way that people tend to operate when sorting manually. Instead of sorting the entire list directly, we first break the original list into m smaller piles or sublists and then sort each pile individually.

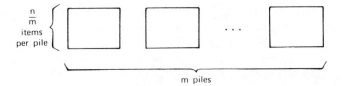

After each of the piles is sorted, we merge them back into a single sorted list.

To sort each individual pile, we can use any $O(n^2)$ sorting technique (e.g., the exchange sort just described). Since there will be n/m items in each little sublist, the approximate time to sort each one will be $O(n^2/m^2)$. There are m of these lists, so the total sorting time will be $O[(n^2/m^2)*m] = O(n^2/m)$. After sorting, we must merge all m sublists back into a single master list. This will involve looking at the top item in each of the m piles to find the largest one. This requires m comparisons. This process must be repeated n times, so the approximate time for the merge phase is $O(m*n)$. The overall time for a merge sort is thus given by

$$O\left(\frac{n^2}{m} + mn\right)$$

Now, by choosing for the value of m the optimum number of piles, we can gain enormously. [Notice, by the way, that if $m = 1$ or $m = n$, the merge sort again becomes an $O(n^2)$ algorithm, and we have gained nothing.] The optimum number of piles is $m \approx \sqrt{n}$.[1] So if we are sorting a list of 50 items we would use about 7 piles; for a list of 10,000 items we would have 100 piles. If we use this value for m in the preceding formula, the order of the merge sort becomes

$$\frac{n^2}{m} + mn$$

$$\frac{n^2}{\sqrt{n}} + n \cdot \sqrt{n} =$$

$$n^{3/2} + n^{3/2} =$$

$$2n^{3/2} =$$

$$O(n^{3/2})$$

The merge sort, using $\sqrt{n}$ piles, becomes an $O(n^{3/2})$ algorithm. For very small lists the computing time difference between $O(n^2)$ and $O(n^{3/2})$ is not great and the choice

---

[1]For those with some knowledge of calculus, the optimum is discovered by taking the derivative with respect to m, setting it to 0, and solving for m. However, this is not necessary for understanding the discussion that follows.

of techniques does not matter greatly. But, as n becomes very large, the difference becomes extremely significant and the merge sort becomes a much more attractive algorithm. In fact, if n becomes enormously large, we may not be able to solve certain problems using the $O(n^2)$ technique because the computing time, t, has become so excessive. This difference is illustrated in the following table, which compares the approximate number of operations needed to sort a list using the merge sort and exchange sort techniques.

List Size, n	Exchange Sort $O(n^2)$	Merge Sort $O(n^{3/2})$
10	100	32
100	10,000	1,000
1,000	1,000,000	32,000
10,000	100,000,000	1,000,000

For small problems, the differences are not that great and it probably is unimportant which technique we choose. However, as the problem gets large (n $\geq$ 1000) the differences become enormous, and the merge sort will solve the same problem 100 times faster! These order-of-magnitude improvements are typical of the gains that can be made by finding a better algorithm. This contrasts sharply with the smaller gains to be made by trying to cleverly speed up the existing program. If any improvements are made, they will typically be on the order of 10 to 30%.

As a final example of this important point, assume that we have six different algorithms, A_1 to A_6, that solve some arbitrary problem P with the following complexities.

A_1: $O(n)$
A_2: $O(n \log_2 n)$
A_3: $O(n^{3/2})$
A_4: $O(n^2)$
A_5: $O(n^3)$
A_6: $O(2^n)$

Assume that the constant of proportionality, c, is approximately the same for all six and is 1 millisecond/operation (large for today's machines). This means that we can do 1000 operations per second of computing time. We can now ask the following question. Given 2 minutes of computing time, t, what is the largest problem that we are able to solve using each of the six algorithms? This is an important way to phrase this type of question, since the limiting factor in solving problems is usually the pragmatic consideration of how much computer time we can afford. The results are shown in Figure 2-18.

Algorithm	Complexity	Largest Problem that Can be Solved in t = 2 minutes (120 seconds)
A_1	$O(n)$	n = 120,000
A_2	$O(n \log_2 n)$	9,000
A_3	$O(n^{3/2})$	2,400
A_4	$O(n^2)$	350
A_5	$O(n^3)$	50
A_6	$O(2^n)$	17

Figure 2-18. Comparison of computing times for t = 2 minutes.

Figure 2-18 shows clearly the enormous difference in efficiency. If we use the merge sort algorithm [which is $O(n^{3/2})$], then for the conditions stated, we could solve a problem about 7 times larger than with the $O(n^2)$ algorithms developed earlier. If we could find and develop an $O(n \log_2 n)$ sorting algorithm we would solve a problem 25 times larger than before in the same time. Finding an algorithm of a lower order should always be our first consideration. Then and only then should we look at improvements in the current algorithm if still more time efficiency is important.

A more thorough treatment of the efficiency of algorithms is beyond the scope of this textbook. What we have tried to do in this section is introduce some fundamental concepts concerning the analysis of algorithms. Even though your knowledge and understanding of these methods of analysis may currently be limited, we hope we have made you aware of some extremely important points concerning algorithms and problem solving.

1. There are quantitative methods for measuring the ''goodness'' of algorithms.
2. There are guidelines to help us choose the best algorithms where alternatives are available.
3. The truly significant gains in efficiency are realized not by trying to make minor changes in the current algorithm but by choosing a better algorithm entirely.

In your future course work in computer science you will investigate this subject in much greater detail.

Style Clinic 2-2

> ### What Is Efficiency?
>
> Programmers (and programming textbooks) used to treat the topic of efficiency solely in terms of shaving every possible statement and microsecond from a program or algorithm. They would spend hours on arcane considerations such as whether it was faster to use
>
> $$A = B + B + B + B$$
>
> or
>
> $$A = B * 4$$
>
> and whether they could save a few milliseconds by using integer values instead of decimal ones. They were proud of the resulting program, which now ran a few seconds faster than before.
>
> This section should make you realize that this is not the proper way to view program efficiency. If minimum computing time is an important factor, worry first about choosing the best possible algorithm. Once that is done, develop the clearest, most straightforward, and most easily understood version of that algorithm. The excessive modification of an algorithm to save a fraction of a second is usually a losing proposition. First, you may find that it usually costs you more money, in terms of the hourly wage of the programmer, than was saved in reduced machine costs. Second, if the tricks that were played to save time were extremely complex, you may find that at some point in the future you are no longer able to decipher what you did! You would have been penny wise and pound foolish.
>
> This discussion does not imply that we tolerate gross inefficiency or total neglect for the concerns of time. It is simply to make you aware of where the real gains in efficiency are made—in the algorithm, not in the coding.

2.4   CONCLUSION

This chapter has provided an overview of algorithms, including their development, representation, and efficiency. Some of the important points we have highlighted are:

1. An algorithm is a procedure for solving a problem. It is composed of unambiguous commands whose order of execution is known, and it is always guaranteed to stop in a finite amount of time.

2.   There are many formats for representing and developing algorithms, and the specific one used by a programmer is not important except as it affects the difficulty of thinking about the algorithm and coding the solution. The ideal format is the one with which the programmer feels most comfortable and that can be converted into the desired programming language with relative ease.

3.   The truly creative part of programming is the design and development of correct and efficient algorithms. The coding phase, which will occupy much of the remainder of this book, can be viewed simply as the process of translating an algorithm into the syntax of a particular programming language.

4.   There is a measure, called the order of the algorithm, that allows us to compare the relative efficiency of one algorithm with other algorithms that solve the same or similar problems.

Chapters 3 to 5 will introduce you to a specific programming language—the language called Pascal.

Style Clinic 2-3

The Fundamental Importance of Algorithms

On simple problems, especially those encountered in introductory programming classes, students frequently go directly from the specification stages to the coding form, eliminating a separate and distinct algorithmic development phase. This tends to reinforce the notion that the important part of programming is coding and programming language syntax. This is not true. The truly important part of programming is developing a correct, elegant, and efficient algorithm in some language-independent representation such as an algorithmic language or a structured flowchart.

Some people have even begun to define computer science as "the study of algorithms and their realization on digital computers."

EXERCISES FOR CHAPTER 2

*1.   Rewrite the shampooing algorithm in Section 2.1 so that it is valid.

2.   Each of the following represents an attempt to write an algorithm that computes the sum of the first 10 integers. State why each is either poor or invalid.

*(a)   START
       set sum to $1+2+3+4+5+6+7+8+9+10$
       write sum
  END OF THE ALGORITHM

 (b)   START
       set n to 10
       set sum to 0
       add n to the sum
       decrement n by 1
       see if $n > 0$
       if it is go back and repeat the previous step
       write sum
  END OF THE ALGORITHM

*(c)   START
       set i to 1
       set sum to 0
       repeat 10 times
           add i to sum
       end of the repeat loop
       write sum
  END OF THE ALGORITHM

 (d)   START
       set i to 1
       set sum to 0
       while $i < 10$ do
           add i to sum
           increment i by 1
       end of the while loop
       write sum
  END OF THE ALGORITHM

*3. Write a valid algorithm to find the sum of the first k integers 1, 2, . . ., k. The value of k will be external input to the algorithm. (Be sure to handle the illegal situation of $k \leq 0$.)

4. Write an algorithm that determines the *mode* of a list of numbers. The mode is the value that occurred most frequently. For example, in

    1 2 2 3 3 3 4 5 5 6 6 7 7 7 7 8

the mode is 7 and has a frequency of 4. You may assume that:

  (a) The values are already sorted into ascending sequence.
  (b) The values will be external input to the algorithm.

(c) If two or more values occur an equal number of times, the mode will be defined as the numerically largest value.

The algorithm you develop should *not* store all the data in a list; it should read in only one value at a time and process that value. The output of your algorithm should be the mode and its frequency.

5. Modify the sequential search in Figure 2-1 so that it finds *every* occurrence of the key value and also produces a second list containing the *location* of every occurrence. For example, if the key were 10 and the list contained

   10 35 12 10 10 5 802 9 10

the output of the algorithm would be a 4 (the number of occurrences) and a list containing the values 1, 4, 5, 9 (the location of those occurrences).

*6. Develop an algorithm to solve quadratic equations of the form $ax^2 + bx + c = 0$ using the quadratic formula

$$\text{Roots} = \frac{-b \pm \sqrt{b^2 - 4ac}}{2a}$$

Your algorithm should handle the regular cases as well as the special cases of:

(a) A double root ($b^2 - 4ac = 0$).
(b) Complex roots ($b^2 - 4ac < 0$).
(c) A nonquadratic equation ($a = 0$).
(d) An illegal equation ($a = 0, b = 0$).

7. Assume that you are given a string of input text of arbitrary length and ending with a "$". Furthermore, assume that you wish to print this text as a set of lines of width no greater than k columns (k will be external input to the algorithm). The rules of our printing also specify that we must never break up a word between lines. (Assume the length of one word will never exceed k.) If a word cannot fit on the current line, print the current line as is and go on to the next line. For example, if k = 20 and the input text was:

   Hello. This is an example of how some textual material might look. . . .

the output would look like:

   Hello. This is an
   example of how some
   textual material
   might look. . . .

8. Modify the algorithm of Exercise 7 so that in addition to printing lines, it will *align* the left and right margins by adding blanks between the words. If the actual length of the current line is n characters, we need to add (k − n) blanks. We should add them as uniformly as possible between all words in the line. (There is a possible ambiguity in this question if there is only one word on the line. Decide what to do in this case.) The output in Exercise 7 would now look like this.

```
Hello.   This   is   an
example of how some
textual        material
might look. . . .
```

*9   (a) Assume that we have two lists that are sorted into ascending order. List A contains m items and list B contains n items. The values of m and n are not necessarily identical. Write an algorithm that merges all items of A and B into a single sorted list C containing all the elements of A and B.

   (b) Modify the algorithm from part a so that it eliminates any duplicate item that appears in both lists A and B. Assume that list A or B itself does not contain any duplicates.

   (c) Modify the algorithm from part a so that it eliminates any duplicate items appearing in both lists A and B *or* that are duplicated within list A or list B.

   (d) What is the time complexity of the merge operations in parts a, b, and c?

10. (a) An alternative type of sort is called the *insertion sort*. If we are sorting a list A into ascending sequence we find the smallest item, place it in the first position of an entirely new list, B_1, and set the value in A to infinity (or some very large value). Then we find the smallest value left in A, move it to B_2, and set it to infinity. When we are done, B is sorted and A is destroyed. Write an algorithm to implement the insertion sort as described.

   (b) What is the time complexity of this algorithm? How much space does it require compared to the other algorithms described in this chapter?

11. (a) Write an algorithm to implement the merge sort described in Section 2.3.

   (b) The fastest sorting algorithms that can be written will be of time complexity $O(n \log_2 n)$. Compare the efficiency of the $O(n^2)$, $O(n^{3/2})$, and $O(n \log_2 n)$ for different values of n. How much time will be gained by using the $O(n \log_2 n)$ algorithm on small lists (n ≈ 25 or 50)? How much will be gained by using them on very large lists (e.g., n > 100,000)?

*12. Write an algorithm to input an integer value N and determine if N is *prime*. (A prime number is an integer N ≧ 1 that is not evenly divisible by any values other than 1 and N.) The output of your algorithm should be either:

'N' is prime

or

'N' is not prime, 'M' is a factor

Make sure that your algorithm operates properly for *all* values of N.

13. Assume that we represented a deck of cards by the integers 1, . . ., 52 using the following assignment.

1 = A♤	14 = A♡	27 = A◇	40 = A♧
2 = 2♤	15 = 2♡	28 = 2◇	41 = 2♧
.	.	.	.
.	.	.	.
.	.	.	.
13 = K♤	26 = K♡	39 = K◇	52 = K♧

Write an algorithm that will input 5 cards, corresponding to a 5-card poker hand, and determine if we have:

(a) A *straight*—any 5 cards in sequence, regardless of suit; for example, A-2-3-4-5, 9-10-J-Q-K.

(b) A *flush*—any 5 cards of the same suit, regardless of rank; for example, 5♡ − 7♡ − 9♡ − 10♡ − K♡.

(c) A *straight flush*—5 cards of the same suit in sequence; for example, 2◇ − 3◇ − 4◇ − 5◇ − 6◇.

The output of the algorithm should indicate whether we had any of the three types of hands. (You can extend the problem to include other poker hands.)

After writing the algorithm, comment on the data representation for the playing cards. Would you have done it differently? Would it have affected your algorithm?

14. Assume that we have N cities, numbered 1, 2, . . ., N, and a *mileage chart* giving the exact distance between any two cities directly connected by a railroad line. (If two cities are not directly connected, the mileage chart contains a 0.) For example, if N = 4 and the railroad connections were

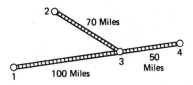

the mileage chart might look like this.

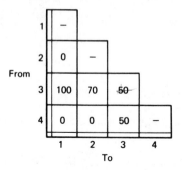

(The chart assumes that trains can always go in either direction on a track.) Develop an algorithm that will input any two indices i, j ($1 \leq$ i, j $\leq$ N; i $<$ j) and determine the total rail mileage from city i to city j. For example, if the input were

1   4

the algorithm should output

150 miles

(Be careful of the pathological case of two cities that are not connected by rail.)

NOTE.

(Questions 15 and 16 ask you to solve the problem that was developed in Section 1.4.2 and whose specifications were given in Figure 1-3.)

15. Assume that we have two lists, x_i and y_i, both containing n items. The *rank correlation coefficient*, r, between the lists x and y is defined as follows.

$$r = 1 - \frac{6 * \sum_{i=1}^{n} (a_i - b_i)^2}{n * (n^2 - 1)}$$

where a_i and b_i are the ordinal rankings of the raw scores contained in x and y, respectively. For example, if n $=$ 4 and x and y are

$x_1 = 52$	$y_1 = 17$
$x_2 = 30$	$y_2 = 93$
$x_3 = 79$	$y_3 = 62$
$x_4 = 60$	$y_4 = 77$

then a and b are

$$a_1 = 3 \qquad b_1 = 4$$
$$a_2 = 4 \qquad b_2 = 1$$
$$a_3 = 1 \qquad b_3 = 3$$
$$a_4 = 2 \qquad b_4 = 2$$

Assume also that there exists an algorithm called:

Rank (x,a)

that takes a set of raw scores in x, determines the proper rankings, and stores them in a. Rank(y,b) will do the same for y and b, respectively. If Rank encounters a raw score of -1, implying a missed examination, it assigns a rank of -1.

Without worrying about how Rank is implemented, write an algorithm to solve the problem whose specifications are contained in Figure 1-3.

16. Develop the algorithm Rank that was used in the correlation assignment in Exercise 15. Rank should assign to a raw score of -1 a ranking of -1 and should handle ties by assigning the average of all the ranks to the scores.

BASIC PASCAL DATA TYPES AND DECLARATIONS

3.1 INTRODUCTION

This chapter begins our introduction to the programming language called Pascal. This language was developed by Professor Niklaus Wirth at the Eidgenossische Technische Hochschule (ETH) in Zurich, Switzerland. The initial report on the language appeared in the literature in 1971,[1] and revised reports describing language improvements appeared during 1972[2] and 1973.[3] The first reference manual intended for use by Pascal programmers was produced in 1974.[4]

Some of the primary motivations behind the development of Pascal were to develop a programming language that would:

1. Be efficient to implement and run on today's computers.
2. Be interesting enough to teach the important concepts of computer programming.
3. Allow the development of well-structured and well-organized programs.

We feel that, taken together, these characteristics make Pascal an outstanding introductory programming language. It will allow us to present the topic of computer programming as a systematic discipline, not as a hit-or-miss art.

Pascal is a general-purpose language that is applicable to a wide range of numeric

[1]N. Wirth, "The Programming Language Pascal," *Acta Informatica,* 1(1), 1971, pp. 34–65.

[2]N. Wirth, "The Programming Language Pascal" (Revised Report), *ETH Tech. Report 5,* Zurich, Switzerland, 1972.

[3]C. Hoare and N. Wirth, "An Axiomatic Definition of the Programming Language Pascal," *Acta Informatica,* 3(1), 1973.

[4]K. Jensen and N. Wirth, "Pascal User Manual and Report," Springer-Verlag, Heidelberg, 1974.

and nonnumeric problems. To place the language in some relation to other well-known and widely used general-purpose programming languages with which you may be familiar, we could say that Pascal has a very loose similarity to both FORTRAN and BASIC except that it has a much richer set of available statements and data types. Pascal is more similar to PL/1 and its variant PL/C, but it is most closely related to ALGOL, since it is a descendant of ALGOL-60.

3.2 THE CONCEPT OF DATA TYPES

One of the most important contributions of Pascal and one of its most fundamental ideas is the formalization of the concept of a *data type*. A data type is a collection of elements that ''belong together'' in that they are all formed in the same way and are treated uniformly.

The most basic data types in Pascal are called *scalar data types,* in which one simply defines or enumerates all the possible constants of that type. This enumeration is always assumed to be ordered. Each constant has exactly one of the following relationships—greater than, less than, or equal—to any other constant of that type. The scalar data types themselves are divided into two classes, the *standard* scalar data types and the *user-defined* scalar data types. The standard scalar data types are the classes of data that are provided automatically by Pascal. There are four of these—integer, real, character, and boolean—and they will be discussed in the following section. The user-defined scalar data types represent new data types that a user can create to aid in solving a specific problem. They will be described in Section 3.4.

The scalar data types just mentioned can be combined to form highly complex *structured data types*. The way in which the scalars are combined and the type of relationship they have to each other determine the particular structured type. Furthermore, the structured types themselves can be combined to form even more sophisticated data structures with exceedingly complex interrelationships. However, regardless of their complexity, all data structures can ultimately be viewed as being composed of the basic building blocks of the language—the simple scalar data types. Structured data types will be discussed in Chapters 7, 9, and 10.

Figure 3-1 summarizes the various data types available in Pascal. One of our goals in this text is to convey an appreciation for the richness of the data-structuring capabilities of Pascal. It is primarily this characteristic that distinguishes Pascal from most popular programming languages.

3.3 THE STANDARD SCALAR DATA TYPES

3.3.1 Integers

The constants of the standard data type integer are the signed whole numbers between some implementation-defined limits. The formal syntax of Pascal integers is shown in Figure 3-4. To avoid having to know the limits for a specific computer,

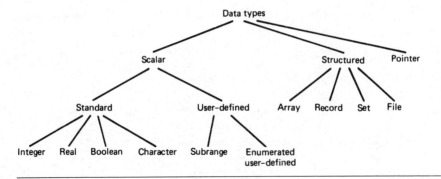

Figure 3-1. The hierarchy of data types in Pascal.

there is a predefined Pascal constant called maxint. The value of maxint is the largest integer constant available on that computer system. For example, on both the UNIVAC 1100 series computers and the PDP-10, maxint is $2^{35} - 1$. This would allow us to write integers with about 11 significant digits. However, be aware that this value may be difficult on other machines.

Some examples of valid Pascal integers are:

```
   27500      (not 27,500)
  - 123
      1
      0
  maxint
    +20
```

Note that a comma cannot be used when writing an integer.

The standard Pascal operators defined for the integer data type are:

+	addition
−	subtraction (and unary negation)
*	multiplication
div	integer division (divide and truncate); 19 **div** 7 = 2
mod	modulus; a **mod** b is the remainder after dividing b into a; 19 **mod** 7 = 5
>	greater than
>=	greater than or equal to
<	less than
<=	less than or equal to
=	equal to
<>	not equal to

The last six operators are called *relational operators*. They operate on any of the standard scalar data types to produce a result that has the value true or false. There are also four standard functions that produce integer results.

abs(i)   the absolute value of the integer i

sqr(i)   i squared

trunc(r)   r is a decimal number. The result is the integer portion of r.
             Trunc(2.61) is 2

round(r)   same as trunc but r is rounded to the nearest integer, round(2.61)
             is 3

3.3.2   Reals

The *real numbers* are the set of implementation-defined decimal values. There are two methods of representing real constants. In *decimal notation* we represent the number with an optional sign, a whole number part, a decimal point, and a fractional part. There must be at least one digit on each side of the decimal point. An alternate shorthand notation permits easy representation of very large or very small real values. This representation is *scientific notation*. The real number is written as a value, called the *characteristic,* multiplied by the appropriate power of 10. Because keypunches and computer terminals cannot type above the line, we cannot use standard algebraic notation for exponents in Pascal. Therefore, to indicate the exponent in scientific notation, we use the letter e. When encountered within a real number, this letter should be read as "times 10 to the power of." There may or may not be a decimal point in the characteristic, but any number in scientific notation is always of type real. As we will see, scientific notation can significantly reduce the keystrokes needed for representing very large or small constants and is a very convenient notation. The following are examples of valid real constants in Pascal. The syntax of real numbers is summarized in Figure 3-4.

3.1415927

−25.0

+0.198

5e6   (this would be the value 5,000,000)

−6.0e−8   (−0.00000006)

+6.08e+27

The following are all invalid real constants.

31   (a valid integer but not a real value)

3.   (no digit to the right of the decimal point)

.00215   (no digit to the left of the decimal point)

−2.427e.2 (only whole number exponents allowed)

As these examples indicate, the rules for forming real values differ slightly from standard mathematical notation. When translating an algorithm into Pascal, be aware of and adhere to those rules.

Each installation will define its own limits on the *range* (the largest and smallest allowable values) and *precision* (maximum number of significant digits) of real numbers. If the real numbers are viewed as a continuous line, four sections of that line will always be unavailable on a computer (Figure 3-2). The shaded areas A and B represent areas with real values too large (either positive or negative) to represent on the computer. Areas C and D represent areas with values too small (i.e., numbers too close to zero) to represent on the computer. The unshaded areas in Figure 3-2 are the set of real numbers that will be available to you in Pascal. Specific values for the exponents, e_1, e_2, e_3, and e_4 will vary from machine to machine and will have to be provided locally. As one example, on the Control Data Cyber 172 Series computers

$$e_1 = 322$$
$$e_2 = 294$$
$$e_3 = 294$$
$$e_4 = 322$$

The operators and functions available for the real data type are listed below.

+	addition
−	subtraction (or unary negation)
*	multiplication
/	real division (the fractional part is not truncated)
abs(r)	the absolute value of the real number r
sqr(r)	r squared
sin(r)	the sine of r
cos(r)	the cosine of r
arctan(r)	the arctangent of r
ln(r)	the natural logarithm of r
exp(r)	exponential function (e^r)
sqrt(r)	the square root of r

In addition, the relational operators discussed earlier are defined and available for use with real values.

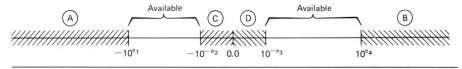

Figure 3-2. The set of available real numbers.

Style Clinic 3-1

Accuracy of Real Numbers

It is not always possible to store real numbers exactly in the internal representation of a computer. Some values just cannot be represented in a finite number of digits. For example, in decimal

$$1/3 = 0.3333333. . .$$

Regardless of where we stop, we will not have the exact representation of 1/3. Our representation will have introduced a small but distinct *truncation error*. If we now perform computations using this truncated value, the results will also be slightly in error. Most computers perform their computations in binary (base 2), not decimal (base 10). However, since binary is a positional numbering system, it also suffers from the same problem.

The impact of these truncation errors is that:

1. Real values computed by your programs may be off slightly in the last decimal places. The analysis of these errors and the methods for approximating their size are complex mathematical problems and are beyond our scope.

2. More important, from our point of view, you should never expect a real value to be *exactly* equal to a particular quantity. You should never test real constants for exact equality. For example, given the truncation error inherent in representing 1/3, the apparently true relationship

$$1/3 + 1/3 + 1/3 = 1$$

would actually be false. If you must test a real value for equality, check instead to see if it is "very close" to the desired value and accept that closeness in place of equality. The comparison

$$\text{if abs}(x - y) \leqq \in$$
$$\text{then write 'x is equal to y'}$$

where $\in$ is an appropriately small real value solves the problem mentioned before.

3.3.3 Characters

The elements of the data type *character* (abbreviated char in Pascal) are all the individual characters that can be represented on a specific machine. Unfortunately, there is currently no single, industrywide standard character set.[5] Therefore character processing can become a highly machine-dependent function for many different reasons.

1. The number of different characters available may vary from one computer to another. Character sets of 64, 128, or 256 distinct characters are not uncommon.

2. The specific characters available on a particular system may differ from the characters available on a different system. The only minimal assumption we can make in Pascal is that regardless of the implementation, we will always have available the 26 capital letters A, . . ., Z, the 10 digits 0, . . ., 9, and the blank character. In practice, the available character set will always be quite a bit larger. Appendix C contains a listing of the characters used in standard Pascal. Your installation may make some changes in this standard set because of local limitations.

3. Internally, the characters are represented by the nonnegative integers 0, 1, 2, . . ., n − 1, where n is the number of distinct characters available. The mapping of the characters onto their corresponding internal integers is called the *collating sequence*. The specific sequence has not been standardized and may be different on different machines. Appendix C lists internal character representations for a number of widely used character sets.

To indicate an element of the data type char, we surround the character with two apostrophes (single quotation marks). To indicate the apostrophe character itself, we simply write it twice. The syntax of the character data type is given in Figure 3-4.

'A'

'<'

'1'   (this is the character 1, not the integer value 1)

' '
.
'
'
'

''''   (the apostrophe character)

You should be careful to recognize that the elements of the scalar data type char are always single characters. Constructs such as 'HELLO' or '***' are not elements of this type but are elements of a more complex data type composed of sequences of characters. That data type, called an *array of characters*, will be described in Chapter 7.

There are four standard Pascal functions particularly useful for processing character data.

---

[5]There is currently a widespread attempt to make the ASCII code (American Standard Code for Information Interchange) a universal standard. However, many machines are not currently using it, and it cannot now be treated as a standard. The ASCII code is shown in Appendix C.

ord(c)	The *ordinal function*. c represents any character in our character set. Ord(c) is the internal integer representation of that character. For example, referring to Appendix C, in the ASCII character set ord('L') = 76.
chr(i)	The *character function*. i is a nonnegative integer. Chr(i) is the external character corresponding to that integer. Again, for the ASCII character set, chr(35) = '#'.
pred(c)	The *predecessor function*. If c is any character, pred(c) is the "previous" character in the character set; that is, chr(ord(c) − 1), except that if c is the first character, chr(0), the predecessor function is undefined.
succ(c)	The *successor function*. If c is any character, succ(c) is the "next" character; that is, chr(ord(c) + 1), except that if c is the last element of the character set, chr(n − 1), where n is the size of our character set, the successor function is undefined.

The pred and succ functions also apply to any scalar data type except real. For example:

pred(7) is 6
succ(9) is 10

Because of the lack of standardization in the ordering of characters, we should realize when applying the relational operators $>$, $<$, $>=$, $<=$, $=$, $<>$ to character data that a relationship that is true on one machine [e.g., 'a' $<$ '5' or '0' $=$ succ('z')] may not be true on all others, thus making it difficult to run the program correctly at other installations. One of the characteristics we will strive for in our examples in this text is *portability*—the ability to transfer a program from one computer to another and successfully execute the program without modification or with only minor modifications.

Style Clinic 3-2 _____

Portable Programs

The earlier discussion of the character data type raised an extremely important point—the idea of *portable programs*. It is frustrating to have a program work well on one computer but fail completely when the inevitable new machine comes along. It is also very nice to be able to share programs developed by other people at other sites. This requires that a program that was written for one computer be easily movable to another.

To achieve portability, we must write programs in the standard version of the language—the language elements that, by agreement or convention, have been adopted for use on all machines. Local language modifications or extensions may be cute and helpful, but using them guarantees that your program will not be easily moved to any other site. In this book we have attempted to adhere to a description of standard Pascal and have avoided mentioning any nonstandard Pascal extensions. Your site no doubt will support some nonstandard features, but use them carefully and with an awareness of what you are doing to your program.

Another limit to writing portable programs is the inclusion of machine-dependent information directly in your program. The use of such information can occasionally be avoided—such as by using maxint in place of 34359738367 or by ascertaining that ord('z') = ord('a') + 25 instead of automatically assuming (incorrectly) that on all machines the letters of the alphabet are in proper sequence and without gaps.

When the use of a particular piece of locally dependent datum absolutely cannot be avoided, organize your program so that this information is easy to locate and change. Do not bury this detail in the depths of your program. A good way is through the use of the **const** declaration (which will be described in Section 3.3.5). For example:

const
    numberofterminals = 2;
    { This value represents the number of terminals on
    this machine. You must change this declaration if
    the number available at your installation is different. }

3.3.4 Boolean

The elements of the scalar data type boolean are simply the two constants true and false ordered so that false < true.

The relational operators operate on the integer, real, char, or boolean data types and produce a boolean result. In addition, there are three operators that can be applied only to boolean values to produce a boolean result.

and	logical conjunction (binary operator)
or	logical disjunction (binary operator)
not	logical negation (unary operator)

They are defined by the tables in Figure 3-3. For example, the value of the expression

(a = 10) **or** *(b > 5)*

p	q	p and q
F	F	F
F	T	F
T	F	F
T	T	T

p	q	p or q
F	F	F
F	T	T
T	F	T
T	T	T

p	not p
F	T
T	F

Figure 3-3. Definition of the boolean operators.

will be true if *either* the variable a is equal to 10 or if the variable b is greater than 5, or both. Otherwise, the expression will be false. Likewise, the value of

not *((a = 1)* **and** *(b = 1))*

will be true if either a is not equal to 1, if b is not equal to 1, or if both a and b are not equal to 1. We will talk much more about the formation of boolean expressions in Section 4.3.

Although **and, or,** and **not** are the only three logical operators provided as a standard part of the Pascal language, all other common logical operations can be implemented by using these three standard relational operators and the knowledge that false < true. For example, if p and q are boolean values:

$p \leqq q$

is exactly equivalent to p⊂q (p implies q).

Finally, there are boolean functions in standard Pascal, called *predicates,* that return a value of either true or false. The only one we will mention now is:

odd(i)   This function is true if the integer i is odd and false otherwise.

The syntax of the four standard scalar types is summarized in Figure 3-4 using a notational device called a *syntax chart.* A syntax chart is simply a way to describe formally the legal syntax of some object (e.g., constant, statement) in a programming language. If you can generate a given object by starting at the left of its syntax chart, following the arrows, and exiting at the right of the chart, that object is said to be

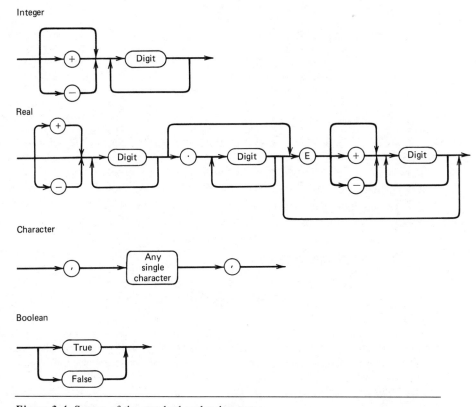

Figure 3-4. Syntax of the standard scalar data types.

syntactically valid. All other objects are invalid. For example, given the following syntax chart for a "silly object,"

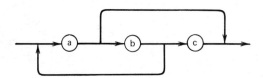

all of the following character strings are legal "silly objects."

a
abc
ababc
aba
ababa

But

        ac
        acb
        abab
        cbc
        baaba

are all illegal "silly objects." There is simply no way to generate these strings from the chart shown.

The rounded symbols in the syntax charts (circles and ellipses) represent terminal symbols that are not defined further. The rectangular symbols are syntactic entities that are further defined in another named syntax chart either in the text or in Appendix A, which contains the complete syntactic description of the Pascal language.

3.3.5   The Const Declaration

The problem with the use of a constant within the body of a program is that it carries no mnemonic value [except for well-known ones such as 3.14 (π) or 2.71 (e)]. Looking at an individual constant rarely gives us a clue to its function or purpose. Frequently it becomes attractive to associate a name with some specific constant and then use the name throughout the program to improve legibility. In Pascal this can be done by using the **const** declaration. The syntax of the **const** declaration is given in Figure 3-5.

The **const** declaration equates a symbolic name with a scalar constant. The indicated name can now be used in place of its corresponding constant throughout the entire program. However, remember that the name still represents a constant value and cannot be changed by any other part of the program, any more than the constant itself could be changed. For example,

```
const
    pi = 3.1415927;
    minimumtaxrate = 0.14;
    blank = ' ';
```

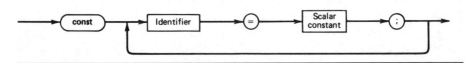

Figure 3-5. Syntax of the **const** declaration.

Now, instead of writing expressions such as

0.14 + increment

and leaving us wondering what the fractional quantity represents, we can write

minimumtaxrate + increment

Nothing has actually changed (both 0.14 and minimumtaxrate are real constants), but the clarity and legibility of the command are greatly enhanced.

In addition to providing increased legibility, the **const** declaration makes it easier to change a program. If we had a dozen occurrences of the same constant in a program, each would have to be located and modified if a change became necessary. With symbolic constants, only the single **const** declaration need be modified.

Style Clinic 3-3 _____

Symbolic Constants

Any scalar constant that either:

    1.   is used frequently within a program
    2.   could possibly be changed in future versions of the program
    3.   is important to an understanding of the logic of a program

should be defined symbolically using a **const** declaration.

3.4   ADDITIONAL SCALAR DATA TYPES

3.4.1   User-Defined Scalar Data Types

The basic data types in Pascal are the four scalar types introduced in the previous section. These scalar types are composed of individual elements, called constants, and the relationship between any two constants of a scalar data type can be described by saying that one constant is always less than, equal to, or greater than any other constant. Thus each scalar data type in Pascal is *ordered*.

Pascal automatically provides four standard scalar data types: integer, real, boolean, and char. Frequently, however, these standard data types are insufficient to describe a particular problem adequately. In some programming languages we may actually be forced to modify or constrain the problem to match one of the available data types. For example, if we wished to work with values that ranged over the days of the week, it would be convenient to have a data type whose constants were sunday, monday, tuesday, wednesday, thursday, friday, saturday, and that were ordered in just that sequence. If such a type existed we could declare variables to be of this data type and let them assume the values of any of those constants—exactly as we did with the standard Pascal types. Statements such as

> set day to monday

or

> if day = saturday or day = sunday then
> write "it's a weekend"

would have a valid meaning in our language, and the intent of the statements would be clear.

If the ability to create this "days-of-the-week" data type were not a part of our language, we would be forced to modify the representation so that we could use an existing standard data type. Most probably this would be done by mapping the days of the week onto the integers 1 to 7. Although this would work adequately and the program could be written, we would have lost the readability inherent in using the day names themselves and would have diminished the clarity of the program.

Perhaps it has occurred to you that we could use a series of **const** declarations to provide meaningful names.

```
const
    sunday = 1;
    monday = 2;
    tuesday = 3;
        .
        .
        .
```

This would allow us to refer to sunday, monday, . . . instead of the integers 1, 2, . . ., and the readability of our program would be enhanced. However, it is a bit awkward and inconvenient to write the sequence of **const** declarations which constitutes the mapping of the names onto the integers. It would be helpful if we could simply name the constants we wished to use without explicitly having to associate each constant with an integer. In a sense, we would like the machine to generate the preceding **const** declaration for us automatically. This is available in Pascal through the use of the *user-defined scalar data type*.

To allow algorithms to be translated into the language most naturally, Pascal permits users to define new scalar data types. To create these new types, we need to provide two specific pieces of information: the constants contained in the data type and their ordering. This information is provided in a Pascal statement called a **type** declaration. The purpose of a **type** declaration is to create totally new data types in Pascal beyond the four standard types introduced in Section 3.3.

The syntax of a type declaration when used to create new user-defined scalar types is shown in Figure 3-6.

The ''identifiers'' contained in the **type** declaration are the constants of the new data type, and ''type-name'' is the symbolic name associated with the new data type. The constants are assumed to have the ordering relationship specified by their left-to-right position in the **type** declaration. A constant is considered greater than all constants to its left and less than all constants to its right.

Examples of user-defined scalar types would include:

```
type
     daysoftheweek = (sun, mon, tue, wed, thur, fri, sat);
     clubmembers = (sybil, benjy, maria, stephanie, rebecca, annie);
     months = (january, february, march, april, may, june, july, august,
                september, october, november, december);
     family = (mother, father, sister, brother);
```

The data type called daysoftheweek, just defined, will be composed of the seven constants called sun, mon, tue, wed, thur, fri, and sat. The ordering of these constants is specified by their position in the **type** declaration. Thus all of the following relations are true.

```
sun < mon
fri > wed
tue = tue
tue <= sat
```

In addition, we can apply the standard functions pred and succ to these newly defined types.

```
pred(wed) = tue
succ(january) = february
pred(father) = mother
pred(sybil) is undefined
```

The only restriction on enumerating the constants of a user-defined scalar type is that each identifier must appear in no more than one user-defined type. This restriction is necessary to guarantee that all operations on these data types are unambiguous. For example, given the following additional **type** declaration:

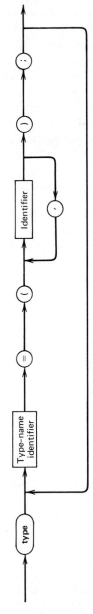

Figure 3-6. Syntax of **type** declaration for user-defined scalar data types.

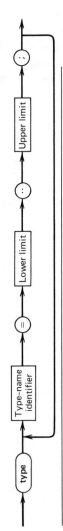

Figure 3-7. Syntax of **type** declaration for scalar subrange data types.

type
      friends = (rebecca, jenny, benjy, kathleen, erik);

the truth of the boolean relation

    rebecca < benjy

is ambiguous, since it depends on which data type we are referring to: friends or club members.

The use of user-defined scalar types can significantly enhance the legibility and clarity of a Pascal program. We will see a number of examples of the use of this data type in upcoming sections.

3.4.2 Scalar Subrange Data Types

Frequently, when choosing the data types we will be using in our program, we find that we really do not need a completely new data type but simply a portion of some existing type. A *scalar subrange* data type is a data type composed of a specified range of any of the other standard or user-defined scalar types, except type real.

We define a subrange type with a **type** declaration of the format shown in Figure 3-7. In Figure 3-7 "lowerlimit" and "upperlimit" are elements of the same standard or user-defined scalar type, termed the *base type,* and lowerlimit <= upperlimit. The new data type is called "type-name" and is composed of only those elements of the base type that lie between lowerlimit and upperlimit inclusively.

Examples of subrange declarations are:

type
      examscores = 0. .100;
      letters = 'a'. .'z';
      digits = '0'. .'9';
      weekdays = mon. .fri; { see section 3.4.1 }
      summer = june. .september; { see section 3.4.1 }
      fall = september. .november; { see section 3.4.1 }

Each of these declarations will create a new scalar subrange data type containing only the constants within the specified range. For example, examscores will be a data type containing the 101 integer values 0, 1, 2. . ., 98, 99, 100. Fall will be a subrange of the data type called months that was created in Section 3.4.1. It will contain the three constants september, october, november.

An obvious question that you may be asking is why we really need a subrange data type. After all, if a portion of an already existing data type is needed, why not simply use the entire data type?

There are two reasons for the new class of data type: increased readability and run-time error checking. If we declare in our Pascal program that a variable called test is of type integer, a reader of that program knows only that test will be able to take on constant integer values in the range $-$maxint to $+$maxint, a very large range. However, if that same variable is declared to be of type examscores, as just shown, we will have significantly increased the information content of our program. Now anyone looking at this program will not only know that the test scores must be integers, he or she will also know that the only possible scores on the tests are between 0 and 100. The judicious use of subrange data types can make statements and declarations much more informative and easier to understand.

In addition to the increased clarity that can be gained by utilizing a subrange data type, there is another extremely useful feature that can be provided to the user: run-time error checking. A subrange data type provides information about the valid range of constants that can be assigned to a value. This information can be used to check the validity of all assignments made while the program is being run. If test were a variable of type examscores, then a statement such as

```
test := 101
```

can be classified as invalid when it is executed.

If a Pascal program is being run in *debug mode,* the system will check all assignments of values to variables declared to be of subrange type. Any attempt to assign an out-of-range value to such a variable will cause an execution-time error and program termination. Entering debug mode is usually done with a special command. Since the exact format of this command will vary from machine to machine, this information will have to be provided by your instructor. The execution of a program in debug mode will naturally increase the computer time needed to execute the program. This is due to the additional run-time checking being performed. This increase may be quite significant. However, in many cases, the extra time can be considered well spent because of its help in locating and correcting errors.

3.5   NAMES IN PASCAL

The previous two sections indicated at least two situations in which we may wish to use a symbolic name in Pascal. In Section 3.4 we indicated that you may define and name a new data type. In Section 3.3.5 we showed why you may want to substitute a symbolic name for a scalar constant. In this section we will talk about a third use— choosing names for Pascal variables. The use of these symbolic names (or, more properly, *identifiers*) is fundamental to all aspects of the language.

There are three distinct classes of names in Pascal.

1. *Reserved Words.* These are names reserved by Pascal for a specific purpose; they cannot be used by a programmer in any other way. These keywords must be delimited by one or more blank characters. The ones we have encountered so far are:

   const   and   or   mod   div   not   type

   Appendix B contains a list of all the reserved keywords in standard Pascal. In this text all reserved words will be set in **boldface type.**

2. *Standard Identifiers.* These are names that have a predefined meaning in Pascal but that may, if necessary, be redefined by the user for another purpose. However, if they are redefined, they cannot be used for the original purpose in the remainder of the program. For example, a user may create and use a symbolic constant named abs. Then, however, the user would no longer be able to use the absolute value function, abs, which is automatically provided as part of the language. Examples of some standard keywords encountered so far include:

   maxint   true   false   integer   succ   abs

   A complete list of standard keywords in Pascal is also given in Appendix B. In this text we will refrain from redefining the meaning of a standard identifier in order to eliminate the confusion that usually results.

3. *User Identifiers.* These are names created by the user that have no other predefined meaning. They may be used to name a wide range of different objects such as new data types, constants, variables, or even entire programs.

The rules for forming a user identifier are given in Figure 3-8. They specify that an identifier must start with an alphabetic character 'A', . . ., 'Z' or 'a', . . ., 'z' (if lowercase is available on your computer) and that it be composed only of alphabetic and numeric characters. No special characters (e.g., +, $, *, ;) are allowed. The user identifier may be as long as desired, but standard Pascal only looks at the first eight characters to determine uniqueness. (Different installations may enlarge the figure somewhat but will never decrease it.) Some examples of valid identifiers in Pascal are:

x
a500
result
thefirstroot
thefirstattempt   (although it may be treated as equivalent to
                                   the preceding one)
thisisanextremelylongidentifier

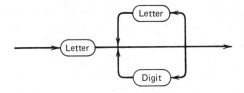

Figure 3-8. Syntax of an identifier in Pascal.

Some examples of invalid user identifiers are:

begin	(a reserved keyword)
1c	(begins with a digit)
stock#	(contains the special character #)
sqrt	(this is actually valid, but now you can no longer access the standard Pascal square root function)

3.6 SCALAR VARIABLES

A *variable* is simply an object that can assume different values during the execution of a program. Alternatively, a variable can be thought of as a location inside the computer that has a name and that can store a value. In Pascal variable names can be any valid user identifier.

It is very important to recognize and remember the distinction between the *name* associated with a variable and the *current value* of that variable.

x | 1.5 |

In the above example the name of the variable is x; its current value is 1.5. The name of a variable is permanent. It is specified only once at the beginning of a program in a declaration we will discuss shortly. The value, however, is quite volatile and may change often during the program's execution. In the algorithmic notation of the previous chapter, any of the following commands:

> increment x by 1
> set x to 2.5
> add 10 to the current value of x
> read in a new value for x

would leave the name of the variable unchanged but produce a new current value.

In some languages there are no restrictions on what type of values we may assign to a variable. For example, in some languages a variable could have the integer value 6 at one point, be changed to the real value -2.71, and then be assigned the boolean value true. Such languages are called *weakly typed* or *typeless*. In these languages the concept of data type is not fundamental, and there are few or no explicit rules associated with data typing. Pascal represents the opposite approach and is termed a *strongly typed* language. This means that:

1. Every scalar variable must be explicitly associated with a single scalar data type.

2. The variable may assume values of only that data type for the duration of its existence.

3. Most operators and functions are defined only for specific data types. Applying them to any other data type is treated as an error.

4. Mixing data types (e.g., adding a character variable to an integer constant) is, with one exception, an error. The exception is the mixing of an integer and a real with an operand that expects two real values.

The beginning Pascal programmer may find the explicit typing requirement awkward and time consuming. However, it has many advantages for both the user and the computer. It enhances the legibility and organization of the program by collecting in a single location, almost as a table of contents, all the variables used in the program and their associated data types. In addition, these required declarations allow the computer to perform extensive error checking during program execution.

To create scalar variables and to associate them with a specific scalar data type, we use the **var** declaration. The syntax of that declaration is shown in Figure 3-9. Without exception, all variables used in a Pascal program must be declared in a **var** declaration. Failure to do so will *always* result in an error.

The "data type name" referred to in the **var** declaration can be either a standard data type (integer, real, boolean, char) or a data type defined by the user in a preceding **type** declaration.

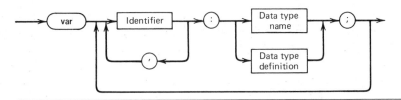

Figure 3-9. Syntax of the **var** declaration.

An example of a **var** declaration is:

var

count, n	:integer;
root	:real;
a,b,c	:char;
day	:daysoftheweek; { see Section 3.4.1 }
people	:family; { see Section 3.4.1 }

Once we have associated a variable with a data type, we have fixed the range of constant values that the variable may assume and the set of operations that we may perform on that variable. For example, the variable count just declared can now take on only integer values. Therefore, operations like

> set count to 9
> add 1 to count
> if count < 1 then write "count is not positive"

are meaningful. But attempts to translate any of the following operations

> set count to the letter 'q'
> set count to true
> set count to monday
> set count to 1.038

directly into Pascal will result in a fatal error. These operations attempt to assign a value of the incorrect type to an integer variable, and this is not allowed in Pascal.

Pascal allows a shorthand notation that combines the effect of a **type** and a **var** declaration into a single declaration. The "data-type name" field of a **var** declaration can always be replaced by the explicit type definition itself. For example, the declaration pair:

type
>   scorerange = 0..150;

var
>   exam : scorerange;

can be replaced by the following single **var** declaration

var
>   exam : 0..150;

The effect of both is identical. The only difference is that in the second case the new data type (the integer subrange 0 to 150) does *not* have an explicit name associated with it.

We are now in a position to distinguish the three classes of operations that are performed on Pascal variables.

1. *Declaring a Variable*. This operation is performed only once at the beginning of the program. It assigns a name to a variable and permanently associates the variable with a data type. It typically does not assign a value to that variable, and no specific initial value (e.g., zero) should be assumed. By making the declaration

    var
      k : integer;

   we reserve a location in memory called k but give it no current value.

   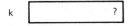

   The values that may eventually be put into k are limited to the valid Pascal integers.

2. *Defining a Variable*. (Also called *assigning a value* to a variable.) This is the process of either creating a value for or changing the current value of a variable. A variable must be declared prior to being defined. When a variable is redefined, the new value will replace the old value, and the old value will be lost. All of the following algorithmic commands are valid ways to define the variable k declared previously.

   Current Value

set k to 3	3
increment k by 1	4
read in a value for k	whatever was on the data card or line just read

   An attempt to do something such as

   set k to 123.456

   is invalid. In the declaration, we stated that k was a variable of type integer. Therefore, when defining k, we must limit it to that class of values.

3. *Referencing a Variable*. This is the process of *using* the current value of a variable in some way.

   write out the current value of k
   if k is equal to 3 then stop
   set j to the current value of k

It should be obvious that a variable must be defined before it can be referenced. Failure to define it will lead to an error. It is also the rule in Pascal (and all other programming languages) that the process of referencing a variable never changes the current value of that variable. In a sense, we can imagine we are making a copy of a variable each time we wish to look at or use its value. We do not change the value by copying it. So, for example, none of the preceding three algorithmic statements would cause a change to the current value of the variable k.

Style Clinic 3-4 _____

Variable Names

All variables used in programs you write should be given mnemonic names that indicate clearly and obviously their exact purpose within the program.

A variable used to store the computed value for daily receipts could be given any of the following names within the program.

> *x*
> *dr*
> *receipts*
> *dailyreceipts*   (assuming no other variable begins with the characters dailyrec)

However, the clarity of the name increases dramatically as we go down the list, and certainly the first two (and possibly the third) should be considered totally inadequate. The use of obscure, nonmnemonic names is a major obstacle to understanding a program. Avoid such names at all costs.

3.7 CONCLUSION

All Pascal programs are made up of two very distinct parts.

1. The *declaration section*, where we describe the data objects that we will be using in our program.
2. The *program section,* where we specify the explicit actions to take on these data objects.

This chapter has presented some of the most basic concepts related to the creation and usage of data (e.g., data types, declarations, constants, variables, and identifiers). All of the declarations that were introduced (**const, type,** and **var**) are part of this declaration section. Additional Pascal data structures will be discussed in Chapters 7, 9, and 10.

Chapter 4 will introduce the basic executable statements of the Pascal language. The purpose of these statements will be to describe exactly how to *process* the data objects that we have just created. When we have completed this description, we will be in a position to write complete Pascal programs.

EXERCISES FOR CHAPTER 3

1. Show the Pascal representation of the following constants.

   * (a) π
     (b) e (the base of the natural logarithms)
   * (c) the fractional value 1/2
   * (d) $6.02 * 10^{23}$
     (e) the number 7
   * (f) the character 7
     (g) the color red
   * (h) 18 billion
     (i) truth
     (j) the blank character

*2. Which of the following are valid Pascal **const** declarations? Identify the error(s) in each of the invalid declarations.

   (a) **const**
   ```
   highvalue = 200;
   ```
   (b) **const**
   ```
   lowvalue = 0 or 1 or 2;
   ```
   (c) **const**
   ```
   firstchar : 'a';
   ```
   (d) **const**
   ```
   greatest = 200.0;
   least = - 100.0;
   ```
   (e) **const**
   ```
   range = 200. .800;
   ```

*3. Write a single **const** declaration for the following values.

   (a) the terminator character '.'
   (b) the integer constant 80 representing the maximum length of a line
   (c) the real constants 0 and 100 representing the range of scores on an examination

4. Write a single **type** declaration to create the following three new data types.

    (a) the integer subrange $(-100, +100)$

    (b) the six New England states

    (c) the lowercase letters of the alphabet

5. Which of the following **type** declarations are illegal? If a **type** declaration is illegal, correct it, if possible.

    * (a) **type** integer = −maxint..+maxint;

    * (b) **type** correlation = 0.0..+1.0;

    * (c) **type** yearinschool = (1, 2, 3, 4);

    (d) **type** colors: (red,blue,green,yellow,pink,chevrolet,brown);

    (e) **type** hyphenatedwords = (pre-set, lower-limit, upper-limit);

6. Which of the following are valid Pascal **var** declarations? Identify the error(s) in each of the invalid declarations and correct them.

    (a) **var**
           1a,2a,3a :char;

    (b) **var**
           a1,a2,a3 :char;
           b1   :real;
           a3   :integer;

    (c) **var**
           a   :integer;
           b   :integer;
           c   :integer;
           abc :real;

    (d) **var**
           resulta, resultb:real;
           count   :integer;
           c1   :char;
           x, y   :real;

*7. Choose reasonable names and write a single **var** declaration for the following values.

    (a) the three real coefficients of a quadratic equation

    (b) the two real roots of that equation

    (c) a boolean value indicating whether or not there was a solution

    (d) an integer value that indicates the data set number

    (e) the primary colors red, yellow, and blue

8. Choose reasonable names and write a single **var** declaration for the following values.

   (a) a six-digit student identification number

   (b) year in school (freshman, sophomore, . . .)

   (c) year of graduation

   (d) grade point average (A = 4.0)

   (e) a variable indicating whether or not all current fees have been paid

9. Rewrite these two declarations so that they accomplish the same operations but using only **var** declarations.

   ```
   type
       list    = (alpha, beta, gamma);
       range   = 'a'..'z';
   var
       a, b        :char;
       greek       :list;
       num         :integer;
       letters     :range;
   ```

10. Classify each of the following character strings as a reserved word, standard identifier, user identifier, constant, or invalid.

    * (a) begin   (h) 1e1
      (b) real   * (i) 1e
    * (c) start   (j) 234
      (d) sqr   * (k) truncate
    * (e) maxint   (l) character
      (f) xyz   * (m) .7
    * (g) e1   (n) 3.

11. Look up the character code used on your computer and state what the result of each of the following expressions would be on your computer.

    (a) ord('q')

    (b) chr(3)

    (c) succ('z')

    (d) pred(ord('#'))

    (e) chr(trunc(sqrt(517)))

12. Using the relational operators and the knowledge that

true > false

implement the following logical operators as defined by the given truth tables.

* (a)   p ≡ q (equivalence)

p	q	p ≡ q
F	F	T
F	T	F
T	F	F
T	T	T

* (b)   p ⊕ q (exclusive - or)

p	q	p ⊕ q
F	F	F
F	T	T
T	F	T
T	T	F

(c) p ⊄ q (negative implication)

p	q	p ⊄ q
F	F	F
F	T	F
T	F	T
T	T	F

ELEMENTARY PASCAL PROGRAMMING

In Chapter 3 we considered some of the fundamental data-oriented aspects of the Pascal programming language: data types, constants, variables, and declarations. We will now add to this framework the additional concepts needed to write complete Pascal programs. This will include arithmetic and boolean expressions, the assignment of values to variables, and techniques for performing input and output operations. We will end this chapter with some simple, but complete, Pascal programs and some general information on how to run them.

4.1 ARITHMETIC EXPRESSIONS

We listed earlier the various arithmetic operators of Pascal. Forming arithmetic expressions with them is very simple. We must, however, pay close attention to the data types we use and the order in which the arithmetic operations are performed.

We will begin with some very simple examples. Suppose that a and b have been declared integer and c and d have been declared real. Each of the following is an acceptable arithmetic expression in Pascal.

Integer Expressions:

a + b
a − 5
*b * 312*
a **div** *3*   (Integer division—the remainder is discarded. If a has the value 7, the value of the expression is 2.)
a **mod** *3*   (The remainder after dividing a by 3. If a is 7, the value of the expression is 1. If a is 9, the value of the expression is 0.)

Each of the preceding expressions produces an integer result.

Real Expressions:

$c + 1.51$
$c - d$
$c * d$
$d / 2.0$ (Real division—the result is a real quantity. If d has the value
                9.0, the value of the expression is 4.5.)

Each of these expressions produces a real result.

Note that in each of these expressions we have used two operands of the same type. That is, regardless of whether the operands were variables or constants, both were real or both were integer. Performing an operation on operands of different types is called *mixing* data types. In all cases except one, the mixing of data types is illegal in Pascal and will cause a fatal error. The one exception is the mixing of reals and integers with an operator that expects two real operators. If a is a real variable and c is an integer, then for each of the following expressions,

$a + c$
$a - c$
$a * c$
a / c
$a < c$ (or any other relational operator)

Pascal will correctly convert the integer operand to a real representation before evaluating the expression.

In all other cases, type mixing is illegal. For example,

$'m' + 1$ (will *not* give an 'n')
$'8' = 8$ (illegal)
$true + 3$ (illegal)

Errors can occur even in cases where the mixing of data types seems harmless. For example, the operators **div** and **mod** require both operands to be integers. Thus, if a is an integer, a **div** 2.0 is invalid, even though the intent seems clear. It is important not to lose sight of the difference between integers and reals. 1 and 1.0 may seem superficially identical, but the computer represents and treats them differently. It is a good idea to exercise care in formulating arithmetic expressions and not rely on Pascal to interpret correctly the intent of a mixed type expression, used accidentally. The habit of consistently using a single data type throughout a given expression will provide an increased sensitivity to data types and also avoid certain kinds of programming errors.

Things would be dull if our arithmetic expressions were limited to precisely the sort of examples just presented: a binary operator and two operands. Fortunately, Pascal permits us to construct arithmetic expressions of arbitrary complexity, as in:

$a * 7 + b$ **div** $2 - k$ **mod** 3 (a, b, k must be integer variables)

or

$c / 1.51 * d - 3.001$ (c, d must be real variables)

It should be obvious that there is an essential consideration in more complex arithmetic expressions such as the last two. In what order are the arithmetic operations performed? Consider the second example just presented. It is not clear what the denominator of the division operation is. It might be 1.51, 1.51 * d, or it might be the entire expression to the right of the division operator, 1.51 * d − 3.001. Clearly, the result of the computation will be different for each case.

In this particular case the denominator is simply 1.51. That is, the division is performed as if we had written

$(c / 1.51) * d - 3.001$

There is more to be said about this example. What will be the multiplier of the quotient obtained from the division? Will it be d or the quantity d − 3.001? We can use parentheses to obtain either effect, but in the absence of parentheses, Pascal will use just d. That is, evaluation will proceed as if we had written

$((c / 1.51) * d) - 3.001$

Pascal utilizes a hierarchy of operators. Certain operators are said to have higher *precedence* than others. In the absence of any other information (i.e., parentheses that would explicitly indicate an ordering), Pascal will evaluate arithmetic expressions so that operators with higher precedence are evaluated before operators of lower precedence. For the operators that we have been considering so far, the precedence rules are:

1. Subexpressions in parentheses are evaluated first.
2. *, /, **div, mod** operations are evaluated next.
3. +, − are evaluated last.

Thus parentheses have the highest precedence, the multiplication and division operations the next highest, and the addition and subtraction operations the lowest. If we write r + s * t, the evaluation will proceed as if we had written r + (s * t) because the multiplication operator has higher precedence than the addition operator.

However, our hierarchy of operators has not resolved all of the uncertainties concerning how expressions are evaluated, since we may have more than one operator of the same precedence. In the expression r / s * t, is the division or the multiplication performed first? To resolve this situation, there is another precedence rule. When there are no parentheses and there is more than one operator of the same precedence, evaluation proceeds from left to right in an expression. Thus, r / s * t is treated as (r / s) * t.

We now have the rules we need to determine the order of evaluation of arithmetic expressions. Consider these examples:

Expression	*Order of Evaluation*
a * 7 + b **div** 2 − k **mod** 3	((a * 7) + (b **div** 2)) − (k **mod** 3)
u − 11.3 * v − w + x	((u − (11.3 * v)) − w) + x
e + f − g * h / k	(e + f) − ((g * h) / k)

In each of these cases we could have originally written the expression with some or all of the parentheses as indicated on the right without changing the order of evaluation. Alternatively, we could have used parentheses to change the order of evaluation of the expression. For example,

*((a * (7 + b)) **div** (2 − k)) **mod** 3*

is a perfectly legitimate arithmetic expression (as long as k does not equal 2) with a meaning that is obviously different from the meaning of the first example.

When translating an expression from an algebraic representation to its Pascal equivalent, we must be very careful to obtain the proper order of evaluation. For example, the well-known quadratic formula is written mathematically as

$$\frac{-b \pm \sqrt{b^2 - 4ac}}{2a}$$

If we transcribe this directly to expressions in Pascal as follows:

*−b + sqrt(b * b − 4.0 * a * c) / 2.0 * a*
*−b − sqrt(b * b − 4.0 * a * c) / 2.0 * a*

we have two syntactically correct statements but the wrong expression! According to the precedence rules of Pascal, what will be computed is

$$-b \pm \frac{(\sqrt{b^2 - 4ac})a}{2}$$

A correct translation of the quadratic formula can be written as follows.

```
(−b + sqrt(b * b − 4.0 * a * c)) / (2.0 * a)
(−b − sqrt(b * b − 4.0 * a * c)) / (2.0 * a)
```

Style Clinic 4-1 _____

Parentheses

After spending a great deal of time describing the precedence rules of Pascal, we will add a new rule of our own. Parenthesize an expression to improve the readability of your program.

When writing an expression such as

```
a / b + c / d + e / f
```

the reader must remember the rules of precedence to interpret it correctly. If that person has forgotten these rules the formula could be misinterpreted. It would have been easier to have written

```
(a / b) + (c / d) + (e / f)
```

Nothing has been changed, but we no longer need to rely on someone's (possibly faulty) memory.

Never sacrifice clarity of expression to minimize keystrokes. Always try to help the reader of your program know what you mean. However, use your common sense to avoid using so many parentheses that you confuse instead of clarify.

```
((((a / b) + (c / d)) + ((e / f))))
```

A single expression of extreme complexity with many adjacent parentheses should be broken into several separate expressions for clarity. After four or five levels of parentheses, it becomes difficult to comprehend what an expression means.

4.2   USE OF STANDARD FUNCTIONS

The Pascal language automatically includes a set of *standard functions* that perform common and useful operations.[1] These functions have already been listed in Chapter 3.

To use a function, we write the *name* of the function followed by an *argument* enclosed in parentheses. The argument is simply the particular value that we want the function to use when performing its computation. For example, sqrt(3.26) would compute the square root of 3.26. In this case, 3.26 is the argument of the function named sqrt.

If we want to make use of the square root that was just computed we would incorporate the function reference into an arithmetic expression. Now the function reference is acting exactly as a simple variable or constant. For example,

(sqrt(3.26) * 7.0) + 3.6

is an acceptable Pascal expression. First, the square root is computed; then that value is multiplied by 7.0; finally, that result is added to 3.6.

In the previous example we used a constant as the argument of the function sqrt. That is actually a special case. In general, the argument of a standard function can be an arithmetic expression of arbitrary complexity. We can say not only sqrt(3.26) but also:

sqrt(x)
sqrt(x + 1.76)
sqrt((x + y) − (x * y) / 2.0)
sqrt(sin(x))

as long as the variables x and y have all been defined and the argument expression evaluates to a nonnegative real value. The order of evaluation of the argument expression will follow the same precedence rules we have already described.

When using a standard function, we must again pay close attention to the concept of data type. However, now it is essential to recognize that there are two data types involved. We must concern ourselves with the data type of the function's argument and also the data type of the function itself (i.e., the data type of the result the function produces). These two types need not be the same. A function can take a real argument and yet produce an integer result [trunc(2.61) is 2], or it may take an integer argument and produce a result of type char [on a Burroughs B90 computer, chr(76) is '<']. Functions that return a value whose data type is different from that of its argument

---

[1]In Chapter 8 we will discuss techniques for writing our own functions to deal with the cases in which the built-in functions are inadequate. This is a very important aspect of programming in Pascal (or any language). However, for now we will limit ourselves to those provided for us by the language itself.

are frequently called *transfer functions*. In addition, some of the standard functions will accept arguments of more than one type. For example, the argument to the standard function sqr can be either real or integer. When using a Pascal function, we must always provide an argument of the proper type.

After making sure that the argument for a function is of the proper type, we are only half done. We must also be concerned with the data type of the result produced by the function. This means that when we incorporate a function reference into an arithmetic expression, we should still have an expression in which all data types are consistent. For example, the sqrt function produces a real result. If a and b are real variables we could correctly write

$a + sqrt(b + 3.5) / 2.0$

Our expression deals consistently with real quantities and does not mix types. Likewise, if m and n are integer quantities,

$m + (1 - n)$ **div** $trunc(2.73)$

is a consistent integer expression. (Remember, trunc produces an integer result.)

In summary, when using a standard Pascal function, we must be aware of the two data types involved: that of the function's argument and that of the function's result. Figure 4-1 summarizes this information for the functions mentioned in Chapter 3. These functions are standardized and are guaranteed to be part of every standard Pascal implementation. However, individual installations may have some additional functions not on this list. That information can be provided by the local computing facility.

4.3 BOOLEAN EXPRESSIONS

Just as we used arithmetic operators to construct arithmetic expressions, we use relational and boolean operators to construct boolean expressions of arbitrary complexity. A *boolean expression* is any expression that has the value true or false.

As with arithmetic operators, we must pay close attention to data types. The relational operators ($<$, $<=$, $=$, $<>$, $>$, $>=$) can be used to compare either real, integer, char, boolean, or user-defined quantities, but in any given comparison, both operands should be of the same type. The result of the comparison is a boolean quantity, true or false.

As indicated earlier, the logical operators (**and, or, not**) operate on boolean values to produce a boolean result.

If we wish to construct a complex boolean expression, the precedence rules of Pascal require us to parenthesize all elementary subconditions except those involving

Function Name	Description	Type of Argument	Type of Result
abs	Absolute value	Integer Real	Integer Real
arctan	Arctangent	Real or integer	Real
chr	Character that corresponds to an integer	Integer	Character
cos	Cosine	Real or integer	Real
exp	Exponential	Real or integer	Real
ln	Natural logarithm	Real or integer	Real
odd	Tests for odd value	Integer	Boolean
ord	Integer representation of a character	Character	Integer
pred	Predecessor	Any scalar type except real	Same type as argument
round	Rounding	Real	Integer
sin	Sine	Real or integer	Real
sqr	Square of argument	Real Integer	Real Integer
sqrt	Square root	Real or integer	Real
succ	Successor	Any scalar type except real	Same type as argument
trunc	Truncation	Real	Integer

Figure 4-1. Standard Pascal functions.

the **not** operation. This might seem to be an awkward requirement, but it is actually a worthwhile programming technique to follow, since it greatly improves the clarity and intent of the expression. For example,

$(a<b)$ **and** $(c=d)$ **or** $(e=0)$

is a boolean expression. It would be invalid if the parentheses were omitted because the **and** and the **or** have higher precedence than the relational operators $<$ and $=$. Even with the parentheses as indicated, the expression could be invalid if the data types of the operands were inappropriate. Variables a and b must be of the same type, c and d must be of the same type, and e must be integer.

In Pascal, if we want to perform a comparison involving an arithmetic expression, such as $a < b + 1$, we once again have the question of the order in which the operators are to be applied. A moment's reflection will reveal that the only valid interpretation for this example is $a < (b + 1)$. The grouping $(a < b) + 1$ would call for the integer value 1 to be added to the boolean constant true or false, a meaningless operation. We will always want the comparison operation performed after the arithmetic operation. This means that in Pascal the relational operators should have a lower precedence than the arithmetic operators.

Of course, the operators **and, or,** and **not** must also have a place in the hierarchy of operators. Figure 4-2 shows the precedence levels for all of the operators discussed so far. When there are several operations at the same level of precedence, the operations are performed from left to right, and the precedence of any operation can be overridden through the use of parentheses.

The major use of boolean expressions is to control the flow of execution through the program. Just as our algorithmic language of Chapter 2 relied heavily on true or false conditions:

if condition then . . .
while condition do . . .

so Pascal relies heavily on boolean expressions to determine the order of execution. We frequently must construct expressions whose truth value is used to decide whether or not we do an operation. For example, if we wished to execute a portion of a program only if the integer variable x was in the range 0 to 25 inclusive, we could test either of the following boolean expressions:

(x >= 0) **and** *(x <= 25)*

or

not *((x < 0)* **or** *(x > 25))*

As a second example of developing boolean expressions, assume that we wished to read input text until one of the following two conditions becomes true.

1. We have looked at 100 characters and have not found the special character that we are looking for.
2. We encounter a '.' or a '!' as the current character.

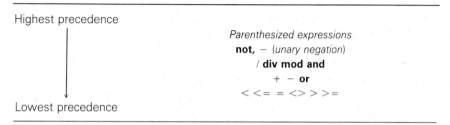

Highest precedence	Parenthesized expressions
	not, − *(unary negation)*
	/ **div mod and**
	+ − **or**
Lowest precedence	< <= = <> > >=

Figure 4-2. Precedence of operators in Pascal.

When either of these conditions occurs, we want to stop.

The boolean expression we might use as our stopping criterion is (assume count is declared type integer, found is boolean, and ch is character):

((count >= 100) **and** *(***not** *found)) ***or*** *(ch = '.') ***or** *(ch = '!')*

This boolean expression has the value true whenever we should stop and is false otherwise. Notice that the boolean variable found is, by itself, a boolean expression. A common programming mistake is to think that all boolean expressions must be formed using either a relational or logical operator. Thus many people might write the second term as

not *(found = true)*

This is redundant and unnecessary (since true = true is true and false = true is false) and indicates a misunderstanding of how to form boolean expressions.

These complex boolean expressions will be extremely important in describing the conditions under which we wish to selectively execute portions of a program or conditions for repetitively executing a loop.

4.4 THE ASSIGNMENT STATEMENT

The *assignment statement* is a Pascal statement that assigns a value to a variable. The form of the statement is shown in the syntax chart in Figure 4-3. (The entire syntax of the Pascal language is summarized in Appendix A.)

We sometimes speak of the symbol := as the *assignment operator*. The expression on the right side of the assignment operator is evaluated using the precedence rules of Figure 4-2 and the current value of any variables referenced in the expression. The result of that evaluation becomes the new current value of the variable on the left side of the assignment operator, replacing any previous value it may have had. Thus the assignment statement is, in effect, a way to *define* a variable and assign it a value. (Later, we will introduce two additional ways to define a variable in Pascal.)

Note, also, that when writing an assignment statement all variables referenced in the expression on the right side of the assignment operator must have been previously defined, perhaps by an earlier assignment statement. If we write

y := x + 1.5

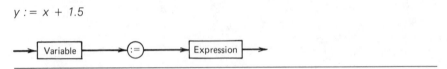

Figure 4-3. Syntax of the assignment statement.

but have never given x a value, this statement is meaningless and cannot be properly executed.

If we have made the following declarations in our program:

var

root1, root2	: real;
vowel	: char;
count, number	: integer;
flag1, flag2	: boolean;

and if root2 has already been defined, each of the following is a valid assignment statement.

```
vowel   := 'e';
count   := 153;
root1   := root2 * 6.71;
flag1   := root2 < 100.0;
number  := (trunc(root2) − 4) * 302 mod 7;
flag2   := odd(round(sqrt(root2 + 1.5)))
```

In each case, the type of the result produced by evaluating the expression is the same as the type of the variable being assigned a value. This is a requirement of the assignment operation. There is, again, one exception to this—an integer value can be assigned to a real variable. In all other cases the data types on either side of the assignment operator must be the same. Thus, if a is a real variable and m is an integer variable, the following is invalid.

$m := a$ { an invalid type-mixing operation }

We could formulate this as a valid assignment statement by writing either m := trunc(a) or m := round(a). In either case, the result of evaluating the function is an integer and can properly be assigned to the integer value m.

There is one very important point to keep in mind concerning the assignment statement. Do not confuse the assignment operation with the notion of mathematical equality which, in Pascal, is denoted by the relational operator =. They are not at all the same! To make this point clear, consider the perfectly acceptable assignment statement k := k + 1. Some people will commonly read this as "k equals k + 1." Unfortunately, the use of the word "equals" connotes the mathematical concept of equality, and this example would seem to be asserting the impossible. This leads some people to think that such an assignment statement is invalid. That is not the case. It is essential to remember that the assignment operation connotes an action. It is providing a value for the variable that appears to the left of the := symbol. This suggests a more illuminating way in which the := symbol can be read: k "gets the value of" k + 1. Although it is a bit more verbose than "equals," it is an alternative that conveys clearly the meaning of the assignment statement.

As some final examples of the formation of valid Pascal assignment statements, the following are Pascal translations of algorithmic primitives used in earlier examples in Chapter 2. In all cases, we assume that the variables used on the right side of the assignment operator have been properly declared and defined.

Algorithmic Primitive	*Pascal Assignment Statement*
Set count to 0	*count := 0*
Increment i by 1	*i := i + 1*
Set top to middle	*top := middle*
Set middle to top plus bottom divided by 2	*middle := (top + bottom)* **div** *2*
Set average to sum divided by number	*average := sum / number*
Set found to true	*found := true*
Compute the two roots of a quadratic equation	*root1 := (−b + sqrt(b*b − 4.0*a*c))/ (2.0*a);* *root2 := (−b − sqrt(b*b − 4.0*a*c))/ (2.0*a)*

4.5 INPUT AND OUTPUT

Input and output are of crucial importance in computer programming. Computers are very adept at performing calculations, but they will do precisely what they are told and no more. We can write a program to perform an intricate calculation flawlessly. However, the results will remain in the computer's memory, hidden from the outside world, unless we include an instruction to display those results. This is the role of the output statements in Pascal. We will also find it helpful to use the output statements to print headings and identifying text along with the output so that it can be more readily understood. In any event, there should always be at least one output statement in every program we write so that we can see the final results.

An input statement allows a program to obtain data values from an external input device such as a card reader or a terminal (see Figures 4-8 to 4-11). As the computer executes the program, these data values are input and assigned to certain variables in the program. This allows a computation to be carried out for a number of different data values without changing the program itself. Only the data cards[2] must be changed.

---

[2]Throughout this section we will use the phrase "data cards" when referring to the external input device. We do not in any way imply that the Pascal input statements apply only to the classical input medium of punched cards. In reality, these "data cards" may be lines typed on a computer terminal or input from some other external device.

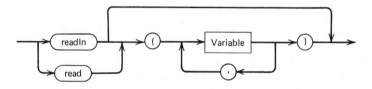

Figure 4-4. Syntax of the input commands.

To illustrate, let us assume that we wish to write a program that computes and prints out the square root of a real number. If the program is written so that the particular number is specified within the program, it will not be terribly interesting. Once we execute the program and obtain the square root, the program is of no further value unless we make an explicit change to the program itself. A better technique is to write the program so that it computes the square root of a variable whose value is obtained through an input operation. This means that the same program can be meaningfully executed many times simply by using a different piece of data each time. Defining a variable by bringing its value in from an external source is termed using *external data*. Defining variables directly in the program itself is usually termed using *internal data*.

4.5.1 Read and Readln Statements

Input operations in Pascal are handled by the two statements read and readln.[3] These two statements operate in a virtually identical fashion; we will describe the read command now and the readln variant a little later.

The syntax of both forms of input command is shown in Figure 4-4.

Zero, one, or more variable names may appear inside the parentheses, with commas separating successive names. The list of variables within the parentheses is called the *read list*. All variables in the read list must be of type integer, real, boolean, character, or subrange. An attempt to input any other data type (e.g., a user-defined scalar) using the standard read command will produce a fatal error. Each of the following is a syntactically legitimate read statement, as long as every variable has appeared in a valid **var** declaration.

```
read(coefficient);
read(socsec, grosspay, dependents);
read(birthrate, deathrate);
read (x, y, z);
```

---

[3]Strictly speaking, read and readln are not statements in the language but special procedures. However, for now we will describe them as if they were statements in the Pascal language.

These input operations will define every variable named in the read list. This is now the second way to define a variable in Pascal. (Using a variable on the left side of an assignment operator was the first method.) There is no limit to the number of variables that can appear in a read statement, although, as a practical matter, a read statement with a great many variables might be too complex to be clear. There is also no limit to the number of read statements that may appear in a program.

The read statement causes the program to examine as many data cards or lines as necessary until a data value has been found for each variable in the read list. The association of a data value from a data card with a variable in the read statement is done entirely on the basis of *position*. The first value found on the data card is associated with the first variable name in the list, the second value with the second variable, and so on. The values provided by the input data must be consistent with the declared data types of the variables. For example, if our program contains three real variables, a, b, and c, and the statement read(a,b,c), we might set up data cards as follows (each line represents an individual data card or line).

1.573   2.0
   − 1.9E6

The result would be that a is assigned the value 1.573, b is assigned the value 2.0, and c is assigned the value − 1900000.0. Note that the data cards contain no indication of the variable names to be associated with the given values. It is essential to remember that the association of values with variables is done entirely by position. If the two preceding data cards were inadvertently reversed, the result of the read would be

a: − 1900000.0
b: 1.573
c: 2.0

We have a great deal of flexibility in setting up our data cards. We can place as many numbers as we like on a card, and we can use as many cards as we wish. The only specific requirements are:

1.   Data values must conform to legitimate Pascal syntax. Thus no commas can appear in numbers and, if a decimal point appears, it must be preceded and followed by at least one digit.

2.   A data value must have a type consistent with the type of the variable that occurs in the corresponding position in the read statement. Again, the only exception is that a value of type integer can be assigned to a variable of type real. Pascal will correctly handle the type conversion.

3.   Successive data values must be separated by one or more spaces. The only exception to this is type char. Since we know that values of this type will

always be of length 1, we do not need to separate them by spaces. As a matter of fact, the space itself is a valid character and can be input as data. Textual input is discussed more fully in Section 4.5.2.

4. A data value must reside completely on one card (i.e., a single value cannot start on one card and be continued on the next one).

As long as these requirements are met, data values can span any number of cards and can be prepared in whatever format is most natural. The computer will continue to read cards until it has found a value for each variable in the read list.

However, even though data cards can be entered in any format, we must remember that the order in which they appear on the card must match exactly the order in which the variable names are written in the read list. If, for example, some inventory data cards had been prepared with part numbers, amount on hand, and unit price, typed in that order,

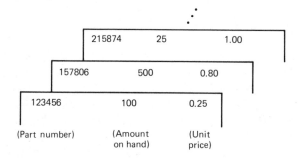

our read statement must have the variables written in that specific order.

read(partnumber, amount, price)

If the order of the variables does not match the order on the data cards, it may result in a fatal error due to a value of the incorrect type being encountered (e.g., a real encountered for an integer variable). Even worse, the program could assign the wrong values to variables and continue executing. This latter possibility is just one example of why *input validation*—ensuring that all input operations were done correctly—is so important. We will have much more to say about this point later.

What happens if there is not an exact correspondence between the number of data values on the current card and the number of variables in the read list? If there are more data values than variables the extra data values are simply not used during this read operation. The values may be read by the next read command, or they may not be used at all.

The situation is different if too few data values to satisfy the read statement are on the current data card. The read command must always find a sufficient number of values to satisfy (i.e., define) every variable included in the read list. If it cannot find all the needed values on the current card, it will automatically proceed to the next one. It will continue in this fashion, processing as many data cards as necessary, until it eventually gets a value of the proper type for every variable. Thus, in our previous example of the inventory cards, we could have just as properly prepared the data as follows.

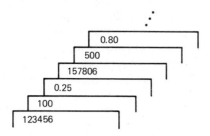

There is one special condition that can occur during a read operation. If at any time during a read operation, we come to the end of all the input data, we say that we have an *end-of-file* condition.[4] Different computer systems have different ways of marking the end of the data (e.g., a special character, a special card), but there will always be some way for the program to detect that it has reached the end, and no more data will follow. Pascal includes a standard boolean function that allows us to test for exactly this situation. We can test whether we have reached the end of any particular file with the standard function eof(filename). This function returns the value true if an end-of-file condition currently exists for the specified filename and false otherwise. The read and readln operations are only defined when the function eof is false. An attempt to perform a read when eof is true is always a fatal error.

In this section we will only be dealing with the special file named input that contains the data cards that we provide with our program or the lines that we enter at a terminal. We can therefore use eof(input) to determine whether all of the data has been read. Because the particular file input plays such a special role in Pascal, it is used as the default file name in many contexts. Thus we can also simply write eof without an argument when we mean eof(input).

In Chapter 5 we will see an example of how this end-of-file test can be used within a program to control the input of data. The basic idea will be to set up the program so that particular instructions (i.e., the read commands) are executed only if the function eof is false, implying that more data cards are available. If we do not do

---

[4]We will discuss the notion of a file more fully in Chapter 10. For now we will simply view a file as a collection of items that are somehow related to one another. When we have exhausted all the items, we have reached the end of the file.

this test for an end-of-file condition we must be absolutely certain to provide enough data values to satisfy all the read statements that the program will attempt to execute. If we do not, the computer will terminate execution because of an error (often with a cryptic and not too helpful error message) when it attempts to input data where none exist.

One final detail about the read comand is the readln variant. (The syntax of the readln was shown in Figure 4-4.) Both the read and readln commands operate in exactly the same manner with respect to the input of data values. The only difference occurs at the very end of the input operation. If we imagine a ''pointer'' moving along the data card looking for values, we can say that the read command leaves the pointer at the position it was in when the read instruction was completed. The readln command advances the pointer to position 1 of the next card or line.

Assume we had the following two data cards.

input pointer

    ↓

  1 2 3

  4 5 6

If the pointer were positioned at the beginning of the first card, the two statements

read(a, b); read(c, d)

would first assign the values

a: = 1
b: = 2

and leave the input pointer where it was when the input operations were completed: just past the integer value 2.

input pointer

    ↓

1 2 3

4 5 6

The second read operation will begin from that position, assign the values

c: = 3
d: = 4

and leave the input pointer on the second card, just past the integer value 4.

However, the two statements

readln(a, b); readln(c, d)

would result in first assigning

a: = 1
b: = 2

and then resetting the "pointer" to the beginning of the second line. This will, in effect, discard the remainder of the first line.

```
    1   2   3
    4   5   6
    ↑
input pointer
```

The second command will result in the values

c: = 4
d: = 5

The input pointer will again be reset to column 1 of the third data card (not shown).
    When preparing our input commands, we must be careful to select the correct statement type—read or readln. In many cases, they will behave in an identical fashion and the choice is not critical, but there are two exceptions.

1.   The read allows different statements to continue reading from the same card. The readln does not. For example, if your data cards are prepared with 4 values per card:

```
    8   0   1234   17
1   5   -6    13
```

You must say either:

(a) *read(a, b, c, d)*
(b) *readln(a, b, c, d)*

(c)

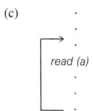

within a loop executed four times. You cannot write:

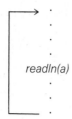

within a loop executed four times because this would improperly discard the last three values on each card.

2. The end-of-file condition will come on (i.e., become true) at different times with read and readln. Assume the '■' character is the special end-of-file symbol on our particular computer system, and the input file contains:

If we write

   read(count)

the input pointer will be left at the position immediately following the number 50, and the boolean function eof will be false. This is because we do not as yet know about the upcoming end-of-file marker. However, if we say

   readln(count)

then, after satisfying the read list, we will try to go to column 1 of the next card. Now we will encounter the end-of-file marker, and the boolean function eof will be set to true. A common programming mistake is to fail to have the eof "switch" come on at just the right time and, as a result, try to do an input operation one time too many. This is yet another example of the off-by-one error mentioned in Chapter 2. We will discuss these errors and how to avoid them in more detail in Chapter 6.

4.5.2 Reading in Text

The read and the readln command can be used for either numeric or textual input. However, there are some conceptual points that are specific to the handling of character-oriented data; we will discuss this point separately.

When reading in either integer or real values with a read or readln, blanks are insignificant. Leading blanks are discarded until we locate the beginning of the next numeric value. If necessary, we will also ignore card boundaries and continue on to the next card or line, searching for a value.

However, when reading in character values, blanks are treated just as any other character, and they are processed identically as all other characters in our character set. If the input to our program is

> . . . . hello there . . . .
>   ↑
>   input pointer

a read(ch) (assuming ch was declared to be of type char) will result in the variable ch being set to blank and the input pointer now pointing to the letter 't.'

This last example points out another fundamental difference between numeric and textual input. Numeric input is variable in length—containing as little as one character (the number 1) or many (the real quantity—123.456789000). However, character input is always of length one. When a character variable is read, the character currently pointed at by the input pointer is assigned to that input variable and the pointer is advanced exactly one position. There is never any need to move the input pointer ahead more than one position searching for the beginning or end of an input value.

A final fundamental difference between numeric and textual input has to do with their treatment of the *end-of-line* (eoln) character. The standard file input can be viewed conceptually as a set of cards (or lines) separated by a special symbol called the end-of-line (eoln) marker. (The specific symbol used to mark eoln is system dependent. However, regardless of what is used, it will always be there and it will behave exactly as described here.)

> cccc . . . . cc ⟨eoln⟩ ccc . . . . cc ⟨eoln⟩. . .   ccccc . . . .
>
> one card or   one card or   c — individual characters
>   line   line   ⟨eoln⟩– end of line symbol

When reading numeric values, the eoln symbol has no importance. In fact, when searching for an integer or real value, if an eoln symbol is encountered, it is automatically skipped, and we continue reading on the new card or line.

When reading in character variables, however, the eoln marker plays an important role. This is because textual input is typically processed as groups of words, lines, and pages. Thus the occurrence of an end-of-line condition is an important situation of which to be aware. (Refer to Section 2.2.4 for an example.)

A standard boolean function called eoln is used to inform us of the presence of an end-of-line condition in an input file.

eoln(file). The function eoln is false if we are *not* currently pointing to an end-of-line character in the indicated 'file.' It is true if we are currently pointing to an end-of-line character. If the file we are referring to is the standard file 'input' then it is only necessary to say eoln.

So, for example, if our input file currently is

> . . . xyz⊂eoln⊃this is the next line . . .
>   ↑
>   input pointer

eoln will be false. If we then executed the following Pascal statement:

read(ch)   { *ch is a character variable* }

the variable ch would be set to 'z' and the function eoln would become true. Since we usually do not want to input the eoln character itself, we not need to skip over it. This is done simply by writing:

readln

The read list is immediately satisfied (since it is empty), and the only effects are to set eoln to false and to take us to the first column of the next card or line.

> . . . xyz ⊂eoln⊃ this is the next line . . .
>   ↑
>   input pointer

The function eoln is useful in working with character-oriented information where we wish to organize the data into lines and pages. We will see numerous examples of textual processing and the eoln function later in the text.

Style Clinic 4-2 _____

Input Validation and Echo Printing

It is imperative that input data be checked immediately for correctness and plausibility. Frequently programs will produce incorrect results that cannot be explained. In actuality, the program itself is perfectly correct, but the data were improper. (This is frequently called *garbage in–garbage out* in computer jargon.)

One simple way to validate the input is to write it back out immediately and check it visually. This is called *echo printing* and should be a part of every program. In addition to aiding in locating errors in data, echo printing has the additional benefit of associating a result in the output listing with the data set that produced it. A program that produces output messages such as

the result is 7

but does not explicitly provide the values that produced this output is extremely difficult to work with and authenticate.

4.5.3 Write and Writeln Statements

As with input, there are two variants of the output command, write and writeln. Their syntax is shown in Figure 4-5.

The write list may contain zero, one, or more items separated by commas. Each item is either an expression of arbitrary complexity or a character string enclosed in single quotation marks ('). If the item is an expression, it is evaluated, and its value is printed. If the item is a character string, it is printed exactly as it appears but without the delimiting quotation mark characters. To print an apostrophe within the character string, we must write two successive ' characters. For example, if a and b are integers having the values 5 and 20, respectively, the statement

write(' a =', a, ', the sum of a and b is ', a+b)

will produce the output

a =   5, the sum of a and b is   25

The statement

write('this ' ' is the quote character')

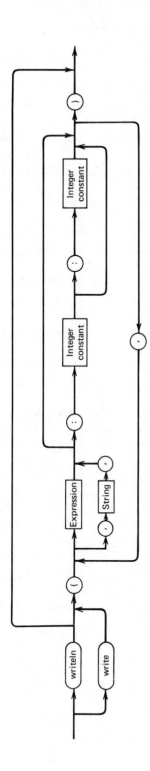

will produce

this ' is the quote character

If a variable (or an expression) is specified in a write statement, the value written will be in accordance with the data type of the expression or variable. Boolean values will be written as true or false, and real values will be written in scientific (power-of-10) notation. A value will be printed with a particular "field width," or number of columns, that is preset for each computer and depends on the data type and the conventions of each local installation. The default field widths used in our examples are listed in Figure 4-6. However, these default values may not apply on every computer, so inquire about the values on your particular machine (or write a simple program that will determine this information).

In our previous example the values of a and a + b were each allocated 10 character positions (or columns) for printing. Although neither number required 10 characters, the computer utilized the entire field by inserting an appropriate number of blanks to the left of the number. We say that such a number has been *right-justified* and that there is *blank fill* on the left. Thus we have nine blanks preceding the number 5 and eight blanks preceding the number 25. The computer will automatically adjust the number of blanks for the particular data type being printed and the number of characters required for printing each value.

We might at times find that the default field widths are inconvenient. For example, perhaps we want to arrange the output in the form of a chart or a table and the default field widths will not achieve the effect we desire. It is a relatively simple matter to override the defaults and specify whatever field widths we need. We simply follow any item in the write statement with a colon and an integer constant that specifies how many columns we wish to use when printing this value. (Remember to allow enough columns for a negative sign, decimal point, and exponent—if appropriate—as well as the actual digits to be printed.) For example, the statement

write(' a = ', a:3, ', the sum of a and b is ', a + b:5)

Data Type	Number of Columns
Integer	10
Real	22 (12 significant digits, exponent is of the form $E \pm dd$)
Boolean	10
Character	1
'text string'	Length of text string

Figure 4-6. Default field specifications in our examples.

will produce

    a =   5, the sum of a and b is   25

As in the default case, if there are not enough characters to fill the field, blanks are inserted to the left. Furthermore, if either an integer or text field is too small to contain the value being printed, Pascal will automatically extend the field to sufficient size.

    This field-width designator can be used much like a "tab setting" to control horizontal placement of values on a line. For example, to print a three-digit integer value in columns 58, 59, and 60, we could write

write(x:60)

The value of x will be right-justified in the 60-column field. Thus, if it were three digits long, it would be preceded by 57 blanks. Headings can also be centered using the field-width designator:

write('x':10, 'sin(x)':10)

will print the character 'x' in column 10 and the 6 character string 'sin(x)' in columns 15 to 20.

    There is another option that applies to the printing of real values. For a real quantity we can specify two "field widths." The first value is the field width we just discussed, which specifies the total number of columns to be occupied by the value being printed. The second "field width" (if present) invokes decimal representation for a real value and specifies the number of significant places to print following the decimal point. For example, if r, s, and t are real variables with values 1.234, -8000.76, and 63.123, the write statement

write(r:6:2, s, t:12)

will produce the following.

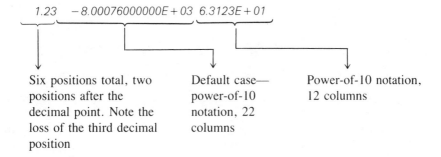

| Six positions total, two positions after the decimal point. Note the loss of the third decimal position | Default case— power-of-10 notation, 22 columns | Power-of-10 notation, 12 columns |

There is one final issue to consider in our discussion of output. Pascal provides a second form of the output command called the writeln. It is identical in every respect to the write command except for one—at the end of the output operation the writeln will insert a carriage return into the output file. This has the effect of terminating the current line and going to column 1 of the next line. The write command leaves the output pointer in its current position, and the next output operation will begin from that point. Thus, if x = 100 and y = 200,

write(' x =', x:5);
write(' y =', y:5)

will produce

    x = 100   y = 200

whereas

writeln(' x =', x:5);
writeln(' y =', y:5)

will produce

    x = 100
    y = 200

The effect of the command

writeln

without any output parameters will simply be to insert a carriage return in the output file (i.e., to start a new line). Likewise,

writeln;
writeln

will give us one more blank line (i.e., double-spacing). By properly utilizing the two field-width designators and the write and writeln commands, we can produce legible and well-organized output. (See Style Clinic 4-3.)

There is one final caution to remember when writing your output commands. Every output device has some fixed-size line length. (The exact length will depend on the characteristics of a specific device. Values of 72, 80, 120, and 132 are common.) An attempt to print more characters on a line than the device can accept will lead to an error. You must remember to terminate the current output line (using the writeln command) before it gets too big to fit on one line of the printed page. If we had an 80 character per line printer, the sequence of statements

```
write(x:25);
write(y:10, z:40:5);
write('this is just too much information')
```

is illegal, since it tries to place 108 characters (25 + 10 + 40 + 33) on one line. We could, for example, change it to

```
write(x:25);
writeln(y:10, z:40:5);
{ this will go to a new line after printing x, y and z }
write('this is not too much information')
```

Be sure to inquire about the line width of the standard output device on your computer system.

Style Clinic 4-3 _____

Output with Style

The output of your program is its reason for being. Most users of a program will be unconcerned with the programmer's ability, cleverness, or ingenuity. They want correct answers that are presented in a clear, easily understandable, highly legible format. Even though a program produces correct answers, if it is difficult to interpret the output listing, the program will be used very little or not at all.

Your first concern should, of course, be making the program correct. As long as it is legible, no one else really cares what the output of a program looks like during its development. However, once the program works, spend some time making the output attractive. Always avoid writing programs that produce output that looks like this.

```
        378245621
.28735E03   3    .4725E2    32.030000
    208.07
```

Always annotate your output with helpful text and place values in groups for increased readability.

(continued on next page)

Social Security No: 378-24-5621   Dependents: 3

Gross pay   = $287.35
Federal tax =   47.25
State tax   =   32.03
Net pay $208.07

The numbers are exactly the same, but the output is much more meaningful. Output such as the latter can be produced in Pascal without a great deal more effort than is required for the former case. (See Exercise 12a.)

4.6   THE OVERALL STRUCTURE OF A PASCAL PROGRAM

We have now discussed some of the basic declarations (Chapter 3) and statements (Chapter 4) that constitute a Pascal program, and we are ready to see how these pieces fit together into a complete computer program.

All Pascal programs will be set up like the model shown in Figure 4-7.

A Pascal program is divided into three distinct parts. The *program heading* is a single statement beginning with the reserved word **program.** The heading assigns a name to the entire program. Additionally, it lists the specific external data files that

```
program name(file₁,file₂, . . ., fileₙ);
    label declaration; { Discussed in Chapter 5 }
    const declaration;
    type declaration; { Discussed in Chapters 3, 7, 9, and 10 }
    var declaration;
    procedure declarations; { Discussed in Chapter 8 }
    function declarations; { Discussed in Chapter 8 }
begin
    statement;
    statement;

        .

        .

        .

    statement
end.
```

Figure 4-7. Model of a Pascal program.

will be used by the program to communicate with the outside world. The use of files other than the standard "input" and "output" will be discussed in Chapter 10.

The *declaration section* of the program contains declarations that describe the data objects that we will be using in the program. We have described three of these: the **const, type,** and **var** declarations. There may be up to six different kinds of declarations in this section, and they are illustrated in Figure 4-7. These declarations must appear in just that order (except that the **procedure** and **function** declarations, if present, may be intermixed in any order).

The *executable section,* which is delimited by the reserved words **begin** and **end**, contains statements that perform explicit actions on the data we have just described. Any of the statements discussed in this chapter (assignment, input, output) may appear in this section. Additional Pascal statements will be introduced in Chapter 5.

Figure 4-7 illustrates some other important points about a Pascal program that should be mentioned.

1. A *comment* is any explanatory information that is added to the program to help a reader understand what is happening. In Pascal comments can appear anywhere in the program where a blank character could be legally placed; they are delimited by the characters { }. On many machines, the brace characters are not available, so Pascal also allows comments to be delimited by the symbol pairs (* *). Comments are never required to make a program correct, but they are absolutely critical in making a program understandable. Style Clinic 4-4 has some important points to make about the proper use of comments.

2. The semicolon (;) is used in Pascal as a statement *separator,* not a statement *terminator.* That is, it is used to separate statements from each other, not to end a statement. Careless use of the semicolon can cause serious program errors. This will be discussed in more detail in Chapter 5.

3. Pascal statements are completely free format and may appear anywhere on a line. More than one statement may be placed on a single line. However, a name or a number may not be divided between lines. If there is not enough space on a line for the whole name or number, leave blanks at the end of that line and begin on the next line. Although Pascal allows complete freedom in preparing your programs, the misuse of this formatting freedom can significantly detract from program clarity. Style Clinic 4-5 discusses the proper use of indentation.

4. A Pascal program ends with the character period (.).

Style Clinic 4-4

Comments

Comments are helpful explanatory notes within the program itself that explain what the program is doing. Good comments can aid enormously in understanding the purpose of a program or a section of code. Unfortunately, good commenting habits are usually the exception and not the rule. For example, when helping a student with a long complex program, an instructor mentioned that it was a difficult program to work with because it did not contain a single comment. The student was quite taken aback and said, ''Of course, it isn't commented yet; I'm not ready to hand it in!'' The student was incorrectly viewing comments only as something the instructor required and that were needed to get full credit on a programming assignment.

Try to learn good commenting habits immediately. Although specific rules for commenting may again be viewed as a matter of personal style, there are some basic dos and don'ts of fundamental importance.

Don't:

1. *Undercomment.* Treat comments exactly as you would a Pascal statement. Use them judiciously and wisely when *first* writing the program. Do not forget about them because they are never actually required, and do not add them later merely because the instructor requests them. Comments can help others to understand your program and even help you to remember what you meant by something you wrote long ago.

2. *Overcomment.* It is a natural human tendency to go to extremes. ''If the instructor asked us to include comments, that's what I'll give.'' The program may become 90% comments, and the actual statements of the program become difficult to find, let alone correct. If this is the case, some of the comments could probably be eliminated or put into a report separate from the program listing.

3. *Rehash Obvious Program Logic.* Do not use comments to restate the obvious purpose of a single Pascal statement.

```
read(number); { Read in a value for number }
if number < 0 { if number is negative print error message }
    then writeln('error')
```

Do:

1. Include an extensive comment block (called a *prologue* or *preface*) right at the top of your program that describes in simple English the

general purpose of the program, who wrote it, and the date it was written. You may want to include some other helpful information here, depending on how the program will be used.

```
program columnalign (text, input, output);
{
    This program takes a character string from
    a file called text and produces 36 character
    lines formatted so that the first and last
    character of each line are nonblank.

        Author:     Benjamin Alan Schneider
        Address:    Harrison Open School
                    Minneapolis, MN
        Date:       1/82                                }
```

2. Use comments to *paragraph* your Pascal program—visually set off and identify logically related segments of a program.

```
{
    This is the data input and validation section
                                                    }
        readln(number);
        readln(x1,x2);
        if x1 < x2
            then writeln(' error in input data ')
        else begin
{
    Here we begin to process class 1 data sets
                                                    }
```

3. Use comments that tell *what* something is or *why* something is being done, not *how* it is being done. Comments should be in simple English and be directed at explaining the higher-level algorithmic functions being performed.

```
{ Search for the octal pattern 63 }
```

is a poor comment unless you are intimate with the problem. It is much clearer to read:

```
{ Look for the character that marks the end of the data }
```

even though they may mean the same thing.

4. Keep the comments current. When you make a change to the program, also change the comments. An incorrect or out-of-date comment can be worse than no comment at all.

Style Clinic 4-5 _____

Indentation

Pascal allows the use of free formatting and multiple statements per line. The excessive misuse of this, however, can lead to a program that is difficult to read. You should quickly adopt good habits of indentation to enhance the readability of your programs and to highlight their logical structure.

For example, the program fragment

```
program sample(input,output); const single = 1;
double = 2; triple = 3; var root1,root2:real;delta:
integer;goodflag,badflag:boolean;
```

is syntactically equivalent to

```
program sample(input,output);
{
        An example of much better
        indentation habits
                                                        }

const
        single = 1;
        double = 2;
        triple = 3;

var
        root1,root2        :real;
        delta             :integer;
        goodflag,badflag  :boolean;
```

but the second example is obviously much more legible than the first. The need for a good indentation scheme will become even more crucial when you begin writing programs with multiple levels of nested logic. So develop the habit early of preparing your program so that it clearly and succinctly reflects the operations you are performing. The specific rules for indenting will, of course, be a matter of personal style, but once chosen, they should be used consistently and should result in a clear and readable program.

4.7   EXAMPLES OF PROGRAMS

We are now in a position to write some simple, but complete, Pascal programs.

Example 1

```
program squareroot(input,output);
{ read a data card that contains a nonnegative real number and print it and its
square root }

var
        inputvalue      :real;
        sqroot          :real;

begin
        read(inputvalue);
        sqroot : = sqrt(inputvalue);
        { note—before invoking the square root function
          we should check that inputvalue > = 0.0. We will learn
          how to do this in the next chapter                          }
        writeln ('the input value was', inputvalue:10:3);
        writeln ('the square root, to three decimal places, is',
                                sqroot:10:3)
end. { of program squareroot }
```

Note that our writeln statements print the result of the computation and the data value that was used in the computation. Furthermore, we are printing both the numerical values and some identifying text. It is good to use both techniques wherever possible because they substantially improve the readability of the output. It might occasionally be impractical to print out all the data values that were input, but there is *never* any excuse for printing results without any identifying text.

Because the program contains several statements, we have separated consecutive statements with semicolons. In Chapter 5 we will discuss the details of where semicolons do and do not belong.

Example 2

```
program charcode(input,output);

{ Read a data card that contains a single character.
  Print the character and its numerical representation (its
  character code). The character should be entered in the
  first column of the first data card or line }
```

```
var
      character:char;
      code:integer;

begin
      read(character);
      code: = ord(character);
      writeln('character ''', character, ''' has the internal code', code:5)
end. { of program charcode }
```

If this program were executed on an IBM 360/370 series computer with the character 'A' punched in the first column of the first data card, the output would be:

character 'A' has the internal code 193

Try it on your computer to see what it produces.

Example 3

```
program compare(input,output);

{ Read a data card that contains two integers.
  Compare the first number with the second and
  indicate whether each of the tests 'less than,'
  'equals,' or 'greater than' is true or false }

var
      a, b:integer;
      less, equals, greater:boolean;

begin
{ Input and echo print the data }
      read(a,b);
      writeln('a = ', a, ' and b = ',b);
{ Perform the three relational comparisons }
      less := a < b; equals := a = b; greater := a > b;
{ Write out the results of the comparisons }
      writeln(' a<b is', less);
      writeln(' a=b is', equals);
      writeln(' a>b is', greater)
end. { of program compare }
```

If this program were executed with the input line

5   9

what would the output look like?

4.8   RUNNING A PROGRAM

In the previous section we coded three examples of complete (albeit simple) Pascal programs. We are now in a position to execute these programs on a computer and produce the desired results.

Obviously, the first step in running a Pascal program on a computer is getting it into a *machine-readable form* that can be input to the computer. The specific form used will depend on which of two very different methods are used to access the computing resources available.

Batch processing was historically the first technique for running programs; it is still a widely used method for running typical student jobs. In most batch-processing environments, the program is first converted to machine-readable form *off-line* (i.e., not linked to the computer). This preparation is usually done on 80 column *punch cards* (Figure 4-8). It is the function of the *keypunch* (Figure 4-9) to translate a keystroke made by the programmer at the keyboard into the combination of punched holes that represents that character and that can later be read by a device called a *card reader*. The relationship between the printed characters and the punch code can be seen in Figure 4-8.

After the program has been prepared and any obvious mistakes corrected, the *program deck,* as it is called, is brought to an *input/output station*. There it may either be entered directly into the computer or collected together with other programs into a batch that is entered as a single unit. Some time later (the exact time typically depends on factors over which you have little or no control, such as the current workload of the computer) results are returned in the form of a listing containing either the desired answers or, more typically, error messages.

Figure 4-8. Standard 80 column punch card.

Figure 4-9. Keypunch.

The most important characteristic of batch processing is that it is impossible to interact with a program while it is being executed. All data must be presented to the computer at the time the job is submitted. Using batch processing, we could not, for example, run a program with a single data set, view the results, choose the next data set based on those results, and continue running the program from that point.

This type of interaction requires a very different technique for accessing computing resources. This other approach goes by many names—*time-sharing, interactive processing,* or *demand processing.* In this environment the conversion to machine-readable form is done *on-line*—by communicating directly with the computer. Usually, the student sits at a terminal containing a keyboard and printing mechanism (Figure 4-10). Alternately, the printer may be replaced by a cathode-ray tube (CRT), which looks much like a television screen (Figure 4-11). Regardless of which type of terminal is available, a keyboard is used to enter and edit the program. When the program is complete, a request is entered to execute the program, and it is usually run immediately. Input may be requested during execution, and any output produced by the program (results, error messages) is displayed on the printer or the screen. After viewing the output, we may make changes in the program or the data. Both program development and program execution are done in an interactive, give-and-take fashion.

Regardless of the approach used, there will be three distinct components to the

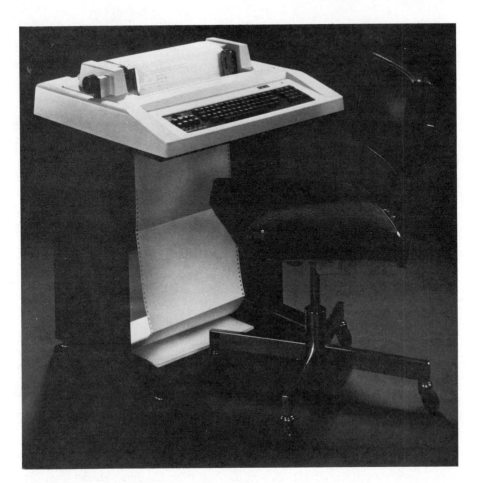

Figure 4-10. Keyboard/printer computer terminal.

completed program deck. The first component is the *program* itself, punched or typed according to the rules of the language. The second component is the *external data* that will be read in by the program. Some programs may not require any external data, so this component should be considered optional. Remember that these data values are not part of the Pascal program. They represent external values to be presented to the program at the time it is executed. In batch processing the data cards are usually separate from and follow the program cards. In a time-sharing environment the input data are keyed in by the user when the program requests it. The request is usually in the form of a *prompt*—a character (e.g., "?") typed out by the computer before it stops to wait for the user to enter the input data.

The third component of the overall program is a set of *system commands*. These

Figure 4-11. Keyboard/CRT computer terminal.

commands provide the computer system with necessary information about who you are and what you want to do. The specific format of these commands varies from one site to another, but the same general information is usually provided.

1. *Personal Identification.* Name, department, course, semester, year.
2. *Accounting Information.* Account number, billing number, budget limit.
3. *Security Information.* Password, privacy code.
4. *Language Information.* The computer language to be used (Pascal, in our case).
5. *Delimiters.* To identify the beginning and end of programs and/or data.
6. *Other Resources.* Other computer resources to be used by this job, such as a filing system, a text editor, or a tape drive.

Figures 4-12 and 4-13 show the first example program of Section 4.7 prepared for batch processing and time-sharing, respectively, for a hypothetical computer. These figures are merely examples to illustrate the points we have been discussing. The actual commands used at your installation will almost certainly differ. The information needed to execute Pascal programs on a particular computer will usually be supplied by your instructor or the local computer center.

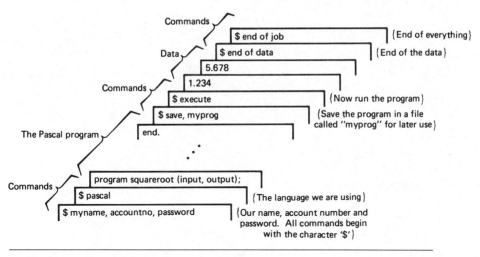

Figure 4-12. Sample batch-processing Pascal program deck.

Style Clinic 4-6

Batch Access versus Time-Sharing

Our previous discussions may have made it seem as if the two methods of running computer programs—batch access and time-sharing—are virtually identical, and that it does not matter which method you choose. This is false.

Throughout this text we have been teaching that computers are used to solve problems. But we sometimes forget that program *preparation* (i.e., keying in and correcting the program and data) is itself a problem. When we do this operation off-line (using punch cards and keypunches), we are failing to let the computer help us with a difficult and complex task. If we enter our program on-line in an interactive fashion, we can take advantage of some very powerful text-oriented facilities provided by most computer systems—things such as text editors, formatters, and filing systems. Also, many computer systems have a number of interactive debugging aids to assist you in locating and correcting program errors.

If time-sharing facilities are available at your installation, you should definitely select this technique *first*. You should become comfortable working on-line at a terminal, interactively preparing your programs and, if appropriate, interactively executing and debugging them as well.

Another important reason for familiarizing yourself with time-sharing is that most of the new applications of computers in the 1980s will function only in an interactive environment where the user and the program must communicate dynamically. Examples of this include data base retrieval systems, word processing, computer-aided design, electronic funds transfer systems, electronic mail, and computerized games.

(Information produced by the computer is in *italics*, with reserved words in boldface. Information typed by the programmer is in the normal typeface.)

```
Account Number: 123456
Password:
■■■■■ (blacked out for security reasons)
Language: Pascal (the language we will be using)
Old or New: New (this will be a new program)
Name: squareroot (the program name)
Ready (we can now type in the program)
0100 program squareroot(input,output);

0200          { read a data card that contains a nonnegative
0300             real number and print it and its square root }
0400 var
0500      inputvalue    :real;
0600      sqroot        :real;
   .         .
   .         .
   .         .

01200 end.
run      (request to execute this program)
mm/dd/yy hh.mm.ss      (date and time)
Pascal system
? 2.0          (a prompt for input)
the input value was 2.000
the square root, to three decimal places, is      1.414
run complete
save,squareroot      (save the program for later use)
ready
(here there can be additional requests to the computer or a sign-off)
goodby
user 123456 signed off
```

Figure 4-13. Sample time-sharing dialogue with Pascal.

EXERCISES FOR CHAPTER 4

1. Assume the following declarations:

   var
   > a,b,c :integer;
   > d   :(red, blue, green);

   Also assume that the following values have been assigned to the preceding variables.

   > a := 10;
   > b := -15;
   > c := 7;
   > d := red

   What is the value of each of the following Pascal expressions?

   *(a) (abs(b - 10) + a **mod** (c - 1))
   *(b) a + 103 **div** sqr(a - c)
    (c) pred(a * 6 + b **div** 5)
    (d) succ(d)
    (e) (2 + a * b **mod** c + 1) < 2

2. Using the declarations from Exercise 1 as well as the following new variables:

   var
   > x,y,z :real;
   > .
   > .
   > .
   > x: = 1.52E1;
   > y: = 0.3;
   > z: = -5.1E3

   what is the value of each of the following Pascal expressions?

   *(a) trunc(x * y + 1.0) - a
   *(b) x / y * 3.4 + z
    (c) abs(sqr(sin(y) + cos(y)) - 0.5)
    (d) round(x) **div** round(y + 1.6) + b
    (e) exp(c - 4)

3. Using the declarations from Exercises 1 and 2 and the following additional declarations:

> **var**
>> *m,n : boolean;*
>> *p   : char;*
>>
>> .
>>
>> .
>>
>> .
>>
>> *m := true;*
>> *n := false;*
>> *p := 'a'*

What are the values of the following expressions?

*(a) *m* **and not** *n*

*(b) *(a>b)* **and** *(b>c)* **or not** *(c=7)*

(c) **not** *odd(c)* **and** *m*

(d) *(x>0.0)* **or** *(y>0.0)* **and** *(z>0.0)*

(e) *chr(succ(ord(p)))* { *use Appendix C.3* }

4. Determine whether the following Pascal expressions are a correct translation of the corresponding mathematical notation. If not, add the necessary parentheses to correct it.

*(a) $k\sqrt{\dfrac{\sin\theta - 1}{\cos\theta + 1}}$ *k * sqrt (sin(theta) − 1.0 / cos(theta) + 1.0)*

(b) $ax^2 + bx + c$ *a * sqr(x) + b * x + c*

(c) $\left(\dfrac{a}{b} + \dfrac{c}{d} - \dfrac{e}{f}\right)^2$ *sqr(a / b + c / d − e / f)*

5. Translate each of the following English or mathematical specifications into a correct Pascal assignment statement. Show the **var** declaration for all variables used in the expressions.

*(a) Taxable pay is gross pay less a fixed deduction of $14 and less $11 for each dependent.

(b) The interest charge is 5% on the part of the balance that exceeds $100 (you may assume that balance $>=$ $100).

(c) Contingency is

$$\sqrt{\frac{x^2}{(N + x^2)}}$$

(d) Amplitude is $\dfrac{A}{2} \sin\left[2\pi(f_c + f_m)t - \dfrac{\pi}{2}\right]$.

(e) The average is $\dfrac{\text{sum of all scores}}{\text{number of scores less the illegal ones}}$.

*(f) Valid is true if and only if the examination score is between 200.0 and 800.0, inclusive.

(g) Done is false unless x is negative, or y is negative, or both x and y are exactly 0, in which case done is true.

6. Assume that we have the following data.

input pointer
↓

53	81	102
−601	0	80
15	9	102

What values will be assigned to the integer variables a, b, c by each of the following input operations? In addition, show where the input pointer would be at the conclusion of each set of input operations. (Assume that each set of input commands is independent and begins with the input pointer in the position shown.)

*(a) *readln(a,b,c)*

*(b) *read(a,b,c)*

*(c) *readln(a); readln(b); readln(c)*

(d) *read(a); readln; read(b); readln; read(c)*

(e) *readln; read(a,b,c)*

7. Write the declarations and the input commands needed to read in data prepared in the following format.

(a) A master payroll card containing a social security number (integer) and a department number (integer), followed by a separate timecard containing hours worked this week (real).

(b) A single student grade card containing a 6 digit student identifier (integer) followed by three letter grades (a, b, c, d, e) all separated by exactly one blank character.

8. Show how the data cards should be prepared if the input commands in our program are written like this.

> **var**
>> *x,y   :integer;*
>> *ch1,ch2 :char;*

  *(a)   *read(x,ch1);*
         read (y,ch2)

  (b)   *readln(x,y);*
        readln(ch1,ch2)

  (c)   *readln(x,y,ch1,ch2)*

  (d)   *readln(x);*
        readln(y);
        readln(ch1);
        readln(ch2)

9. Assume that the variables w, x, y, z have been declared to be of type integer and that the symbol '■' represents the end-of-file condition. If our input data is as follows:

input pointer

```
13    80
21     9
■
```

for each of the following input sequences, give the value assigned to each variable and the value of the boolean function eof on completion of the entire sequence. Also state whether or not the sequence would lead to an error condition caused by attempting to perform a read (or readln) while eof is true.

  *(a)   *read(w);*
         read(x);
         read(y);
         read(z)

  (b)   *readln(x,y,z)*

  (c)   *read(w,x);*
        read(y,z)

  (d)   *readln(x);*
        readln(y);
        readln(z)

10. Assume our input was currently:

input pointer

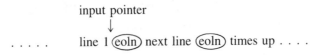

. . . . .   line 1 ⓔⓞⓛⓝ next line ⓔⓞⓛⓝ times up . . . .

For each of the following input sequences, give the value assigned to each variable, the value of the boolean function eoln, and the final position of the input pointer on completion of the input sequence. (Assume ch1 and ch2 have been declared to be of type char.)

(a) *read(ch1); readln*

(b) *readln; read(ch1)*

(c) *read(ch1,ch2)*

(d) *readln(ch1,ch2)*

(e) *readln(ch1); readln(ch2)*

11. Show the *exact* output produced by each of the following output sequences. Assume that we are presently at the beginning of a new line and that the referenced variables have the following values. (Use the defaults shown in Figure 4-6.)

> *x := 1.23456*
> *y := 567.89*
> *z := 10*
> *c := '$'*

*(a) *writeln(x,y,z); writeln(c)*

*(b) *writeln(x:15:1, y:8:3, z)*

(c) *write(x:15); write(y:15); write(c:3)*

(d) *writeln(x:16:4); writeln(y); writeln(z:1)*

12. Show the output commands needed to produce the following output formats. Assume the necessary values have already been computed and stored in the indicated variables.

(a) Produce the more legible tax report shown in Style Clinic 4-3. The variables are called:
> ssnumber, dependent, gross,
> fedtax, statetax, net

(b) Variables: month, year, amount, tax, total.

> *Date: mm/yy*
>
> | *Gross Amount* | *$xxx.xx* |
> | *Tax* | *$xxx.xx* |
> | *Grand Total* | *$xxx.xx* |

*(c) Variables: count, average, high, low.

total number	*average*	*range*
xxxx	*xx.x*	*xx.x — xx.x*

(d) No variables are needed, but assume your character set includes the characters ' − ', '|', and '>' (ASCII 95, 124, 62).

13. Write a complete Pascal program to input a data card containing three values.

    (a) A real value corresponding to the amount of a loan in dollars and cents (the principal).

    (b) A real value corresponding to the interest rate of the loan.

    (c) An integer quantity, N, giving the number of payment periods per year N >= 1.

The program should compute the loan payment required for each pay period to repay the outstanding principal in one year at the indicated interest rate in N equal payments. The formula for doing this is:

$$\text{Payment} = \frac{p(1 + i) + 25}{N}$$

where
$$p = \text{principal}$$
$$i = \text{interest rate}$$
$$N = \text{number of pay periods per year}$$
$$\$25 = \text{annual service charge}$$

The program should print out the input data and the answer in some nice, legible format.

Now attempt to run this program on the computer facilities available at your installation. If appropriate, run the program in both a batch access and time-sharing mode. Familiarize yourself with all aspects of the operations policy of your computer center. This would include:

· Location of keypunches and computer terminals.

· Operating procedure for keypunches and terminals.

· Location of program submission stations.

· Commands required for program preparation, execution, and storage.

· Availability of consulting help and documentation.

THE FLOW OF CONTROL

5.1 INTRODUCTION

At the end of Chapter 4 we wrote some complete but simple programs. We view these programs as simple not so much because of their limited length, but because of their structure: they are what we term *straight-line programs*. That is, they reflect operations that are simply sequential in nature. The general model of these straight-line programs is:

Read a data value.

Compute an intermediate result.

Use the intermediate result to compute the desired answer.

Print the answer.

Stop.

Although we might occasionally need to solve a real problem of this kind, more often than not we will find that such a simple structure is not appropriate for our problem.

In our discussion in Chapter 2 we saw that most algorithms rely heavily on the techniques of *iteration* and *conditional branching*. Since most real-world problems require these techniques, we will find that most computer programs make abundant use of them.

The *control statements* of a programming language allow us to alter the normal sequential flow of instructions within our programs and allow us to accomplish these repetitive and decision-making operations. Pascal contains an extensive set of control statements, and we are now in a position to examine them in some detail. In addition to the extensive range of data structures available in Pascal, it is the wide range of control structures that most sharply distinguishes Pascal from other high-level programming languages.

5.2 THE COMPOUND STATEMENT

The *compound statement* is used in Pascal to indicate that a sequence of statements is to be executed in sequential order. The general form of the compound statement is shown in Figure 5-1. Notice that the reserved delimiters **begin** and **end** surround the statements that make up the compound statement. For example,

```
begin
    readln(num1, num2);
    sum := num1 + num2;
    diff := num1 − num2;
    writeln(sum:10, diff:10)
end { of compound statement }
```

is a valid compound statement. Observe the use of semicolons (';') to separate successive Pascal statements. This is important. A semicolon is not part of a Pascal statement. It simply serves as a statement *separator*. It is also important to recognize that **begin** and **end** are not Pascal statements. They are reserved words that designate the beginning and the end of a compound statement. Thus, in our example we used a semicolon between the readln statement and the assignment statement, a semicolon between the two assignments, and another semicolon between the assignment and the writeln statement. We do not have a semicolon after the **begin** or before the **end** because there is nothing to separate. (Remember, **begin** and **end** are not statements, but reserved words.)

What would happen if we placed a semicolon between the writeln statement and **end**? This would appear to be an error, because the semicolon would not be separating two statements. However, Pascal includes a construct called the *empty statement* that will come to our rescue in this particular case. The empty statement is simply a syntactic construct that Pascal uses when necessary to try to make sense of a program or statement that might not be strictly correct. We will now look at a particular

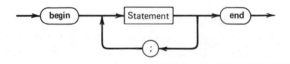

Figure 5-1. Syntax of the compound statement.

example—a compound statement with an extra semicolon. Try to find the empty statement that will permit a correct interpretation of our compound statement.

```
begin
    root1 := (−b + discriminant) / (2.0 * a);
    root2 := (−b − discriminant) / (2.0 * a);
end                                    The empty statement will be inserted here.
```

In this example the existence of the empty statement permits a proper interpretation of our compound statement, despite what appears to be a violation of the rule for the use of semicolons. The extra semicolon is viewed as separating the second assignment statement from the empty statement. However, this discussion does not mean that we should become casual in our use of semicolons. The empty statement will not always be able to undo the damage caused by misplaced separators. We should still be careful and use these statement separators only where they belong—between two Pascal statements.

The compound statement is really quite simple: a group of Pascal statements, separated from one another by semicolons, and bracketed by the reserved delimiters **begin** and **end.** Since a compound statement will be processed in the obvious order (sequentially), why do we need it? In our upcoming discussions of some of the more sophisticated control statements in Pascal, we will see that in several places the syntactic description will call for a single "statement." This indicates that any individual Pascal statement is permissible. But what if we want to use several statements at that point in our program, instead of being restricted to just one? There is no problem if we simply group the statements together as a compound statement (i.e., bracket the statements with **begin** and **end**) because of the following fundamental principle. Since the compound statement is treated as only one statement, Pascal will always accept a compound statement wherever any individual statement is allowed. We will see some examples of this in the next few pages.

5.3 ITERATIVE STATEMENTS

It is usually the case that one part, and perhaps several parts, of an algorithm need to be executed repetitively. In our discussion of algorithms we represented this notion by means of the **while** and **repeat** constructs. We can now examine three different statements that allow us to accomplish repetition in Pascal.

5.3.1 The While Statement

The Pascal **while** statement permits a program segment to be repeatedly executed as long as a specified condition is true. The syntax of the statement is shown in Figure 5-2a. A boolean expression is any expression that produces a value of true or false

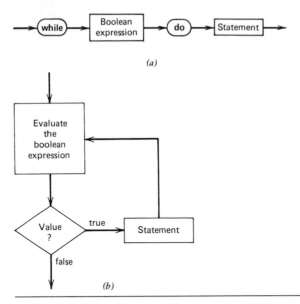

Figure 5-2. (*a*) Syntax of the **while** statement. (*b*) Behavior of the **while** statement.

(see Section 4.3). The boolean expression is initially evaluated. If it is true, then the statement (which may be any statement, including a compound one) is executed. The cycle is then repeated as the boolean expression is again evaluated and a decision is made about whether to execute the statement. The execution of the **while** statement is complete when the boolean expression in the **while** clause is evaluated and found to be false. The overall operation of the **while** statement is summarized in Figure 5-2*b*.

As a simple example, consider the program on the following page (Figure 5-3), which computes the sum of the first 100 integers. It should be clear that this program computes the sum $100 + 99 + \cdots + 2 + 1$ and then prints out the sum. Note the use of the compound statement to designate that we wish to have two statements executed if number > 0. The first of these statements adds another number to the sum, while the second statement modifies the variable called number so that it will have the value needed for the next cycle. Observe that the last number added to the sum is 1. Once number reaches 0, the condition number > 0 is no longer true and the compound statement after the **do** is not executed.

As another example, we consider a program (Figure 5-4) that deals with character data. We will read one character at a time, keeping a running count of characters until a period is reached. (For this example we will assume that we are certain the input file does contain the character '.' In general, we would not make such an assumption.) Note that two read statements appear in this program. The first one, before the **while,** provides an initial value for the variable currentchar so that the test specified by the

```
program total(input,output);
{
      program to find the sum of the integers
      100,99,...,1                        }
var
      number : integer; { counter running from 100 down to 1 }
      sum        : integer; { the running sum }
begin
      sum := 0;
      number := 100;
      while (number > 0) do
      begin
            sum := sum + number;
            number := number − 1
      end; { of the while loop }
      writeln(' the sum of the first 100 integers is ', sum)
end.
```

Figure 5-3. Program to compute the sum of the first 100 integers.

```
program countchars(input,output);
{
      read characters from the standard file input
      until we encounter a period.
      We will count the number of characters
      read, excluding the period.
                                                        }

const
      period = '.';

var
      count            : integer;     { the count of the characters on the line }
      currentchar     : char;        { the current character we are looking at }
begin
      count := 0;
      read(currentchar);
      while (currentchar <> period) do
      begin
            count := count + 1;
            read(currentchar)
      end; { while loop }
      writeln(' the number of characters on the line is ', count)
end. { program countchars }
```

Figure 5-4. Program to count characters.

while can be performed the first time. (Otherwise, currentchar would be undefined.) The second read statement provides a new value for currentchar for the next iteration of the **while.** A very common programming error when using the **while** is failing to define a value needed to initially evaluate the boolean expression. For example,

```
{ read and sum up integers until the first
    negative value occurs. This loop is incorrect }
sum := 0;
while (number >= 0) do
begin
    readln(number);
    sum := sum + number
end
```

The above loop will not execute properly. When the **while** loop is first entered we must immediately test whether the value of the integer variable number is nonnegative. However, number is not given a value until we enter the loop (through the readln). The program will halt because of a reference to an undefined variable. We can correct this problem by writing the loop in the following way.

```
sum := 0;
readln(number); { get the first value }
while (number >= 0) do
begin
    sum := sum + number; { tally the value just read }
    readln(number) { set up for the next iteration }
end
```

It is also important to realize that the statement(s) after the **do** might *never* be executed at all. If the specified boolean condition is false initially, the body of the **while** statement will be skipped (see Figure 5-2*b*). Consider this program fragment.

```
{ read in a positive value for k and compute
    k! = k * (k − 1) * . . . * 2 * 1. Caution —
    k! gets large very, very quickly              }

readln(k);
factorial := 1;
while (k > 0) do
begin
    factorial := factorial * k;
    k := k − 1
end { while loop }
```

The statements within the body of the **while** loop will be executed only if a positive data value is provided for k.

Notice that the **while** loop as just written is always guaranteed to terminate. We can only enter it with a positive value for k and, on each pass through the loop, we subtract one from k and store that value back into k. This decrementing of the variable k guarantees that the boolean expression (k > 0) will eventually become false and that the loop will ultimately terminate. It is absolutely imperative that, during the construction of a loop, we include statements inside the body of the loop that will eventually allow us to exit. If we fail to do this, we will be trapped inside an "infinite loop"—one of the most common programming errors. For example,

```
read(upperbound);
count := 1;
{ now repeat a certain set of operations until the
  counter 'count' equals the value of upperbound }
while (count <> upperbound) do
begin
      .
      .
      .   { perform some processing operation }
      .
      .
      count := count + 1 { tally one more iteration }
end
```

This is a dangerous loop to write. If the initial value of the variable upperbound is either negative or 0, count (which is taking on the values 1, 2, 3, . . .) will *never* equal upperbound and the loop would, in principle, run forever. (In actuality, the loop would halt with a fatal error either when the value in count overflowed or when we ran over our maximum time limit. See Style Clinic 5-1.)

Always check that the loops you write will eventually terminate and will terminate at the proper time. This will save you untold grief.

5.3.2 The Repeat Statement

The **repeat** statement is similar to the **while** statement: an indicated statement (or group of statements) is repeatedly executed, and a specified test is performed to determine when the repetition is to stop. (The syntax of the **repeat** is shown in Figure 5-5a.) However, there are two principal differences between the **while** and **repeat.**

1.   The **while** performs the test *before* each cycle; the **repeat** performs the test *after* each cycle.

2.   These two statements consider the test to be performed from opposite points of view. One statement performs repetition **while** a certain condition is true;

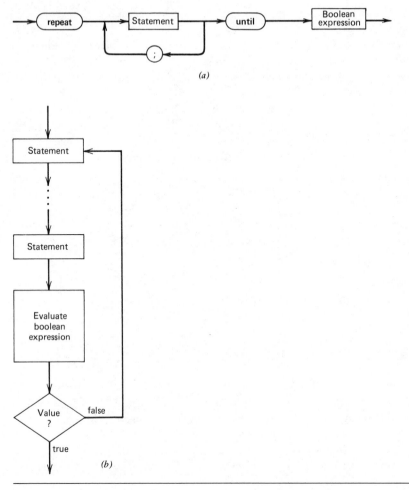

Figure 5-5. (*a*) The syntax of the **repeat** statement. (*b*) The behavior of the **repeat** statement.

the other statement performs repetition **until** (i.e., it **repeats** . . . **until**) a certain condition becomes true. This difference is clearly shown by comparing the behavior of the **while** loop in Figure 5-2*b* with the diagram in Figure 5-5*b*.

Style Clinic 5-1 _____

Too Low a Time Limit?

Suppose you submit a program for execution and find that the output contains a message similar to

*** time limit exceeded — execution terminated ***

Apparently your program was using too much computer time and did not conclude normally. When you originally submitted your program, you specified a time limit (probably supplied by your instructor). This limit prevents any one program from monopolizing the computer for too long, thereby providing a reasonable level of service for all users. But your program did not finish, so apparently the time limit you provided was too low. You should resubmit the program, this time with a higher time limit, right? Wrong!

Although a mistaken time limit is a possibility, it is most unlikely. Do not be fooled by what appears to be a ridiculously low time limit. Computers are fast! On a large computer system a time limit of 2 to 5 seconds might be ample for a class assignment. On a smaller system 10 or 15 seconds might be appropriate. In any case, for class assignments in a beginning course, you will usually be dealing in milliseconds or seconds, not minutes. You should first proceed on the assumption that the time limit provided by your instructor is adequate.

What, then, is the problem? Your program is probably caught in an *infinite loop*. It is performing a repetitive operation (perhaps a **while** statement or one of the other repetitive statements that we will discuss), and the condition for terminating the repetition has not become true. You probably forgot to alter one or more variables inside the loop, and it is impossible for the boolean condition ever to achieve the necessary value.

You should not run your program again with a higher time limit. Nothing will change, and you will only be wasting time—yours and the computer's. Find the mistake in your program. Carefully examine every repetitive section of the program and note the condition under which each repetitive statement terminates. What data values are you using in this execution of the program? Will the repetitive statements terminate?

It is interesting to note that the syntax explicitly permits a sequence of statements, and we do not have to use a compound statement to achieve this. This comes about because the statements to be repeatedly executed are bracketed by the two reserved words **repeat** and **until.** Therefore there is never any uncertainty about which statements are to be repeated. Of course, if we wish, we could still bracket our statement sequence with **begin** and **end** as in:

repeat
> **begin**
> S_1;
> S_2;
> .
>
> .
>
> .
>
> S_n
> **end**

until *boolean expression*

This is not wrong, but it is redundant.

When using a **repeat** statement, there will always be at least one execution of the statement sequence, because the test for completion is performed at the end of the cycle, not at the beginning. For example, if we were to write:

> *readln(k);*
> **repeat**
> > *statement1;*
> > *statement2*
>
> **until** *(k < 0)*

statement1 and statement2 would always be executed once, even when a negative data value has been read in for k. In fact, even if a negative value has been given to k initially, if either statement1 or statement2 alters k so as to make it nonnegative, the loop will still continue. The iteration will terminate only when k is left with a negative value after all the statements in the body of the loop have been executed.

Figure 5-6 on the next page shows the use of a **repeat** statement in a program that computes the average of a set of 20 numbers read from data cards. We have set up the program to read a data value and add it to the sum, performing each step 20 times. The variable named count is used to keep track of how many repetitions there have been. When count reaches 20, the loop ends, and the average is computed. Note that when we use a **repeat** loop, we specify the condition that will terminate the repetition. Contrast this with the **while** statement, in which we specify the condition for continuing the repetition.

You may be wondering why we wrote the last statement as average := sum/ count instead of average := sum/20.0. We certainly could have used the second form. However, by using the variable count instead of the constant 20, we will find it easier to modify our program in the future. For example, suppose we want to compute the

```
program mean(input,output);

{ program to compute the average of 20 real values
  read in from cards                                    }

var
    average     : real;       { the average of all values }
    count       : integer;    { a counter to count up to 20 }
    sum         : real;       { the sum of all values }
    value       : real;       { the input value just read }

begin
    sum := 0.0;
    count := 0;
    repeat
        readln(value);
        writeln(' input value = ', value:15:3);
        count := count + 1;
        sum := sum + value
    until count = 20;
    average := sum/count;
    writeln(' average = ', average:15:3)
end. { program mean }
```

Figure 5-6. Program to compute averages.

average of 100 numbers instead of 20. We only need to make one change to our program. We would write

```
until count = 100;
```

(Of course, we would also have to provide 100 data values instead of 20, but that is a change to the data, not the program.) Clearly we would have had to make a second change if we had used the constant 20 in the division operation on the next line.

This may seem like a small point, but it does illustrate a very important principle of computer programming. Even if the specific problem does not demand it, it is usually a good idea to write programs with as much generality as possible, as long as the increased generality does not result in an overly complicated program. It should be possible to take a program that computes an average of 20 values and convert it with a minimal amount of work to a program that works for any number of values. We will use the term *program generality* to describe a computer program that works correctly on variations of a problem with little or no modification to the program itself. The fewer the changes, the less opportunity there is for introducing errors.

For example, we can use a **const** declaration to give a symbolic name to the constant representing the number of pieces of input data.

const
   howmany = 20; { the number of pieces of input data }

Now, to make a change, we no longer have to search through our program for all occurrences of the constant 20—a highly error-prone operation. Instead, we must only make a single change to the **const** declaration at the beginning of the program. For example, if we write:

const
   howmany = 100;

then our program will compute the average of 100 numbers. (Remember we would still need to provide the 100 required data values.)

We can carry this concept of generality further. We can write a program that will work for any number of data values without requiring any modifications to the program. How do we do it? Simply by agreeing to provide one additional piece of data: the number of values we will be using during that particular program run. For example, if we want the average of 20 numbers, our first line of data would contain the number 20. We would then provide the 20 numbers whose average we seek. If we want to run our program again to find the average of 100 numbers, our first data value would be 100 and, of course, we would follow that with the 100 required values. Our program would work for both cases without change. It would look like the one in Figure 5-7 on page 153.

It is interesting to note that this version of the program is not very different from the one in Figure 5-6. Instead of being the constant 20, howmany has become a variable whose value is set by reading a line of data each time the program is run. The only changes are to the data; the program need not be touched.

This is an interesting programming technique, but we should note that it is appropriate only if the number of data values is relatively small. Experience has shown that if the number of data values is large, the user of the program might very well count incorrectly and provide the wrong data value for the variable howmany. Computers can count more reliably than people can. It is usually a much better idea to set up a program so that it simply continues to read data values until there are no more, regardless of how many that might be. There are two techniques for doing this.

The first technique uses a construct called the *signal card*. This is a data card or input line that contains a value that could not properly appear on any other data card. The user adds this card to the end of the data set, and the program is written to test for the appearance of this value. For example, if the values to be averaged were examination scores in the range 0 to 100, then a value of -1 could be used to signal

program *mean(input,output);*

{ find the average of a set of real data values. The
number of values is specified on the first card }

var

average	*: real;*	*{ the average of all test scores }*
count	*: integer;*	*{ counter from 1. .howmany }*
howmany	*: integer;*	*{ number of test scores }*
sum	*: real;*	*{ sum of all the real scores }*
value	*: real;*	*{ the individual data values }*

begin
    readln(howmany); { find out how many data values.
                    We should really check this value to
                    make sure it is positive. We will
                    do this later in the chapter }
    writeln('there are', howmany, 'data values');
    sum := 0.0;
    count := 0;
    repeat
        readln(value);
        writeln(' data value = ', value);
        sum := sum + value;
        count := count + 1
    until *count = howmany;*
    average := sum/howmany;
    writeln(' the average is = ', average:15:3)
end.

Figure 5-7. Modified program to compute averages.

the end of the data. The program would use the occurrence of this signal card as the criterion for loop termination.

The second technique utilizes the *end-of-file* (designated eof) that we introduced in Chapter 4. We can continue to execute a loop in Pascal until the boolean function eof becomes true. This would indicate that no more data values are available. If we were to revise our program along these lines, it would appear as in Figure 5-8 on page 154. Now our data values will consist only of the numbers that are actually used in computing the average. We do not have to count these values and punch an additional data card for howmany, and we do not have to remember to place a signal card at the end of the data values. The program will continue reading data values until none are left. The issues we have just discussed concerning program generality are summarized in Style Clinic 5-2.

```
program mean (input,output);

{ program to find the average of a set of real numbers.
  Data values will be processed until we encounter the
  end-of-file condition. }
var
     average        : real;      { average of all data values }
     count          : integer;   { to count how many data values }
     sum            : real;      { sum of all data values }
     value          : real;      { the data value just read }
begin
     sum := 0.0;
     count := 0;
     repeat
         readln(value);
         writeln(' data value = ', value);
         sum := sum + value;
         count := count + 1
     until eof(input); { eof would be sufficient, the file input is assumed }
     average := sum/count;
     writeln(' there are ', count, 'values');
     writeln(' the average is ', average)
end.
```

Figure 5-8. Use of eof as an end-of-file indicator.

Style Clinic 5-2 _____

End-of-Data Indicators

We have discussed several ways in which a program can be made aware of the number of data values to be processed.

1. The number can be built directly into the program through an explicit constant, as in

    while *count* < 20 **do**
    .
    .
    .

2. The number can be referred to through a **const** declaration, as in

```
const
     limit = 20;
       .
       .
       .
while count < limit do
```

3. The count can be read from the input data.
4. Data can be read until a signal card is encountered.
5. Data can be read until end-of-file is encountered.

We can make some very worthwhile observations. Alternatives 1 and 2 should rarely be used, because they needlessly restrict the usefulness of the program. We must change the program even for trivial changes in the problem statement.

Alternatives 3, 4, and 5 provide the generality we seek, but alternative 3 is very error-prone. There is simply too great a chance that at some time a user will count incorrectly and the program will produce incorrect results.

Alternatives 4 and 5 are the methods of choice. They provide the desired generality, and they are easy to use. Of course, the user must always re-member to add the signal card to the set of data values, so alternative 5 is probably the very best technique, since it requires no action whatsoever by the user. (Note that alternative 4 would be appropriate if the program is to process several sets of data during a single program run. The signal card would represent an "end-of-set" condition for each set of data.)

5.3.3   The For Statement

In our discussion of the **while** statement we looked at a program that computed the sum of the first 100 integers (Figure 5-3). We will rewrite that example, making some relatively trivial changes.

```
sum: = 0;
n    := 1;
while n <= 100 do
begin
    sum := sum + n;
    n := n + 1
end;
writeln(' sum = ', sum)
```

(In this version we are performing the computation $1 + 2 + \ldots + 100$ instead of $100 + 99 + \ldots + 2 + 1$, as before. This requires a different initialization for n as well as a different condition for the **while.**)

If we look at this example, we see that we are repeatedly executing the assignment statement sum : = sum + n under circumstances in which the variable n is one greater with each iteration. We also know exactly how many repetitions there will be. These facts allow us to rewrite this program segment with a bit less effort by using a Pascal control statement called the **for,** another kind of iterative statement. It is different from the **while** or **repeat** because it automatically includes the following operations.

1. An initialization of a special variable called the *control variable,* which will be used for counting loop iterations. The control variable can be of any *ordinal* data type (integer, boolean, char, user-defined, or subrange).
2. A test of the control variable before each iteration to determine whether the proper number of iterations have been completed.
3. An automatic incrementing of the control variable after each iteration.

If we rewrite our most recent example using a **for** statement instead of a **while** to control the repetition, we have the following.

```
sum := 0;
for n := 1 to 100 do
    sum := sum + n;
writeln(' sum = ', sum)
```

In addition to replacing the **while** with the **for,** we have eliminated the two statements, n := 1 and n := n + 1. Both of these operations are performed automatically by the **for** statement itself.

The **for** statement repeatedly executes the statement sum : = sum + n as n varies from 1 to 100. But let us examine, step by step, exactly what happens.

1. The control variable n is initialized to 1 (the *initial value*).
2. The control variable n is compared to 100 (the *final value*). Since n is *less than or equal to* this value, the statement after the **do** is executed. This statement, which can of course be a compound statement, constitutes the *body* of the loop.
3. The control variable n is incremented by 1.
4. Steps 2 and 3 are repeated until n exceeds 100, the *final value*. When n reaches a value greater than the final value, the statement after the **do** is no longer executed. The computer has completed executing the **for** statement, and the program continues with the statement following the **for.**

The syntax of the **for** statement is shown in Figure 5-9*a*, and its operation is summarized in Figure 5-9*b*. The body of the loop, which may be a compound statement, is repeatedly executed while the control variable ranges from the initial value up to the final value as it is incremented through its successors. The initial value and final value need not be constants. Any expression of the proper ordinal type is acceptable. However, we must be careful. These expressions are evaluated only once, when the **for** statement is first encountered. It is therefore meaningless to use an expression that will in any way depend on the repetitive execution of the statement that follows the **do.** For example, we can write:

for *i* := *k* + *1* **to** *k* + *(j*2)* **do** *statement*

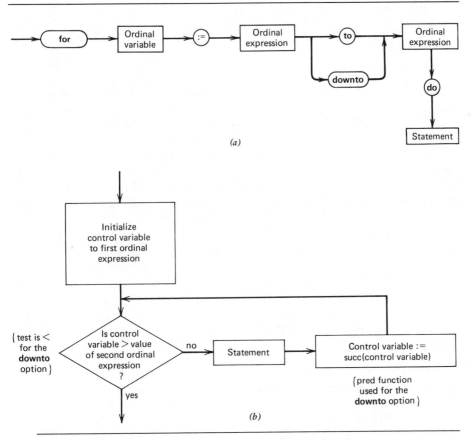

Figure 5-9. (*a*) Syntax of the **for** statement. (*b*) Behavior of the **for** statement.

Since the two expressions will be evaluated only when the **for** is first encountered, k must already be defined. Otherwise, there would be no initial value to assign to i. The variable j must also be defined, since the final value will be established at this time. Any future changes made within the **for** loop to k or j will not be reflected in the final value, since that has already been fixed.

There are some important points to keep in mind concerning the control variable. First, this variable must never be altered by the body of the **for.** The control variable will be automatically updated by the built-in mechanism of the **for** statement, and that is the only way it can be changed. We may use the value of the control variable, for example, in an arithmetic computation, but we may not change it. This means that it cannot appear on the left side of an assignment statement or in a read or readln statement. Consider this example.

```
sum: = 0;
for i: = firstvalue to lastvalue do
begin
    sum := sum + i;
    i := i + 5 { this is invalid }
end
```

The body of the **for** is a compound statement that consists of two assignment statements. The first is perfectly legitimate. It merely references (i.e., uses) the value of i, the control variable. The second assignment statement is invalid because it seeks to change i. That is something we are not allowed to do.

You may be wondering about what happens to the control variable after the **for** statement has finished processing. Strangely enough, the control variable, in a sense, disappears! More precisely, we say that upon completion of the **for** statement, the control variable is *undefined*. This may appear strange, since we would normally expect its value to be one greater than the final value. This is not the case. If for any reason we wish to reuse that variable, we must re-establish a value for it. Of course, a readln or an assignment statement would suffice for this purpose. But as an interesting special case, you might note that the variable could reappear as a control variable in another **for** statement (recall that the first operation done by a **for** is to set the control variable to the indicated initial value).

If we look back at the program in Figure 5-7, which computes the average of a set of numbers, we might note that a **for** statement could be used in place of the **repeat.** The **for** statement could be used to automatically execute the loop as the value of count goes from 1 to howmany in steps of 1.

```
for count : = 1 to howmany do
begin
    readln(value);
    writeln(' data value = ', value);
    sum := sum + value
end
```

In general, a loop is well suited to being implemented using the **for** statement if it satisfies the following two criteria.

1. We know explicitly how many times the loop will be executed (since we must place a specific value in the final value field).
2. The loop cannot terminate abnormally or terminate before we have completed the specific number of iterations (since the only criterion for loop termination is control variable $>$ final value).

Before we leave our discussion of repetitive statements, we should mention an alternative form of the **for** statement that uses the clause **downto** in place of **to.** (See Figure 5-9*a.*) This statement is similar to the **for** statement we have already discussed, except that it counts ''down'' instead of ''up.'' That is, the control variable is checked to see if it is *greater than or equal to* the final value; if it is, the statement is executed, the control variable is *decremented* by using the predecessor function, and the cycle is repeated. In all other respects, it is the same as the previous version of the **for** statement.

For example, on a test with a range of 0 to 100, we could print the number of people who received each possible score, *from highest to lowest,* as follows.

```
for score := 100 downto 0 do
begin
    write ('score of',score);
        .
        .        { compute and print out the number of
        .          people who received this score }
        .
end { for loop }
```

This loop will be executed 101 times with the control variable score having the values 100, 99, 98, . . ., 2, 1, 0.

Style Clinic 5-3 _____

Off-by-One Errors

A common programming error is to pay too little attention to the exact number of times a loop will be executed. We often set up a loop that is correct in its basic structure but produces incorrect results. This is frequently because the loop is executed once too often or once too seldom. We say there is an *off-by-one error.*

Continued on next page

Consider this simple attempt to find the sum of the first n positive integers.

```
sum := 0;
number := 1;
while number < n do
begin
    sum := sum + number;
    number := number + 1
end
```

This loop will produce an incorrect result. It is actually computing the sum of the first n − 1 positive integers. We should have written

```
while number <= n do
    .
    .
    .
```

The nasty thing about off-by-one errors is that they usually do not generate error messages—just wrong answers. To make things worse, we may not immediately recognize that the results are incorrect. An error of this kind can be difficult to detect once a program has proceeded to the testing stage. Obviously, a good set of test cases with known answers will be a tremendous help. We may not always have such handy test cases, however.

What can we do about off-by-one errors? We can prevent them by carefully examining every program loop we write as soon as it is written. If we wait until the entire program is written and only then begin to check out the program by running test cases, it is possible we will never be aware of a mistake. As soon as we write a loop, we should examine the conditions for the first and last cycles of the loop and ask how many times the loop will be executed. These assessments should be made automatically for every loop in every program. Developing this habit will save a lot of grief later on.

5.4 CONDITIONAL STATEMENTS

In our discussion of algorithms, we made use of two primitives for the selection of alternative courses of action: if/then and if/then/else. As we will now see, these two primitives correspond directly to two statements available in Pascal. Although we could view these two statements as just two different forms of a single statement—with the **if/then** being a special case of the **if/then/else**—we will, for now, discuss them separately. These statements, along with a third called the **case** statement, allow us to write Pascal programs that execute sections of code only if certain conditions are satisfied.

5.4.1 The If/Then Construct

The syntax of the Pascal **if/then** is shown in Figure 5-10a. The meaning of this should be apparent. The statement (which may, of course, be a compound statement) will be executed if and only if the boolean expression has the value true. The statement will not be executed if the boolean expression is false. This behavior is summarized in Figure 5-10b. For example, we might write

if $a > 0$ **then** writeln(' a= ',a)

to write the value of a only if a is positive. Or

if switch **then**
begin
    c := a * b;
    writeln(a,b,c)
end

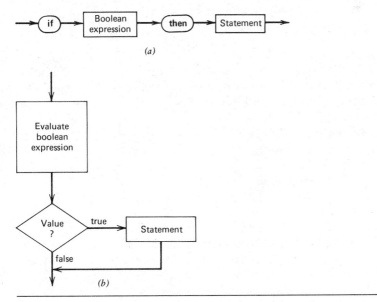

Figure 5-10. Syntax and behavior of the **if/then** statement. (a) Syntax of the **if/then.** (b) Operation of the **if/then.**

would execute the compound statement only if the boolean variable switch had the value true.

We can use the logical operators **and, or,** and **not** to construct complex boolean expressions as the basis for our decision. For example, to execute statement s when all of the conditions c_1, c_2, . . ., c_i are true, we could write

if *(c₁)* **and** *(c₂)* **and** . . . **and** *(cᵢ)* **then** s

To execute statement s when any one condition is true, we would write

if *(c₁)* **or** *(c₂)* **or** . . . **or** *(cᵢ)* **then** s

These compound conditions can be built up to any desired complexity. For example, if we wished to write out the value of x only when it was nonnegative and not a multiple of 10, we might write

if *(x >= 0)* **and not** *(x* **mod** *10 = 0)* **then**

To test to see if the real variable exam is in the range 200 to 800 inclusive, we could write

if *(exam >= 200.0)* **and** *(exam <= 800.0)* **then**
    .
    .   *{ score is between 200 and 800 }*
    .

In setting up compound conditions we must be careful to write out exactly each test that we want to perform. A common programming error is to attempt to apply a type of ''distributive'' law to the test and write

if *a < b* **and** *c* **then** *a := a + 1*

in which the intention is to test for the two conditions a < b and a < c. If that is what we want, then we must write it explicitly.

if *(a < b)* **and** *(a < c)* **then** *a := a + 1*

Now a will be incremented only if both conditions are true.

Note that we allow any Pascal statement to be the one that is conditionally executed, including another **if** statement. This would lead to the construct

if *condition-1* **then if** *condition-2* **then** *statement*

Now the indicated statement would be executed only if both condition-1 and condition-2 were true. This could clearly be extended to any number of conditions. Compare these two constructs.

1. **if** *(a < b)* **and** *(a < c)* **then** *a := a + 1*
2. **if** *a < b* **then if** *a < c* **then** *a := a + 1*

Both are legitimate Pascal statements and both have the same ultimate effect—to increment a only if a is less than both b and c. But there is a subtle difference between them, and we should be aware of what the difference is. In construct 1 the tests are done at the same level; in construct 2 one test is subordinate to the other. Thus, in the first case, both tests are always performed.[1] In the second case, a is compared to c only if it has already been determined that a is less than b.

One of the most important uses of an **if** statement is in checking data values for validity. It is not at all uncommon to use a computer program that is "correct" and yet obtain incorrect or meaningless results because incorrect data values were provided. In almost every program there are certain checks that can be made to guarantee that data values fall within an allowable range. If the data values are outside this range, the program should print an informative message instead of trying to carry out the computation with meaningless values. Of course, the data values might well be in the allowable range and still not be the values we intended, but that is why we should always echo-print the input data. That way a simple inspection of the computer output will disclose data values that were "valid" but still not "correct." (These topics will be pursued in more detail in Chapter 6.)

The particular tests for validity that have to be performed will depend on the problem to be solved. We will consider a particular example so that we can discuss several alternative ways to structure these tests.

Suppose we have three integer variables, x, y, and z, whose values will be input to the program. Suppose further that the values must fall within the following ranges if the computation is to be meaningful.

x: must be positive.

y: must be greater than 10.

z: must be between 50 and 100, inclusive.

---

[1]We might note that some implementations might perform only as many tests as necessary to ascertain that the entire expression is true or false (thus if a were not less than b, a might not be compared to c), but this sort of optimization would vary from one system to another. As programmers, we cannot make any assumptions about this.

We might write the following Pascal statements.

```
{ Read and print data values }
readln(x,y,z);
writeln('x = ', x, 'y = ', y, 'z = ', z);
```

```
{ Perform the computation if the data values are valid }
if (x > 0) and (y > 10) and (z >= 50) and (z <= 100) then
begin
{ Carry out the computation }
end
```

That is one way to handle the situation. However, suppose we also wanted to print out an informative message if any of the data values are invalid. We could make the printing of the message contingent on the data being invalid, as indicated by this conditional statement.

```
if (x <= 0) or (y <= 10) or (z > 100) or (z < 50) then
    writeln('invalid data')
```

Note that each test has been changed to test for invalid data, and **or** has been used instead of **and.** The overall condition will now be satisfied if any one of the subconditions is satisfied.

This will take care of printing the informative message, but we still need a mechanism to prevent the program from continuing with the computation. We could introduce a boolean variable for this purpose. If we begin the program with this variable being false and set it to true if the data values are invalid, we can accomplish our objective. If we analyze this situation carefully, we see that there are two actions that are to be conditionally performed: the printing of an error message, and the computation, which is the principal objective of the program. Interestingly, these two actions arise from complementary conditions. If the data are invalid, we want to print the message and not do the computation; if the data are valid, we want to do the computation and not print the message. In either case we want to do one action but not the other. Figure 5-11 on the top of the next page shows how this can be accomplished using an **if/then** and an auxiliary boolean variable. In the next section we will discuss the **if/then/else** statement, which will allow us to achieve the same results much more easily and naturally.

5.4.2   The If/Then/Else Construct

The **if/then/else** statement is a construct that allows us to select one of two alternative statements by evaluating a specified boolean condition. The form of the statement is shown in Figure 5-12a. If the boolean expression is true, statement-1 is

```
{ Read and print data values }
error : = false;
readln(x, y, z);
writeln('x = ', x, 'y = ', y, 'z = ', z);

{ Check for invalid data }
if (x <= 0) or (y <= 10) or (z < 50) or (z > 100) then
begin
    error : = true;
    writeln('invalid data')
end; { if statement }

{ Perform computation if data are valid }
if not error then
begin
{ Carry out the computation here }
end
```

Figure 5-11. Checking for valid data using an **if/then.**

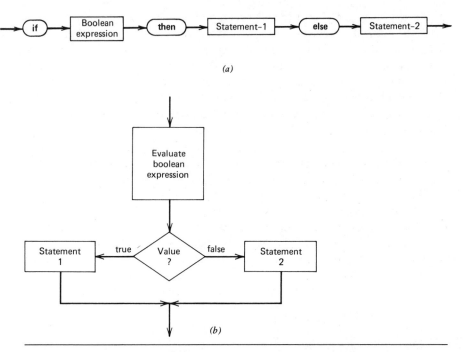

(a)

(b)

Figure 5-12. Syntax and behavior of the **if/then/else** statement. (*a*) Syntax. (*b*) Operation.

executed and statement-2 is skipped. If the boolean expression is false, statement-1 is skipped and statement-2 is executed. Thus, one and only one of the two statements will always be executed. For example, if we write

if $a > b$ **then**
    large := a
else
    large := b

we would assign the greater of a and b to large. What happens if a = b? Since the condition tests specifically for a greater than b, the boolean expression would be false and the second statement (the one following the **else**) would be executed. It is important to remember that one of the two statements will always be executed.

The **if/then/else** mechanism is perfectly suited for the task we illustrated in Figure 5-11. Since we have alternative courses of action and we always want to perform one of them, but never both, the **if/then/else** is ideal (Figure 5-13).

When either (or both) of the conditionally executed statements are compound statements, it becomes especially important to exercise some care in positioning the various parts of the **if/then/else** so that the intent of the entire construct can be readily grasped. It is quite common to have a nested sequence of **if/then/else** statements. Such a sequence can be readily understood by the reader of a program only if some consistent indentation scheme is followed. (Of course, the program will be understood by the Pascal compiler no matter how it is laid out, but it is important to write programs that can be readily understood by people too.) There are many different indentation schemes that can be used, and the specific details are not important as long as you pick a reasonable scheme and use it consistently. Figure 5-14 at the top of the next page shows two particular schemes that we find useful, but we emphasize that any approach that clearly depicts the flow of control is acceptable.

```
{ read and print data values }
readln (x,y,z);
writeln ('x = ', x, 'y = ', y, 'z = ', z);

{ check for invalid data }
if (x <= 0) or (y <= 10) or (z < 50) or (z > 100) then
    writeln ('invalid data, processing will be skipped')
else
begin
    writeln ('valid data, processing begins')

        ·       { carry out the computations here }
        ·

end { of the else clause }
```

Figure 5-13. Checking for valid data using the **if/then/else.**

```
if condition then                          if condition
begin                                      then begin
    { indent next line three spaces }
              .                                        .
              .                                        .
              .                                        .
end { then clause }                                  end
else                                       else begin
begin                                                .
    { indent three spaces }                          .
              .                                        .
              .                                        .
              .                                        .
end { else clause }                                  end

        (a)                                        (b)
```

Figure 5-14. Possible indentation schemes for conditional statements.

Either of the above layouts allows our eyes to quickly find the alternative clauses, and mentally skip the one that will not be executed. This matter of indentation and program layout may seem like a small mechanical point, but in a large program with several nested conditional statements, it can be a tremendous aid to comprehension. (In this text, we will use the indentation scheme shown in Figure 5-14*a*.)

Look at the following set of nested conditional statements

```
if a < 3.5 then begin if (b < 2.0)
or (c <> 60.0) then begin
c := a * b − 9.7; writeln ('c = ',
c) end else b := b − 1 end else S
```

and try to determine under what conditions we execute statement S. In its current format, this is not an easy task! However, if we rewrote the above fragment as

```
if (a < 3.5) then
begin
    if (b < 2.0) or (c <> 60.0) then
    begin
        c := a * b − 9.7;
        writeln ('c = ', c)
    end
    else
        b := b − 1
end
else
    S
```

the conditions for executing S become much more clear—namely, a $>= 3.5$.
Consider this Pascal statement.

if $a < 0$ **then if** $b < 0$ **then** $b := b + 1$ **else** $a := a + 1$

(We have deliberately written this on one line to make our point.) What is the meaning of this construct? If you think the answer is obvious, look again, because two different interpretations are possible. To which **if** does the **else** belong?

In Figure 5-15 we have inserted **begin** and **end** to indicate the two possible meanings and we have used indentation to highlight these meanings. Note that the difference in meaning is significant. In alternative 1, a is incremented only if a is negative and b is nonnegative; in alternative 2, a is incremented only if a is nonnegative. Which meaning is correct?

This well-known ambiguity is usually called the *dangling else* problem. To resolve it, Pascal uses the first interpretation: an **else** is always associated with the innermost **if.** There is a lesson to be learned here. Sometimes the addition of a redundant **begin** and **end** can help to clarify the meaning of a construct. Just as it pays to use parentheses to make the meaning of an arithmetic expression obvious, it sometimes helps to use **begin** and **end** to bracket parts of a control construct even if the **begin** and **end** might not be technically necessary. Note also that, in Pascal, there can never be a ';' before the reserved word **else,** because **else** is not a statement.

Figure 5-16 is a complete Pascal program to compute and print employee paychecks. It illustrates both the iterative and conditional statements that we have introduced so far in this chapter.

```
1.   if a < 0 then
     begin
         if b < 0 then
             b: = b + 1
         else
             a: = a + 1
     end
2.   if a < 0 then
     begin
         if b < 0 then
             b: = b + 1
     end
     else
         a: = a + 1
```

Figure 5-15. The dangling else problem.

```
program paycheck(input,output);

{ program to read a timecard containing employee id number, hourly rate, hours
  worked this week, and number of dependents, and print out the pay earned for
  this week }

const
      minimumwage = 3.35; { federal minimum wage }

var
      dependents  : integer;   { number of dependents for this employee }
      federaltax  : real;      { the amount of federal withholding tax }
      gross       : real;      { pay before taxes }
      hoursworked : real;      { hours worked this week }
      id          : 0..99999;  { employee id number }
      netpay      : real;      { pay after taxes }
      payrate     : real;      { hourly payrate }

begin
{ We are going to repeat the following for every employee
  until we run out of data                                    }
      while not eof do
      begin
            readln (id, payrate, hoursworked, dependents);
            writeln (id, payrate, hoursworked, dependents);
            { validate the data }
            if (payrate < minimumwage) or (hoursworked < 0.0) or
                  (hoursworked > 168.0) or (dependents < 0) then
                  writeln (' illegal data for employee ', id,
                              ' no paycheck will be issued ')

            else
            begin { data is ok. first compute gross pay }
                  if (hoursworked > 40.0) then
                        gross := (payrate * 40.0) + (payrate * 1.5 *
                        (hoursworked − 40.0))

                  else
                        gross := payrate * hoursworked;

                  { federal tax will be 14% of gross pay less $10.00 for each
                    dependent }
                  federaltax := 0.14 * gross − (dependents * 10);
                  if federaltax < 0.0 then federaltax := 0.0;

                  { compute net pay as gross pay less deductions }
                  netpay := gross − federaltax;
                  writeln (' net pay for employee, ', id, ' is ', netpay:10:2)
            end { else clause on valid data }
      end { while loop on eof }
end. { program paycheck }
```

Figure 5-16. Program to print paychecks.

Style Clinic 5-4

Clarifying the Flow of Control

Are you wondering if indentation alone can be used to convey the intended meaning of a construct like the one in Figure 5-15? Be careful—indentation can convey a meaning to the program reader, but it cannot force a meaning on the computer. For example, suppose we rewrite the second of our possible interpretations, using good indentation but omitting **begin** and **end.**

```
if a<0 then
    if b<0 then b:=b+1
else
    a:=a+1
```

Things are not what they appear to be! The indentation suggests one meaning, but the computer is oblivious to the indentation. The actual meaning is that of alternative 1; the **else** is associated with the nearest **if,** regardless of how we choose to lay out the program on the printed page. If we want the meaning of alternative 2, we must state it explicitly, using **begin** and **end.**

```
if a<0 then
begin
    if b<0 then b:=b+1
end
else
    a:=a+1
```

In summary, we must remember that a good indentation scheme is important because it can help the reader understand the control flow of a program. But indentation cannot change the flow of control, and we never want the indentation to suggest a meaning that is not the proper one. Therefore, if there is ever any doubt as to the meaning of a particular construct, resolve that doubt with an explicit indication of intent, even if it means being somewhat redundant.

5.4.3 The Case Statement

Unlike the **if,** which allows a selection of two alternatives, the **case** statement allows a program to select one statement for execution out of a set of alternatives. During the execution of the **case** statement, only one of the possible statements will be executed; the remaining statements will be skipped. The syntax and operation of the **case** statement is shown in Figure 5-17.

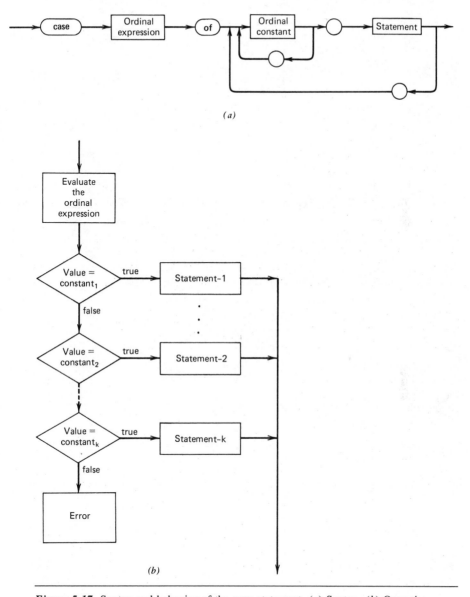

(a)

(b)

Figure 5-17. Syntax and behavior of the **case** statement. (*a*) Syntax. (*b*) Operation.

For example,

```
{ Assume j is an integer variable }
case j of
     1      :      a: = a + 1;
     2,3    :      b: = b + 1;
     5,     :      c: = c + 1;
     6,8,10 :      d: = d + 1
end
```

The **case** statement will execute one (and only one) of the assignment statements based on the value of j. If j is 1, a will be incremented; if j is 2 or 3, b will be incremented; if j is 5, c will be incremented; if j is 6, 8, or 10, d will be incremented. Only one statement will be executed and the rest will be ignored. The program will then continue with the statement following the **end.**

An obvious question has probably occurred to you. What happens if j does not have one of the values 1, 2, 3, 5, 6, 8, or 10? It might be nice if nothing at all happened, that is, if the entire **case** statement were ignored. However, that is not what happens. If the **case** statement is executed at a time when j does not have one of the indicated values, the effect of the **case** statement is *undefined*. We simply do not know what will happen, and we can make no assumptions whatsoever. This means that we can use a **case** statement only if we know in advance all the possible values that the selector expression can have. If we know all the values, we can list them as possibilities, and the **case** statement will always do something meaningful. Of course, if the number of possible values is quite large, it may be impractical to list them all. In such a situation we may not be able to use the **case** statement.

Let us look at the general form of the **case** statement.

```
case expression of
     cll: statement; { cll = case label list }
     cll: statement;
        .
        .
        .
     cll: statement
end
```

Each cll ("case label list") is a list of constants (separated by commas) of the same type as the selector expression (any ordinal type is allowed). The items in each list indicate the values of the selector expression for which the associated statement is to be executed. We can have as many items in a case label list as we like (in any order), and we can have as many lists as we like, although a given constant can appear in only one list. Also, any of the associated statements can be a compound statement.

Note that an **end** terminates the **case** statement. This is one of the two places in Pascal where an **end** appears without a matching **begin.** After writing a fairly lengthy program it is not uncommon to get an error message during the first run of the program, indicating an improper number of **begin**s and **end**s. In checking your program, remember that it is not required to have each **end** balanced by a **begin.** If your program has **case** statements, each one will terminate with an **end,** which matches the **case** instead of a **begin.**

Keep in mind that **case** statements are not restricted to situations in which the selector expression is based on integer values. Suppose that currentchar is a char variable and at some point in a program we have ascertained that currentchar contains one of the vowels. If we want to execute a different statement for each of the possible values of currentchar, we can write

```
case currentchar of
    'a':statement-1;
    'e':statement-2;
    'i':statement-3;
    'o':statement-4;
    'u':statement-5
end
```

(Remember that this is reasonable only if we are certain that currentchar has one of the five indicated values. If the **case** statement is executed when the variable has any other value, the result will be unpredictable.)

If the variable day has been defined as follows:

```
var
    day : (mon,tue,wed,thur,fri,sat,sun);
```

then a payroll program that pays time-and-a-half for work done on Saturday and double time for Sunday could use a **case** in the following way.

```
case day of
    mon,tue,wed,thur,fri    : payrate := 1.0;
    sat                     : payrate := 1.5;
    sun                     : payrate := 2.0
end { case }
```

We will now look at a specific example in which a **case** statement might be helpful. Suppose we consider a simplified version of a real estate tax computation. We will consider a situation in which the tax rate varies with the assessed value of the property, as follows.

Assessed Value	Tax Rate
< $20,000	3% of assessed value
$20,000 – $29,999	4% of assessed value
$30,000 – $59,999	5% of assessed value
≥ $60,000	6% of assessed value

Because we have four possible tax rates, we might want to use a **case** statement to select the appropriate rate. Since the assessed value could presumably be any positive number, we might at first glance think we would have to list a very large number of possibilities in the case label lists. Even if we had the patience, we could not list all the possibilities, since there is no upper bound.

A simple programming technique can solve our problem. Instead of using the assessed value as the selector expression, we will use a value computed from the assessed value. In particular, we can map 10,000 assessed values into a single integer if we divide the assessed value by 10,000. For example,

    20000 **div** 10000   yields 2
    20001 **div** 10000   yields 2
    20500 **div** 10000   yields 2
    29999 **div** 10000   yields 2

and so on. In this manner we can deal with the positive integers 1, 2, 3, . . . instead of all the numbers in the 10,000s, 20,000s, 30,000s, ... But we still must be careful. Since there is no upper limit on the assessed value, there is no upper limit on our integers. A value of $60,000 will yield 6 when divided by 10,000, but a value of $100,000 will yield 10 when divided by 10,000. Larger assessed values will result in still larger values for our selector expression. We will solve this problem by performing a special test before executing the **case** statement: if the value of the selector expression exceeds 6, we will reset it to 6, since any assessed value greater than $60,000 is in the highest tax bracket.

Our **case** statement will now look like this.

```
category : = value div 10000;
if category > 6 then category : = 6;
case category of
    0,1  :      rate : = 0.03;     { $0 – $19,999 }
    2    :      rate : = 0.04;     { $20,000 – $29,999 }
    3,4,5 :     rate : = 0.05;     { $30,000 – $59,999 }
    6    :      rate : = 0.06      { ≥ $60,000 }
end;
tax : = value * rate
```

Note that as long as the assessed value is a positive number, our **case** statement has dealt with all of the possibilities. The selector expression is guaranteed to have a value between 0 and 6. (You might try rewriting this fragment so it works properly even if a negative assessed value is accidentally provided. Print an error message if value < 0.)

Let's incorporate this into a complete program that will read an assessed value (an integer) from a data card and compute the appropriate tax. The program will continue processing data cards until a negative or zero signal value is encountered for an assessed value. Note that the program will be set up to process any positive data value; any nonpositive value will stop the program. The program appears in Figure 5-18.

```
program taxes (input,output);

{ program to compute property tax from the assessed value of the property }

var
    category  : integer;      { one of 6 possible tax categories }
    rate      : real;         { tax rate from 3 – 6% }
    tax       : real;         { actual tax }
    value     : integer;      { dollar value of the house }

begin
    readln(value);
    while (value > 0) do { a zero or negative value is a signal to terminate }
    begin
        category := value div 10000;
        if category > 6 then category := 6;
        case category of
            0,1  : rate := 0.03;   { $0 – $19,999 }
            2    : rate := 0.04;   { $20,000 – $29,999 }
            3,4,5: rate := 0.05;   { $30,000 – $59,999 }
            6    : rate := 0.06    { >= $60,000 }
        end; { case }
        tax := value * rate;
        writeln (' assessed value = ', value);
        writeln (' tax is ', tax:12:2);
        readln (value) { get the next data value }
    end { of while loop }
end. { of program }
```

Figure 5-18. A program for computing property tax.

5.5 UNCONDITIONAL BRANCHING

We have seen how **if/then, if/then/else,** and **case** statements allow us to alter the execution flow of our program to execute a statement conditionally. We will now discuss a mechanism that allows us to alter the control flow unconditionally. An *unconditional branch* is a jump to another point in the program without making a test or satisfying any specific condition. The idea is fairly simple, but we will see that the need for this unconditional transfer seldom arises in a program that has been well thought out.

There are two aspects to the mechanism of unconditional transfer of control. One is the statement that performs the actual transfer, the other is a labeling mechanism that uniquely identifies the place in the program to which the transfer is made.

5.5.1 Statement Labels

If we are interested in transferring to a particular point in a program, we must label that point with a *statement label*, an unsigned integer placed before any Pascal statement and followed by a colon.[2] For example,

150: a := a + 1

affixes the label 150 to the assignment statement. The syntax of the **label** declaration is shown in Figure 5-19*b*.

We can attach labels to as many statements in a program as we like as long as each label is unique. However, the only reason for using a label is to indicate a place in the program to which an unconditional transfer will be made. Since we will see that the need for these unconditional transfers is rare, it follows that most programs should contain very few labels. In fact, most of the time there will be none.

[2]Each implementation defines a range of values for statement labels. In standard Pascal, labels can consist of up to four digits, so the possible labels range from 1 to 9999. We will adhere to this limit.

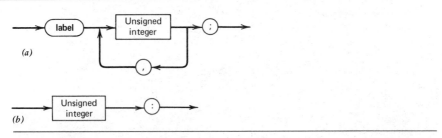

Figure 5-19. Syntax of statement labels and the **label** declaration. (*a*) **Label** declaration. (*b*) Statement label.

There is one more aspect to defining a statement label. All statement labels must appear in a **label** declaration at the beginning of the program. This declaration appears before the **var** and **const** declarations. The syntax of this declaration is shown in Figure 5-19a. For example, if our program made use of 15 and 25 as statement labels, we would write

label *15,25;*

We should note that statement labels are not the same as integer constants that might appear in a case label list, despite the similarity in syntax. Statement labels appear in the **label** declaration, and they designate places to which a program can transfer. Case labels appear in the context of a **case** statement, and they designate the values for which the associated statements will be executed. Thus, despite the apparent similarity in syntax, 10 and 15 are not being used as duplicate labels in this example.

```
label 10, 15;
var
     k : integer;
     .
     .
     .

10:     statement-1;
        case k of
                5: statement-2;
                10: statement-3;
                15: statement-4
        end;
15:     statement-5
        .
        .
        .
```

Of course, since this might be confusing to the reader, it is not considered good programming style. In this situation it would be prudent to select numbers other than 5, 10, or 15 for statement labels. This will lead to a more readable program.

5.5.2 The Goto Statement

To accomplish an unconditional transfer, we simply write

goto *statement label*

where statement label is a label that appears in both the program and a **label** declaration. The execution of the **goto** statement causes the program to continue execution at the point of the statement label. For example,

goto *100*

will cause execution to continue at the statement with the label 100.

We have already made reference to the fact that the **goto** statement will not often be needed in a Pascal program. No doubt you are wondering why. After all, the **goto** seems like a simple idea that is relatively easy to use.

Yes, the **goto** is a simple idea—and that is its downfall. The **goto** is, in a sense, just a building block used in the creation of more interesting control structures. In Pascal these more sophisticated control structures (**while, repeat, for, if/then/else,** and **case**) are directly available as part of the language. We need not synthesize them with **goto** statements. Which of the program fragments in Figure 5-20 conveys its meaning more clearly? Both program fragments perform exactly the same operations, but the **if/then/else** and **while** statements give a clearer indication of what is happening. In the second fragment, we have used four **goto** statements, four statement labels, and two **if** statements to achieve the identical results. We are actually using some primitive building blocks to construct a more interesting structure. Since these struc-

```
i := 0;
while (i < 100) do
begin
    if (i < 50) then
        { process the first 50 iterations one way }
    else
        { process the next 50 iterations a different way };
    i := i + 1
end
```
(a)

```
    i := 0;
20: if i < 50 then goto 10;
    { process the last 50 iterations }
40: i := i + 1;
    if (i >= 100) then goto 30;
    goto 20;
10: { process the first 50 iterations }
    goto 40;
30:
```
(b)

Figure 5-20. Comparison of the structure of two code fragments. (*a*) Properly structured code. (*b*) Poorly structured code.

tures are directly available in the language as the **while** statement and the **if/then/else,** it makes more sense to use the structured statement. It is easier to write and provides a clearer indication of what is happening. A program that uses only the high-level control structures of Pascal and has few (or no) **goto**s is written in a style that is called *structured code*.

In a similar manner, we could synthesize all the other control statements (**repeat, for, if/then/else, case**) using only **if/then** and **goto** statements. This might be an interesting exercise, but it would not be a productive way to go about writing programs. Our programs will be easier to write (and read) and more apt to be correct if we utilize the higher-level structures that are built into the language. The rich set of control structures in Pascal distinguishes it from many other programming languages.

Theoretically, we do not need the **goto** statement at all. Any Pascal program can be written entirely without **goto** statements. Then why is it present in the language? In some circumstances it may be awkward to achieve a certain effect without a **goto** statement. Thus, occasionally the use of a **goto** statement will allow us to write a program that is clearer than it would be without it. We need a bit of insight as to when the **goto** statement may be able to help us.

When we discussed algorithms, we introduced a number of constructs that served as convenient building blocks. We have seen that these constructs have direct analogs in our programming language, and it is convenient to think in terms of these constructs—**while, repeat, for,** and so on—when we write computer programs. However, on rare occasions it happens that the natural structure of our algorithm has to be broken, usually to deal with some type of exceptional condition. These breaks in the overall algorithmic structure can sometimes be handled more easily with **goto** statements.

It is not possible to catalogue all of the situations in which a **goto** statement might properly be used, except to say that they almost always involve a special circumstance of one sort or another and usually involve a forward jump within the program. (A backward jump, which by definition is a loop, can almost always be better expressed by one of the structured statements.) For example, in the process of performing a lengthy calculation, we might find that an unacceptable intermediate result has occurred (e.g., a negative value where one was not permitted). This might make it meaningless to continue with the rest of the computation. It might be appropriate to print an error message and jump to the end of the program. Of course, if this action can be conveniently incorporated into the algorithm with a structured statement (e.g., **if/then/else**), it would make sense to do so. Sometimes, however, it is a bit awkward to use a structured statement to deal with this situation.

As a concrete example of what we are describing, let us look again at the issue of data verification. In Figure 5-13 we showed how an **if/then/else** can be used to handle this. The test would be constructed to look for invalid data. The **then** clause would print an error message, while the **else** clause would contain virtually the entire program.

> **if** *test for invalid data*
> **then**
>   *print an error message*
> **else**
>   *carry out the computation*

This can be awkward if the program is fairly long. We may not find it particularly convenient or very readable to have an entire program contained in the **else** clause of an **if/then/else** statement. Subsequent control statements will require additional levels of indentation, and we might find it difficult to format our program in a readable way. In a situation such as this we might want to use an **if/then** to check for invalid data and, if appropriate, print a message and jump to the end of the program to avoid the computation. The outline of our program would look like the one in Figure 5-21. Note that the statement label (''100:'') occurs at the very end of the program. It is actually labeling the empty statement that exists between the colon and the **end**. When the program transfers to statement 100, there is nothing to execute (since the empty statement does nothing), and the program stops.

Notice that we have inserted a comment near the **goto** that explains where we are going. One of the problems with a **goto** statement is that as you read a program and

```
label 100;
        .
        .
        .

begin
{ Read and print data values }
readln(. . .);
writeln(. . .);

{ Check for invalid data }
if "data invalid" then
begin
     writeln('error — invalid data');
        goto 100 { Jump to end of program to terminate execution }
end;
{ The computations begin here }
        .
        .
        .

100: end.
```

Figure 5-21. Using a **goto** in data verification.

encounter a **goto,** you do not know exactly where you are going (until you find the label), and you do not know why you are going there. It is a good idea to include a comment near the **goto** that provides this information. This can be a great help in following the flow of the program.

In summary, then, the situations in which an unconditional branch may be useful will almost always have the following two characteristics.

1. A long forward branch, frequently to the end of the program unit.
2. A branch caused by an error, an abnormal condition, or a break in the normal flow of operations of the algorithm.

However, this does not mean that all early loop exits should be implemented with the **goto.** There is often a temptation to use a **goto** statement when it is necessary to exit from a loop before the normal loop condition is satisfied. For example, suppose that we are reading in characters, one at a time, checking to see that they are alphabetic, counting them, and printing them out. We must continue these operations either until we encounter a nonalphabetic input character or we come to the end-of-file. We might initially be tempted to use a **goto** to handle the abnormal exit that occurs when we encounter nonalphabetic input.

```
count : = 0;
while not eof do
begin
    read(ch);
    if (ch < 'a') or (ch > 'z') then goto 1;
    count : = count + 1;
    write(ch)
end; { while loop }
1:
```

The previous example, however, is not a desirable use of the **goto** statement. If the loop is large, we may not be able to see where the **goto** is taking us. More important, the intent of the loop is not clearly expressed by the boolean condition in the **while** statement. Looking at the **while** statement, it appears at first glance that the only criterion for termination is reaching the end of file.

There is a much better and lucid way to handle the problem of an early exit from a loop. We can use a boolean variable in the loop expression to help control the execution of the loop. A conditional statement inside the loop can be used to set this variable to the appropriate value so that the loop is exited after the terminating condition occurs. In our example, we might use a boolean variable called alphabetic, which has the value true when all input is in the range 'a' to 'z.' The variable is set to false if illegal input is encountered.

```
alphabetic := true;
count := 0;
while alphabetic and (not eof) do
begin
    read(ch);
    if (ch < 'a') or (ch > 'z') then
        alphabetic := false
    else
    begin
        count := count + 1;
        write(ch)
    end { else clause }
end { while loop }
```

In this loop it is clear that there are two distinct termination conditions. Note that the use of a suggestive name for the boolean variable greatly enhances the readability of the code.

The programming technique of using a boolean variable to terminate a loop instead of using a **goto** to exit is a good one to become familiar with. It is another instance in which avoiding a **goto** statement can lead to a program that is much more readable.

Keep in mind that a **goto** statement will be helpful in a relatively small number of cases. We should always try to design and implement our programs in terms of higher-level control constructs and use the **goto** only when the natural flow of the program must be broken. If you find yourself writing a Pascal program that contains many **goto** statements, you should stop and think. You have probably not thought out the program carefully enough. The excessive use of **goto** statements will result in a program that is difficult to comprehend.

Style Clinic 5-5

The Goto Controversy

You may be interested to know that the **goto** statement has been an area of debate among computer scientists. The "**goto** controversy" has contributed to the development of an important movement called *structured programming*. Although structured programming does not yet have a fixed definition, its most important concerns are for the types of control statements needed in a programming language and the relationship between certain control structures and a program's clarity. As in any new movement, there are proponents of extreme positions. In the area of structured programming, one of these extreme positions is that the inclusion of *any* unconditional branch in a program is inherently bad. Our position is not related to the worth of a statement itself, but to the overall clarity of the resulting program. If a particular situation lends itself naturally to an unconditional branch, use it.

Style Clinic 5-6 _____

Which Loop Primitive Should I Use?

In this chapter we have introduced three statements for performing iteration in Pascal—the **while, repeat,** and **for.** You will need to choose the appropriate one when you begin writing your programs. In many cases it won't matter, but these two guidelines can assist you in making the right choice.

1. The **for** loop is the least flexible statement and should never be used when there are two or more criteria for loop termination. You will get yourself in the following bind.

    ```
    { loop can terminate after 100 iterations or upon
      encountering a negative value }
    for i := 1 to 100 do
    begin
        readln (x);
        if x < 0 then ????
        else
            { process this data value }
    end { for loop }
    ```

    What do we put in for the question marks? It will have to be an unconditional branch. If we had selected a **while** or **repeat,** the loop termination conditions could have been phrased as

    ```
    while (count <= 100) and not (x < 0) do
    ```

2. When choosing between the **while** and **repeat** take a careful look at the *null case*—the situation in which there are no data to process. The **repeat** loop will always execute the loop body at least once and may not correctly handle the null case.

5.6 CASE STUDY—ROOT FINDING

In this section we will go through the complete development of a computer program
that uses many of the ideas that we have presented so far in the first five chapters.

The problem we will address in this case study is finding the root of an equation,
a very common and important problem in mathematics. To represent an equation we
will use the notation $f(x)$. For the purposes of this case study, $f(x)$ can be anything
we want: for example, $f(x) = x^2 - 2x + 1$, $f(x) = \sqrt{x^3 - 9.2}$, $f(x) = \sin^2(x) + x^{8.8}$. The *root* of an equation is defined as a point x^* such that the value of the equation
at that point is 0, that is, $f(x^*) = 0$. For example, the two roots of the equation $f(x)$
$= x^2 + x - 12$ are 3 and -4. Pictorially, we can view a root of an equation as a
point where the graph of that equation crosses the x-axis.

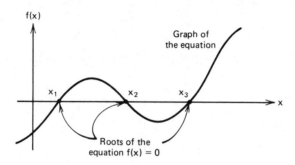

There are literally dozens of well-known algorithms for finding the roots of an
equation. In fact, the ancient Greek mathematicians studied this problem over 3000
years ago. The technique that we will use in this case study is called the *method of
false position* (sometimes referred to by its Latin name *regula falsi*).[3] The basic
principle behind this technique is that we have two points, x_1 and x_2, that lie on
opposite sides of the root. We then draw a line (called a *secant*) between the points
$f(x_1)$ and $f(x_2)$, and call the point where that secant crosses the x-axis x_3. This operation
is shown in Figure 5-22 at the top of the next page.

---

[3]Note that the method of false position is considered by mathematicians to be a poor technique for
locating roots, and better algorithms do exist. We have selected this method because it is easy to understand and
describe and does not require a knowledge of calculus. Our purpose in this case study is to study programming,
not mathematics.

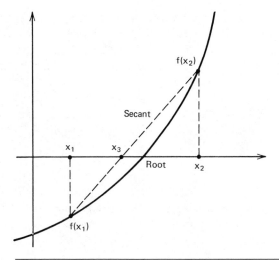

Figure 5-22. Definition of the method of false position.

As we see in this figure, the new point x_3 will usually lie closer to the root than either of the original points x_1 or x_2. We now discard the previous point that lies on the same side of the root as x_3 (x_1 in Figure 5-22) and repeat the process just described, but this time using points x_3 and x_2.

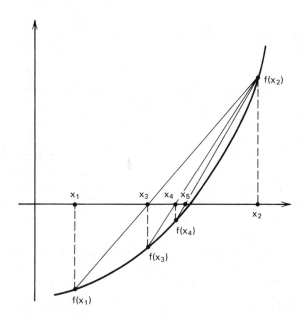

As the diagrams show, we will be generating a series of points x_3, x_4, x_5, x_6, . . . that are getting closer and closer to the actual value of the root. This type of repetitive-solution technique is called an *iterative solution*. We will never get an exact answer, but we keep moving closer and closer to the answer and stop when we have reached the desired level of accuracy.

The "desired level of accuracy" can be expressed in a number of different ways. In this case study, we will say that we are satisfied with the accuracy of the result when the value of the function at the most recent point is "near enough" to 0. That is, if x_i is the most recent point generated, then

$$| f(x_i) | < \epsilon$$

where ϵ is some small positive number and represents the desired accuracy.

There is a special case that we should be aware of: a function with no root at all!

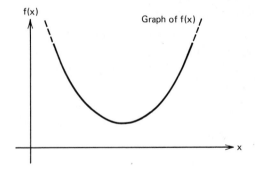

When faced with this situation, our program should print out something like

*** sorry, but I cannot find a root ***

A second special case occurs when we try to locate a root to a degree of accuracy beyond what is possible on our machine. For example, given a value of $\epsilon = 10^{-15}$ (implying an error of less than 1 part in a million billion!), we may never achieve accuracy to this level, because of round-off and truncation errors inherent in doing finite arithmetic on a computer. In this case, we might possibly iterate "forever" trying to achieve something that is inherently impossible. To prevent this, we must add a second criterion to our loop termination—reaching some program-defined upper bound on the number of possible iterations.

The formal specification statement for the problem just described is given in Figure 5-23. We will now develop an algorithm to solve this problem.

You are to write a program to find a real root of an arbitrary equation f(x). If the equation has more than one root, the program should find any one root and then halt. If the equation has no roots, the program should print the following message.

*** sorry, I cannot find a root ***

The program should allow the user to specify the accuracy desired, where accuracy is defined as

$| f(r) | < \epsilon$

where r is the approximation of the root and ϵ is a small positive value provided as input to the program. When the program finds a root to this degree of accuracy, it should print out the message.

root = xxx.xxxx to an accuracy of .xxx

Figure 5-23. Specifications of the root-finding problem.

At the highest level, the problem is quite easy to formulate (a high-level algorithm is shown in Figure 5-24a). However, now we must begin to refine these higher-level constructs into our basic algorithmic primitives.

START
      get a pair of points x_1 and x_2 that lie on opposite
         sides of a root
      read in ϵ, the desired accuracy
      set root-found to false
      while not (root-found) do
         determine point x_3 using the method of false position
         if x_1 and x_3 are on the same side of the root then
            set x_1 to x_3
         else
            set x_2 to x_3

         compute the accuracy we have obtained
         if accuracy $< \epsilon$ then
            set root-found to true
      end of the while loop
      write out the answer
      stop
END OF THE ALGORITHM

Figure 5-24. (*a*) Highest level of the root-finding algorithm.

For example, looking at the first line in Figure 5-24a how might we get initial values for the points x_1 and x_2 on opposite sides of the root? There are a number of ways. A simple method would be to ask the *user* to provide these two input values and have the program check that they actually do lie on opposite sides of the root. (We can quickly see if they lie on opposite sides of the root by checking the sign of the equation at points x_1 and x_2. They will be different if they are on opposite sides.) If these points are not acceptable, we will ask the user to try another pair of values.

```
set gooddata to false
while not gooddata do
        read in values for x₁ and x₂
        if x₁ and x₂ are on opposite sides of the root then
                set gooddata to true
        else
                write 'these values are not valid starting points, please try again'
        end of the while loop
```

However, to avoid having an infinite loop in the situation where there is no root anywhere, we should allow the user some way to exit gracefully from the loop. One reasonable way would be to say that if the user enters a pair of values for which $x_1 = x_2 = 0$, we will interpret that as a signal that he or she is giving up on ever finding an interval containing the root (see Figure 5-24b).

```
set gooddata to false
set giving-up to false
while not gooddata and not giving-up do
        read in values for x₁ and x₂
        if x₁ and x₂ are both 0 then
                set giving-up to true
        else
                if x₁ and x₂ are on opposite sides of the root then
                        set gooddata to true
                else
                        write out an appropriate message about either trying
                                again or giving up
        end of the while loop
```

Figure 5-24. (b) Refinement of the input section of root-finder algorithm.

The technique for finding the point x_3 using the method of false position is simply to solve the following equation.

$$x_3 = \frac{x_2 f(x_1) - x_1 f(x_2)}{f(x_1) - f(x_2)}$$

where $f(x_1)$, $f(x_2)$ is the value of the equation f at the points x_1, x_2.

We must realize that this formula is undefined if $f(x_1) = f(x_2)$, since this causes a division by 0. The secant will be parallel to the x-axis and will never cross it. However, since we have already checked that $f(x_1)$ and $f(x_2)$ have different signs, this situation cannot occur. We can now define the expansion of the operations to determine the point x_3 (line 6 of Figure 5-24a).

> Compute the value of the function at point x_1.
> Compute the value of the function at point x_2.
> Set x_3 to $(x_2 f(x_1) - x_1 f(x_2)/f(x_1) - f(x_2))$.

We can now see that the process of discarding the old point that lies on the same side of the root as the new point is simply a question of checking signs and discarding the point that has the same sign as the new value x_3. The expansion of this operation (lines 7 to 10 of Figure 5-24a) is shown in Figure 5-24c.

There is a special case we should look at which we mentioned earlier. In the **while** loop of Figure 5-24a, the only criterion for termination is finding the root. However, it is possible for us to enter the loop but never be able to locate the root. This situation occurs when we try to locate a root to an accuracy beyond what is possible on our computer. For example, if we provide a value of $\epsilon = 0.000000000001$ (an error no greater than 1 trillionth!), we may never be able to achieve this level of accuracy because of the inherent round-off errors that occur when we do real arithmetic on a finite computer. In this case, the loop might iterate "forever." To prevent this, we should probably add a second criterion to our loop termination, such as reaching some program-defined upper bound on the number of iterations.

> if($f(x_1) < 0$ and $f(x_3) < 0$) or
> ($f(x_1) > 0$ and $f(x_3) > 0$) then
>   set x_1 to the value of x_3
> else
>   set x_2 to the value of x_3

Figure 5-24. (c) Expansion of the operation to discard a previous point.

```
set count to 0
while not (root-found) and (count < maximum) do
        .

        .

        .
    increment count by 1
end of the while loop
```

We have completed the algorithmic development of the problem and can now put the pieces together to form a complete root-finding algorithm. This algorithm is shown in Figure 5-25 on page 191.

With our algorithm developed, we are in a position to begin to code our Pascal program. Our algorithmic notation is actually so close to Pascal that this process will be relatively straightforward. Our only concerns will be the technical details of Pascal syntax. We will have to select legitimate names for all our variables (ϵ is not acceptable as a Pascal identifier), and we will have to provide suitable declarations for all of our identifiers.

We can now clearly see the advantage of working with an algorithmic notation before writing the program in Pascal. The details associated with a programming language need not concern us during the algorithm development phase. We do not want to be distracted by the details of semicolons, reserved identifiers, type declarations, and so on while we are working at this higher level. Only when we are generally satisfied with the algorithmic solution should we become involved with the constraints imposed by a particular programming language.

In Figure 5-26 on pages 192-193 we have written a complete program [except for substituting an actual formula for f(x)], but we are not done. We must check out our program with a few well-chosen test cases to see whether it will perform correctly. Unfortunately, in all but the most trivial programs, testing will not guarantee that our program is perfect. We can find out whether our program performs properly for a few test cases, but that will not ensure that the program will work in all cases. In general, we will want to run a number of test cases, checking out the program for data values that are valid and invalid. Most of these tests can be made by simply letting the computer execute the program, but it is usually a good idea to test at least one case by *hand-simulating* the program. This simulation can often uncover bugs in the program before it has even been prepared for execution, when corrections will be easier to make.

We will now hand-simulate one test case, using "reasonable" data values. This should provide some assurance that at least the basic concept underlying the program is valid. (Chapter 6 will discuss the topic of testing programs in much greater detail.)

The key to hand-simulating a program is good organization. You should start with several clean sheets of paper (trying to work in an unused corner of some scrap paper can be disastrous!). You should have a scratch pad and an electronic calculator for computing immediate results. It is important to start at the beginning of the program

START
    set gooddata to false
    set giving-up to false
    while not gooddata and not giving-up do
        read in values for x_1 and x_2
        if x_1 and x_2 are both 0 then
            set giving-up to true
        else
            if x_1 and x_2 are on opposite sides of the root then
                set gooddata to true
            else
                write out an appropriate message to try a new
                    pair of points or to give up

    end of the while loop

    if giving-up then
        write out an appropriate message that you couldn't
            locate an interval containing a root and you gave up
    else
        read in ϵ the desired accuracy and maximum number of iterations
        set root-found to false
        set count to 0
        while not(root-found) and (count < maximum) do
            determine point x_3 using the method of false position
            if $(f(x_1) < 0)$ and $(f(x_3) < 0)$ or
                $(f(x_1) > 0)$ and $f(x_3) > 0)$ then
                set x_1 to the value of x_3
            else
                set x_2 to the value of x_3
            increment count by 1
            compute the accuracy
            if accuracy < ϵ then
                set root-found to true
        end of the while loop
        if root-found then
            write out the answer and the level of accuracy
        else
            write out that we could not find the answer in
                the maximum number of iterations
    stop
END OF THE ALGORITHM

Figure 5-25. Finished root-finder algorithm.

```
program rootfinder (input, output);
{ program to find roots of an equation using the method of false position. the
  user must provide the equation, f(x), and the absolute accuracy desired        }

const
      maximumcount = 100; { if we don't find the root after this many iterations
                            we will quit }

var
      count     : integer;  { iteration count }
      epsilon   : real;     { the relative accuracy desired }
      givingup  : boolean;  { switch to tell us if we are giving up locating a valid
                              interval }
      gooddata  : boolean;  { switch to determine if input is valid }
      rootfound : boolean;  { switch to tell us if answer has been found }
      x1,x2     : real;     { an interval containing the root }
      x3        : real;     { the new point computed by method of false
                              position }

begin
      { let's first locate an interval containing the answer }
      gooddata := false;
      givingup := false;
      while not gooddata and not givingup do
      begin
            writeln('please enter the two starting points');
            read (x1, x2);
            if (x1 = 0.0) and (x2 = 0.0) then
                  givingup := true
            else
                  { note the user will either have to replace the notation f(x) with the
                    actual equation desired, or will have to provide the function called
                    f. we will explain how to do this latter operation in Chapter 8     }
                  if ((f(x1) <= 0.0) and (f(x2) >= 0.0)) or
                     ((f(x1) >= 0.0) and (f(x2) <= 0.0)) then
                        gooddata := true
            else
            begin
                  writeln('sorry, the points provided do not lie on opposite');
                  writeln(' sides of the root — please try again ');
                  writeln(' enter 0 , 0 to terminate input ')
            end { else clause }
      end; { while loop }
```

```
if givingup then
begin
     write('sorry, terminating program because of failure');
     writeln('to find a valid starting interval')
end
else

begin { solving the problem }
     writeln('please enter the desired accuracy');
     read(epsilon);
     rootfound : = false;
     count : = 0;
     while not rootfound and (count < = maximumcount) do
     begin
          x3 : = (x2 * f(x1) − x1 * f(x2)) / (f(x1) − f(x2));
          if f(x3) = 0.0 then { we found the root exactly! }
               rootfound : = true;
          if ((f(x1) < = 0.0) and (f(x3) < = 0.0)) or
               ((f(x1) > = 0.0) and (f(x3) > = 0.0)) then
               x1 : = x3
          else
               x2 : = x3;
          count : = count + 1;
          if (abs(f(x3)) < epsilon) then
               rootfound : = true
     end; { while loop }

     if rootfound then
          writeln (' root = ', x3, 'to accuracy', epsilon)
     else
          writeln('sorry, unable to find the root within', maximumcount,
                    'iterations')
end { else clause on solving problem }
end. { program rootfinder }
```

Figure 5-26. Program rootfinder.

and faithfully carry out the steps exactly as they appear. It is all too easy to obtain false conclusions by doing several steps at a time because you "know what has to be done." What often happens if you try is that you carry out the instructions that you were thinking about when you wrote the program, instead of the actual instructions that you wrote down.

We present next the sequence of intermediate values obtained when the rootfinder program was hand-simulated for a particular test case. We used an electronic calculator to compute values. The number of significant figures is small because we intended

only to verify the reasonableness of the program, not to obtain a very precise answer—
we will let the computer do that.

The test of the rootfinder program in Figure 5-26 follows.

$f(x) = x^2 - 10$ (Note: Roots are approximately $\pm 3.1827. \ldots$)
We will use as our initial input
$\qquad x_1 = 1 \qquad x_2 = 15$
$f(1) \;\; = -9$
$f(15) = 215$

Since they have opposite signs, they lie on opposite sides of the root, and they are
valid input.

Let us assume that we now input $\epsilon = 0.2$.

x_1	x_2	x_3	Count	Root-found	Accuracy $|f(x_3)|$	ϵ
1	15	1.750	1	false	6.938	0.2
1.750	15	2.164	2	false	5.317	0.2
2.164	15	2.474	3	false	3.879	0.2
2.474	15	2.700	4	false	2.737	0.2
2.700	15	2.851	5	false	1.873	0.2
2.851	15	2.956	6	false	1.262	0.2
2.956	15	3.026	7	false	0.842	0.2
3.026	15	3.073	8	false	0.558	0.2
3.073	15	3.104	9	false	0.366	0.2
3.104	15	3.124	10	false	0.239	0.2
3.124	15	3.137	11	true	0.159	0.2

Note that our hand-computed answer is 3.137. The value of $|(3.137)^2 - 10|$ is about
0.159, within the requested accuracy of $\epsilon = 0.2$.

You may find it worthwhile to hand-simulate rootfinder with a different set of
data to gain experience with this testing technique.

EXERCISES FOR CHAPTER 5

1. For each of the problems listed, write a Pascal fragment first using a **while** and
   then a **repeat.**

   (a) Read in and print out characters from a card until the occurrence of a ''
   or eoln.

   (b) Read in integers from a card. Count the number of positive and negative
   values. Stop when you encounter a value of 0.

(c) Find the greatest integer whose square is less than 142,619.

(d) Find the sum of the first k odd integers.

2. Explain why it is difficult to do parts a to c in Exercise 1 using a **for** statement. Write part d from Exercise 1 using a **for** loop.

*3. The following program fragment uses **goto** statements needlessly; a structured statement would be much clearer. Rewrite this fragment using a **for** statement and then a **while** statement.

> currentvalue := 150;**goto** 20;
> 10: currentvalue := currentvalue − 1;
> 20:   S;   { S is any valid Pascal statement }
>   **if** currentvalue > 15 **then goto** 10

4. Write a complete Pascal program to find all integer solutions to the equation

$$3x + 2y - 7z = 5$$

for values of x, y, and z in the range 0 to 100.

*5. Let v1 and v2 represent boolean variables and let s1, s2, and s3 represent Pascal statements. Suppose that one of the statements is to be executed based on the values of the boolean variables, as follows.

	v2 t	v2 f
v1 t	s1	s2
v1 f	s3	s3

Set up a conditional statement to achieve this effect.

*6. Write a complete Pascal program to compute the average of all legal examination scores. A legal score is one in the range 0 to 150. Your program should read scores until an end-of-file condition occurs and then produce as output:

(a) The average of all legal scores.

(b) The number of legal scores.

(c) The number of illegal scores.

(Be sure your program works properly even when there are no legal scores.)

7. The Fibonacci series is defined as

$$n_0 = 1, \qquad n_1 = 1$$
$$n_{i+2} = n_{i+1} + n_i \qquad i = 0, 1, 2, \ldots$$

Thus, the first few Fibonacci numbers are

1, 1, 2, 3, 5, 8, 13, . . .

Write a complete Pascal program to compute and print the first k Fibonacci numbers, where k is input to the program. (Your program should work properly even if k $<=$ 0.)

*8. Temperatures on the Celsius (or centigrade) scale are related to those on the Fahrenheit scale by the formula

$$c = \frac{5}{9}(f - 32)$$

Write a complete program that prints the Celsius equivalent of Fahrenheit temperatures in the range low to high where low and high are input to the program. The increment size of the table should also be input to the program.

9. Write a program that reads text and produces encoded text by replacing each character with the character that occurs five positions "later" in the character set. (Thus, considering the typical ordering for alphabetic characters, 'a' would be replaced by 'f,' 'b' by 'g,' etc.) This replacement should "wrap around" the end of the character set so that there is a well-defined replacement for each character. (That is, the character that occurs at the end of the character set should be replaced by the character in the fifth position. You will have to know how large the character set is on your computer.) Read text and print the encoded form until an end-of-file condition occurs.

10. Write a complete program that computes the minimum number of coins and bills needed to make change for a particular purchase. The cost of the item and the amount tendered should be read as data values. Your program should indicate how many coins and bills of each denomination are needed for change. Make use of these denominations.

Coins: $0.01, $0.05, $0.10, $0.25
Bills: $1, $5, $10

11. Write a program to determine the frequency of each vowel in some English language text. The input will consist of sentences running over a number of lines. The end of the text is indicated by the special symbol '*' that will not appear anywhere else in the text. The output of the program should be the input text and the percentage of characters that were equal to 'a,' 'e,' 'i,' 'o,' 'u.' Blanks and punctuation marks should not be treated as characters and should not be included in the total.

12. Write a program to count the total number of words in some English language text. The input will consist of text running over a number of cards or lines. The end of the text will be indicated by the end-of-file condition becoming true. Your program should count the number of words in the entire input, where a word is defined as any sequence of nonblank characters bounded on either side by one or more blank characters. (Therefore things like +1.2, real-life, don't, and 1,000,000 are all counted as one word.) The output from your program should simply be the number of words in the text.

13. The area of a circle with a radius of 1 is π, and the area of a square that just contains the circle is 4. Therefore, if a large number of points is chosen randomly in the square, the fraction of those points that fall within the circle will be approximately $\pi/4$. Assuming the existence of a standard real-valued function called random that returns a random number, r, between 0 and 1, write a program to compute an approximation to π.

14. Assuming random is a standard real-valued function that returns a random number, r, between 0 and 1, write a program that approximates the probabilities for rolling the values 2 to 12 with two dice. Use a **case** statement in the program.

15. Write a Pascal program to process the weekly payroll of the Brooks Leather Company (BLC). For each employee of BLC your program will compute the gross pay, deductions, and net pay. This information is to be clearly printed in the output along with certain summary information for the entire payroll.

    Each week BLC punches a data card for each employee that includes the following information.

Social security number	(9 digits)
Hourly pay rate	(xx.xx)
Number of exemptions	(0 to 19)
Health insurance code	(1, 2, 3, or 4)
Hours worked	(xx.x)

    Using this information, your program should carry out the following computations.

    (a) *Gross Pay.* Regular pay for the first 40 hours and time-and-a-half beyond that up to a limit of 54 hours in any given week.

    (b) *Deductions.* Let g represent gross pay and t taxable pay. Let e represent number of exemptions.

    (i) Federal income tax withholding is defined as
    Let $t = g - \$14.00 * e - \$11.00$
    Withholding $= t * (0.14 + 2.3 \times 10^{-4} * t)$

    (ii)   State income tax withholding
          State withholding is defined as 31% of the amount withheld for federal income tax.

    (iii)   Social security tax
          $16.70 or (7.7% of g), whichever is smaller.

    (iv)   Health insurance
          1—No coverage
          2—Employee coverage ($2 per week)
          3—Family coverage ($7.50 per week)
          4—Major medical coverage ($13 per week)

(c) *Net Pay.*   Gross pay less all deductions.

For each employee, your program should produce an output report in a legible format with each item clearly labeled.

After the last employee has been processed, your program should print a summary report that includes the number of employees processed, total gross pay, total deductions of each type, and total net pay.

Your program must be capable of processing an arbitrary number of data cards and should perform reasonable operations for all data sets regardless of how meaningless they are. (For example, what if deductions exceed net pay? What if taxable pay is negative? Be careful to check those and similar situations and decide the appropriate action.)

16.   Assume that another program has already computed the mean, m, and standard deviation, σ, on a homework assignment for our class. We now wish to write a program that assigns letter grades to the individual homework scores. The input to this program will be m and σ followed by student grade cards containing an identification number (integer) and a score, s. The rules for assigning letter grades are as follows.

If S is Greater Than	But No More Than	Letter Grade
$M + \dfrac{3}{2}\sigma$	100	A
$M + \dfrac{\sigma}{2}$	$M + \dfrac{3}{2}\sigma$	B
$M - \dfrac{\sigma}{2}$	$M + \dfrac{\sigma}{2}$	C
$M - \dfrac{3}{2}\sigma$	$M - \dfrac{\sigma}{2}$	D
0	$M - \dfrac{3}{2}\sigma$	F

17. A very typical "real-world" programming operation is not to write a new and complete program from scratch, but to modify an existing program so that it meets new specifications. Modify program rootfinder of Figure 5-26 so that it performs the operations listed below. (You may choose to implement some or all of them.)

    (a) It checks to ensure that ($\epsilon > 0.0$) and prints out an error message if it is not.

    (b) If the program cannot find a root after "maximumcount" iterations, it prints out the current interval (x_1, x_2) and says this is the best approximation it can get.

    (c) After successfully finding one root, it lets the user start over and try to find a new root with a new starting interval.

    (d) The program itself tries to locate the starting interval (x_1, x_2) instead of requiring the user to do this.

RUNNING, DEBUGGING, AND TESTING PROGRAMS

6.1 INTRODUCTION

At the end of Chapter 4 we presented some simple, straight-line Pascal programs, and we discussed how to prepare programs for computer processing. In Chapter 5 we added a sufficient number of Pascal control statements to be able to write relatively interesting and nontrivial programs such as the case study on root finding.

You should now have sufficient knowledge of both algorithm development and the Pascal language to attempt to solve some interesting problems on your own using these tools. This chapter will discuss some of the important aspects of programming that come into view only after the program is written: running, debugging, testing, and maintaining programs.

Our discussion will be general enough to apply to any computer system. However, there are certain details (e.g., the format of error messages and the availability of debugging aids) that differ from one system to another, so, where appropriate, you will need to obtain specific information that applies to your particular computer system.

6.2 PROCESSING THE PROGRAM

One of the nice features of programming in a high-level language like Pascal is that it can be done with almost a total lack of understanding of what a computer is and how it actually operates. Machine-dependent details of Pascal, such as maximum integer size and internal character codes, are few in number and can be learned easily without probing deeply into computer design. This is as it should be. There is no reason why someone who wants to write a computer program should have to understand the electronic circuitry of a computer, any more than someone learning to drive a car should have to understand how the internal combustion engine works.

Nevertheless, you will occasionally find it helpful to know something about what the computer is doing with your program. Our goal in this section is to look at the processing of a program from a macroscopic, not a microscopic, point of view. We will outline the general sequence of events that takes place when the computer begins to process your program. This knowledge can be particularly helpful to you as you try to understand error messages that the computer produces.

The Pascal language or, for that matter, any of the high-level languages mentioned in Chapter 1, cannot be directly ''understood'' by any computer. That is, no computer can directly execute the commands of those languages. Programmers write in these high-level languages because they are convenient. Their English words, their natural algebraic notation, and their use of the familiar decimal numbering system are all helpful to the programmer. However, a program written in one of these high-level languages, called a *source program,* must be translated into an equivalent program in the internal machine language of the computer. That program is called the *object program.* The process of translating a source program in some high-level language into an equivalent object program in machine language is called *compilation.* Compilation is done by a computer program called, naturally enough, a *compiler.* The input to the compiler is a program (a source program) and the output of the compiler is another program (the object program) and a *program listing.* The program listing is simply a printed representation of the program that was presented to the compiler for translation. This listing may also include error messages and other information from the compiler about the translation process. Although using one program (the source) as data for another program (the compiler) to produce still another program as output (the object program) may seem strange, it is inherently no different from using alphanumeric data as input for an ''ordinary'' program to produce alphanumeric results.

After compilation we begin the second phase of running a program on the computer: *execution.* During this step, the computer will sequentially execute the machine language commands contained in the object program. Any input data requested by the object program will now be read and any output produced will be printed. Figure 6-1 summarizes how a program is executed.

You might wonder why we bother going through the compilation phase at all. If we were to write directly in machine language, the computer could execute the program directly without wasting time performing a translation. The reason that is never done is quite obvious if one simply looks at a typical machine language translation of a Pascal statement. The machine language used for this example is MIX,[1] which

---

[1]D. E. Knuth, *MIX: The Design of a Typical Computer and its Assembly Language, with Programming Problems and a Glossary of Basic Computer Terminology*, Addison-Wesley, Reading, Mass., 1970.

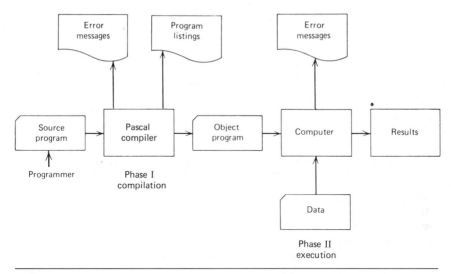

Figure 6-1. Overall program execution.

is frequently used to introduce students to topics in computer organization, but our conclusion would be the same regardless of the machine language we had chosen.

The example in Figure 6-2 on the following page should make it obvious that machine languages are completely devoid of any useful user-oriented features that are available in high-level languages like Pascal. There are no symbolic variable names, no algebraic notation, and no high-level control statements (e.g., **while** or **case**). There are not even any words to help us to understand what is going on. The enormous difficulty of writing machine language programs makes it worthwhile to spend a few extra seconds of machine time to have a compiler translate typical student Pascal programs into the machine language of a particular computer.

In fact, we will concern ourselves with the object program only if we have developed a program that will be run very often. It might be foolish to translate such a program every time we wish to execute it, because the wasted time could eventually become significant. To avoid this, we usually translate the finished program once and store the object program itself in a program library. When we wish to run the program, we can execute it directly without using the compiler to translate it. This use of an object program also explains why program generality is so important. In the previous chapter we talked about how to set up programs that handle, without modification, variations in the original problem. We can now see why this is so important. In the "real world," we frequently do not have direct access to the Pascal source program. We may be limited to working with the translated version that is stored in the program library. This version can be modified only with the greatest of difficulty. (Imagine trying to modify the program fragment in Figure 6-2*b*.)

	Location	Contents
	1000	00001
	1001	0999 0 5 08
	1002	1006 0 0 40
if a > 0 **then**	1003	1000 0 5 01
a := a + 1	1004	0999 0 5 24
else	1005	1008 0 0 39
a := a − 1	1006	1000 0 5 02
	1007	0999 0 5 24
(a)		(b)

Figure 6-2. Comparison of Pascal and machine language instructions. (*a*) Pascal. (*b*) Machine language.

Since student programs (once working) are rarely run more than once or twice, the need to store the object program is rare, and this feature may not be frequently used or even allowed. In most student programming environments, the computer proceeds directly from compilation to execution without any intermediate commands. You will usually be unaware of the existence of these two distinct phases in the running of your program.

6.3   DEBUGGING

The process of *debugging* involves discovering, locating, and correcting all errors that cause a program to produce either incorrect results or no results at all. A beginning programmer usually does not realize (but quickly becomes aware) that program debugging is the single most time-consuming phase in the overall program development process. Studies on the development of large programming systems indicate that it is not uncommon for 50 to 75% of the overall programming time to be spent on finding and correcting errors. This percentage is probably accurate for student jobs as well.

You should not think that your work is almost done when you have coded the program and entered it into the machine. Instead, you have just begun. In extreme cases, programs have been scrapped because they could not be effectively or economically corrected. Sometimes *bugs* (programming errors) become so deeply ingrained in programs that programmers, in frustration, give up on ever being able to find the errors and instead resort to issuing instructions on how to get around the problems! These are the kinds of bad habits and ''almost-working'' programs that you should learn to avoid from the beginning.

There are many reasons debugging can consume so much time, but two are of primary importance. First, it should be obvious that the ease of finding errors in a program is directly related to the clarity and lucidity of the structure of that program.

Programs with complex, intricate, and "jumpy" logic are much more difficult to work with and to debug. To understand what we mean, see how much time it takes you to find and fix the bug in the following fragment, which was supposed to print out the largest of three unequal data values x, y, z.

```
        if x > y then goto 1;
        if y > z then goto 5;
        goto 2;
1:      if x > z then goto 2;
        goto 4;
5:      write(y);
        goto 3;
2:      write(x);
        goto 3;
4:      write(z);
3:          { remainder of the program }
```

(In case you have not spotted it, the error is in the third line. It should be a branch to label 4.) Program segments like the one just shown greatly complicate debugging. Unfortunately, programs like this have, in the past, been all too common.

When these programs are large (hundreds or thousands of lines long), it becomes almost impossible to follow the flow of control through the program. The many **goto** statements create too many logical paths for the mind to keep track of. It is much easier to find and correct errors when well-structured statements (and indentation) clearly delineate the control paths. For example, consider the same program segment (with the same error) coded using the **if/then/else** construct.

```
if x > y then
begin
    if x > z then
        write (x)
    else
        write (z)
end
else
begin
    if y > z then
        write (y)
    else
        write (x)
end
{ remainder of the program }
```

It is easier to find the error because it is easier to see the conditions that had to be met in order to reach a particular section of the program.

The second main reason that programmers encounter difficulty during debugging is that, unfortunately, debugging has usually not been taught in the same systematic manner that has characterized the teaching of algorithms, data structures, and languages. These latter subjects are presented quite formally with a great deal of organization, rules, and well thought out examples. However, debugging has been treated almost as "black magic." Students are rarely given formal instruction about exactly what procedures to follow when their programs fail. This has usually led to a great deal of confusion, wasted time, frustration and, ultimately, incorrect and undebugged programs. This is totally unacceptable, since in most application areas a partially debugged program is no better (and sometimes worse) than no program at all.

Our objective in this chapter will be to classify the approaches to debugging so that, when the inevitable errors do occur, you will have some logical, organized method for finding their causes—other than scratching your head and heading for the instructor's office.

Style Clinic 6-1 _____

Clear Programs and Software Engineering

It is a fundamental principle of debugging that the single most useful debugging aid is a well-written, well-organized, well-structured and well-documented program. This fact is the reason for our overriding concern with teaching good programming habits and style. It is also one of the reasons for the recent increase in interest in languages similar to Pascal that allow clear and natural expression of program structure. And, finally, it is the reason for the rapid growth of *software engineering*, an area of computer science that deals with the tools and techniques needed for the efficient and systematic implementation of correct programs.

6.3.1 Syntax Errors

Syntax errors are among the most common errors made in programming and the easiest to find and correct. A *syntax error* is any violation of the grammatical rules of the programming language. For example, the Pascal syntax for the **if/then/else** construct is

if *boolean expression* **then** *statement* **else** *statement*

All statements of this type must adhere to this format without exception. Therefore, all of the following violate a syntactic rule of Pascal (assume a and b are boolean values and x is real).

1. **if** *a* **and** *b* **then**
  write (a);
 else
  write (b)

 { Misplaced semicolon }

2. **if** *a* **and** *b* **then**
  write (a); write (b)
 else
  write (a)

 { Two statements placed where only one should be }

3. **if** *x* + *1.3* **then**
  write (x)
 else
  write (y)

 { A real expression placed where a boolean expression should be }

Syntax errors are easier to correct than other error types because they usually produce a helpful error message that gives a clue about what is wrong. These error messages are produced by the Pascal compiler while it is attempting to translate a Pascal program into machine language. Any grammatical mistake will cause problems when the translation is performed. The compiler will attempt to produce a message indicating where the mistake is and what it believed the mistake to be.

Figure 6-3 on pages 208-209 is a listing of a Pascal program that contains numerous syntactic (as well as other) errors. This example shows how errors are printed on a particular system. You may be using a system that prints error messages in a different form, but the information provided should be comparable.

Figure 6-3 highlights most of the major points that you should be aware of when working with syntactic error messages.

1. Some of the error messages produced are quite clear and explicit about the nature of the mistake. For example, on line 320 of the program, Pascal gives error message 55—"**to**" or "**downto**" expected. A quick glance at the **for** loop shows that we did not adhere to the correct syntax.

 for *control variable* : = *initial value* [**to/downto**] *final value* **do** *statement*

On line 340 we get the error message "identifier not declared," with the pointer pointing at the variable val. Looking at the **var** declaration on line 210, we see that there is no variable declaration for val. There is a declaration for value, however, and some simple checking would convince us that we mistakenly changed names in midstream.

2. Unfortunately, the meaning of many error messages is not always as clear, concise, and helpful as the first examples might indicate. Some of the error messages tell us nothing more than that an error occurred. It is left up to us to determine the cause. For example, on line 370 we get the cryptic message

```
00100     program average(input,output);
00110
00120     { this program computes the sum of examination scores
00130       in the range 0 to 100. the number of exams is
00140       contained on the first card }
00150
00160     const
00170         lowrange = 0;
00180         highrange = 100;
00190
00200     var
00210         value        :integer;
00220         number       :integer;
00230         sum          :integer;
00240         avg          :integer;
00250         error        :integer;
00260
00270     begin
00280         readln(number);
00290         sum := 0;
00300         writeln(number, 'data items');
00310         error := 0;
00320         for i := 1, number do
00330             readln(val);
00340             if val >= lowrange and val <= highrange
00350             then
00360                 sum := sum + val;
00370             else
00380                 error := error + 1
00390         end;
00400         avg := sum div number - error;
00410         writeln('average of the scores is', avg)
00420     end.
```

```
ready
run
000041  00320      for i: = 1,number do
*****                 ↑ 104,155    ↑ 55
000042  00330        readln(val);
*****                        ↑ 104
000046  00340      if val > = lowrange and val < = highrange
*****                 ↑ 104                 ↑ 104    ↑ 59
000046  00360        sum: = sum + val;
*****                          ↑ 104
000046  00370          else
*****                    ↑ 6
000046  00390      end;
*****                ↑ 6
***** eof encountered
```

compiler error messages:

6:	illegal symbol
55:	"to" or "downto" expected
59:	error in variable
104:	identifier not declared
155:	control variable must not be formal

Figure 6-3. Sample Pascal syntactic error messages.

"illegal symbol" and the pointer pointing at the reserved identifier **else.** What is wrong and how are we to find the problem? First, we should compare the statement from the program with the legal Pascal syntax for that statement type. Element by element, we compare the **if** statement on lines 340 to 380 with the allowable syntax of the **if/then/else** statement.

if boolean expression **then** statement **else** statement

Usually the comparison will lead us to the cause of the error—in this case, the incorrect semicolon at the end of line 360. If a thorough check of the offending statement fails to identify the error, we should next check the statements immediately before and immediately after the one supposedly in error. Many syntax mistakes are caused either by the erroneous termination of statements or by statements that are accidentally run together and considered by the compiler as one. Finally, we should check out all other statements related in any way to the one in error. For example, we should check the **var** declaration for all variables contained in the statement, matching **begin/end** pairs, **then** and **else** clauses of **if** statements, or **repeat/until** pairs.

Line 390 also contains the cryptic message "illegal symbol." Using your knowledge of the syntax of a **for** statement and some of the clues just cited, work through the program to determine what is causing that error message.

3. There is not always a one-to-one relationship between error messages produced and corrections that need to be made. Frequently, a single error will generate numerous error messages. For example, our error in failing to declare the variable named val caused an error message to be produced every time val was referenced throughout the program—lines 330, 340, and 360. Be aware that some of the causes for the error messages you encounter will have already been corrected by earlier corrections of other mistakes. For example, the two errors 104 and 155 on line 320 are both caused by our single failure to include the control variable i in the **var** declaration.

4. You may require a second run to eliminate all syntactic mistakes. Frequently, a syntax error is missed by the compiler because of the presence of other mistakes on that same line. For example, line 340 will still cause syntactic problems after the error described in Figure 6-3 is corrected. (The precedence is improper. Parentheses are needed around the two relational operations.) After the second compilation, all, or nearly all, of the syntax errors should be corrected.

6.3.2 Run-Time Errors

When the program is grammatically correct and produces no syntactic error messages, there is still no guarantee that, because of the possibility of a run-time error, it will produce correct results. A *run-time error* is any error that causes abnormal program behavior during execution. The statement in line 400 of Figure 6-3,

avg : = *sum* **div** *number* − *error;*

is grammatically correct and will not produce any error message. However, if number has the value 0, this statement will attempt a division by 0, which will result in program termination. This fact will not be apparent until the program is actually executed, and that is why it is termed a run-time error.

In addition to division by zero, some of the most common run-time errors include:

1. **Case** statement expressions not corresponding to one of the **case** labels.
2. Real to integer conversion, where round(abs(real))>maxint.
3. Sqrt(x) or ln(x) when x < 0.
4. Subrange out of bounds.
5. Array indices out of bounds (this will be discussed in Chapter 7).

As with syntactic errors, run-time errors also produce some type of error message. For example, unless the following feature is explicitly suppressed by the programmer, all of the above run-time errors would produce a *post-mortem dump*. This condensed

Style Clinic 6-2 _____

How **Not** *to Debug Programs*

There are many valid approaches to debugging programs. There is one approach that is utterly wrong—blindly trying something, anything, because you do not know what else to do. Too often, after a cursory glance at a program fails to reveal the cause of a problem, you start groping in the dark for any advice, whether good or bad, on how to proceed. You start listening to and heeding worthless advice like, "Hey I think somebody once tried _____ and it might have worked," or "Throw in _____ ; it probably won't hurt." The result is that the error is still there, your program is getting needlessly confusing, and you have wasted valuable computer time.

The error is obviously being caused by some incorrect operation. Until you have an indication or a clue about what, specifically, that incorrect operation is or how to go about finding it logically, it makes no sense to change or rerun the program. Use the program listing and results along with a textbook or reference book, the debugging aids discussed in this chapter, and your own experience to identify the likely cause of the error before you begin making changes. In the unlikely event that you still can't isolate the problem and are unsure how to proceed, seek out competent, professional advice. Reject any advice that is not based on a rational plan for finding the problem. Suppress the urge to make a quick correction. Run-time errors can be symptomatic of serious flaws in your program.

One final comment: be extremely suspicious of suggestions to rerun the program without changes because the error may have been caused by a "machine mistake." Such hardware malfunctions are rare, and the rerun will more than likely produce the same problems and leave you in the same predicament.

history of the state of the machine at the time of abnormal termination is intended to help the programmer find out what happened. Although the format may vary from one system to another, this dump usually includes:

1. A message indicating what caused the termination.
2. Which program unit you were in. As we will see in Chapter 8, programs will typically be composed of more than one unit, each with its own name.
3. Where within that program unit the error occurred. (This information may

be given in terms of the object program and not your source program, so it might not be too helpful.)

4.   The names and current values of all variables in that program unit.

If we were to correct the program in Figure 6-3 and run it for a data set where the variable named number is 0, the output might appear as in Figure 6-4 below.

The preceding discussion explained how Pascal helps you to recover from abnormal terminations. However, it is wrong to expect Pascal to help you recover; you should prevent abnormal termination by using the foolproof programming techniques mentioned throughout the text. When you write and develop programs, you should insert checks for illegal or invalid operations wherever necessary.

For example, the computation of the discriminant of the well-known quadratic formula is given by the following formula.

$$\sqrt{b^2 - 4ac}$$

This could be computed by the following Pascal statement.

discriminant : = sqrt(b*b − 4.0*a*c)

Since square roots are undefined for negative values, this statement runs the risk of

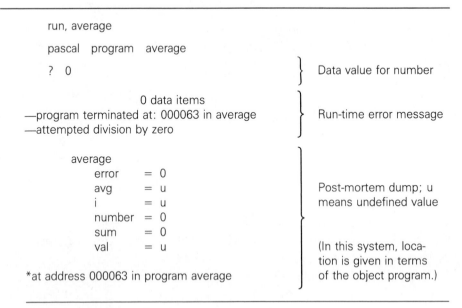

Figure 6-4. Sample output from a run-time error.

abnormal termination if $(b^2 - 4ac) < 0$. A much better way to perform this computation would be:

```
discsqr : = b*b − 4.0*a*c;
if discsqr < 0.0 then
      writeln('the roots are complex −
                program cannot continue')
else
begin
      discriminant : = sqrt(discsqr)
              ·
              ·      { remainder of the program }
              ·
```

By preventing run-time errors before they occur instead of waiting until they do, we gain the ability to recover in the program itself and continue processing instead of stopping irrevocably. Even if the program does nothing more than write an appropriate error message before stopping, it is usually easier to figure out what went wrong. This is because you are now interpreting a message that you produced instead of trying to interpret a message produced by the computer system that may or may not be clear.

Style Clinic 6-3 _____

Robustness

A *robust* program is one that produces meaningful output for *any* set of input data, regardless of how incorrect or implausible. Robustness is a very desirable property because it allows the program to maintain control, produce meaningful messages, and, if possible, keep on going. (See Style Clinic 6-4.) To write a robust program you should carefully check before you perform any potentially "dangerous" operations that could result in a run-time error. The occurrence of a run-time error is usually an indication of a poorly written program.

6.3.3 Logic Errors

By the time you have eliminated the syntax and run-time errors from your program, you will probably have invested a fair amount of time and effort. You will have made a few computer runs and spent a great deal of time hand-simulating the program, interpreting error messages, and preparing corrections. Therefore it is only natural for you to be overjoyed at the first run that actually produces some results.

However, you should realize that you have now reached the point where you are ready to begin locating and correcting the most difficult and time-consuming errors in the programming process: logic errors. A *logic error* is simply an incorrect translation of either the problem statement or the algorithm. An excellent example of a logic error is the following Pascal translation of the well-known formula for computing the two roots of quadratic equations.

$$r = \frac{-b \pm \sqrt{b^2 - 4ac}}{2a}$$

```
discriminant = (b*b) − (4.0*a*c);
if (discriminant >= 0.0) and (a <> 0.0) then
begin
    root1 := −b + sqrt(discriminant)/(2.0*a);
    root2 := −b − sqrt(discriminant)/(2.0*a)
end
```

The two assignment statements contained in the **then** clause are syntactically acceptable and would not cause any error messages. However, they would produce wrong answers. Those two lines are not a correct translation of the desired quadratic formula. Instead, they translate the following:

$$r = -b \pm \frac{\sqrt{b^2 - 4ac}}{2a}$$

The two assignment statements for root1 and root2 should have been written as follows:

```
root1 := (−b + sqrt(discriminant))/(2.0*a);
root2 := (−b − sqrt(discriminant))/(2.0*a)
```

Another example of a logic error is the following Pascal fragment that seeks to find the sum of "countfield" values. It is syntactically correct, but produces wrong answers.

```
readln(countfield);
if countfield > 0 then
begin
    for i := 1 to countfield do
    begin
        sum := 0;
        readln(number);
        sum := sum + number
    end; { for loop }
    writeln('sum of', countfield, 'values is', sum)
end { if statement }
```

Do you see the error? The initialization of the variable sum was mistakenly placed inside the **for** loop. The loop will compute only the sum of the last value provided as input.

Both of these examples indicate why logic errors are so difficult to correct. You will typically have no clue about what is happening except that the program produces a wrong final value. There will usually be no indication about which section of the program is in error and no message to help determine what type of mistake you have made. Sitting down with paper and pencil and hand-simulating the program (i.e., playing computer and doing step by step what the program says) may help. In many cases, however, the program will be too complex or the mistake too subtle for you to be able to find the error in this way. Instead of allowing frustration to set in, you should begin to use your debugging tools.

By far the most powerful and useful debugging tool in Pascal (aside from a well-written program!) is the good old-fashioned output statement we introduced in Chapter 4.

> *writeln(values)*   *write(values)*

Too often we tend to think of the write and writeln statements only as vehicles for writing out final answers. This is completely false. An output operation can be used to write out any values whatsoever—including intermediate results that may aid in locating mistakes. An important rule to remember is that there is (up to some point of diminishing returns) a direct relationship between the amount of output produced by a program and the ease of debugging that program. A 1000 line Pascal program that should have produced a value of 1, but instead printed 2, would probably leave us wondering even where to begin to look for errors. If the same program had included output statements that produced intermediate results describing how the computations were proceeding, we would probably find the task considerably easier.

Style Clinic 6-4 _____

Instrumenting Your Program for Errors

Anyone who believes that his or her program will run correctly the first time is either a fool, an optimist, or a novice programmer. Inevitably, there will be errors. You should anticipate their occurrence and prepare for them by having all necessary tools included in your program *from the start*. Always try to get the most information you can out of each computer run.

The most important tools to include from the beginning are well-placed output statements to produce intermediate results on the status of the computation. Avoid writing long, complex programs that contain only a single output statement as the last line. Include a sufficient number of well-placed write statements to facilitate finding the errors that may occur.

A common programming trick is to make these debugging write statements conditional on the value of a boolean switch:

if *debugging* **then** *writeln (. . .)*

Now we can turn on or turn off our debugging mechanism by simply setting the value of the boolean variable called debugging.

debugging : = true

or

debugging : = false

The write statements in your program that are intended to find errors instead of print final answers are sometimes called *debugging instruments* and are a very important programming tool.

Therefore our primary concern is not whether to include statements to produce intermediate output, but where to put these statements. Although this is partly a matter of personal style and other considerations (size of the program, time available, and the cost of paper), there are certain general guidelines to follow.

Because Pascal contains such a wide range of control statements (**if/then/else, while, repeat, case, for, begin/end**), most well-written Pascal programs will be composed entirely of single-entry, single-exit program units that we will call *blocks*. A well-structured block is a group of statements that begins execution at the first line, performs some useful computation, and exits from the block upon completion of its last line. There are no jumps into or out of the middle of the block. A block can be nested inside other blocks, but each one will follow the single-entry, single-exit restriction. If we construct a program in this way, we will find that it is easy to read and debug because we can readily identify the control paths through the program. Examples of properly nested blocks are shown in Figure 6-5.

The first goal of debugging is to isolate an error to a specific block in the program. We can accomplish this by initially bracketing a few of the outer blocks with output statements. Prior to entering the block, we print the current value of all important variables that are referenced in the block. After exiting, we print the current value of all variables defined or redefined within the block. Since a well-structured block will not have any unconditional jumps into or out of it, we can determine whether the statements within that block are correct or whether they contain an error. When we find that one block contains an error, we can narrow our search even more. Since a block may contain other blocks nested inside, we bracket some inner blocks with output statements to check if they are correct. We continue until the error becomes obvious or we have isolated the problem to an area small enough to be traced through by hand.

There are two other general guidelines concerning the placement of output statements during debugging.

1. It is a good idea to *echo-print* all input data immediately. Your program may be producing erroneous results not because it is wrong but because you are feeding it garbage. Although most of the output statements used for debugging will be removed or turned off (see Style Clinic 6-4) when the program is completed, the echo-prints are quite useful and should probably remain. They will allow the user to associate any particular result with the data set that produced it.

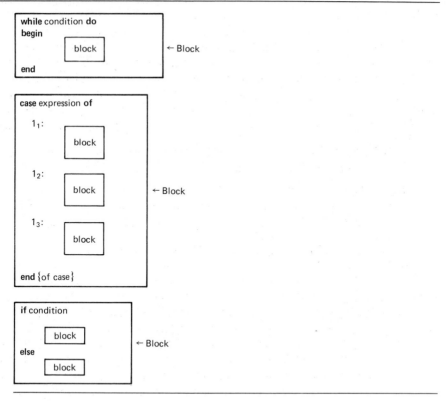

Figure 6-5. Examples of nested program blocks.

2. Be very careful when placing an output statement *within* instead of *around* a highly repetitive loop. You may be flooded with output, and meaningful values can be lost or overlooked. If you produce too much output, you might be unable to find the specific information you need. If you must place a write statement inside a highly repetitive loop, consider printing a value only every nth iteration.

```
for i := 1 to 5000 do
begin
    if (i mod 50) = 0 then writeln (. . .)
    { The writeln will be executed every 50th iteration }
            .
            .
            .
```

As an example of what we have been discussing, let us assume that we ran the corrected program from Figure 6-3 with the following data set.

```
    5      { The number of scores }
   70
   80
 -50      { An invalid value }
   90
  110      { An invalid value }
```

We would expect the program to produce an answer of 80, the average of the three valid scores: 70, 80, and 90. The actual output produced by the program would be:

5 data items

average of the scores is 46

Assuming that we have not already spotted the error, what would we do? The way to proceed would be to insert some additional output statements in the program. For example,

```
335 writeln('val =', val);
385 ;writeln('sum =', sum, 'error =', error)
```

With these two lines included, we now get the following output.

```
5 data items
val   = 70
sum = 70        error = 0
```

```
val  =  80
sum  =  150       error  =  0
val  =  −50
sum  =  150       error  =  1
val  =  90
sum  =  240       error  =  1
val  =  110
sum  =  240       error  =  2
average of the scores is 46
```

By comparing what the program produced with what we expected, we see that through line 385 everything has proceeded correctly. However, at line 410, we have produced an incorrect average. Therefore we know that the problem must be with the single assignment statement at line 400. A careful check of that statement would show the problem to be a missing set of parentheses leading to an improperly evaluated expression. The statement should have been:

avg := *sum* **div** *(number − error);*

Rerunning the program with this change produces the correct result. The use of strategically placed output statements within a program is the most systematic way to isolate and find logic errors.

In addition to output statements, some computer systems provide special debugging aids. However, since these aids are not really part of the Pascal language, they may not be available on your specific computer system. You should check into the local availability of the aids described in the following paragraphs.

One of these useful debugging aids has already been mentioned—the post-mortem dump. Whenever a Pascal program terminates abnormally, output similar to that in Figure 6-4 will be produced. However, it is not necessary to wait for an abnormal termination to get this potentially useful information. Some versions of Pascal include a procedure named halt that will terminate a program and produce a post-mortem dump. During debugging, you may wish to use the halt procedure to guarantee that even upon normal termination all variables have the correct values.

Another useful debugging aid available on some computer systems is a type of dump called a *snapshot dump*. A snapshot dump produces the same general information as the post-mortem dump—the current values of all important variables—but does not cause program termination. Using some special "snap" procedure, you indicate in the program that you wish to produce a snapshot dump. Your program will be temporarily suspended, the dump produced, and the program will continue at the point immediately following the request for a snap.

Finally, we should mention what is probably the most useful automatic debugging aid—an *automatic trace* feature. The automatic trace is a way to have the computer system produce a running commentary of exactly what the program is doing. In a way it is similar to inserting a writeln command after every statement in the program. The exact output produced by these automatic trace aids varies from system to system and depends on the type of statement currently being executed. Since a complete trace of an entire program would usually produce an excessive amount of output, an on/off switch is usually included. When you wish to investigate a specific portion of a program, you execute some type of ''trace on'' command [e.g., trace(true)] prior to entering that portion. The full trace output will be produced until the program encounters a ''trace off'' command [e.g., trace(false)]. If the system you are using has a trace feature, become acquainted with it. It is a quick and powerful technique for helping to locate and correct programming errors. However, if you do use it, do so wisely. Indiscriminate tracing can use an enormous amount of time and paper, which is both expensive and ecologically unsound. As a general rule, remember that it is almost never appropriate to trace either an entire program or a highly repetitive loop.

Style Clinic 6-5

Get All the Information You Can

When you build tests into your program to guard against abnormal termination at run time, you keep control of the situation. In addition to printing a meaningful message that will be easy to interpret, you might also want to reset any variables that have inappropriate values that will allow the program to continue.

For example, if a test indicated that your program was on the verge of trying to find the square root of a negative number, you might want the program to print a message and then replace the negative value with zero. This will allow your program to continue, and you may obtain useful information about the rest of the program. Perhaps there is an error further along that you will be able to find during this program run instead of during the next run.

You should always try to get as much information as possible out of each program run. Whenever possible, reset invalid values (always print a meaningful message when you do this!) and keep going.

6.4 PROGRAM TESTING

The process of *program testing* is concerned with proving that a computer program will produce correct and meaningful results for all possible input data. This goal, however, is generally impossible to achieve for any but the smallest programs. All that testing can actually determine is when a program is working incorrectly. Some computer scientists are developing techniques that formally prove that a program is correct, but their work is not yet complete enough to analyze large, practical programs. Currently, we must still proceed by testing.

In a way, finding mistakes in a program is not unlike using a pitchfork to look for someone in a haystack. By shoving the fork into the haystack, we will know without a doubt when we have found someone! However, we can never be completely sure that the haystack is empty. What we do then is put the fork into the stack a sufficient number of times and places to satisfy ourselves that the probability that someone is inside the haystack is infinitesimally small. But a small, clever, and lucky person might still escape detection.

In effect, we use a ''pitchfork'' made of data during the testing phase. Since we cannot guarantee correctness, we must convince ourselves that the probability of a program being correct is very, very large. We do this by testing the program with a sufficient number of interesting data sets to see whether the program produces correct answers. If it does, we tentatively say that it is correct, and we release it for general use. Obviously, there is still a small chance that there may be errors that went undetected because no data set tested for them. That is why *program maintenance* is important. Program maintenance involves the continuing responsibility for monitoring a program's operation in the field, correcting any errors found through continued use, and issuing the appropriate corrections to all users of the program. It is not unusual in the case of large, complex programs for an installation to be issuing *patches* (program updates to correct errors) 2, 3, or even 4 years after the program has entered general use.

Therefore the most important aspect of program testing is choosing the specific data sets with which to test the program. Too often, quantity of test data is accepted in place of quality. A program that worked on 1000 sample runs should not be accepted as correct solely because 1000 may be considered by some to be a large number. If, in fact, all 1000 cases tested the same logical part of the program, all we would know is that that specific part is probably correct. We would know nothing at all about the remainder of the program. Our objective in testing is to select test cases that exercise all parts of our program. This requires a perception of the different logical paths that exist in the program. Of course, we know that the logical paths can be identified most readily in a program that uses clear control structures, and that is another reason for writing well-structured programs. Test cases can be broken up into roughly four classes, and we must ensure that we validate our program with a selection of data from all four.

The *valid* cases represent data sets that are logically meaningful to our program and for which the program should produce correct answers. Our first set of tests should be designed to ensure that our program does indeed work correctly on the valid data sets, because these cases will probably represent the great majority of input.

We must examine our program carefully and make sure that we have at least one test case for each *flow path* in the program. A flow path is a unique sequence of statements executed while proceeding through a program. For example, given the following **program segment:**

```
begin
    S₁; { The Sᵢ are any Pascal statements }
    S₂;
    if boolean expression then
        S₃
    else
        S₄;
    S₅
end
```

there are two possible paths in proceeding from **begin** to **end**: either the sequence S_1, S_2, S_3, S_5 or the sequence S_1, S_2, S_4, S_5. Whenever we have an **if/then/else** construct, we create two distinct flow paths corresponding to the execution of either the **then** clause or the **else** clause.

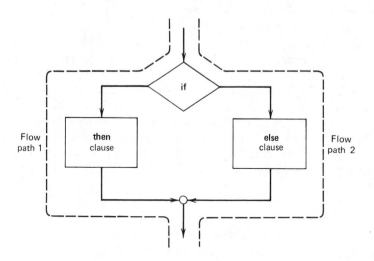

In a similar manner, the **case** will create n flow paths, where n is the number of alternatives contained in the **case** statement. The **while** loop will create two flow paths—corresponding to executing or skipping the statements in the loop body.

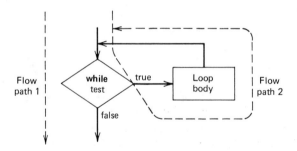

Our test data should be selected to test each of these different paths through the program.

For example, assume that we were developing a payroll program to produce employee paychecks from hourly timecards. After examining the logic of the program we would initially test the program with data sets chosen from each of the following distinct classes.

1. No overtime, standard deductions.
2. No overtime, special deductions (e.g., credit union).
3. Overtime pay.
4. Regular social security deduction.
5. Maximum social security deduction (pay exceeds the maximum wage base).
6. No dependents.
7. One or more dependents.

.

.

.

(Other distinct cases)

(In actuality a program of this complexity would probably be developed and checked out in stages; it would not be tested only as a single large unit. However, the testing at each individual stage would still proceed along the lines discussed here. This point will be discussed further in Chapter 11.)

Thus it can require a large number of test cases to check all valid alternatives. The creation of these test data can become a time-consuming task, which is a good reason for keeping program units small and compact (another point we will discuss further in Chapter 11). The number of flow paths in a program grows *very very* quickly. If you wait until a program has grown to 500 or 1000 lines before you begin to test it, you will never be able to test it as thoroughly as we have described here. You will probably end up with a program filled with undiscovered bugs. Test your program in small pieces. After writing 50 lines or so, stop coding and test what you have written so far. Testing smaller pieces will reduce the total debugging and testing time needed.

The second class of test cases represents a subset of the valid cases. However, it is such an important subset that it is usually treated separately. These are the *boundary* cases—the data sets that represent the extremes of the valid problems that our program will accept or the exact point at which a decision will be made. Many common programming errors (e.g., the off-by-one error mentioned in Chapter 5) show up only when tested with these boundary conditions. Examples of these extremes might be: working with a list as long or as short as the program allows, working with the first or last item in a list, or setting a variable to its largest or smallest allowable value.

In our hypothetical payroll program we would want to ensure that we had at least one data case that tested each of the following typical boundary conditions.

1. Gross pay exactly equal to the social security wage base maximum.
2. Hours worked equal to the maximum allowed by company policy.
3. Persons in the highest and lowest tax brackets.
4. The first and last entries in the payroll file.
5. Deductions exactly equal to the total earnings, leaving a net of 0.

The previous two classes of test data represent the valid, meaningful conditions of the problem. However, as everyone is aware, errors do occur—because of a misinterpretation of the problem, a misunderstanding of what was intended, or simply a manual error in reading and entering the data. It is imperative that our program perform meaningful operations for all data sets, even those that seemingly violate the conditions of the problem. This characteristic, called robustness, was mentioned in Style Clinic 6-3. The last two classes of data values are used in testing the robustness of our program.

The *special* or *unusual* cases represent conditions that are not necessarily invalid, but for which normal processing cannot be completed or some special or unusual handling may be required. When the program cannot produce the normal answers, it still should perform some meaningful recovery action. This may include sending an error message to the operator, making an entry in an error log, or having the computer drop the data card into a special hopper. In our payroll problems such special cases might, for example, include:

1. Hours worked equal to 0.0 (on vacation? sick? mispunched?).
2. Total deductions exceeding employee's gross pay (who makes up the difference?).
3. Pay rate of $108.50 per hour (highly improbable; could it be $10.85?).
4. Deductions claimed greater than 1 but an "individual" health plan (Is the person unaware of this? Should we warn him or her?).

The final phase of testing should be on the *invalid* cases—those situations that are utterly meaningless and that violate physical reality or the statement of the problem. Although these cases should never occur when the program is operating, "Murphy's Law" will usually prevail. Our program must be completely impervious to and insulated from the effects of bad data, no matter how pathological. The possibility of abnormal termination for any data set whatsoever is a sign of a poorly written program. To ensure that our program does indeed display these characteristics, we might conclude the testing phase of the payroll program with something like the following classes of data.

1. Hours worked < 0.0 or > 168.0 (number of hours in a week).
2. Dependents < 0.
3. Timecard for a nonexistent employee.
4. Two timecards for the same employee.
5. Pay rate < 0.00.

When we have completed our testing, what have we proved? As we stated at the beginning of this section, we have not proved the absolute correctness of our program, but we have shown that the program operates correctly on a wide range of test cases. From this we extrapolate to the statement that the program will operate satisfactorily for all possible data sets. If we have designed and chosen the test data carefully, this extrapolation will, for the most part, be valid, and we can hope that further modifications to correct undetected errors will not be needed.

Style Clinic 6-6

Graceful Degradation

The invalid cases bring into play a characteristic that we might call *graceful degradation:* a program should "do nothing" in a reasonable way. Invalid data values should result in a meaningful error message and, if at all possible, an assumption that allows the program to continue. Perhaps the invalid data can be reset to an acceptable value or perhaps the data should be ignored. In any case, let the error message indicate clearly what action is being taken. Your program should be designed so that it will always behave gracefully— it should never "blow up" when it is faced with the unexpected.

6.5 DOCUMENTATION AND MAINTENANCE

Documenting and maintaining programs are two very important aspects of the programming process. Unfortunately, these items usually receive scant attention in an introductory programming course, because they do not have direct relevance to the environment in which student programs are written. Nevertheless, we will discuss them because we believe that programmers who are aware of them will write better programs.

One of the mistaken ideas held by too many programmers is that the documentation for a program should be written only after the program is "finished." That is a very dangerous point of view! It will certainly lead to inadequate documentation and might very well result in an incomplete or incorrect program. Documentation is a continuous process. It starts when we first begin to formulate a clear problem statement and continues as we devise a solution, express the solution algorithmically, and code the algorithm as a computer program. The proper point of view is that documentation is an inherent part of a program. It is therefore meaningless to assert that documentation should be written after the program is finished.

Most programs that are written by professional programmers are used in a production environment. This means that once a program is deemed operational, it is used on a regular basis, usually by people other than the author(s). For example, programs to process payrolls, maintain inventories, or handle hotel or airline reservations are invariably used by people who did not write them. Moreover, these people are usually not even programmers. In this sort of environment we can see the need for two different kinds of documentation: user documentation and technical documentation.

User documentation provides the information that one needs in order to use a program. This information includes a number of different items.

1. A description of the application area of the program—what will this program do?
2. A description of the input data that the program requires.
3. A description of the output produced by the program.
4. A description of the commands needed to start the program.
5. If appropriate, a description of the kinds of interactions that are possible with the program.
6. An explanation of all the messages that the program can produce.
7. A discussion (in nontechnical terms) of the performance capabilities and limitations of the program.

Note that the user documentation is much more than the list of commands needed to invoke the program. A great deal of information must be provided to enable the potential user to determine whether or not the program is suitable. Perhaps the program is not capable of handling certain special cases that happen to be of interest at this time, or perhaps the program is based on an algorithm that performs efficiently only when the number of data items does not exceed a certain value. These matters must be addressed in the user documentation.

When a person has determined that a particular program is the one that is needed, the user documentation should explain how to use it. Since a user may know very little about programming (perhaps nothing at all), there is no need for this part of the documentation to describe the internal workings of the program. The user wants (and needs) to know everything that must be done to use the program, but he or she is not interested in the technical details of its implementation. The program is simply a tool for the user.

However, we do want to maintain a description of the technical details, and we do this in the *technical documentation*. This documentation is addressed to programmers who might be faced with the task of modifying the program at some time. Perhaps a bug will become apparent after the program has been placed into use, or a decision may be made to enhance the program by adding a new feature. In either case, good technical documentation is a necessity.

This documentation is usually in two parts. First, the program listing and the comments that we included as we coded the program are an integral part of the technical documentation. This information is addressed to someone who knows how to program and is interested in examining in detail what the program does. In extreme cases (e.g., when a program is small and not very sophisticated) the listing (if done well) may be all the technical documentation needed. However, this will often not be the case. Most of the time it is appropriate to prepare a separate document that provides further technical information. This document usually includes program design information of a global nature. For example, there will usually be a list of procedures and functions (these terms will be defined in Chapter 8) and a brief explanation of the purpose of each one. There will also be a description of the data items that are accessible from different program units and often there is a chart that depicts the relationships between the program units.

This information provides a general outline, as well as a few specific details, of the overall program structure. Further details are obtained by reading the comments and the text of the program itself. Needless to say, it is a tremendous aid if the program adheres to the rules for good style, such as the use of appropriately structured statements, well-placed and meaningful comments, meaningful names for identifiers, and a consistent and clear indentation scheme.

Now we are in a good position to see why documentation should take place throughout the programming process. Most or all of the user documentation should be written before any coding is done. The user documentation represents a functional description of a program, and it can serve as a set of specifications to the programmer. If the programmer has done a good job of problem analysis, these specifications can be very useful in keeping things on course during the coding phase. Of course, it is always possible that some changes will need to be made as the implementation proceeds, and these changes must be reflected in a revised user document. However, if the user document requires a large number of changes once the implementation is under way, that should serve as a warning. It is quite likely that inadequate attention has been given to the analysis of the problem.

Once the problem has been analyzed and a user document has been prepared, the programmer can proceed with the development of the algorithms. It is at this stage that much of the technical documentation can be written. Indeed, if more than one programmer is involved, it is essential to prepare a technical description of the proposed implementation. It is simply impossible to coordinate the activities of several programmers without such a document. Even if only one person will be doing the coding, a technical description prepared before the coding has started will be invaluable. The coding task will be much more organized and the technical documentation will be of a higher quality when the project is completed.

As implementation proceeds, changes to the technical documentation are apt to be more numerous than changes to the user documentation. But, again, if the technical documentation needs a high degree of change, it is a bad sign. It is probable that too little time was devoted to the development of an algorithmic solution. Remember that it is always a bad practice to rush into the coding phase. The result will be an incorrect, inadequate, or incomprehensible program.

When the implementation is complete and the final full-scale testing has been done, it is appropriate to review all the documentation and make certain that it is in order. If the documentation is to be of any value, it must describe the program accurately. It may be appropriate to run some performance tests to obtain a measure of the speed and capabilities of the program. This information should be added to the user documentation, since it could have an important bearing on the suitability of the program for some users.

Why are we so concerned with documentation? There are several reasons, and they should now be apparent. Good user documentation is essential if a program is to be a useful tool. We may have designed and coded an outstanding program, but what good is it if no one can figure out what it does or how to use it?

Good technical documentation is essential for maintaining a program. We may decide at a future date to add features to the program, or we may have to find and correct errors in the program, both of which can be virtually impossible if the technical documentation is inadequate. There have been many instances of a program being thrown out entirely because it would have been too expensive or difficult to change.

Finally, good documentation can be educational. When we are faced with the task of designing and coding a program, we may be able to learn a great deal by studying the documentation of a similar project.

We began this section by observing that the topics of documentation and maintenance are not usually discussed in detail in an introductory programming course. That is because a student programming environment is somewhat artificial. Problems are usually presented in a form in which most of the analysis has already been done.

The problems are of modest size and when the programs are complete, they are executed once or twice and then usually discarded. This means that there is little need for detailed documentation, and there is almost never any program maintenance.

Do not be shortsighted. Things will be different as you write larger and more complex programs (perhaps in more advanced courses, certainly in the "real world"). For now, you should keep in mind the ideas we have discussed in this section. If you begin applying them now (in a modest way for modest programs), your programs will be the better for it.

6.6 CONCLUSION

This chapter has discussed the overall transition from a potential solution written in Pascal to a computer program that produces the desired results. This transition has three distinct phases. Debugging involves locating and correcting all syntactic, run-time, and logic errors in the program. This requires knowledge of a systematic, logical approach to debugging and of the debugging tools that are available. Next, there is the testing phase, which involves showing that the program is indeed correct. This phase requires a knowledge of the specifications of the problem and the techniques for designing program test data. Finally, there is documentation and program maintenance, which simply acknowledges that it may, at some time in the future, be necessary to change a program either to fix a bug or add a feature. It involves the continuing responsibility for monitoring, correcting, and updating programs that have already been released for general use.

Style Clinic 6-7 _____

Overall Program Development

Although the operations described in this chapter may not be considered as creative or challenging as some of the earlier operations (e.g., algorithm development), they are nevertheless just as important in the overall solution of a problem. Too often, interest in a problem wanes once the "interesting" aspects are complete. The dirty work—debugging and testing—are poorly and sloppily done. This leads to poorly tested, poorly documented, and poorly maintained programs. Such programs are useless. A competent programmer must always view the problem-solving process from start to finish and be willing to carry out all the programming operations discussed in Chapter 1. The programming tools and techniques discussed in the present chapter are critically important to the programmer.

EXERCISES FOR CHAPTER 6

*1. Using the syntax diagrams in Appendix A, state whether the following Pascal statements would or would not cause a syntax error. Assume that all necessary variables have been correctly declared and defined.

    (a) **while** $x < 1$ **and** $y <> 2$ **do** *readln(ch)*

    (b) **for** $i := 1$ **downto** n **do** *sum := sum + i*

    (c) **if** *testflag* **and** *(i <= n)* **then**
       else *writeln ('done')*

    (d) *circlearea := pi*r**2*

    (e) **repeat**
       begin
          $x := y; y := z; z := x + y;$
       end;
       until $z > 1000$

    (f) *root := −b + sqrt(disc)/2a*

    (g) **if** *count := 0* **then**
       writeln ('empty file')

    (h) *writeln; writeln; writeln*

    (i) **var** *i, j, k = integer;*

    (j) **case** *i* **of**
       begin
          $0, 1 : j := j + 1; k := k + 1$
            $2 : j := sqrt(j + k); k := 0$
          $3, 4 : j := abs(j + k); k := −1$
       end

    (k) **if** *count < 15* **then**
          $a := a + 1;$
       else
          $b := b + 1$

*2. Find and correct all of the errors in the following program. Characterize each error as either a syntax, run-time, or logic error.

```
line
number
  1        porgram sample(input,output);
  2        { This program computes the sum of the integers from 1 to k.
  3          k is read as a data value }
  4        var k, sum : integer;
  5              readln(k);
```

```
 6              sum := 1
 7              for i = 1 to k do
 8                  sum = k
 9              writeln('the sum from 1 to k is', sum)
10        end.
```

*3. Assume that you have entered the following program.

```
00100    program fibonacci(input, output);
00110    { This is a first attempt at a program to
00120      generate the fibonacci sequence x(i) = x(i − 1) +
00130      x(i − 2), i = 2, 3, . . .; x(0) = x(1) = 1. We will stop
00140      when we come to some user-specified upper limit }
00150    var i, x, y, z, linit : integer;
00160    begin
00170        readln(limit); writeln('index fibonacci number');
00180        i := 0; x := 1; writeln('i:6, x:15);
00190        i := 1; y := 1; writeln(i:6, y:15);
00200        while (z < limit) do
00210            z := x + y { This will determine the next number
00220                           in the fibonacci sequence        }
00230            i := i + 1; writeln(i:6, z:15);
00240            y := z;
00250            x := y { These last two statements set up for
00260                       the next iteration                 }
00270            end;
00280        writeln('end of the fibonacci sequence');
00290        writeln('a total of ', i, ' numbers were generated)
00300    end. { Of fibonacci }
```

After giving the command to run the program, the computer produced the following error messages.

```
pascal   program   fibonacci
00471    00170     readln(limit); writeln(' index fibonacci number');
***                        ↑ 104
000035   00180     i: = 0; x: = 1; writeln('i:6, x:15);
***                                                   ↑ 202
000037   00190     i: = 1; y: = 1; writeln(i:6, y:15);
***                    ↑6 ↑4
000056   00200     while (z<limit) do
***                              ↑ 104
000057   00230     i: =i+ 1; writeln(i:6,z:15);
***                ↑ 59
000073   00270         end;
***                    ↑ 6
```

```
000117   00290        writeln('a total of',i,'numbers were
                                 generated)
***                                        ↑ 202
***   premature end of source file
compiler error messages:
   4:     ")" expected
   6:     illegal symbol
  59:     error in variable
 104:     identifier not declared
 202:     string constant must not exceed source line

error(s) in Pascal program
```

Locate and correct all the syntactic errors in the program.

4. Assume that after making all the necessary changes to the program in Exercise 3, you attempted to run the program and got the following run-time error message:

```
?100
index           fibonacci number
     0                1
     1                1

—program terminated at: 00053 in fibonacci
—attempt to reference an undefined variable

fibonacci
       i      =      1
       x      =      1
       y      =      1
       z      =      u
    limit     =     100

end of program fibonacci
```

Discuss how you would go about determining what the error was. Discuss your use of hand-simulation, the program output, the dump, and writeln commands in helping you to locate the problem. Locate and correct this run-time error.

5. Again, assume that you have corrected the run-time error discussed in Exercise 4. Now when the program is run, it produces the following output.

```
?   100
index            fibonacci number
    0                    1
    1                    1
    2                    2
    3                    4
    4                    8
    5                   16
    6                   32
    7                   64
    8                  128
end of the fibonacci sequence
a total of               8 numbers were generated
```

(a) Instead of printing out 100 numbers as we had requested, the program only printed out 8. In addition, the numbers it did print are incorrect. Discuss how you would go about finding and correcting this logic error. In your answer discuss the role that hand-simulation, the program output, and additional writeln commands would play in helping you correct the mistake.

(b) After correcting the error(s) from part a, test the program to see if it works properly under all possible conditions. If not, suggest necessary changes to make the program more secure against pathological conditions.

6. Suppose that the rootfinder program at the end of Chapter 5 was executed with the following data:

$$f(x) = x^2 - 15x + 56$$
$$x1 = 0$$
$$x2 = 50$$
$$epsilon = 0.005$$

However, instead of producing the correct result,

root = 7.0 (or root = 8.0)

it produces:

cannot find a root in this interval

Discuss your approach to finding why rootfinder is apparently not operating properly. You should discuss the roles of trace statements, additional output statements, and hand-simulation in helping you find the problem.

7. Write the user-level documentation for the program rootfinder in Figure 5-26 so that a user will be able to use the program properly and intelligently by merely reading this documentation.

8. Modify program average in Figure 5-7 so that it does the following.

   (a) Checks the value of howmany and produces an error message if it is non-positive. It may take any other recovery action you think appropriate for this situation.

   (b) Accepts data values only in the range [low, high] inclusive, where low and high are user-specified parameters and high > low.

   (c) Prints the number of legal scores used in computing the average.

   (d) After processing one set of data, repeats the process for another set and continues until end-of-file.

   After making these modifications, design test data to test all possible paths through the program. State what type of case (valid, boundary, special, invalid) each data set is intended to represent. Write the user documentation for average so that it could be used easily by others.

9. If you have not already done so, implemen⁺ one or more of the program rootfinder changes suggested in Exercise 16 of Chapter 5. These operations are a good example of typical program maintenance operations—going back and updating or improving an existing program. After implementing these changes, discuss how you feel you might have been helped by having good, complete technical documentation on the rootfinder program.

10. A good example of the difficulty that can be encountered with program maintenance is working with an unfamiliar program whose details are not fully understood. Exchange a program that you have written with a similar program written by someone else, and agree on some interesting, nontrivial modification that each of you will then make to the other's work. After completing the modification, write the necessary user documentation. Discuss the style and organizational characteristics of the program that aided (or hindered) the maintenance process.

STRUCTURED DATA TYPES— ARRAYS

7.1 INTRODUCTION

The scalar data types that were introduced in Chapter 3 (integer, real, boolean, character, subrange, and user-defined) could properly be called *simple* types. This is because variables of these scalar types are limited to assuming only a single value at a time and no higher-level relationships between scalar variables are possible. For example, when we make the declaration

var
    x, y : integer;

we are simply stating that x and y are two unrelated variables that will take on integer values. The declaration implies nothing at all about any inherent relationships between x and y. For example,

    1.   Is x logically related to y? If so, how is it related?
    2.   Does x come "before" or "after" y in any sense?
    3.   Is x in any way subservient to y?
    4.   Does the value of x limit the value of y in any way?

Frequently, we want to indicate in our programs that values are not independent and unrelated but are part of a unified collection of related data. For example, we might want the x and y just discussed to be treated as a pair of integer values (x,y) that are always operated on as a unit. These higher-level relationships cannot be created with simple scalar data types. Instead, we need a way to define more interesting and more complex data representations called *structured data types*.

235

Structured data types are complex higher-level data types that are built from collections of simple scalar data types and that contain some additional relationships between the various elements of that scalar type. These relationships, together with the rules for constructing elements of a higher-level type, are how we categorize the various structured data types available in Pascal.

As we mentioned when discussing control statements and scalar data types, the provision for higher-level data types is another example of Pascal's extraordinary range of power. There are five distinct varieties of structured data types available in Pascal.

1. Arrays.
2. Records.
3. Sets.
4. Files.
5. Pointers.

In this chapter we will discuss only the first of these data types—the array. In Chapters 9 and 10 we will introduce all of the remaining data types available in Pascal.

In addition to the previously listed structured types, we can also create a number of additional data representations because of a very important principle of Pascal— all of the structured data types in Pascal can be defined in terms of other structured data types. Therefore, instead of constructing our higher-level data structures only from scalar building blocks (such as integers or reals), we can build them from other high-level types. This leads to complex hierarchical structures, such as:

1. Arrays of arrays of arrays.
2. Arrays of records.
3. Records containing arrays.
4. Files of records.
5. Arrays of sets.
    .
    .
    .

Ultimately, however, all of these complex higher-level data types can be viewed as being constructed from the simple Pascal scalar data types.

An understanding of the enormous data structuring capabilities available in Pascal is essential for taking advantage of the full power of the language. The richness of the data typing facilities is one of the major features that distinguishes Pascal from other high-level languages.

7.2 ARRAYS

With the scalar data types that we introduced in Chapter 3, we are required to give each variable a unique name. There are times when this is extremely cumbersome. For example, to read in 10 character variables with a single read statement would require something like this.

var
> a, b, c, d, e, f, g, h, i, j : char; { the names are horrible, but so is the
> technique! }
> .
> .
> .

readln(a, b, c, d, e, f, g, h, i, j)

To find out whether any of these variables have the value ';' we would need to write something like this.

if *(a = ';')* **or** *(b = ';')* **or** *(c = ';')* **or** *(d = ';')* **or**. . .

If these operations are a cumbersome way of handling 10 items, imagine the problems of working with 100 or 1000! What we need is a data structure in which we can refer to a collection of data objects of identical type by a single name. In Pascal this type of data structure is called an *array*. The structure of an array is diagrammed in Figure 7-1.

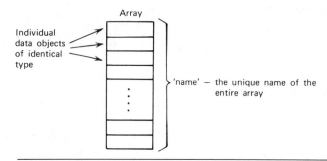

Figure 7-1. Organization of an array.

However, since a single "name" now refers to a collection of objects, we must be careful to avoid ambiguous operations such as:

name := name + 1 { name is an array structure so this is ambiguous }
if *name = 3* **then** *x := x + 1 { this is also ambiguous }*

In these two examples, the particular element or elements of the array name we are referring to is unclear—the first, the third, all of them? Therefore, when referencing an element of an array, the name will always be composed of two distinct parts: the array name itself and the *array index* (which is frequently termed a *subscript*). This subscript is like a "pointer" into the array, specifying the particular element of the array we are referring to. The subscript is enclosed in square brackets immediately after the array name.

> *name*[*subscript*]

To create an array data type, we use the following **type** declaration:

> **type**
> > *type-name* = **array** [t_1] **of** t_2;

where both t_1 and t_2 are either data type names or data type definitions. t_1 specifies the data type of the values to be used in the subscript field. It must be a scalar data type other than real. (In most cases it will be a subrange of the data type integer.) This field indicates how we are going to be accessing the individual elements of an array and how many objects will be contained in the array (i.e., how big the array is). t_2 specifies the data type of the identical objects that are stored in the array. It is important to remember that we cannot store elements of different data types (e.g., real and boolean) in the same array.

Once we have defined this new data type, we can create the actual arrays using the **var** declaration, as shown in the following examples.

Example 1

> **type**
> > *sample1* = **array**[1. .100] **of** integer;
>
> **var**
> > *x : sample1;*

These declarations state that x will be a 100 element array of integers. The first element will be accessed as x[1], the second as x[2], . . . , and the hundredth element as x[100].

Example 2

> **type**
> > *sample2* = **array**[− 5. .5] **of** *char;*

var
    y : sample2;

The variable y will be an 11 element array of characters. The first element will be accessed as y[− 5], the second as y[− 4], . . . , and the eleventh as y[5].

Example 3

type
    sample3 = **array**[*daysoftheweek*] **of** *integer;*

var
    z : sample3;

If daysoftheweek is the user-defined scalar type we created in Section 3.4.1, z will be a 7 element integer array. The first element will be referenced as z[sun], the second as z[mon], . . . , and the seventh as z[sat]. The contents of the array z will be integer values.

Example 4

type
    sample4 = **array**[*char*] **of** *0. .200;*

var
    w : sample4;

The exact length of w will depend on the size of the character set of the computer you are using. For example, if you are using a computer in the IBM/360 or 370 series, w will contain 256 elements. The first element can be accessed as w[chr(0)], the second as w[chr(1)], . . . , and the 256th can be accessed as w[chr(255)]. The value of any array element is an integer between 0 and 200, inclusive.

Now that we know how to create an array, how can we utilize it to avoid the cumbersome constructs that we wrote at the beginning of this section? Assume that we have the following declarations:

type
    string = **array**[*1. .10*] **of** *char;*

var
    alpha : string;

and we wish to read 10 values into the array alpha. If we say

read(alpha[1], alpha[2], alpha[3], . . .)

we are no better off than we were before, and the use of an array has gained us nothing. However, if we say

read(alpha[i])

and we repeatedly execute the read statement just given with the value of i ranging from 1 to 10, we have gained enormously. By using a variable subscript, we can operate successively on all elements of the array merely by changing the current value of the subscript. All that is necessary to complete our work is to decide how best to assign the necessary values 1, 2, 3, . . . , 10 to the variable i. In Section 5.3.3 we introduced the **for** statement, which automatically initializes, increments, and tests a scalar variable. The **for** loop would be an ideal method of controlling the index of an array, especially when we know exactly how many elements of the array we will be processing. The previous example of reading in an array could now be written

for *i :* = *1* **to** *10* **do** *read (alpha[i])*

The **for** loop will cause the read statement to be executed 10 times, each time reading one character and putting it into the next slot of the array. The first time the loop is executed, i will have the value 1 and we will read a character into alpha[1]. The second time through, the loop i will be 2 and we will read a character into alpha[2]. If the next 10 characters on the current data card were

hello ruth

the array alpha would look like:

h	alpha [1]
e	alpha [2]
l	alpha [3]
l	alpha [4]
o	alpha [5]
	alpha [6]
r	alpha [7]
u	alpha [8]
t	alpha [9]
h	alpha [10]

If we wished to count the number of times the letter "l" occurred anywhere within alpha, we could again use the **for** construct and a variable subscript to search through the entire array.

count : = *0;*
for *i :* = *1* **to** *10* **do**
    if *alpha[i]* = *'l'* **then** *count :* = *count* + *1*

The first time through the loop, i will have the value 1 and we will compare alpha[1] to the constant ''1''. The second time through the loop, i will have the value 2 and we will compare alpha[2] to ''1'', and so forth.

The use of a variable in the subscript field of an array reference is actually a special case. Any expression is allowed in the subscript field of an array reference as long as it evaluates to a scalar value of the proper type. For example, to search the even-numbered elements of the array alpha in reverse order, we could write:

```
count := 0;
for i := 5 downto 1 do
    if alpha[2*i] = '1' then count := count + 1
```

Now, as i takes on the values 5, 4, 3, 2, 1 the subscript expression (2*i) takes on the values 10, 8, 6, 4, 2, and we will search the even-numbered elements in reverse order.

In some cases control of the subscript may be better handled by either a **repeat/ until** or a **while** statement. This is especially true in cases where we do not know exactly how many elements of the array we will be processing. For example, suppose that instead of automatically reading in 10 characters, we wish to keep reading characters into the array until we come to the end of the sentence, denoted by a period. We could write the following.

```
i := 0;
repeat
    i := i + 1;
    read(alpha[i])
until alpha[i] = '.'
```

The **repeat** loop will now read characters into the array alpha one at a time until the last character read is a '.' When we leave the loop, the variable i will contain the total number of characters read in, including the period.

There is a serious problem, however, with this last example. If you look back at the original **var** declaration for alpha, you will see that it is a 10 element character array. In the previous example, if we have not encountered a period within the first 10 characters, the subscript i will become 11 and we would attempt to execute read(alpha[11]). There is no such element, since the subscript falls outside the bounds of the array. This is a fatal error. In some systems this type of error terminates a program immediately. In others, the program continues processing with unpredictable results. Regardless of what your local system does, however, this situation must be avoided. It is always invalid to attempt to access an array element that is outside of its predefined limits. Your programs should be constructed so as to prevent this from occurring. This is another example of foolproof programming, which we have stressed repeatedly.

In our second example it would have been much better to write

```
i := 0;
repeat
    i := i + 1;
    read(alpha[i])
until (alpha[i] = '.') or (i = 10)
```

Now the loop will terminate either when we encounter the end of sentence marker ('.') or when we reach the upper limit of the array.

There may appear to be another solution to the problem of overrunning arrays. If we do not know how long to declare an array when we write the program, why not simply postpone the decision until we do know? For example, if the number of elements to be put into an array were contained on the first data card, it would be nice if we were able to write

```
type
    list = array[1 . .n] of integer; { this is not allowed }

var
    table   :list;      { an n-element array }
    n       :integer;   { a variable specifying the size of the array }
    i       :integer;

begin
    readln(n); { read in the length of the array }
    for i := 1 to n do
    begin
        readln(table[i]); { read in the next array element }
        .
        .       { process the array }
        .
```

What we are trying to do in this example is say that the size of the array will become known when the program is run. However, declarations such as this are illegal in Pascal. When an array is declared in Pascal, the necessary memory space is reserved during compilation. (Refer to Section 6.2 and Figure 6-1.) Therefore the Pascal compiler must know exactly how much space is needed when it processes the **type** declaration. In the previous example, the value of n will not be known until the program is actually executed and a data value is read. Therefore that declaration is invalid. All array declarations must be given in terms of scalar constants (which may be symbolic constants defined using a **const** declaration).

What can we do if we wish to set up an array whose exact length is unknown? We can plan for the worst case by setting up an array large enough to handle the longest list the program will ever encounter. Although it is invalid to attempt to access more of an array than we declared, it is always acceptable to leave part of an array unused. In Figure 7-2 on the next page, which finds and prints the largest and smallest elements within an array as well as the average of all the elements, we have declared the array to be 100 elements long. If the actual list size is not more than 100, the program will run correctly. If we wish to run the program for a list that has a length greater than 100, we would need to make a single change to the **const** declaration on line 6 of the program.

This example raises an interesting and fundamental question about using arrays: When and why do we need them? The problem in Figure 7-2 can be solved without arrays. The program could be written so that it reads in only a single value at a time, and performs all necessary computations on that one value. The program would look something like this.

```
count := 0;
big := − maxint;
small := maxint;

while not eof do
begin
    readln (num); { read in a single value }
    if num > big then big := num;
    if num < small then small := num;
    total := total + num;
    count := count + 1
end;

average := total/count { should probably check that count <> 0 }
```

One major difference, however, becomes obvious. In the first example in Figure 7-2, which uses arrays, when we have completed the program the original data are still available in the array called table. In the second example, the original data, except for the last item, have been destroyed. Each new value read into the scalar variable num overwrites the previous value. One of the primary considerations in determining the need for an array (or some other high-level structure) is this: Is it necessary to retain the original data for use in later operations? The program in Figure 7-2 is not the best choice to illustrate the need for the array structure, since there is no obvious reason to save the data. However, a slightly different version makes this need quite obvious. Assume that we wish to scan a list to find the largest value. We then wish to scan it again to find the second largest, and so on until we have found all items in numerical order. This is basically the sorting problem that we have discussed several times and whose algorithms are outlined in Section 2.3. Now the need for an array becomes quite obvious, since we will be making numerous passes over the original list to put it into numerical order. If we lose the data after the first pass, we will be unable to complete the sorting process. The exchange sort algorithm in Figure 2-17, when translated into Pascal, would look like the program in Figure 7-3 on pages 246-247.

```
program findextremes (input, output);
{ program to find the largest, smallest, and average of
  values from a list of no more than 100 values. an array
  structure will be used to hold the elements        }

const
      maxsize = 100; { maximum length of the array }

var
      average    :real;          { average value }
      big        :integer;       { largest value }
      count      : 0. .maxsize;  { actual length of the array }
      i          :integer;       { for loop index }
      small      :integer;       { smallest value }
      table      : array[1. .maxsize] of integer;
      total      :integer;       { sum of all values }

begin
      count := 0;
      while not eof and (count < maxsize) do
      begin
          count := count + 1;
          readln(table[count]);
          writeln(table[count])
      end;

      { the main algorithm begins here. first check if
        the list had any items placed in it }

      if count > 0 then
      begin
          big := table[1];
          small := table[1];
          total := table[1];
          for i := 2 to count do
          begin
              if table[i] > big then big := table[i];
              if table[i] < small then small := table[i];
              total := total + table[i]
          end; { for loop }
          average := total / count;

          writeln(' largest value =', big);
          writeln(' smallest value = ', small);
          writeln(' average value = ', average)
      end { then clause on count > 0 }
      else
          writeln(' list is empty')
end. { of program findextremes }
```

Figure 7-2. Program to find the largest, smallest, and average values in an array.

```pascal
program sort (input, output);
{ program to read in and sort a list of real values into descending numerical
  sequence using exchange sort in section 2.3 }

const
    maxsize = 500; { maximum array length }

type
    range = 0. .maxsize;
    listtype = array [range] of real;

var
    big        :real;       { stores the largest value }
    i          :range;      { loop index }
    length     :range;      { size of array }
    list       :listtype;   { the list to be stored }
    location   :range;      { stores the index of the largest value }
    pointer    :range;      { loop index }
    temp       :real;       { used during interchange }

begin
    length := 0;
    while not eof and (length < maxsize) do
    begin
        length := length + 1;
        readln (list [length])
    end;

    { see if the list was empty }

    if length = 0 then
        writeln('empty list, cannot sort')
    else

    { the actual sorting algorithm begins here }

    begin
        for pointer := 1 to length - 1 do
        begin
            big := list[pointer];
            location := pointer;
            { find the largest item in the list from position
              pointer + 1 to length }
            for i := pointer + 1 to length do
                if list[i] > big then
                begin
                    big := list[i];
                    location := i
                end;
```

Continued on next page

```
        { now exchange the largest value with the item at
          position pointer }
        temp := list[pointer];
        list[pointer] := list[location];
        list[location] := temp
   end; { for loop }

   writeln(' the sorted list');
   for i := 1 to length do
        writeln(list[i])
end { else clause on length > 0 }
end. { program sort }
```

Figure 7-3. Program to do exchange sort.

7.3 MULTIDIMENSIONAL ARRAYS

In the previous section we defined an array as a collection of identical elements known by a single name. For those identical elements we have so far limited ourselves to the scalar data types: integer, real, char, boolean, and user-defined. We will now generalize this to say that the elements of an array can be any data type—including another array. A *multidimensional array* should not, therefore, be considered a new data type but simply a generalization of the array structure introduced in the previous section.

As an example of a multidimensional array, suppose we wished to define a five-element data structure called score. Each element would itself be a three-element integer array containing values in the range 0 to 100. This type of structure is called a *two-dimensional array*. Graphically, it would look like Figure 7-4 on page 247.

To create this structure in Pascal, we could say

type
      score = **array**[1. .5] **of array**[1. .3] **of** 0. .100;

However, this type of declaration is quite cumbersome, so Pascal provides a shorthand notation:

type
      score = **array**[1. .5, 1. .3] **of** 0. .100;

In general, a two-dimensional array is created using the following **type** declaration:

type
      type-name = **array**[t_1, t_2] **of** t_3;

where t_1 is an ordinal data type[1] that gives the subscript range of the first dimension (whose size is termed the number of *rows*), t_2 is an ordinal data type specifying the subscript range of each row (whose size is termed the number of *columns*), and t_3 is the *base type*—the data type of each identical scalar object in the array. Once the data type has been defined, we can create instances of these two-dimensional arrays using the **var** declaration.

Example 1

type
        sample5 = **array**[0. .10, −5. . +5] **of** char;

var
        a1 : sample5;

The variable a1 will be a two-dimensional array with 11 rows, indexed 0,1, . . . , 10, and 11 columns, indexed −5, −4, . . . , + 5. This will result in a total of 11 × 11 = 121 elements, each of which is a character.

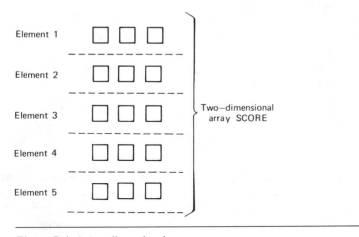

Figure 7-4. A two-dimensional array.

[1]Remember that in Pascal, the ordinal data types include all the scalar data types except real—integer, boolean, character, user-defined, and subrange.

Example 2

type
    sample6 = **array**[*1. .25, (red,white,blue)*] **of** *real;*

var
    a2 : sample6;

The variable a2 will be a two-dimensional array with 25 rows and 3 columns. The 25 rows will be indexed by the integers 1, 2, . . ., 25. The 3 columns will be accessed by the 3 user-defined constants red, white, and blue. Each element of the array will be a real number.

To refer to an element stored in a two-dimensional array we must, as before, use both an array name and a subscript. However, a single subscript is now insufficient. Looking back at Figure 7-4, we can see that when we write score[3], we are referring not to one object but to three. To locate a single object uniquely within the array, we must identify it by its row and its position within that row. In general, when we make a reference to array-name[i,j], we are referring to row i, and element j of that row. For example, to work with the second element of the third row of the array in Figure 7-4, we would refer to score[3,2]. The elements of the fourth row would be called score[4,1], score[4,2], and score[4,3]. To reference the 11 elements of the first row of the array a1 whose declaration was shown above, we would write:

    a1[0, −5], a1[0, −4], . . . , a1[0,5]

The 25 elements of the second column of the array a2 declared earlier would be indexed in the following manner.

    a2[1,white], a2[2,white], . . . , a2[25,white]

The generalized enumeration of the elements of a two-dimensional array is shown in Figure 7-5.

As with the one-dimensional arrays discussed in the previous section, the real power of a two-dimensional array comes from being able to use expressions in place of constants as subscripts. Since we now have two subscripts, we will be required to define each one explicitly. This can be done by using a **for, repeat/until,** or **while** loop, as in the previous examples. We have the additional problem, however, of determining the *order* in which to change the two subscripts. The sequence in which we modify subscript values determines the order in which we will process elements in the array. In a one-dimensional array we can, by definition, move in only one dimension (although we have a choice of a forward or backward direction). This is shown in Figure 7-6a. With a two-dimensional array, we can move either horizontally (by rows) or vertically (by columns). This is diagrammed in Figure 7-6b.

type
    $arraytype$ = **array**$[a_1..a_m, b_1..b_n]$ **of** *"basetype"*

$$a_1, b_1 \quad a_1, b_2 \cdots a_1, b_n$$
$$a_2, b_1 \quad a_2, b_2 \cdots a_2, b_n$$
.

.
.

$$a_m, b_1 \quad a_m, b_2 \cdots a_m, b_n$$

where the a_i and b_i are elements of an ordinal data type and $a_m >= a_1$ and $b_n >= b_1$

Figure 7-5. Enumeration of elements in a two-dimensional array.

Assume, for example, that an array called score holds examination scores for a class of 30 students. Each row of score contains three examination scores for a single student. The declarations to create this structure would be as follows.

const
    $examcount$ = 3; { *number of exams per student* }
    $classcount$ = 30; { *number of students in the class* }

var
    score : **array** $[1..classcount, 1..examcount]$ **of** *integer;*

If we want the average score for each student on the three exams, we will need to process the array by rows. This implies holding the row subscript fixed while the

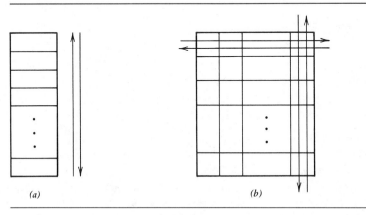

(a)   (b)

Figure 7-6. Possible movements through an array structure. (*a*) One dimension. (*b*) Two dimensions.

column subscript varies from 1 to the total number of scores (in this case, 3). This can be accomplished by the following Pascal statements.

```
for i := 1 to classcount do
begin
    sum := 0;
    for j := 1 to examcount do
        sum := sum + score[i,j];
    average := sum div examcount;
    writeln('average of student no. ', i, 'is', average)
end { of for loop }
```

Since the inner **for** loop will be executed to completion for each value of i in the outer **for** loop, we will handle one complete row and only then move on to the next row.

If, instead, we wanted an overall class average for each examination, we would need to process the array by columns. This would involve holding the column subscript fixed while the row subscript ranged from 1 to the total number of students in the class (in this case, 30).

```
for i := 1 to examcount do
begin
    sum := 0;
    for j := 1 to classcount do
        sum := sum + score[j,i];
    average := sum div classcount;
    writeln('average of exam no.', i, 'is', average)
end { of for loop }
```

These examples illustrate two important principles to remember when working with multidimensional arrays:

1. Use an appropriate control structure (e.g., **for, while,** or **repeat/until**) to control the values assigned to each subscript expression.
2. Ensure that the order in which the subscripts are being modified is correct for the problem being solved.

We have explained multidimensional arrays by using the specific example of a two-dimensional array. As you might expect, however, all of our comments generalize completely to arrays of arbitrarily high dimension, bounded only by the limitation of the memory available on your computer system. These higher-dimensional arrays allow a greater representation of interrelationships between data objects. For example, assume that we wished to store examination scores of students in five different classes. We could make score an array of two-dimensional arrays—in effect, a *three-dimen-*

sional array. Each array element would represent a single class and would be an array of student scores on a number of examinations. There would be as many elements as there are different classes.

const
numberofclasses	*= 5;*	*{ five separate classrooms }*
classcount	*= 30;*	*{ thirty students per classroom }*
examcount	*= 3;*	*{ three exams per student }*

var
       score : **array**[*1. .numberofclasses, 1. .classcount, 1. .examcount*] **of** *integer;*

The array would look like Figure 7-7. Notice that each element of this three-dimensional array is a two-dimensional array of the type shown in Figure 7-5. When we

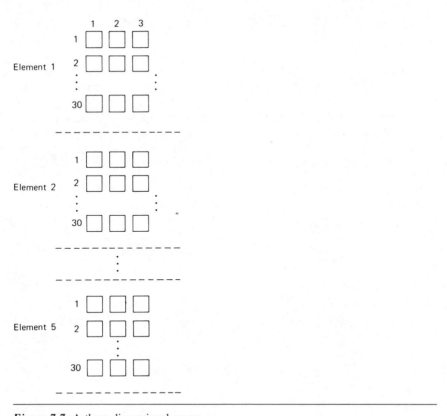

Figure 7-7. A three-dimensional array.

refer to score[2,5,1], we mean the first examination of the fifth student in class number two.

The following is a fragment of Pascal code to read in a class identification number (in the range 1 to 5) and count how many students in that class received a perfect score of 100 on any examination.

```
readln(class);
if (class >= 1) and (class <= 5) then
begin
    perfectcount := 0;
    for i := 1 to classcount do
        for j := 1 to examcount do
            if score[class,i,j] = 100 then
                perfectcount := perfectcount + 1
end { if statement }
else
    writeln ('illegal class identification number')
```

We could continue this process and add a fourth dimension, in which case the entire three-dimensional data structure of Figure 7-7 would simply be the first element of a higher-level four-dimensional array. A reference to score(3,2,5,1) might refer to the first examination of the fifth student in class number two, of the third school.

The syntax of the **type** declaration for an array of arbitrary dimensionality is shown in Figure 7-8.

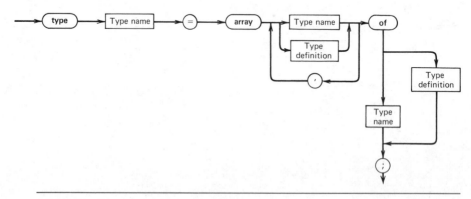

Figure 7-8. Generalized array declaration.

Style Clinic 7-1

Efficiency and Multidimensional Arrays

Multidimensional arrays allow you to create interesting data structures describing a complex set of relationships. But a word of caution is in order—they can quickly use up an enormous amount of memory space. The seemingly innocuous declaration

```
var
     x : array[0. .50, 0. .50, 0. .50] of integer;
```

will require an allocation of $51 \times 51 \times 51 = 132,651$ memory locations. That may be more memory locations than are available in your computer.

Before creating a very large multidimensional array, be particularly sure that the entire array is really needed. If it is, and you are squeezed for space, some of the space-saving alternatives you should consider are:

1. *Sharing the Same Space.* If two arrays of the same type are used at different times, that is, if you finish using the first array before you need the second, then consider simply using a single array for both purposes. However, we caution against doing this unless absolutely necessary. It can lead to errors that are extremely difficult to find and correct.

2. *Overlays.* If it is impossible to fit the entire array structure in memory at once, consider bringing in a portion of it at a time and working with just that portion. Each new segment will overwrite, or *overlay*, the previous segment when it is brought in. (This is not a Pascal programming technique. Instead, it is a facility that may be provided by the *operating system* of your computer. Ask your instructor or computer center for details.)

3. *Packing.* When storing information in a memory location, it is not uncommon for much of the memory space to be unused. For example, most computers allow anywhere from two to six constants of type char to be stored in a single location. However, the normal storage of array elements is one element per memory location. Thus, if a particular computer permits four characters per location, the word pascal would internally look like the following:

This has wasted 75% of the available space. To avoid this waste, Pascal allows you to create *packed arrays* that minimize wasted space by packing information as tightly as possible. If the array just shown were a packed array, it would be stored internally as:

To create a packed array structure, simply add the optional reserved word **packed** to the **type** declaration.

type
> *type-name* = **packed array**[t_1, t_2. . .] **of** *basetype;*

Alternatively, arrays can be packed or unpacked dynamically in the program by using the standard Pascal functions pack and unpack described in Appendix B.

The use of a packed array will have no effect on the logic of a program. You work with and manipulate the array in exactly the same fashion. It is Pascal's job to access the individual array elements properly. Be aware, however, that when you use packed arrays you gain *space* (a reduction in the total amount of memory space needed to contain the program) at the expense of *time* (an increase in the computer time required to execute the program). It takes additional time to isolate and fetch an array element from a packed array, and that makes the program run more slowly. Whether or not the time lost invalidates the savings in space will depend on the particular problem and the particular computer.

7.4 CASE STUDY—ENCRYPTION/DECRYPTION

One of the more interesting applications of computers is the encoding and decoding of messages to prevent unauthorized usage of information. (And it's not just the FBI and CIA that are interested. Hospitals, corporations, and research centers also encode personal or sensitive information.)

The process of converting *plaintext* (the original natural language text) into *cyphertext* (the encoded, unintelligible message) is called *encryption*. The reverse process, converting cyphertext into plaintext, is called *decryption*.

One of the most simple types of encryption schemes is the *substitution cypher* in which each letter in the plaintext is mapped into a different letter of the alphabet. For example, using the rule that each letter of the alphabet is changed into the letter that is two positions beyond it in the alphabet, (a → c, b → d, . . . , x → z, y → a, z → b), we would encrypt in the following way:

encryption   this is a message.   decryption   (plaintext)
    ↓   vjku ku c oguucig.   ↑   (cyphertext)

We will develop a program that takes cyphertext and attempts to decrypt it by assuming that it has been encrypted using a simple substitution cypher.

The decoding technique is based on the fact that the letters of the alphabet do not occur with the same frequency. In English, the letter 'e' is the most common, 't' is the second most common, and so forth, until 'z,' which is the least common. Thus, as a first approximation to decrypting cyphertext, we could count the frequency of occurrence of each letter in the cyphertext and attempt to relate these frequencies to the known standard frequencies of letters in the English language. For example, if 'q' were the most common letter in some cyphertext, then we might try changing all 'q's to 'e's. Similarly, we could do this for all 26 letters.

Let us set up a 26 × 2 character array, called frequency. The first column of this two-dimensional array will be initialized to the letters in their natural alphabetic ordering—a, b, c, ... The second column will contain the letters ordered by their standard frequency of occurrence in English—e, t, n, r, . . . (Figure 7-9*a*). Let us also set up a second one-dimensional array, called count, that will contain the frequency counts of all letters in the cyphertext. We will go through the cyphertext, one character at a time, and tally the total number of occurrences of each character. (This is shown in Figure 7-9*b*.) We will now sort the count array into descending order and, as we interchange values in count, we will interchange the corresponding rows in column 1 of the frequency array. The result is that column 1 of the frequency array will contain the letters of the cyphertext ordered by their frequency of occurrence (Figure 7-9*c*). We can now perform a substitution by replacing each letter in column 1 of the frequency array with the corresponding letter in column 2. This should give us a first approximation to the contents of the secret message.

The algorithm to implement what we have just described is shown in Figure 7-10. However, this is simply the first stage of the decryption process. Unless we are phenomenally lucky, the output of this initial decoding operation will not be the correctly decrypted message. It will have some letters that match properly, but many letters will be incorrect.

Frequency 1	Frequency 2		Count		Frequency	Frequency		Count		Frequency	Frequency
1 a	e	1	43		a	e	1	127		d	e
2 b	t	2	1		b	t	2	122		h	t
3 c	n	3	114		c	n	3	120		m	n
4 d	r	4	127		d	r	4	114		c	r
5 e	o	5	109		e	o	5	111		y	o
6 f	a	6	18		f	a	6	109		e	a
.	.		.		.	.		.		.	.
.	.		.		.	.		.		.	.
.	.		.		.	.		.		.	.
26 z	z	26	62		z	z	26	1		b	z
(a)					(b)					(c)	

Figure 7-9. The operations involved in decryption.

For example, after applying the algorithm from Figure 7-10 to the message shown at the beginning of this case study, the first part of our algorithm might produce something like this.

vjku ku c oguucig   (cyphertext)
thiw iw a mkwwagk   (first attempt at plaintext)

START
    construct the frequency array as shown in Figure 7-9a
    initialize the count array to all 0's
    read the letters of cyphertext into cypher[1], cypher[2], . . .
        cypher[n]
    write out the cyphertext
    for i := 1 to n do
        update the count field of the letter stored in cypher[i]
    sort the count array into descending order, and perform the
        identical operations on column 1 of the frequency array
    for i := 1 to n do
        look up letter cypher[i] in column 1 of the frequency array
        message[i] := the letter in column 2 of the same row
    write out the partially decoded message
END OF ALGORITHM

Figure 7-10. Algorithm for part 1 of the decryption operation.

What we need to do now is refine and improve our initial approximation and move toward a correct interpretation of the message. This is a very difficult operation for a computer program to perform automatically (and certainly too difficult to do in this case study), so we will ask this to be done by the user. Our program will now expect the user to study the output and provide "clues" as to how to properly do the substitutions to arrive at a correct message. These clues will be in the following format:

c_1, c_2 { where c_1, c_2 are both letters a. .z }

The interpretation of this input is a request to the computer to change all occurrences of the character c_1 in the cyphertext into the character c_2, *instead of* the character it is now using. For example, looking at the previous cyphertext and partially correct plaintext, we see that the letter 'u' is currently being changed into the letter 'w.' This does not seem to be the correct substitution ("thiw iw . . ." does not make sense). Instead, it seems that the cyphertext letter 'u' should be replaced by the letter 's'. We can accomplish this by entering the following line.

? u,s

If this is the only change requested, the program should now produce the following output.

vjku ku c oguucig   (cyphertext)
this is a mkssagk   (plaintext)

Again, we can study the output and decide what changes we wish to make now. The one additional input line

? g,e

should now alter the program to produce the correctly decrypted message.

Implementing these clues in our program is quite simple. When the user inputs the character pair, c_1 c_2, we will look up character c_1 in column 1 of the frequency array, and change the corresponding character in column 2 to c_2. We will continue to read in these clues until the user inputs some special flag indicating that there are no more changes and that he or she wishes to see the plaintext. (We will use the character '-' to represent this "end of clues" signal.)

An algorithm to implement this second phase of the decoder is shown in Figure 7-11.

```
START
    correct := false
    while not correct do
        { assume the character pair -,- indicates the completion of clues }
        read in c₁, c₂
        while c₁ and c₂ are both <> '-' do
            look up c₁ in column 1 of the frequency array
            change column 2 of the frequency array to c₂
            read in a new c₁ and c₂
        for i := 1 to n do
            look up letter cypher[i] in column 1 of the frequency array
            message[i] := letter in column 2 of the frequency array
        write out the decoded message
        ask the user if the message is correct and if yes,
            set correct to true
    end of the while loop
END OF THE ALGORITHM
```

Figure 7-11. Algorithm for the second phase of the decryption operation.

A complete program to implement these two algorithms is shown in Figure 7-12. The reader should look closely at that program, especially the creation and manipulation of the one- and two-dimensional arrays, the concept that was introduced in this chapter.

Another point to notice about the program in Figure 7-12 is that it is relatively long (about 150 lines) and reasonably complex. Also, you will notice that there are segments of identical code that are repeated a number of times within the program, for example,

1. Looking up a letter in the frequency array.
2. Changing cyphertext to plaintext on a character-by-character basis.
3. Writing out the plaintext message.

In the next chapter we introduce a programming technique that helps to reduce the difficulty of designing and coding large programs and also eliminates the need for repeating identical code segments. It is one of the most fundamental and powerful ideas in computer programming—the *subprogram*.

program *decode (input, output);*
{ program to decode a cypher created using a simple substitution
* method. the first phase uses frequency counts of letters to*
* make the substitutions, while the second phase prompts the*
* user for clues about how to improve the guess   }*

const
> *max = 100; { maximum length of the cypher is 100 characters }*

var
big	*:integer;*	*{ used in sorting count }*
ch	*:char;*	*{ used for reading input }*
char1,char2	*:char;*	*{ input clues provided by user }*
correct	*:boolean;*	*{ switch to terminate phase 2 }*
count	**:array** *[1..26]* **of** *integer;*	
cypher	**:array** *[1..max]* **of** *char; { the cypher text }*	
found	*:boolean;*	*{ switch during table look-up }*
frequency	**:array** *[1..26, 1..2]* **of** *char;*	
i, j	*:integer;*	*{ for loop indices }*
length	*:0..max;*	*{ length in characters of cyphertext }*
location	*:integer;*	*{ used in sorting count }*
message	**:array** *[1..max]* **of** *char; { the decoded message }*	
response	*:char;*	*{ response by user about correct message }*
separator	*:char;*	*{ character separating char1, char2 }*
temp	*:integer;*	*{ used during interchange }*
tempchar	*:char;*	*{ used during interchange }*

begin
> *{ initialization section. user will have to provide two*
> * data cards containing abcd...xyz, etnr...kjz   }*
> **for** *i := 1* **to** *26* **do**
> > *count[i] := 0;*
> **for** *i := 1* **to** *max* **do**
> > *message[i]:= ' ';*
> *writeln('please enter the letters in alphabetic order');*
> *readln;*
> **for** *i := 1* **to** *26* **do**
> > *read(frequency[i,1]);*
> *write('please enter the letters in order of their');*
> *writeln('frequency in English.');*
> *readln;*
> **for** *i := 1* **to** *26* **do**
> > *read(frequency[i,2]);*
> *writeln('please enter the encrypted message');*
> *readln;*

Continued on next page

```
{ input the entire encoded message one line at a time.
  input will end when we read in max characters or
  when we encounter the character '*' in the message }
i := 0;
read(ch);
while (ch <> '*') and (i < max) do
begin
      i := i + 1;
      cypher[i] := ch;
      if eoln then
          readln; { discard the end-of-line marker }
      read(ch)
end; { of while }
writeln('the complete message is as follows');
length := i;
for i := 1 to length do
      write(cypher[i]);
writeln;
{ now tally the characters and keep the count in the count array }
for i := 1 to length do
begin
        { the following assignment statement changes the characters
          'a'..'z' into the integers 1..26. warning: this only
          works if these letters are contiguous in the character
          field. it will not work if there are gaps between letters }
        j := ord(cypher[i]) − ord ('a') + 1;
        if (j >= 1) and (j <=26) then
            count[j] := count[j] + 1
end; { frequency count }

{ now sort the count array. let's use the exchange sort shown in figure 7-3 }
for i := 1 to 25 do
begin
        big := count[i];
        location := i;
        for j := i + 1 to 26 do
            if count[j] > big then
            begin
                big := count[j];
                location := j
            end;
        temp := count[i];
        count[i] := count[location];
        count[location] := temp;
        { let's interchange column 1 of the frequency array }
        tempchar := frequency[i,1];
        frequency[i,1] := frequency[location,1];
        frequency[location,1] := tempchar
end; { sorting phase }
```

```
{ now let's change the cyphertext into plain text }
for i := 1 to 26 do
begin
    for j := 1 to length do
    begin
        if cypher[j] = frequency[i, 1] then
            message[j] := frequency[i,2]
    end { inner loop }
end; { outer loop }

{ write out the partially decoded message }
writeln('the decoded message is as follows');
for i := 1 to length do
    write(message[i]);
writeln;

{ this is the end of phase 1 of the algorithm. now let's ask user
  for some clues to improve the first guess }
correct := false;
repeat
    write('please input clues of the form c1,c2 where c1 and c2');
    writeln('are any alphabetic characters');
    writeln('enter -,- to terminate the input');
    readln;
    read(char1, separator, char2);
    while (char1 <> '-') and (char2 <> '-') do
    begin
        found := false;
        i := 1;
        while (not found) and (i <= 26) do
            if char1 = frequency[i, 1] then
            begin
                frequency[i, 2] := char2;
                found := true
            end
            else
                i := i + 1;
        readln;
        read (char1, separator, char2)
    end; { while loop }

    { now let's attempt to decode the message again }
    for i := 1 to 26 do
    begin
        for j := 1 to length do
        begin
            if cypher[j] = frequency[i, 1] then
                message[j] := frequency[i, 2]
        end { inner loop }
    end; { outer loop }
```

Continued on next page

```
{ write out the decoded message }
writeln('the decoded message is as follows');
for i := 1 to length do
    write(message[i]);
writeln;

{ finally, let's ask the user if the message is correct as it now stands }
writeln ('is the message correct ? please enter yes or no');
readln;
read(response);
if response = 'y' then
    correct := true;
until correct;
writeln('end of decrypting operation. thank you')
end. { of program decode }
```

Figure 7-12. The complete decoding program.

EXERCISES FOR CHAPTER 7

1. For each of the structures described below, provide the required declarations and code needed to perform the specified initialization.

   *(a) An array named price is to contain the prices for each of 300 items stocked by a small store. Initialize all entries to zero.

   *(b) A 10 × 10 integer matrix, initialized to ones on the diagonal and zeroes elsewhere.

   (c) An array of 26 integers, indexed by the characters 'a' to 'z' and initialized to all zeroes.

   *(d) An array of months (jan, feb, . . .). Each month contains the dollar sales volume for every single day of that month.

   (e) A three-dimensional array called brains. The first dimension is indexed by (male, female), the second dimension is indexed by age in years (18. .100), and the third dimension is indexed by I.Q. level (75. .150). The values contained in the individual elements are the percentage (0 to 100) of people of that sex and age with that I.Q. level. For example, brains (female, 21, 140) would be the percentage of 21-year-old females with I.Q. scores of 140.

2. (a) Write a program that reads values into the brains array of Exercise 1e. The input will be in the following format.

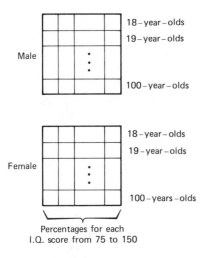

Percentages for each
I.Q. score from 75 to 150

(b). Validate that for each (sex, age) pair the percentage of all 75 possible I.Q. scores totals 100.0. (Assume that the percentage for the I.Q. score of 75 includes all those with scores below 75, and the percentage for the I.Q. score 150 includes all those with scores above 150. Thus for every (sex, age) pair, the total should be 100.0.)

*3. Assume that you are given a 10 element array of characters. The values in the array are limited to the characters ' + ', ' − ', and '0' through '9'. The characters represent a signed Pascal integer in valid syntactic format. Write a Pascal fragment that converts the characters in the array into the correct integer value. The character string is terminated by the end of the array or the first blank character.

4. Write a Pascal program that reads in a one-dimensional integer array and sorts that array using the *bubble sort*. The bubble sort compares adjacent pairs of values a_i, a_{i+1} to see if they are in order. If not, the two values are interchanged. We do this pairwise comparison on the entire list (a_1, a_2) (a_2, a_3) . . . (a_{n-1}, a_n). This is called a *pass*. If at any time during a pass at least one interchange was made we will need to make an entirely new pass. The method terminates when no interchanges are made during a pass. (Try to determine whether this technique is more or less efficient than the exchange technique in Figure 7-3.)

5. (a) Write a Pascal procedure to *merge* two sorted one-dimensional arrays into a single master array. Assume that you have two lists, a_i and b_i, each sorted into ascending order. Write a program to produce a new list, c_i, that contains every item from lists a and b and that is still sorted into ascending order.

(b) Do the same problem as in part a, but now your program should eliminate *duplicates*. That is, if the same value appears in both list a and list b, move only one value to the new list c and discard all other identical copies.

6. Write a Pascal program that first reads, row by row, an n × n two-dimensional array, where n is an input parameter. The program should then determine whether the array just read falls into any of the following special classes.

   (a) Symmetric.
   $$a_{ij} = a_{ji} \text{ for all i,j}$$
   (b) Upper triangular.
   $$a_{ij} = 0 \text{ whenever } i < j$$
   (c) Diagonal.
   $$a_{ij} = 0 \text{ whenever } i <> j$$

   Print out the array and state whether or not it belongs to any of the classes just listed.

7. A *sparse matrix* is defined as a two-dimensional array in which the great majority of elements are 0. It is very wasteful to store these sparse matrices as arrays, since so few of the elements actually contain meaningful information. A more efficient way to represent an m × n sparse matrix is as a k × 3 array in which we store the row index, the column index, and value of only the nonzero elements of the original array. This is called a *reduced representation*. For example, the matrix

   ```
   0  0  0  1   0
   3  0  0  0   0
   0  0  0  0   0
   0  0  0  0   0
   7  0  0  0 -22
   ```

   could be more efficiently stored as

   ```
   1  4   1
   2  1   3
   5  1   7
   5  5 -22
   ```

   Write a Pascal program that reads, one row at a time, a sparse two-dimensional m × n matrix and produces and prints the reduced representation of that matrix. At what percentage of nonzero elements does this reduced representation actually become more inefficient than a regular array representation?

8. Write a Pascal program that reads a sequence of characters into an array and counts the number of *words* in that text. A word is any sequence of non-blank

characters bounded on either side by at least one blank character. For example, given the following text:

Jefferson School is on Hennepin Avenue.

the output should be:

The above sentence contains 6 words.

(You may wish to go back and reread Section 2.2.4, which describes the development of an algorithm for just this problem.)

*9. (a) Write a Pascal program to compute the mean and standard deviation of a set of test scores. The standard deviation, σ, is defined as:

$$\sigma = \sqrt{\frac{\Sigma(x_i - \bar{x})^2}{n}},$$

where x_i is the test score
$\bar{x}$ is the mean
n is the number of scores
Σ means summation

(b) Repeat the same problem as in part a, but do input validation to ensure that:

(i) All examination scores are in the range 200 to 800. Do not accept test scores outside this range.

(ii) There is at least 1 legal score. If not, print an error message that there were no valid scores.

10. While the reduced matrix representation of Exercise 7 does decrease the amount of space needed to represent an m × n matrix, it does increase the complexity of the programs that manipulate those matrices. (See Style Clinic 9-2.)

Write two Pascal procedures to add and multiply matrices represented in the reduced form described in Exercise 7. Matrix addition and multiplication are defined as follows:

Addition: If A is m × n and B is m × n
then C = A + B means
$$c_{ij} = a_{ij} + b_{ij} \qquad i = 1 \ldots m$$
$$j = 1 \ldots n$$

Multiplication: If A is m × p and B is p × n
then C = A × B means
$$c_{ij} = \Sigma_k(a_{ik} * b_{kj}) \qquad k = 1 \ldots p$$

11. Write a complete Pascal program to read input cards containing names in the following format.

cccc. . . .   cccc. . . .   cccc. . .   c = any alphabetic character

first   middle   last
name   name   name

All three names may be of arbitrary length and there will always be one or more blanks between each name. The first and last name will always be present, but the middle name may be omitted, in which case there will only be two names on the card. All three names fit on a single line of 80 characters.

After reading in a name, print it out in the more standard "report-oriented" format.

ccccc,   cccc   c.

last   first   middle
name   name   initial

where 'last-name' and 'first-name' include only the first 15 characters of each. Additional characters beyond 15 are not printed. The middle initial is the first letter of the middle name followed by a '.' If the middle name is not present, this field is omitted.

Continue printing names until you come to the end of file. As an example, the following input card:

Rebecca . . . . Allison . . . Schneider   (. means blank)

will result in the following output line:

Schneider, Rebecca A.

Chapter 8 _____

FUNCTIONS AND PROCEDURES

8.1 INTRODUCTION

In the case study at the end of Chapter 5, we developed a program called rootfinder to find roots of arbitrary equations. This program required the evaluation of a formula, which we called f(x), at three different places within the algorithm. This fact was not belabored since, at the time, it was only incidental to the development of the example. However, we now wish to examine this aspect of rootfinder in depth, because it will lead us into a rich and beautiful concept in computer programming: the *subprogram*.

Observe first that, as it is currently written, rootfinder is not ready to be run on a computer because the statements

if *((f(x1) <= 0.0)* **and** *(f(x2) >= 0.0))* **or** . . .

.

.

.

x3 := (x2 * f(x1) − x1 * f(x2)) / . . .

.

.

.

if *(abs(f(x3)) < epsilon)* **then** . . .

will produce errors when the program is compiled, since the symbol f has not been defined. Of course, the problem is easily solved. To handle the example worked out in the chapter (finding the root of $x^2 − 10$), we simply change the statements just given so that they directly compute the desired equation. For example, the last line would be rewritten as follows:

if *(abs(x3 * x3 − 10.0) < epsilon)* **then** . . .

But what happens if f(x) is more complicated? The function f(x) could be, for example, an enormously complex computation arising out of a problem in engineering design, statistical analysis, or economic optimization. The specifics are not really important here. The point is that the function f(x) could easily require hundreds or thousands of lines of code. Now the value of a subprogram facility becomes evident. In the first place, the sheer tedium of replicating this much program text several times makes us wish to write the code just once and use it wherever we need it. We cannot use a simple **goto** statement to jump to the code that will evaluate the function because we also need to keep track of where to resume processing after completing the function. To be sure, we could keep track if we really wanted to, but the result would be very clumsy.

Suppose, for example, that we have a very complicated formula f and wish to determine whether f(x) (the value of the formula at the point x) is larger than f(y) for two numbers x and y that are to be read in. We could use the program compare shown in Figure 8-1.

```
program compare (input, output);
{ Read two numbers, x and y, and determine whether f(x)
  is larger than f(y) }
var
      x, y, fx, fy : real;
begin
      readln(x,y);
            .
            .
            .

      { Several hundred statements that compute f(x). The
        variable x appears in some of them, and finally the result
        is assigned to the real variable fx }
      fx := { final expression };
            .
            .
            .

      { The same several hundred statements as above that
        compute f(y). This time the variable y appears instead of x in those
        statements that contained x. Finally the result is assigned to the real
        variable fy }
      fy := { final expression };

      if fx > fy then
            writeln(' f(', x, ') is larger than f(', y, ')')
      else
            writeln(' f(', x, ') is not larger than f (', y, ')')
end.
```

Figure 8-1. Program compare using replicated code.

The program in Figure 8-1 would be quite tedious to write out. However, the most significant problem with this program is not actually the labor required to produce all that code. The major problem is clarity.

The abstract algorithm for compare is quite simple.

> read x and y
> set the variable fx to the value f(x)
> set the variable fy to the value f(y)
> compare the values of fx and fy
> write a message telling whether fx is greater than fy

Four statements in the Pascal program represent that algorithm.

```
readln(x,y);
fx := . . .;
fy := . . .;
if fx > fy then writeln . . .
```

In Figure 8-1, however, some of these statements are separated from each other by hundreds of lines of code whose purpose is to compute the function f. In a full program listing, the statements that reflect the important and fundamental steps of the algorithm would each be separated by several pages, and the main theme of the program would be obscured by the large volume of code that is, in fact, subservient to these four statements. Figuratively, we have lost the melody in the orchestration.

In Figure 8-2 we have eliminated both the replicated code and the separation of the important statements by using **goto** statements to transfer control. The code needed to compute the function f appears just once, and the statements that drive the algorithm are localized at the end of the program.

However, the program outline shown in Figure 8-2 is totally unacceptable. In the first place, we could do without the confusion caused by the many labels and jumps. Keep in mind that if all of the several hundred statements used to compute the function f were listed, it would be even more difficult to follow the logical flow of the program. The destinations of some of the **goto** statements would be separated by several pages from the **goto** statements themselves. A second problem is that if we wished to modify the program to handle three input variables and three function evaluations, we would have to add still more labels and jumps and elaborate on the code that returns control to the proper place in the program after each evaluation. We would be adding code not only in the section that evaluates the function, but also in the driving portion at the end. The approach pictured in Figure 8-2 will only lead to confusion and an illegible, unreadable program.

A third and greatly superior alternative for writing the compare program is available. Pascal (and most other languages) allows us to define independent program units called *subprograms*. As we will see, this mechanism permits the construction of

```
program compare(input, output);
{ Read two numbers, x and y, and determine whether f(x) is larger than f(y) }
label 1, 2, 11, 12;
var
        x, y, fx, fy, inputvalue, resultvalue : real;
                              returnvalue : integer;

begin
        goto 1;
2:      { compute f }
                    .

                    .

                    .
        { Several hundred statements to compute f(inputvalue).
          The variable inputvalue appears in some of them, and
          finally the result is assigned to resultvalue }
        resultvalue := { final expression };
        { Now figure out how to get back to the correct spot }
        if returnvalue = 11 then goto 11
        else goto 12;
1:      readln(x,y);
        inputvalue := x;
        returnvalue := 11;
        goto 2;
11:     fx := resultvalue;
        inputvalue := y;
        returnvalue := 12;
        goto 2;
12:     fy := resultvalue;
        if fx > fy then
                writeln (' f(', x, ') is larger than f(', y, ')')
        else
                writeln(' f(', x, ') is not larger than f(', y, ')')
end.
```

Figure 8-2. Program compare using **goto** statements.

programs consisting of thousands or even tens of thousands of lines of code that are nevertheless clear and quite comprehensible. We do this by successively dividing the problem into smaller, simpler, and more manageable subproblems. This is quite similar to the approach we use with any large writing task, including, for example, the writing of this textbook. We initially decompose this large and awkward task into smaller subtasks (chapters, sections, subsections), simplifying our job considerably. We will quickly see that the most compelling reason for defining a subprogram is not just to avoid the repetitious code of Figure 8-1, or to avoid the unnecessary **goto** statements of Figure 8-2, but to group sequences of closely related statements into conceptual entities that can subsequently be dealt with as single units.

These units are often referred to as program *modules,* and the process of breaking a large, complex algorithm into independent modules is called *modularization.* The advantage of such an approach in the compare program, for example, is that once the function f is defined and verified to be correct, it is no longer necessary to be concerned with how it works. The higher-level portion of the compare program can be written to compare the values of any function, f, at two points without regard for how f itself operates. In fact, because the module called f is viewed at this level in an abstract sense, it is possible and (as we will see later) quite desirable to code these higher-level, more general parts of the program first. This process of developing a program module in terms of other, lower-level modules is a key point in the development technique called *top-down program design* which was mentioned in Chapter 2. The subprogram facility in Pascal is fundamental to the effective use of the top-down design method.

Figure 8-4 (in the next section) shows the program compare written with a separate program module (called a function) used to compute the value of the formula, f. Notice how the fundamental aspects of the algorithm are grouped together and clearly delineated within the program. The example of Figure 8-4 is certainly easier to read and understand than either of the two previous approaches. In this chapter we will be learning how to write and use the subprogram features available in the Pascal language.

To summarize, then, the advantages of the subprogram in computer programming are:

1. To reduce or eliminate the need for repetitive sequences of identical code. We will now be able to write a sequence of code just once and activate it as many times as necessary.

2. To increase the clarity of a listing by removing low-level details from the main flow of program logic and placing it in separate units.

3. To provide a means for decomposing large programs into a collection of smaller and more manageable subprograms, facilitating the implementation of very large complex tasks.

4. To provide a unit of program sharing. The subprograms of a single large task need not all be written by the same person. Some may be developed by others and shared through program libraries. (We have already made use of this feature when calling sqrt, abs, sin, . . . from the Pascal library.)

As you can see, the subprogram is one of the most important and powerful tools in computer programming.

In Pascal there are two types of subprograms: *procedures* and *functions.* In the next section we look at an example of a function. Most of the discussion, however, applies to both types of subprogram, and we discuss the minor differences between them in the subsequent section.

8.2 FUNCTIONS

8.2.1 Function Declaration

A *function* is an independent program unit in Pascal. Unlike a **while** or **for** loop, which are merely parts of a larger program, a function has its own declarations for labels, constants, types, variables, and even other subprograms. Here is an example of the function f that would be needed to make the rootfinder program acceptable to the Pascal compiler.

```
function f(point : real) : real;
{ This is an example of a function f(x) supplied by the
  user of rootfinder to evaluate his or her own formula }
begin
    f := sqr(point) − 10.0
end; { of the function f }
```

This is called a *function declaration* because it defines the name that is to denote the function. It must appear immediately after the **var** declarations of the program. Let us examine the function declaration for f in detail. Following the reserved word **function** is an identifier that names the function. In this case the one-character name f is used. Any valid user identifier may be chosen. (See Style Clinic 8-1 for a discussion on how to choose good function names.) Following the name is a list of identifiers called *formal parameters*. These parameters describe both the variables that constitute input to the function and their data type. This list is enclosed in parentheses. In this example, there is only one parameter, called point, of type real. In general, there can be any number of parameters of any type, including none at all, and we will see many examples to come. Finally, we have the data type of the result that will be computed by the function. In this case, the result is of type real. The result of a function may be any scalar data type. The entire line beginning with the word **function** and ending with the semicolon is called the *function heading*.

Figure 8-3 shows the formal syntax of a **function** declaration in Pascal.

Following this heading is a sequence of statements that describes the operations to be performed on the input parameters when the function is executed. These statements may contain any valid Pascal construct and, like a program, must have a **begin/end** pair. However, somewhere within these statements, a value must be assigned to the function name itself. This is the means by which the result of the computation is communicated back to the program that activated the function. A similar effect was achieved in Figure 8-2 by using the variable resultvalue to pass information between different parts of the program. In the example just given, the assignment of a value to the function name is the only statement present.

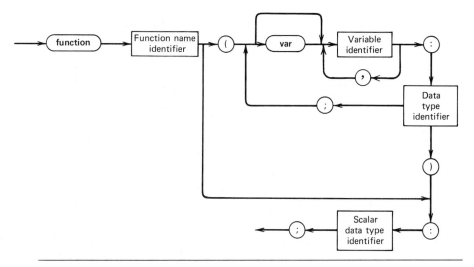

Figure 8-3. Syntax of a **function** declaration in Pascal.

8.2.2   Invoking a Function

The purpose of a function subprogram is to describe a computation to be performed on a set of input data. It is very important to note that no actual computation is performed as a result of merely writing out the function itself. The actual execution of statements in the function takes place only when the function is *invoked,* that is, when it is referenced within the main program. For example, the following assignment statement:

newvalue : = f(x)

is an example of a function invocation for the function f at the beginning of Section 8.2.1. The single line

if *f(x)* > *f(y)* **then** . . .

actually contains two invocations of the function f.

A function is invoked by using it within an arithmetic or boolean expression exactly as if it were a variable or a constant. You must be careful to ensure that the expression you are writing is consistent in terms of the data type of both the argument and the result. For example, the function f written earlier takes one real argument and returns a single real result. Therefore all of the following would be correct invocations of the function f.

var
 x, y, z : real;
 .
 .
 .
 z := 1.0 + sqrt(f(y))
 .
 .
 .
 if f(x) >= 1.38 **then** z := z + f(x – 1.0)
 .
 .
 .
 writeln (f(z + 2.0):10:2)

However, the following invocations are incorrect.

 z := f(x) + 'c' { adding a real value to a character }
 x := f(1) { integer parameter instead of a real }

Figure 8-4 shows the compare program implemented using a function declaration and invocation.

Although the programs in Figures 8-2 and 8-4 look considerably different, their behavior with respect to the computer is remarkably similar. The first statement executed in Figure 8-4 is the readln statement in the main program. When the boolean expression

 f(x) > f(y)

is encountered, the following events occur.

1. The value of x is transferred to point and control transfers to the function f.
2. The value of f(x) is computed and saved and control passes back to the boolean expression in the main program.
3. The value of y is transferred to point and control again transfers to the function f.
4. The value of f(y) is computed and saved and control again returns to the boolean expression where the two values f(x) and f(y) are then compared using the relational operator >.

The variables fx, fy, and returnvalue and all the labels declared in Figure 8-2 are not needed in Figure 8-4. In fact, they still exist in some sense at the machine level, but their roles are handled automatically. As Pascal programmers, we are now free to think in terms of the construction of algorithms from subalgorithms without having

```
program compare (input, output);
var
      x, y : real;

      function f (point : real) : real;
                    .
                    .
                    .
      begin
                    .
                    .
                    .
                  { here there may be several hundred Pascal
                    statements to compute the value of f at the
                    place called point. The variable point appears
                    in some of these and finally the result is
                    stored in f }
            f := { result of the computation }
      end; { of function f }

begin { the main program begins here }
      readln (x,y);
      if f(x) > f(y) then
            writeln ('f(', x, ') is larger than f(', y, ')')
      else
            writeln ('f(', x, ') is not larger than f('y. ')')
end. { program compare }
```

Figure 8-4. Program compare using functions.

to burden ourselves with considerations of subprogram linkage, transfer of data, or return techniques.

Returning to our example subprogram for rootfinder, we note that the formal parameter point is quite different from any other variable we have dealt with before. Although it appears within an executable statement just as any other variable might, there is no **var** declaration for it. Nor does it appear to have been initialized. In every example program presented so far, each variable that occurred within an expression on the righthand side of an assignment statement must have previously had a value assigned to it, usually by means of an assignment statement or a read statement. In this case, however, point acquires a value when the function f is invoked, and the value it assumes is the value of the actual parameter used in the call to the function. In the statement

      newval := f(x);

the variable x is termed the *actual parameter*. Here, x is a variable of type real, and it has acquired a value before it is used as an actual parameter in the function invocation. The actual parameter (x, in this case) in the function invocation corresponds to a formal parameter (point) in the function declaration. Formal parameters are used merely as placeholders to indicate where the actual parameters will be placed when the subprogram is called. We distinguish between formal and actual parameters to make clear this notion of placeholding. Until now, we have been able to trace the logical flow and execution of a program by reading it from beginning to end. When we come upon a function declaration, however, we are looking at lines of code that we cannot think of as being executed in place (i.e., just after the **var** declaration). Its execution will be deferred until the function is invoked. Only then do the formal parameters become associated with values, which are obtained from the actual parameters.

The names of actual and formal parameters need not be the same. The correspondence between formal and actual parameters is established solely on the basis of position. The first actual parameter in the invocation replaces the first formal parameter in the function heading, the second actual parameter replaces the second formal parameter, and so on. This positional relationship is shown in Figure 8-5.

The number of formal and actual parameters must match. For example, the main program in Figure 8-6 utilizes a function that checks whether the three characters provided as actual parameters are in alphabetical order. When the order of the actual parameters is changed, however, the same function can be used to check for reverse alphabetical order.

An alternative way of writing the function heading for inorder is

function *inorder(x, y, z:char) : boolean;*

Formal parameters of the same type need only be separated by commas and have their

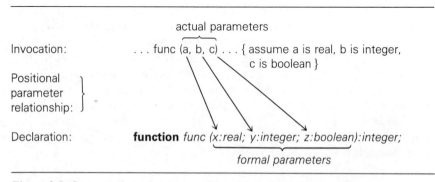

Figure 8-5. Correspondence between actual and formal parameters.

```
program checkorder (input, output);
{ read three characters and report whether they are in
  alphabetical order. loop until reading '***'        }

var
    c1, c2, c3      :char;
    working         :boolean;

function inorder (x:char; y:char; z:char) : boolean;

{ the function inorder returns true if and only if
  x <= y <= z                                    }

begin
    if x <= y then
        inorder := y <= z
    else
        inorder := false
end; { inorder }


{ the main program starts here }

begin
    working := true;
    while working do
    begin
        readln(c1, c2, c3);
        write(c1, c2, c3);
        if (c1 = '*') and (c2 = '*') and (c3 = '*') then
            working := false
        else
            if inorder (c1, c2, c3) then
                writeln ('are in order')
            else
                if inorder (c3, c2, c1) then
                    writeln ('are in reverse order')
                else
                    writeln ('are not in order')
    end { while loop }
end. { program checkorder }
```

Figure 8-6. Positional dependence of formal and actual parameters.

type specified once. Semicolons are used to separate the type field from the parameter that follows it. For example, we might write

```
function of manyparams(x, y, z:real; i, j:integer;
    list:arraytype):char;
```

As a matter of syntax, subprogram declarations must follow all variable declarations. Finally, an invocation of a function may appear anywhere in a program that a variable of the same type may appear.

As one final example, Figure 8-7 shows a function, called lookup, that searches an array called 'list' with 'length' elements to locate the first occurrence of a specified 'key.' The function returns the index of where that key occurred in the array or returns a 0 if the key is not found.

```
{ function lookup assumes that the calling program
  has made the following declaration:
type
     arraytype = array [1. .max] of integer;
                                                                   }

function lookup (list:arraytype; length:integer;
     key:integer):integer;

var
     found   :boolean;        { these local declarations will be discussed in Section
                                8.5 }
     i       :integer;

begin
     found  := false;
     i      := 1;
     while (i <= length) and not found do
     begin
         if list[i] = key then
             found := true
         else
             i := i + 1
     end;
     if found then
         lookup := i
     else
         lookup := 0
end; { function lookup }
```

Figure 8-7. Function to search a table.

8.3 PROCEDURES

Frequently, we wish to use a subprogram not to compute and return a single scalar value, but to perform a number of operations and return a set of values. For example, a substantial portion of a program might serve the purpose of printing the results of a computation. The development of the necessary code rests on considerations for the formats to be used for titles, headings, and result values. However, these detailed decisions are not needed in order to deal with the more general notion of output. Just as the main portion of the compare program could be written without explicit knowledge of the function f, so the main portion of any program could invoke the printing of a report without explicit information about the format of that report.

In Pascal, a *procedure* is also an independent program unit. In general, procedures and not functions are more often used to create program modules. One reason for this is that a procedure invocation is a statement in itself. Thus, for example, with appropriate declarations, the following is a valid main program:

```
begin
    inputdata;
    computeresults;
    writereport
end.
```

The body of the program consists solely of calls to three procedures called inputdata, computeresults, and writereport.

To understand the required syntax for Pascal procedures, let us look at a simple example. The writereport procedure just mentioned might be used to print the average distance that students in a class live from school. The following procedure declaration could be used.

```
procedure writereport (distance:real);
{ Procedure to print out the average distance to school }
begin
    writeln;
    writeln('average distance to school is', distance:10:1)
end; { procedure writereport }
```

The syntax of a procedure heading is shown in Figure 8-8.

The major difference between this declaration and the one shown in Figure 8-3 is that we do not specify a data type for the procedure itself, since the procedure name, unlike the function name, is not used to return an explicit value. The procedure name is used only for identification purposes. All values that are returned by a procedure are returned through the actual and formal parameters.

A procedure is invoked by writing the name of the procedure followed by the list of actual parameters that are to be passed into the procedure. The positional association between formal parameters in the procedure declaration and actual parameters in the procedure invocation is identical to the function relationship shown in Figure 8-5.

The following is an example of an invocation of the procedure writereport just given.

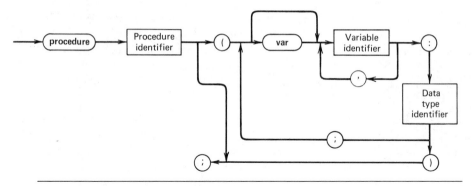

Figure 8-8. Syntax of the **procedure** heading.

```
sum := 0.0;
count = 0;
while not eof do
begin
      readln(dist);
      sum := sum + dist;
      count := count + 1
end;
avg := sum/count; { count <> 0 }
writereport(avg)
```

Notice that in the case of a procedure, it is not necessary (or even allowed) to assign a value to the procedure name. Also, note that a function name is always used as a component of an expression, but a procedure name is a valid statement by itself.

When the last line of the previous program fragment is executed, the following events will occur.

1. The value of the actual parameter, avg, will be transferred to the formal parameter, distance, and control will be transferred to the procedure write-report.

2. The procedure will be executed to completion. (In this case, that will be two writeln commands.)

3. Control will be returned to the statement immediately following the procedure invocation and the program will continue from that point.

Like the function, the statements that can be used when writing a procedure include *every* valid Pascal statement—assignment, input/output, iterative, conditional, and even another procedure call.

Style Clinic 8-1

A Note on Writing Readable Main Programs

Names chosen for subprograms should indicate very clearly what the subprogram does. A reader should be able to get a clear idea of what a program does just by looking at its main, or driving, portion. A reader should be required to look at the subprogram declarations themselves only to learn how these subprograms work.

For example, the following program is quite meaningless because the code for the procedures and functions is not shown.

```
program dosomething(input, output);
{An appropriate comment here would also be helpful}
type
     arraytype = array [1..100] of real;

var
     avg : real;
     thedata : arraytype;
           .
           .
           .
     { Declarations for step1, step2, step3, and step4 would go here }
begin
     step1(thedata);
     step2(thedata);
     avg : = step3(thedata);
     step4(avg)
end.
```

However, if we were just to change the names of the four subprograms so that the main program reads as follows, it is quite obvious what the program is doing.

```
program avgdisttoschool (input, output);
{ A comment should be here, but the point is that
subprogram names should be informative too }
           .
           .
           .
begin
     get (thedata);
     checkAllValuesPositive (thedata);
     avg : = average (thedata);
     writereport (avg)
end.
```

8.4 PARAMETERS

A subprogram may be thought of as a program within a program. As such, it may do all the things that any program can do, such as input, output, declare variables, and even define and invoke subprograms of its own. This property, along with a capability known as variable parameters, which is described shortly, enables us to define a program structure that is the crux of the modularization process used to write large, complicated programs. We describe the variable parameter mechanism first and then, in the next section, study block structure.

The point of *variable parameters* is that a means is provided by which a subprogram can obtain the initial value of an actual parameter and change its value as well. The importance of this ability to program structure is that it opens the communication lines not just into the subprogram but back to the calling program as well. Without variable parameters, the only piece of information that could be returned is a function value. With variable parameters, any amount of information can move both into and out of the subprogram including such powerful data types as multidimensional arrays.

The parameters we have used until now are known as *call-by-value* or simply *value parameters*. To illustrate the difference and the way each kind works, think of a subprogram as a clerk at a desk with an in-basket and an out-basket. Behind this clerk is a file cabinet (the computer memory) in which each file folder contains a single number. Whenever we provide a set of values to the in-basket (an invocation of the subprogram), the clerk performs a prescribed set of operations using those values. In the case of a function, the clerk places a single result value in the out-basket. We may provide input to the clerk in either of two ways. Using value parameters, we go to the file cabinet, look up the required input values, copy them onto a separate sheet of paper for the clerk to use, and drop them in the in-basket. We then lock the cabinet so that the numbers on file cannot be altered. The clerk may use only the values provided in supplying us with a result in the out-basket. Any changes made to these values do not change the original, which is safely locked up in the filing cabinet.

However, with variable parameters, instead of placing the needed values in the in-basket, we identify which file folders in the file cabinet contain these values and make these folders directly available for the duration of the computation. Since the clerk has access to the folders themselves, the original numbers stored there can be modified or deleted if the process being performed requires such changes. When the operation is finished, we may go to the file cabinet and examine the current contents of the folders we originally specified, thereby obtaining any results that may have been placed there.

The syntax for specifying variable parameters requires the reserved word **var** to precede the variable parameter name in the procedure or function declaration. To indicate that a parameter is passed by value, we simply omit the reserved word **var** before the parameter name.

With call-by-value, the formal parameter is initialized to the current value of the actual parameter. In a sense, we can think of making a "copy" of the actual parameter, initializing that copy to the current value of the actual parameter, and giving the copy to the procedure. However, the actual parameter is now inaccessible to the procedure and any changes to the formal parameter do not cause changes to the actual parameter, only to the local copy. For example,

```
procedure example (x : integer);
begin
    x := x + 1;
    writeln(x)
end;
```

If we invoke the procedure example by saying

```
a := 1;
example(a);
writeln(a)
```

the output will be

```
2
1
```

The actual parameter a is being passed by value. Therefore the formal parameter x in the procedure will be initialized to the value 1. However, the assignment statement in the procedure increments only that copy; the value of a is still 1. When we return to the main program and print out the value of a, it will be unaffected by the call to the procedure.

When using variable parameters, the formal parameter is actually *replaced* by the actual parameter, and the formal parameter acts only as a placeholder. Every modification of the formal parameter in the procedure will end up being a modification to the value stored in the actual parameter. For example,

```
procedure example (var x : integer);
    { x is now a variable parameter }
begin
    x := x + 1;
    writeln(x)
end;
```

Now the parameter is being passed as a variable (notice the reserved word **var**). If we activate the procedure by saying

```
a := 1;
example(a);
writeln(a)
```

then every use of the formal parameter called x in procedure example will be replaced by the actual parameter name 'a.' (Actually, it is memory addresses that are being replaced inside the computer, but we can think in terms of names.) Now the increment of x becomes an increment of the variable a and the output produced will be

2
2

The general rule for choosing parameter types is to use value parameters to pass values into a subprogram and variable parameters to return them. Each mode has certain attributes associated with it, and the choice of which to use should be based on which attributes are needed. Value parameters do not allow the value of the actual parameter to be changed. Therefore they should be used when the values of actual parameters must be protected from accidental or intentional change. However, this same feature means that results cannot be transferred back to the calling program through these parameters. On the other hand, variable parameters can be used to pass values into a procedure and must be used for returning results. However, because a return path is possible, the protection of actual parameters is lost when this calling mode is used. Changes to the formal parameters will cause corresponding changes to the actual parameters.

Figure 8-9 shows a procedure to take a list called 'list1' of length 'size1' and produce a second list, called 'list2,' containing only the nonnegative elements of list1. The final length of 'list2' is called 'size2.' Since list1 and its size are not modified by the procedure, we can pass them as value parameters to prevent them from being accidentally changed. List2 and its length are results computed by the procedure and are to be returned to the calling program. They *must* be passed as variable parameters to allow them to be returned.

Another way of looking at the difference between parameter types is to understand that in the case of value parameters, only the value of the actual parameter is passed to the formal parameter, which then assumes that value. We are really dealing with two distinct variables, one within the subprogram and the other outside. In the case of variable parameters, the value exists in only one place. Even though the actual and formal parameters may be two different symbolic names, both refer to the same entity. In fact, this is true even if both formal and actual parameters coincidentally have the same name.

If the formal parameter of a procedure is a variable parameter, then the corresponding actual parameter must be a variable. If the formal parameter is call-by-value, then the corresponding actual parameter may be any expression whose value has the appropriate type. In this regard, a variable is just a simple case of an expression. For the procedure heading:

procedure *f (val : real;* **var** *ref : real);*

```
procedure copy (list1 : arraytype; size1 : integer;
    var list2 : arraytype; var size2 : integer);

var
    i    :integer;        { index into list1 }
    j    :integer;        { index into list2 }

begin
    j := 0;
    for i := 1 to size1 do
    begin
        if list[i] >= 0 then
        begin
            j := j + 1;
            list2[j] := list1[i]
        end
    end; { for loop }
    size2 := j
end; { procedure copy }
```

Figure 8-9. Example of parameter passing mechanisms.

the following statements are valid invocations of the procedure f.

```
f(x,y);
f(1, a[5]); { assuming a is an array of reals }
f(sin(y) + 0.5, z);
f(3.0*z − 2.0 + sqrt(x), r);
```

The following are examples of invalid invocations.

```
f(x,1);          { not valid because constants cannot be passed into a variable
                   parameter }

f(z, sin(y));    { expressions cannot be passed into a variable parameter }
```

As a final example, Figure 8-10 shows a complete main program and procedure declaration for reading in and sorting a list of real values using the exchange sort technique. This example illustrates procedure declarations, procedure invocations, and parameter passing mechanisms.

```
program order (input, output);

{ program to read, sort, and print a list of real values.
  the table must have fewer than 100 elements                          }

type
    list = array [1..100] of real;

var
    k       :integer;       { for loop index }
    size    :integer;       { the number of elements in table }
    table   :list;          { the table of values to sort }

procedure readdata (var data : list; var size : integer;
                         maxsize : integer);

{ procedure to read in a list and return the list and its
  size. the procedure will terminate either when we reach an
  end-of-file or when we reach the maximum length of array      }

var
    i : integer;

begin
    i := 0;
    while not eof and (i < maxsize) do
    begin
        i := i + 1;
        readln (data[i] );
        writeln ('input value =', data[i] )
    end;
    size := i
end; { of procedure readdata }

procedure sort (var data : list; size : integer);

{ procedure to sort the list called data into
  descending order                                                     }

var
    big        :real;        { holds biggest value found during a pass }
    i, j       :integer;     { for loop indices }
    location   :integer;     { location of that largest value }
    temp       :real;        { used for interchanging values }
```

```
begin
    for i := 1 to size − 1 do
    begin
        big := data[i];
        location := i;
        for j := (i + 1) to size do
        if data[j] > big then
            begin
                big := data[j];
                location := j
            end;

        { now interchange }

        temp := data[i];
        data[i] := data[location];
        data[location] := temp
    end
end; { procedure sort }

{ main program begins here }

begin
    readdata (table, size, 100);
    if size = 0 then
        writeln ('no data provided. cannot sort')
    else
    begin
        sort (table, size);
        writeln ('sorted table');
        for k := 1 to size do
            writeln (table[k]);
    end
end. { program order }
```

Figure 8-10. Sample program using procedures.

Style Clinic 8-2 _____

Efficiency and Parameter Passing Techniques

There is one exception to the parameter passing mechanism just discussed. Frequently, large high-level data structures such as

var
　　　　x : **array** [*1..1000*] **of** *integer;*

need to be passed as variable parameters instead of by value, even if they are used only as input parameters to a subprogram. The reason is that the call-by-value mechanism entails the making of a duplicate copy of the input parameter. This copying is cheap enough for simple scalar types, but copying large structured values, such as the array x just given, can be extremely costly in terms of memory space. Passing this array by value would require an extra 1000 memory locations.

If space is at a premium, you should think carefully before using the call-by-value technique on very large data structures.

8.5 BLOCK STRUCTURE

A *block* is a sequence of declarations, a **begin,** a sequence of statements that describes actions to be performed on the data structures described in the declarations, and an **end.** Pictorially, a block can be represented as follows:

```
    declaration;
        .
        .
        .
    declaration;
begin
    statement;
        .
        .
        .
    statement
end
```

We can see from the previous diagram that a Pascal program consists of nothing more than a program heading followed by a block. Indeed, one of the purposes of a program heading is to give the block that follows a name. Furthermore, each subprogram declared within a block also contains a heading and a block, so a Pascal program becomes a hierarchical construction of named blocks. The complete program itself is often referred to as the *outer block,* while each subprogram constitutes an *inner block.* Any program can have many levels of nesting of blocks within blocks, so the terms *inner* and *outer* must be used in relation to a particular subprogram.

The usefulness of this kind of structuring lies not just in the potential it provides for modularizing the computation, but in its ability to protect data that are the exclusive concern of one set of modules from encroachment or contamination by other modules. This protection is accomplished by the fundamental rule of block structuring—all data values declared at the beginning of a block are accessible to all executable statements that are part of that block, including statements belonging to inner blocks, *but to no others.* The program skeleton in Figure 8-11 demonstrates this mechanism.

```
program blockstructure (input, output);
var
     a0 : real;
     b0 : real;
     c0 : real;

procedure block1;
var
       a1 : real;
       b1 : real;
       c1 : real;

          function block11 : real;
          var
              a11 : real;
              b11 : real;
              c11 : real;
          begin { code for block 11 }
             .

             .

             .
          end; { of block 11 };
     begin { code for block 1 }
        .

        .

        .
     end; { of block 1 };
```

continued on next page

```
    procedure block2;
    var
        a2 : real;
        b2 : real;
        c2 : real;
    begin { code for block 2 }
            .
            .
            .

    end; { of block 2 };

begin
        .
    · { here is the main program }
        .

end.
```

Figure 8-11. Example of block structure.

The identifiers a0, b0, and c0 are declared in the outer block of the program called blockstructure. They are therefore accessible to all levels of the program and are termed *global*. The variables a1, b1, and c1 are declared in block1, so they are available only within that block. They would be available in block1, but could not be referenced from block2 or from the statements of the program outer block. The variables a11, b11, and c11 can be referenced by statements within block11 but no others. An identifier declared in a block is said to be *local* to that block, while an identifier that is accessible in an inner block by virtue of its having been declared in an outer block is said to be *global* to the inner block. In Figure 8-11, the variables a1, b1, and c1 are local to block1, global to block11, and not defined in block2 or in the program's outer block.

We also refer to the block in which an identifier is declared as the *scope* of that identifier. In the example just given, the scope of a0, b0, and c0 is the entire program; the scope of a1, b1, and c1 is block1; and the scope of a2, b2, and c2 is block2. In other words, the scope of an identifier is that portion of a program in which the definition of the identifier is valid.

Two very important points about block structure should be emphasized here. The first is that both global variables and variable parameters provide a means of getting data into and out of a subprogram. The second point, whose importance bears further emphasis, is that local variables provide a means of protecting data from undesirable accessing. The value of this feature is that it allows us to write subprograms without undue concern for the program environment in which those subprograms will exist. We need only declare variables local to the subprogram to assure ourselves of control over the subprogram we are writing. Name conflicts—the declaration of an identifier with the same name in an inner and outer block—are automatically resolved by a convention known as *name precedence*. The rule is that an identifier always refers to the variable of most limited scope. Another way to say this is that a reference to a variable always refers to the most recent, or innermost, declaration of that variable. Any global variables represented by the same identifier become inaccessible and simply retain whatever values they had when the new variable was declared. To demonstrate this mechanism and its use, let us put together a program to read in a two-dimensional array and then find both the largest element it contains and the row and column subscripts that reference that element. We begin with the main program shown in Figure 8-12 and work inward.

After reviewing the main program of Figure 8-12, we can see that we now need a procedure, rowread, to read one row of the array, and another procedure, rowmaximum, to find both the maximum element of a row and its location. Note that the use of rowmaximum requires that max and index be variable parameters because these are results returned to the main program. Note also that the problem now consists of two smaller, independent subtasks. The two required procedures might be written as shown in Figure 8-13.

If the two modules were placed into the main program arraymax immediately after the variable declarations, we would have a complete and valid program. The most important aspect of this example is that the two procedures operate only on their own parameters and local variables. Therefore, while writing them, we need not be concerned with the variable names used in the rest of the program. We are thus able to concentrate entirely on the immediate subalgorithm.

Note, for example, that rowread contains a **for** loop using the control variable k, but the procedure itself is invoked in arraymax within another loop also using the variable k. There is no problem here, because k is declared locally inside rowread. So, even though we have two variables referenced by the same identifier, the program will still work properly. The name precedence rule ensures that neither variable will interfere with the other. Within the procedure rowread, we are referring to the 'local' k declared within the procedure. In arraymax, we are now referring to the 'global' k declared in the main program. If k had not been declared locally, the program would no longer execute properly. This is because both the outer loop and the inner loop would indeed be using and modifying the same variable.

The procedure rowmaximum demonstrates another aspect of name precedence. Outside the block for this function, the name table refers to a two-dimensional array; but inside the block, it refers to a local real variable. Even though the function was called with the actual parameter table, inside the block the formal parameter matrix has assumed the role of the array table. Again, there is no confusion between the array table outside the block and the real variable table inside as far as Pascal is concerned. Finally, notice that the procedure rowmaximum also declares and uses a local variable called k. Again, there is no problem. In rowmaximum, any reference to the variable k will refer to the 'local' k declared within the procedure.

However, one final comment should be made about the coding techniques used

```
program arraymax (input, output);

{ program to read in a 10 × 10 array of reals and locate the
  maximum value and the row and column index of its position }

const
    size = 10; { the size of array we are testing }

type
    a = array [1. .size, 1. .size] of real;

var
    biggestsofar    :real;          { the overall biggest element }
    column          :integer;       { column index of overall largest value }
    index           :integer;       { column index of largest value in a row }
    k               :integer;       { index of current row }
    max             :real;          { the biggest element in one row }
    row             :integer;       { row index of overall largest value }
    table           :a;             { the 10 × 10 array }

begin
    biggestsofar := − (maxint); { initialize biggestsofar to a
                                   very small number          }
    for k := 1 to size do
    begin
        { read in one row of array called table }
        rowread (table, size, k);

        { find the largest item in that row }
        rowmaximum (table, size, k, max, index);

        { now see if that value is the current biggest one }
        if max > biggestsofar then
        begin
            { reset values because we have found a new biggest value }
            biggestsofar := max;
            row := k;
            column := index
        end
    end; { for loop }

    { now print results }
    writeln ('maximum element = ', biggestsofar);
    writeln ('at row = ', row, 'column = ', column)
end. { program arraymax }
```

Figure 8-12. Main program for arraymax.

procedure *rowread (***var** *table:a; size:integer; rownum:integer);*

{ read one row of array. we should also check here for legality of the input data. we will omit these details for reasons of focusing on other issues }

var
     k : integer; { local variable used as loop index }

begin
     for *k := 1* **to** *size* **do**
        read (table [rownum, k]);
     readln;
     for *k := 1* **to** *size* **do**
        write (table [rownum, k]:10:2);
     writeln
end;

procedure *rowmaximum (matrix:a; length:integer; rownum:integer;*
                     var *big:real;* **var** *index:integer);*

{ procedure to find the largest element in row 'rownum' of table 'matrix' and return the value in 'big' and the column index in 'index'   }

var
     k   :integer;   { local variable used as loop index }
     table   :real;   { table is a local real variable—not the same as the
                                  array variable declared in the outer block }

begin
     table := matrix [rownum, 1];
     index := 1;
     for *k := 2* **to** *size* **do**
        if *matrix[rownum, k] > table* **then**
        begin
           table := matrix [rownum, k];
           index := k
        end;
     big := table
end; *{ of procedure rowmaximum }*

Figure 8-13. The procedures rowread and rowmaximum.

Style Clinic 8-3 _____

Side Effects

The alteration of a global variable by a subprogram is called a *side effect*. Although it is at times appropriate to let procedures act on global data, the practice should always be followed with great care and discretion, and beginning programmers should probably avoid it altogether. It is too easy to build in unnecessary complications or even outright errors. Such problems tend to arise because the actual behavior of subprograms that have side effects can be quite different from what we expect when we invoke them. Consider, for example, the following program. The problem is that the value returned by the function s depends not only on its parameter but on how many times the function itself has been called before. The output printed by this program is

        0   1   2   3   4

yet the main program makes it appear that the same value will be printed five times.

```
program sideeffect (input, output);
{ an illustration of side effects }

var
    g : integer;

function s (x : integer) : integer;
begin
    s := x + g; { the global variable g is referenced here }
    g := g + 1; { and altered here. this is a side effect }
end; { of function s }

begin
    g := 0;
    writeln (s(0), s(0), s(0), s(0). s(0))
end.
```

We cannot caution too strongly about the dangers posed by functions or procedures that have side effects. Use them only with care and when you have a specific reason for doing so. The accidental alteration of global values during the invocation of a subprogram can be an extremely difficult error to detect and correct.

Style Clinic 8-4 _____

> ### *Global Variables Versus Formal Parameters*
>
> In the program arraymax, the variable index declared in the outer block and
> the formal parameter index in the procedure rowmaximum are two distinct
> variables that just coincidentally have the same name. In other words, the
> formal parameter might just as well have been called inx, columnnumber, or
> anything else. However, if the heading had been:
>
> > **procedure** *rowmaximum (matrix:a; length:integer;*
> > *rownum:integer;* **var** *big:real);*
>
> the procedure would still work because the identifier index inside rowmaxi-
> mum would then refer to the global variable index declared in the outer block.
> The resulting calling sequence is shorter, and we have a little less writing to
> do when we call the procedure. But we have introduced a side effect. In this
> case, the use of the global variable to pass information out is not entirely
> unacceptable, because the global variable index is used only as a means of
> conveying information between rowmaximum and the program's outer block.
> The danger now, however, is that an unsuspecting programmer who wishes
> to make a change to the program or the subprogram might use the name
> index for his or her own purposes as well. If arraymax were a very large
> program, the cause of the subsequent troubles could be very difficult to trace.
> So, although global variables and formal parameters can both be used to pass
> information into and out of a subprogram, formal parameters should probably
> be the preferred method unless there is a compelling reason to do otherwise.

in Figures 8-12 and 8-13. We intentionally chose identical names for variables serving
different roles to illustrate parameter passing and name precedence with local and
global variables and to indicate that Pascal can resolve these problems. However, as
is probably obvious, this is poor programming style and can lead to a great deal of
confusion on the part of a reader. Even though the program will operate properly, its
clarity and legibility could have been significantly improved by choosing more de-
scriptive names that, whenever possible, do not conflict between modules.

8.6 FUNCTIONS AND PROCEDURES AS PARAMETERS

Besides value parameters and variable parameters, it is possible to pass procedure
names and function names themselves into other subprograms. The method is to use
the reserved word **procedure** or **function** in the subprogram heading to specify the

parameters appropriately, just as we use the reserved word **var** to indicate variable parameters. The type of each function parameter must also be stated. To illustrate, let us define a function that returns as a result the maximum value of two other functions.

```
function findmax (function f,g:real; x:real):real;

{ a function that takes on the larger of the values
  f(x), g(x) for any arbitrary functions f, g that take one
  real parameter and return a real result                     }

var
    fval : real; { value of f(x) }
    gval : real; { value of g(x) }

begin
    fval := f(x);
    gval := g(x);
    if fval > gval then
        findmax := fval
    else
        findmax := gval
end; { function findmax }
```

Notice that the declarations of function parameters f and g in findmax do not include the parameter list. A major restriction on the parameters of subprograms themselves used as parameters (the parameters of f and g above) is that these parameters can only be call-by-value. No variable parameters, function parameters, or procedure parameters are allowed in subprograms used as parameters.

Similarly, we may pass the name of a procedure as a parameter to a subprogram. This facility might be used, for example, when any one of several validity checks is to be performed on input data. The name of the appropriate check procedure could be passed into the input subprogram, and a boolean flag set if the check fails.

```
program sample (input, output);
{ this program illustrates the use of procedure names as
  parameters to other procedures }

var
    a, b, c     :real;
    flag        :boolean;      { set by check1 and check 2 }
    monthend :boolean;

procedure check1(x, y, z : real);
{ performs one type of validity checking on x, y and z
  and sets flag accordingly }
```

begin
.

.

    flag : = *true;* { *if data are ok* }
.

.

    flag : = *false;* { *if data are bad* }
.

.

end; { *procedure check1* }

procedure *check2(x, y, z : real);*
{ *performs a different type of validity check on x, y, and z*
 and sets flag accordingly }
begin
.

.

    flag : = *true;* { *if data are ok* }
.

.

    flag : = *false;* { *if data are bad* }
.

.

.

end; { *procedure check2* }

procedure *readdata* (**var** *x,y,z:real;* **procedure** *check);*
{ *this procedure reads in three real values and validates them*
 using a checking procedure passed in as a parameter }
begin
    readln (x,y,z);   { *input the data* }
    check (x,y,z);   { *check them for correctness* }
    if *flag* **then**. . .
       { *process the correct data* }
    else
       { *data are incorrect* }
    end;

{ *the main program begins here* }
begin
  · { *assume that we use checking procedure check1 for*
  · *weekly data and procedure check2 for month-end data* }
  ·

```
if monthend then
     readdata (a,b,c,check2)
else
      readdata (a,b,c,check1)
    .
    .
    .
end. { program sample }
```

Because parameters of procedures passed as parameters must be call-by-value, the only way that one procedure passed as a parameter to another can communicate results back is through global variables. This is a necessary exception to our discussion in Style Clinic 8-4 about avoiding global variables.

Style Clinic 8-5 _____

Signal Flags

After invoking a procedure, we must be careful to check that it did indeed work properly before going ahead and using any values returned by the procedure. Therefore, a subprogram must always be able to inform the calling program of the outcome of any attempted operation. Merely writing an error message is insufficient.

```
if x < 0.0 then
     writeln ('illegal value for x')
else
     y := sqrt(x)
```

The user will be able to see the message, but the program that invoked this procedure will have no way of knowing whether the sqrt operation was successfully completed. An attempt to reference the variable y could then lead to a run-time error. One way to determine whether a subprogram execution was successful is to include a parameter whose sole purpose is to say, "Yes, the program produced results," or "No, it did not produce results." These parameters are usually called *signal flags* and their use in subprograms is extremely important.

Using the boolean signal value ok, we could write the previous operations as follows.

```
procedure takeroot (x:real; var y:real; var ok:boolean);
begin
    if x < 0.0 then
        ok := false
    else
    begin
        ok := true;
        y := sqrt(x)
    end
end; { of takeroot }
```

The main program can now use the signal flag to determine the appropriate action to take.

```
readln (val);
writeln (val);
takeroot (val, result, flag);
if flag then
    writeln ('the answer is', result)
else
    writeln ('attempt to take the square root of a negative number')
```

8.7 RECURSION

Pascal permits procedures or functions to invoke themselves, a technique known as *recursion*. This capability offers an approach to problem solving not available in many programming languages. In the case of a function, recursion is indicated by the appearance of the function name as part of an expression. For example, the following function computes x^n using the recursive definition $x^n = x * x^{n-1}$.

```
function power (x:real; n:integer):real;

{ compute x raised to the power n recursively. the function always returns 0 for
  x = 0 }

begin
    if x = 0.0 then
        power := 0.0
    else
        if n = 0 then
            power := 1.0
        else
            if n < 0 then
                power := power(x, n + 1) / x
            else
                power := power(x, n - 1) * x
end; { of power }
```

The first two assignment statements (on lines 6 and 9) simply serve to return a function value (0.0 or 1.0). However, the last two assignments (on lines 12 and 14) contain recursive calls on the function called power.

A recursive call of a function will cause the program to remember exactly where it was in evaluating the current invocation of the function, save that information, and re-execute the function all over again. When we finish the recursive invocation, we must go back and complete any invocations that had been previously interrupted, and finish them in the reverse order that they were interrupted. (That is, we start executing the most recent function invocation that was saved.)

Let's see what happens when we say

power(x,2) { compute x^2 for some value of x }

This will cause us to invoke a function call

power(x,1)

which, in turn, generates a

power(x,0)

At this point, the sequence of information saved because of the recursive calls can be viewed as follows.

1. Interrupted in the computation of power(x,2) at the last line of the function
2. Interrupted in the computation of power(x,1) at the last line of the function

The evaluation of power(x,0) does not cause a recursive call but simply produces the real value 1.0. We will now begin to complete all previously interrupted function invocations. First, we must complete invocation number 2 (from above) and finish the evaluation of power(x,1). This evaluation does not generate a recursive call but simply the real value

1.0 * x { for some real value x }

Next, we complete invocation number 1 and evaluate power(x,2), which becomes

(1.0 * x) * x = x^2 as desired

All previous invocations of the function power have been completed and we are done.

As this example illustrates, recursion can sometimes be very expensive in terms of memory space and overhead, requiring the saving of a great deal of information. (Imagine computing x^{20} this way!) This is especially true if simple iterative schemes exist to solve the same problem. In this case, a trivial iterative algorithm exists to compute x^n.

```
{ product is a scalar real variable }
product : = 1.0;
for i : = 1 to n do
        product : = product * x { for n >= 0 }
```

The advantage of recursion is that many problems in computer science are defined in terms of recursive relationships, and these recursive problems usually end up with simple and elegant recursive solutions. For example, Figure 8-14 shows a *binary tree,* a very common data structure. It has *nodes,* represented by the circles with the name of the node written inside and, at most, two pointers coming from each node. These pointers are called the *left pointer* and the *right pointer* of the node. The very top node of the tree is called the *root.* You are probably familiar with this type of data structure from charts that show the chain of command in corporations, although we would probable allow more than two pointers coming from each node in such charts (otherwise, they would be top-heavy with management!)

Assume we are given the problem of developing an algorithm to trace through a binary tree and print out the name of every node. An iterative algorithm for this is certainly a nontrivial problem, and the answer is not immediately obvious.

If we wish to solve the problem recursively, our first step would be to attempt to define the problem recursively—that is, in terms of itself. A tree has one very nice property that allows us to do this quite easily: if we follow a pointer from one node to another, what we are left with is still a tree. For example, in Figure 8-14, if we follow the left pointer from node A, we are left with the tree shown on the top of page 302.

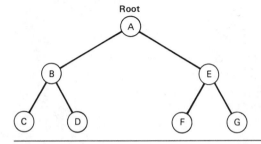

Root

Figure 8-14. Example of a binary tree.

If we follow the left pointer of B, we are left with the following one-node tree.

Finally, if we attempt to follow the left pointer of this tree, we come to the trivial case—an empty tree.

This characteristic allows us to write the recursive algorithm 'Search-a-tree,' which is shown in Figure 8-15. The parameter to this algorithm is a pointer to the root of the tree we are currently searching. Initially, it will point to the root of the entire tree (node A in Figure 8-14).

The recursive approach has led us to an elegant four-line solution to a quite complex problem. You should trace the algorithm, using the techniques discussed earlier, with the tree shown in Figure 8-14. The algorithm search-a-tree will produce the following output.

c
b
d
a
f
e
g

In addition to the obvious recursion discussed so far, less direct forms are also possible. A procedure p1 might not call itself directly, but might instead invoke another procedure p2 that subsequently calls p1.

```
algorithm search-a-tree(pointer to the root)
begin
      if "the pointer does not point to an empty tree" then
            search-a-tree(left pointer of root)
            write out the name of the root
            search-a-tree(right pointer of root)
end
```

Figure 8-15. Recursive algorithm for searching a binary tree.

In general, if a procedure p1 references another procedure called p2, then p2 must be declared before p1 uses its name. Otherwise, an unidentified symbol would occur. This is not a serious restriction; however, it does require a special construct to handle the situation in which two subprograms call each other. This special construct is called a *forward declaration,* and it is the same as any subprogram declaration with the subprogram body replaced by the single word "forward" (Figure 8-16). The complete declaration occurs later in the declaration section with the heading reduced to just the procedure or function name.

This section has only briefly discussed the topic of recursion. This is an interesting and very powerful programming tool and will be covered in much greater depth in advanced courses in programming and problem solving.

```
{ the following line is the forward declaration of func }
function func(x,y:real):real; forward;

procedure proc (var r1,r2:real);
begin
    .
    .
    .                   { this is the statement that requires
    z := func(a,b)        the forward declaration }
    .
    .
end; { procedure proc }

function func; { note the abbreviated function heading }
begin
    .
    .
    proc(u,v) { this is indirect recursion }
    .
    .
end; { function func }
```

Figure 8-16. Skeleton of a program illustrating forward declarations.

8.8 EXTERNAL SUBPROGRAMS

Two additional kinds of procedure and function declarations are available in some implementations of Pascal. Because they depend to some degree on the particular computer installation, an exact description of these features is not possible here. However, we can give a general, machine-independent discussion.

The idea is to provide a means whereby programmers can share subprograms. This facility allows the construction of *libraries* of general-purpose subprograms that can be conveniently made available to every user of the computer. Typical examples of the contents of such collections might include debugging tools, general-purpose input/output programs, sorting programs, plotting packages, and a variety of mathematical and statistical functions and procedures.

In order to use a library routine written in Pascal, we substitute an *external declaration* for the usual procedure or function declaration. The appearance is similar to a forward declaration, except that the identifier "extern" is used instead of forward. For example, if a procedure called plot was currently available in a program library, we might utilize it as follows.

```
program graphics (input, output);
    .
    .
    .

procedure plot (x,y:real; pen:integer); extern;

{ the main program begins immediately }
begin
    .
    .
    .

    plot (x,y,1);
    .
    .
    .
```

No procedure body for the procedure plot appears in the program. The Pascal system will locate the procedure plot stored in a library and include it automatically in your program. Some special commands, meaningful only to the individual computer system being used, may also be required to specify which of several libraries is to be used. The method for adding new subprograms to a library is also installation-dependent. Be sure to check with your local computer center about the availability and use of external procedures and program libraries.

Finally, it should be mentioned that global variables are not an allowable method of communication between a main program and an external routine. The only means of communication is by formal parameters—either value or variable parameters.

Style Clinic 8-6 _____

The Importance of Library Routines

The ability to incorporate external subprograms into a main program is one of the most valuable properties a programming language can have. Without it, sharing programming tools and ideas would be severely limited. Most computer installations maintain extensive libraries of generally useful routines such as mathematical operations, input/output routines, graphics packages, statistical analysis programs, and sorting and searching routines. Before undertaking the construction of any substantial program, it is a good idea to find out whether helpful library subroutines are available. There is no point in developing a routine that already exists.

    Likewise, if you have developed a program that may possibly be of interest to a number of other people, consider putting it in a program library for general use. This will, of course, require that you produce good user documentation so people will know that the program exists, what it does, and how it may be used.

8.9 CASE STUDY—PAYROLLS

In this case study we concentrate on the use of procedures and functions and, most importantly, how they can be of help in implementing large, complex computer programs. This was a point that was stressed in the very beginning of the chapter.

    Let's assume that we have a card file of weekly payroll information. For every employee in the company we have a single data card containing the following seven pieces of information.

1. Social security number (integer).
2. Hours worked this week (real).
3. Hourly pay rate (real).
4. Dependents (integer).
5. Year-to-date gross pay (real).
6. Year-to-date withholding tax (real).
7. Year-to-date social security tax (real).

We are to write a Pascal program to read in the payroll data on one employee; compute gross pay, all deductions, and net pay; print out a payroll check for that employee; update all year-to-date information; and finally, print out this newly updated year-to-date information to produce a "year-to-date report."

While this is not a very large problem, it is complex enough to benefit from having a well-organized solution. Attempts to leap directly into the coding without any planning or organization will probably result in failure or unnecessary difficulty.

At the highest levels, the problem we have defined is quite easy to describe. This top-level solution is shown in Figure 8-17.

```
program payroll (input, output);

{ program to compute employee payrolls from a
   master payroll information file          }

var
      dependents   :integer;      {number of dependents}
      gross        :real;         { gross pay for one employee }
      hours        :real;         { hours worked }
      netpay       :real;         { net pay for one employee }
      ok           :boolean;      { used in validating input }
      payrate      :real;         { hourly payrate }
      socsec       :real;         { social security tax for one employee }
      ssnumber     :integer;      { social security number }
      tax          :real;         { federal tax for one employee }
      ytdgross     :real;         { year-to-date gross pay }
      ytdsocsec    :real;         { year-to-date social security contribution }
      ytdtax       :real;         { year-to-date withholding }

begin
      while not eof do
      begin
            readdata (ssnumber, hours, payrate, dependents, ytdgross, ytdtax,
                          ytdsocsec);
            ok : = validate (hours, payrate, dependents);
            if not ok then
                  errorhandler
            else
            begin
                  computegross (hours, payrate, gross);
                  computedeductions (hours, payrate, dependents,
                                    gross, tax, socsec);
                  computenet (gross, tax, socsec, netpay);
                  printcheck (ssnumber, netpay);
                  update (gross, ytdgross, tax, ytdtax, socsec, ytdsocsec);
                  printytdreport (ssnumber, ytdgross, ytdtax, ytdsocsec)
            end { else clause }
      end; { while clause }
      writeln ('end of payroll processing')
end.
```

Figure 8-17. Top-level solution for the payroll program.

We have solved our payroll problem by defining a total of nine lower-level subprograms for handling various aspects of the problem. These subprograms are:

readdata: To read one employee data card from the standard input file.

validate: To check portions of the input data for legality. The function validate will return true if the data are valid and false otherwise.

errorhandler: A procedure to process all erroneous payroll information.

computegross: A procedure to compute gross pay for one employee, including the computation of overtime pay.

computedeductions: A procedure to compute the two deductions of federal withholding tax and social security.

computenet: A procedure to compute net pay.

printcheck: A procedure to print an employee paycheck containing employee name and net pay.

update: A procedure to update the three year-to-date totals and check that the employee has not exceeded the maximum social security contribution in any one year.

printytdreport: A procedure to print the final updated year-to-date report.

Even though the final version of the payroll program may result in hundreds of lines of detailed code, the top-level solution of Figure 8-17 is easy to read and understand. It is quite clear what has been done and what remains to be done to solve the problem. The "solution" of Figure 8-17 would be a correct one if the nine procedures and functions just defined actually existed and worked correctly. Therefore we must now begin to implement the nine lower-level subprograms that we have created and defined. This will involve obtaining a number of additional lower-level details (e.g., how to compute federal withholding tax, at what point overtime begins) that were not necessary earlier.

The process of fleshing out the details of previously unwritten, lower-level subprograms is called *stepwise refinement*. As we refine and develop lower-level routines, we typically become less concerned with *what* to do and more concerned with *how* things must be done. We start looking at finer and finer details of the solution. But, because we have already designed the higher layers, we know how these details fit into the overall picture. We are not swamped with seemingly unrelated and unimportant data.

Figure 8-18 on pages 308 and following shows the Pascal code for four of these nine lower-level routines.

```
function validate (hours:real; pay:real; exemptions:integer):boolean;

const
    maxexempt = 15;      { maximum number of exemptions is 15 }
    maxpay    = 25.0;    { maximum payrate = $25 per hour }

begin
    validate := true;
    if (hours < 0.0) or (hours > 168.0) then { 168 hours/week }
        validate := false;
    if (pay < 0.0) or (pay > maxpay) then
        validate := false;
    if (exemptions < 0) or (exemptions > maxexempt) then
        validate := false
end; { function validate }



procedure computegross (hours, payrate:real; var grosspay:real);

const
    regulartime = 40.0; { overtime begins after 40 hours }

var
    overtimepay :real;       { amount of overtime pay }
    regularpay  :real;       { pay for the first 40 hours }

begin
    if hours > regulartime then
    begin
        regularpay := regulartime * payrate;
        overtimepay := (hours - regulartime) * payrate * 1.5
    end
    else
    begin
        regularpay := hours * payrate;
        overtimepay := 0.0
    end;
    grosspay := regularpay + overtimepay
end; { procedure computegross }
```

```
procedure computedeductions (hours:real; rate:real; exemptions:integer;
                             gross:real; var fedtax:real; var sstax:real);
```

const
```
    deduc      = 10.0;   { the deductions per dependent for computation of
                           federal tax }
    ssrate     = 0.072; { social security tax is 7.2% of gross }
    ssbase     = 34.0;   { maximum weekly contribution is $34.00 }
```
var
```
    taxable : real; { taxable pay }
```
begin
```
    { first determine taxable pay, which is gross pay less $10.00 per dependent }
    taxable : = gross − deduc * exemptions;
    if taxable < 0.00 then { person has no taxable pay }
        fedtax : = 0.0

        { now compute federal tax. the percentage of withholding depends on
          the amount of taxable pay and goes from 14 to 70. let's assume a
          function exists to determine this percentage value }
    else
    begin
        rate : = ratecomputation(taxable) / 100.0 ; { convert it to a fractional
                                                      value 0.0-1.0 }
        fedtax : = rate * taxable
    end;
        { social security tax is 7.2% of gross or $34.00 per week, whichever is
          less }
    sstax : = ssrate * gross;
    if sstax > ssbase then
        sstax : = ssbase
end; { procedure compute deductions }
```
continued on following page

```
procedure printcheck (ssnumber:integer; net:real);

{ procedure to print checks for employees }
var
    day     :integer;
    found   :boolean;
    i       :integer; { for loop index }
    month   :integer;
    name    :array [1..30] of char; { employee's name }
    year    :integer;

    procedure date (var month, day, year: integer):extern;

        { external procedure to provide today's date }

begin { procedure print check }
    { let's first look up employee's name in table of
      social security number − name pairs        }
    findname (ssnumber, name, found);
    if not found then
        writeln('cannot produce check for id number', ssnumber,
                'name not found')
    else
    begin
        writeln (month, '-', day, '-', year);
        write ('pay to the order of');
        for i := 1 to 30 do
            write (name[i]);
        writeln;
        writeln ('$', net:10:2)
    end { else clause }
end; { procedure printcheck }
```

Figure 8-18. Four second-level procedures for the payroll program.

We have now written four of the nine subprograms that were defined by the initial refinement. In the process of doing this, we have defined an additional three lower-level routines.

ratecomputation: A function that takes as input the amount of taxable pay earned and returns as the function value the proper percentage of withholding on that amount of earnings.

findname: A procedure to look up a social security number in a table and return the employee's name as a 30-character array.

date: Procedure to return today's date. This procedure was declared as external. (It is a very common library routine on most computer systems and most likely will exist on your local computing facility.)

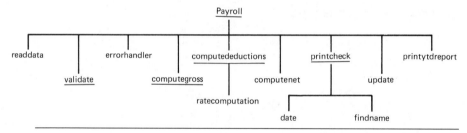

Figure 8-19. Organization of the payroll program.

The procedures that were just developed illustrate some key points about subprograms and the top-down development process. First of all, even though we have defined a total of a dozen subprograms and have written a total of about 110 lines of code, the program logic is quite easy to follow, and it is very easy to understand what we have done. We are not lost in a welter of "picky" details or unsure about what needs to be done next. Our task is clearly set out before us and we know exactly what is left to do to complete our job. The top-down development process lets us "stay on top of" our problem and effectively manage the developing solution. Also, notice that the lower-level routines we are beginning to define are becoming more and more concerned with the finer details of the problem. This is exactly as it should be. During the early stages of development we can concentrate on the general high-level aspects of the problem. Only later in the development do we need to begin to ask questions concerning the essential but "messy" lower-level details.

Figure 8-19 shows the overall organization of the payroll case study up to this point. The underlined names are modules that were coded here. Exercise 17 at the end of the chapter asks you to complete the development of this program.

We will have much more to say about program development in Chapter 11. Also, like the topic of recursion, program design methodology is an extremely complex topic that will be covered at greater length in advanced courses in computer science.

EXERCISES FOR CHAPTER 8

*1. Describe the scope of all the variables used in the following program fragment.

```
program outer;
var
    a : integer;
    b : integer;
        .

        .

    procedure p1;
    var
        b : integer;
        c : integer;
            .

            .

    end; { of p1 }

    procedure p2;
    var
        c : integer;
        d : integer;
            .

            .

        procedure p3;
        var
            e : integer;
                .

                .

        end; { of p3 }
            .

            .

    end; { of p2 }
begin
        .

        .

        .

end. { of outer }
```

2. Consider the following two procedures.

```
procedure swap1 (x,y:real);
var
      t : real;
begin
     t := x;
     x := y;
     y := t
end;

procedure swap2 (var x,y:real);
var
      t : real;
begin
     t := x;
     x := y;
     y := t
end;
```

If a has the value 1.2 and b has the value 1.5, what is the result of each of the following invocations?

(a) `swap1(a,b);`
`writeln(a,b)`

(b) `swap2(a,b);`
`writeln(a,b)`

*3. Given the following procedure:

```
procedure silly (x:integer; var y:integer);
var
      z : integer;
begin
     x := 5;
     y := 6;
     z := 7
end; { of silly }
```

what is the output produced by the following three lines?

```
x:= 1; y:= 2; z:= 3;
silly(y,x);
writeln(x, y, z)
```

*4. Given the following program

```
program mainline (input, output);
var
      a : integer;
      b : integer;
      c : integer;

procedure proc1;
var
      a : integer;
      c : integer;

      procedure proc2;
      var
          b : integer;
      begin
          a := 4;
          b := 5;
          writeln ('inside proc2, values for a, b, and c are currently',
                      a, b, c)
      end; { of proc2 }

begin { of proc1 }
      c := 6;
      writeln ('inside proc1, values for a, b, c are currently',
                 a, b, c);
      proc2;
      writeln ('still inside proc1, values for a, b, c are currently',
                 a, b, c)
end; { of proc1 }

{ main program begins here }
begin
      a := 1;
      b := 2;
      c := 3;
      proc1;
      writeln ('inside main program, values for a, b, c are currently',
                 a, b, c)
end. { of main program }
```

what would be the exact output of the program if it were executed? (If any of
the writeln commands attempt to print an undefined quantity, just indicate that
with the symbol '***' and keep tracing.)

5. What is the output that will result from the execution of the following program?
Denote undefined variables by '***'.

```
program block (output);
var
        a : integer;
        b : integer;
        c : integer;

        procedure p1 (var x:integer; y:integer);
        var
                b : char;
                c : char;
                d : char;

                procedure p2;
                var
                        x : integer;
                        y : integer;
                begin
                writeln ('in p2:', x:3, y:3, a:3, b:3, c:3, d:3);
                a := ord(b)
                end; { of p2 }

        begin { p1 }
                d := 'x';
                writeln ('in p1:', x:3, y:3, a:3, b:3, c:3, d:3);
                x: = y; y: = 0; b: = chr(a); c: = chr(x);
                p2;
                writeln('out p1: ', x:3, y:3, a:3, b:3, c:3, d:3)
        end; { of p1 }

begin { program block }
        a: = 1; b: = 2; c: = 3;
        p1(a,b);
        p1(b,c);
        p1(c,a)
end; { of block }
```

*6. Assume that we had a procedure that merged two sorted lists a and b and produced a new master list c containing all the elements of both a and b. The parameters to the procedure are:

(a) a—a 50 element integer array.

(b) asize—an integer value giving the number of elements in a ($0 <=$ asize $<= 50$).

(c) b—a 2000 element integer array.

(d) bsize—an integer value giving the number of elements in b ($0 <=$ bsize $<= 2000$).

(e) c—the new master list. It will be a 2050 element integer array.

(f) csize—the number of elements placed into the list c ($0 <=$ csize $<= 2050$).

(g) switch—a signal flag (see Style Clinic 8-5) set to true if the merge operation was successful, and set to false otherwise.

For each of the seven parameters to the procedure merge, state what parameter passing mechanism (variable or value) you would probably use.

*7. Given the following recursive function

```
function dunno (m:integer):integer;
var
      value : integer;
begin
    if m = 0 then
        value := 3
    else
        value := dunno(m – 1)+5;
    dunno := value;
    writeln ('current values of m and value are', m, value)
end; { of dunno }
```

what output is produced by the following statement?

```
writeln(dunno(3));
```

8. What is the output produced by the following program?

```
program rec(output);

    function p(x:real; n:integer):real;
    begin
        writeln(' in p: ', x:6:1, n:3);
        if n = 0 then
            p := 1.0
        else
            if odd(n) then
                p:=x*sqr(p(x,n div 2))
            else
                p:=sqr(p(x,n div 2));
        writeln('end of p')
    end; { of function p }

begin
    writeln(p(2.0,13))
end. { of program rec }
```

*9. Write a subprogram that computes the value of an investment p after n years of interest at rate r compounded quarterly. Should your subprogram be a procedure or a function? Should the parameters be passed by value or as variables?

10. Write a procedure that accepts a character string and returns the same character string with all blanks deleted, along with an integer that indicates how many blanks existed in the input string. What will be the parameters of the procedure and what will be their type and passing mechanism?

11. Write a complete Pascal function that computes sin(x) using the approximation formula.

$$\sin(x) \approx \frac{x}{1!} - \frac{x^3}{3!} + \frac{x^5}{5!} - \frac{x^7}{7!} + \ldots$$

The number of terms of the series to be used should be a parameter of the function. For example, sin(y, 3) should compute sin(y) using the first three terms of the series.

12. Write a complete Pascal function that *integrates* another function f(x) between two points a and b. To integrate a function means to determine the total area contained under its curve.

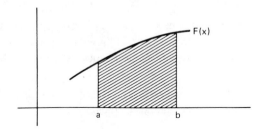

One way to do this is to approximate the area using a number of rectangles.

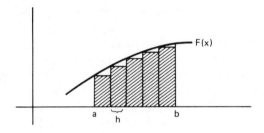

Obviously, the more rectangles used, the better the approximation. If we assume that there are n rectangles, then the approximation to the integral I can be written as

$$I = h(f(a) + f(a + h) + f(a + 2h) + \ldots + f(a + [n - 1]h))$$

where h is the width of each rectangle and is defined as

$$h = \frac{b - a}{n}, \quad n > 0$$

Your function should be able to integrate an arbitrary function f between any limits a and b.

13. Write a Pascal program to solve the following problem.

Read in a list of integer values from data cards. Each data card may contain one or more integer values and the end of the entire data set will be indicated by an end-of-file. Every value read should be in the range 200 to 800. Print out the following two pieces of information.

(a) The list in ascending order.

(b) The first, second, and third quartiles. The first quartile is the score that has 25% lower scores and 75% higher scores. The second quartile (median) is the score that has 50% below and 50% above. The third quartile is the score that has 75% lower and 25% above.

In order to write this program you may assume that there is a procedure called "bubblesort" and a function called "median" with the following capabilities.

Bubblesort. This procedure will sort an integer array into ascending order using a technique called the bubble sort.

Median. This function will accept an integer array in ascending order and return as a result the value of the median, or middle, element.

After writing the main program assuming that these two subprograms exist, write the specifications for the two modules "median" and "bubblesort." These specifications should include the parameters that are required and the operations that must be performed. When this problem is completed, go on to Exercise 14.

14. (a) Write the Pascal procedure called "bubblesort" that was described in Exercise 13. The bubble sort technique sorts a list by comparing the first and second items in the list and exchanging their positions if they are out of order. It then compares the second and third items, the third and fourth, and so on, until it has compared all items in the list. This entire operation is called a single *pass*. This is repeated until the list is eventually in order. Here is a simple example.

10	10	10
30	25	25
25	30	26
78	26	30
26	78	78
Exchanges during pass 1	Exchanges during pass 2	Sorted list

Your procedure should work for any integer array up to a limit of 200 elements.

(b) Write the Pascal function "median" that was described in the previous exercise. Now test the entire program composed of the main program from Exercise 13 and the two subprograms from Exercise 14.

15. A student was given the job of writing a Pascal procedure to find the average of a list of up to 200 examination scores in the range 0 to 150. Here is what was produced.

```
procedure avg;
begin
    total: = 0.0; average: = 0.0; bad: = 0;
    if (number<1) or (number>200)
        then writeln(' improper number of scores ')
        else begin
            i: = 1;
            while i <= number do
                begin
                if(list[i]<0.0) or
                  (list[i]>150.0)
                    then bad: = bad + 1
                    else total: = total + list[i];
                i: = i + 1
                end;
            average: = total/(number − bad);
            writeln('the average is',average)
            end
end; { of avg }
```

*(a) Assume that the procedure avg was going to be put into a program library and used by different people. Within this context, discuss the poor programming habits and poor style displayed by the procedure as it is currently written.

(b) Rewrite avg to remedy these problems.

(c) Write the documentation needed for avg so that it can be intelligently and properly utilized.

16. In Section 7.4 we developed a program to do decryption of messages using a simple substitution cypher. Look back over that listing (Figure 7-12) and decide how that program might be better organized and easier to follow with the aid of procedure and function subprograms. Rewrite that program using the subprograms that you have identified and named. Discuss the advantages that you see between the cypher program as it was developed in Chapter 7 and the modularized version that you developed for this exercise.

17. Complete the development of the payroll program begun in Section 8.9. Write all the subprograms identified in Figure 8-18 and add any new ones you feel might be useful.

Chapter 9

MORE STRUCTURED DATA TYPES—RECORDS AND SETS

9.1 INTRODUCTION

In Chapter 7 we introduced the first Pascal structured data type, called the array. It was a very useful and important data structure and allowed us to expand significantly the types of programs we could develop and the problems we could solve. In many programming languages (BASIC, FORTRAN) the array is the *only* structured data type available. However, one of the major distinguishing features of Pascal is its enormous wealth of both scalar and structured data types (refer to Figure 3-1 for a summary of all data types available in Pascal). In this chapter we introduce two new data types—the *record* and the *set*—and give extensive examples of their usage. In the next chapter we introduce two additional data structures—the *file* and the *pointer*.

9.2 RECORDS

9.2.1 Simple Record Structures

We have seen that an array can be a useful data structure because it allows us to refer to a collection of identically typed objects by a single name. There are many times, however, when we wish to deal with a collection of elements that are not all of identical type. For example, the following is a typical collection of academic information about a single student:

1. *Name:* A 20 element array of characters.
2. *Year in School:* An integer between 1 and 4.
3. *Grade-point Average:* Real.
4. *Fees Paid:* Boolean.

However, we could not place this information in a four-element "student array" because the data types of the elements are not identical.

Pascal deals with this problem by providing another structured data type called a *record*. In a record structure, the individual components, called *fields,* may have different types. A record can have any number of fields, and each field is given a unique name called the *field identifier*. The syntax of the **type** declaration to create a record structure is shown in Figure 9-1.

In Figure 9-1 the "field identifiers" are any valid Pascal identifiers, and the "type definition" can be *any* Pascal scalar or structured data type, including an array or another record. (This recursive use of data structures is very important and we will discuss it at length a little later.)

As an example of the syntax of a record structure, let us create a student record with the academic information described at the beginning of this section.

```
type studentrec = record
        name : array [1. .20] of char;
        year  : 1. .4;
        gpa   : real;
        fees  : boolean
    end; { studentrec }

var student : studentrec;
```

The variable "student" is now a record structure with four component fields called name, year, gpa, and fees. Notice that these fields do not have to be identical in type and can be either scalar types (integer, real, boolean) or other structured types (a 20 element array, in this example).

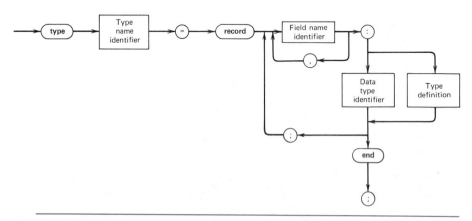

Figure 9-1. Syntax of the **record** structure.

As a second example we define a record structure to store the current date.

```
type date = record
     dayname    : (mon, tue, wed, thur, fri, sat, sun);
     month      : (jan, feb, mar, apr, may, jun, jul, aug, sep, oct, nov, dec);
     day        : 1..31;
     year       : integer
end; { date record }

var today, tomorrow, yesterday : date;
```

Now the three variables today, tomorrow, and yesterday are all identical record structures with four component fields—dayname, month, day, and year.

Accessing the elements of a record is quite different from accessing the elements of an array. There are no subscripts with the record structure. Instead, access into the record is via a *path-name* using the following syntax:

```
record-variable-name.field-identifier
```

This notation allows us to access the individual field of "record-variable-name" called "field-identifier." For example, to set today's date to Sunday, July 4, 1982, we could do the following.

```
today.dayname    := sun;
today.month      := jul;
today.day        := 4;
today.year       := 1982
```

The field-identifier in a path name must explicitly name the component we are referring to. We cannot use a variable to designate the component. This error is frequently made because we wish to perform an operation on a record similar to the following operation on arrays.

```
for i := 1 to 100 do
     sum := sum + x[i];
```

As i varies from 1 to 100, we will process every element of the array. Thus, some people think it would be nice to do something similar with records, and "index through" the field names.

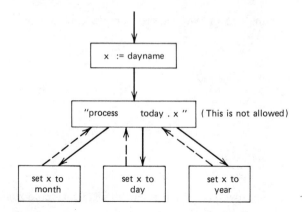

This type of variable path-name is illegal and is not allowed in Pascal. We must explicitly name the component we are accessing by its fixed and unique field name. Thus, in comparing records to arrays we see that, with records, the accessing method is somewhat more restrictive, but the record provides a more flexible structure since its components can be of arbitrary type.

If the field we are specifying is a simple scalar type, then the field name will be a single identifier (as in the components of record type date). However, if the field we are referring to is itself a structured type, then the field name will need to be more complex in order to identify exactly the individual components. Referring back to the definition of the record structure studentrec, the path-name:

student.year

refers to an integer quantity in the range 1 to 4. However,

student.name

refers to a 20 element character array. In order to identify any individual character within that array we must use, in addition to the field name, the standard subscript notation discussed in Chapter 7.

student.name[1], . . . , student.name[20]

The following is an example of how we might initialize the four fields of the student record described earlier.

```
for i := 1 to 20 do
    read (student.name[i]);
student.year := 1; { freshman }
student.gpa := 4.0;
student.fees := true
```

If you look back at the examples we have done so far, you will probably notice that the path-name syntax can be quite cumbersome. We frequently find ourselves writing the identical preface to a sequence of path-names, as in:

yesterday.dayname
yesterday.month
yesterday.day
yesterday.year

This repetition can be cumbersome and bothersome.

Pascal has a statement to deal with just this problem—the **with** statement. The syntax of the **with** is shown in Figure 9-2. The scope of the **with** is the statement following the reserved word **do** (which can, of course, be a compound statement). Within the scope of the **with** statement, all fields in the record variables mentioned in the **with** can be referred to by their field identifiers only. Pascal will build the correct path name to properly access that field. For example, we could rewrite the examples of this section in the following way.

```
(a)  with student do
     begin
         for i := 1 to 20 do
             read(name[i]);
         year  := 1; { freshman }
         gpa   := 4.0;
         fees  := true
     end { with }

(b)  with today do
     begin
         dayname   := sun;
         month     := jul;
         day       := 4;
         year      := 1982
     end { with }
```

The **with** statement provides a convenient shorthand notation to reduce the burden of accessing and processing record structures.

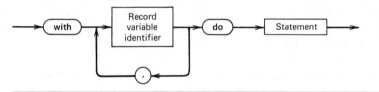

Figure 9-2. Syntax of the **with** statement.

We will conclude this section with an example of the use of records in a program. We will write a procedure called inventory that does some elementary inventory management. Assume that for each part in our inventory we maintain the following data.

```
type partrec     = record
     partnum      : integer;   { part number }
     description  : array [1. .20] of char;
     onhand       : integer;   { quantity on hand }
     unitcost     : real;      { unit cost in dollars }
     orderamt     : integer;   { amount to order when short }
     ordered      : boolean    { is this part backordered }
end;
```

The procedure we will write should take an integer variable called amount, the part record for a single part, and perform the following operations.

1. If amount is positive, this represents a shipment *into* inventory. We should increase the amount on hand, and print out the total dollar value of these parts.

2. If amount is negative, this represents a removal *from* inventory. We must ensure that we have a sufficient supply on hand and, if not, order more parts to replenish our supply. (Assume that the actual ordering is done by a procedure called orderproc not written here.)

The procedure to accomplish this is shown in Figure 9-3. (We have deliberately omitted the use of the **with** statement to provide additional examples of path-name syntax.)

9.2.2 Hierarchical Record Structures

We stated in the previous section that a field of a record can be any arbitrary data type. We gave examples of fields that were scalar variables and fields that were arrays. We will now generalize that even further to say that a field of a record can be anything, *including another record.* For example, a Pascal record declaration to create a mailing record might look like the declarations in Figure 9-4 on page 328. The variable parcel is now a record structure with three fields called name, address, and postage. The first two of these fields are themselves record structures with three and five fields, respectively. These subfields could theoretically have been additional nested record structures.

The path name into a hierarchical record must now specify *all* intermediate record structures that must be traversed to arrive at the desired field. For example, the nine fields of the variable parcel would be accessed with the following path-names.

```
procedure inventory (var part:partrec; amount:integer);

{ example of the use of record structures to do simple
  inventory management                                              }

var
    i       : integer;    { for loop index }
    value   : real;        { total dollar value of part inventory }

begin
    if amount > 0 then { shipment into inventory }
    begin
        part.onhand := part.onhand + amount;
        value := part.unitcost * part.onhand;
        writeln('part no', part.partnum);
        for i := 1 to 20 do
            write (part.description[i]);
        writeln;
        writeln ('total value = $', value:12:2)
    end
    else
        begin { shipment out of inventory }
            if part.onhand < abs(amount) then
            begin
                { order the missing part using the
                  procedure orderproc not shown here }
                orderproc (part.partnum, part.orderamt);
                part.ordered := true;
                { take what you can out of inventory }
                part.onhand := 0
            end
            else
                part.onhand := part.onhand − abs(amount)
        end
end; { procedure inventory }
```

Figure 9-3. Inventory program to demonstrate use of records.

```
parcel.name.first[i] (i = 1, . . ., 25)
parcel.name.last[i]
parcel.name.middle
parcel.address.streetnum
parcel.address.streetname[i]
parcel.address.city[i]
parcel.address.state[i]
parcel.address.zip
parcel.postage
```

```
type string = array [1. .25] of char;

     mailrecord      = record

          name          : record
               first    :    string;
               last     :    string;
               middle :    char
                         end; { name record }

          address       : record
               streetnum    : integer;
               streetname  : string;
               city             : string;
               state           : string;
               zip              : integer
                         end; { address record }

          postage :      real
     end; { mailrecord }

var parcel : mailrecord;
```

Figure 9-4. Hierarchical **record** declaration.

In these large hierarchical structures, the path names can get quite long and complex, as we just saw. In this environment, the proper use of a **with** statement can save quite a lot of writing. The Pascal fragment in Figure 9-5 shows how we might use the **with** statement along with the previous record structure to print out mailing labels in the following format.

```
last, first middle.
street address
city, state
zip
```

We can go even further with this idea of building complex, hierarchical data structures. What if, instead of maintaining information about only a single parcel, we had an entire collection of parcels, each of which was described by identical mailing information. This leads us back to the **array**—a collection of identical elements. This time the identical elements are the mailrecords that we described in Figure 9-4.

To create the data structure that we just described, we would write the following.

```
with parcel.name, parcel.address do
begin
     for i := 1 to 25 do write (last [i]);
     write (', ');
     for i := 1 to 25 do write (first[i]);
     write (' ', middle, '.');
     writeln;
     write (streetnum:5, ' ')
     for i := 1 to 25 do write (streetname[i]);
     writeln;
     for i := 1 to 25 do write (city[i]);
     write (', ');
     for i := 1 to 25 do write (state[i]);
     writeln;
     writeln (zip:5)
end { with }
```

Figure 9-5. Example of a **with** statement and a hierarchical record.

```
const
     max = 500; { maximum size of the parcel array }

type
     parcelarray = array [1. .max] of maiirecord;

var
     dailymail : parcelarray;
```

Now dailymail is a 500 element array in which each element is the mailrecord described earlier. The path name to any individual field must now include this additional level of structure.

> dailymail[1].name.last[1]. The first character of the last name on the first parcel.
> dailymail[5].address.zip. The zip code portion of the address of the 5th parcel.
> dailymail[500].postage. The amount of postage for the 500th parcel.

This discussion points out a very important principle in Pascal. Both the **array** and the **record** data structures are totally recursive; that is, they can be defined in terms of each other to build up very complex, but very interesting, structures. If we look at the type dailymail, we see that:

1. It is an array of records.
2. The records contain subfields that are themselves records.
3. These inner records contain fields that are arrays.

This type of hierarchical construction of data structures is very common in Pascal and is a point that will be covered in additional detail in courses in data structures and advanced programming techniques.

9.2.3   Record Variants

There is one final area of discussion related to the Pascal record structure. *Record variants* allow us to set up a record whose precise structure may be slightly different for different variables. For example, suppose we want to set up an array of records that contains student enrollment information for a university. The components of the record might be:

1. Name.
2. Student identification number.
3. Grade-point average.
4. Year started.
5. Receiving financial aid?
   If so, how much this year and how much on a cumulative basis?
   If not, has the student received financial aid in the past?

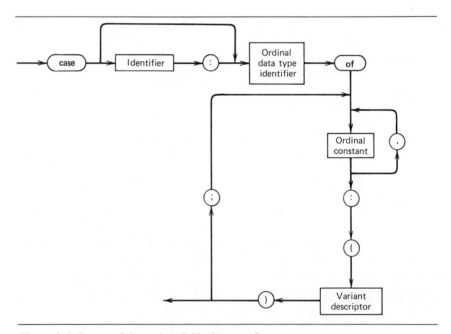

Figure 9-6. Syntax of the variant field of a **record** structure.

The last component is of particular interest. If a student has received financial aid, we want to record this year's amount and a cumulative total. Of course, there is no need for entries in these areas if a student is not currently receiving aid, so these fields need not be present for all students. However, in this case, we want to record whether the student has ever received financial aid. We call this kind of information *variant fields*.

We can set up a record structure with variant fields by using a **case** statement to specify the circumstances under which each variant is used. Each variant has associated with it a list of components, and each component has a type. The components and their types are enclosed in parentheses, and all of the variants are listed after the invariant portion of the record structure. Component names cannot be duplicated, even in different variants. The syntax of the variant portion of a record is shown in Figure 9-6.

As an example, we will create the student enrollment structure discussed earlier.

```
type studentrecord = record
    name          : array [1. .20] of char;
    id            : integer;
    gpa           : real;
    yearstarted   : integer;
    financialaid  : boolean;
    case financialaid of     { the variant field }
        true    : (currentamt : real;
                        total : real);
        false   : (pastaid : boolean)
end; { studentrecord record }

var sheldon : studentrecord;
```

If a student has received financial aid, then the field financialaid will be true, and two additional fields will exist: currentamt and total. If financial aid is false, then only one additional field—the boolean variable pastaid—will be in the record.

Because the variant part depends on the component financialaid, which is defined in the same record structure, we can achieve a slight economy of notation by combining the declaration of financialaid with the **case** clause.

```
case financialaid : boolean of
    true    : (currentamt : real;
                    total : real);
    false   : (pastaid : boolean)
```

The previous example declares financialaid to be a field in the record *and* it uses it as the selector for the appropriate variant field.

If financialaid is true, then we can reference the following two fields.

sheldon.currentamt
sheldon.total

If financialaid is false, then we can reference

sheldon.pastaid

When creating a record structure with variant fields, you must keep the following two rules in mind.

1. There can be only one variant field in a record. (However, there can be any number of alternatives for that variant.)
2. The variant field must be the last field of the record, following all invariant fields.

As a second example of variant record structures, we show the creation of a record structure for storing marital information:

```
type status = (married, divorced, widowed);

    maritalrec          = record
        name            : array [1. .20] of char;
        age             : integer;
        sex             : (male, female);
    case maritalstatus : status of
        married    : (length : integer;
                      children : integer;
                      spousesname : array [1. .20] of char);
        divorced   : (divorcedate: record
                            month: integer;
                            year: integer
                          end);
        widowed  : (yearofdeath : integer;
                    insurance : boolean)
    end; { marital record }
```

The record data structure will also be used in a more interesting example in the case study shown in Section 9.4.

9.3 SETS

When we worked with the array and the record data structures we did so by manipulating the individual elements of the structure. We never worked with the entire array or record at one time or with a single operation. For example, if we wished to search an array, we would do so by looking at each individual array element and comparing it to the desired key. If we wanted to fill a record we would separately input a value into each field of the record.

A *set* is a Pascal structured data type that, like the array and record, is a collection of elements. However, unlike the array or record, we do not index and access the individual elements that belong to a specific set. Instead, we work with the entire set as a single structure.

The elements that comprise any particular set are chosen from a collection of objects termed the *base type*. To create a set data type in Pascal, we use the **type** declaration shown in Figure 9-7. The base type of Figure 9-7 must be an ordinal data type—integer, boolean, char, or user-defined (or a subrange thereof).

The following are examples of syntactically valid **type** declarations.

```
type colors = (red, blue, yellow, green, purple, orange, white);

    letterset = set of 'a'..'z';
    colorset = set of colors;
  numberset = set of 1..100;
```

In the latter three examples the base type is a subrange of char, colors, and a subrange of the integers, respectively.

We may now create variables of these newly declared types. Values assigned to these variables will be sets whose elements (called *members*) are chosen from the specified base type. To indicate a set constant, we use the syntactic notation shown in Figure 9-8 on the top of the next page.

For example, consider the following declarations.

```
var
      a,b,c: letterset; { from previous declarations }
       x,y: colorset;
        z: numberset;
```

Now a, b, c, x, y, and z are variables that can be assigned the value of a set with members of the appropriate base type. If we wished to make the variable called a the set containing the vowels, we would write the following.

```
a := ['a', 'e', 'i', 'o', 'u']
```

Figure 9-7. Syntax of the **set** declaration.

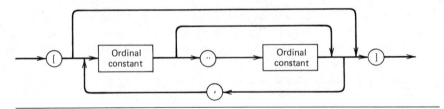

Figure 9-8. Syntax of set references.

If we wanted x to be a set containing the primary colors, we could write

> *x := [red, blue, yellow]*

Likewise, all of the following are valid set assignments.

> *b := ['a'..'d', 'f'];* { *this set will contain the characters 'a', 'b', 'c', 'd', 'f'* }
>
> *c := [ ];* { *this is called the empty set* }
>
> *y := [white];*
>
> *z := [1, 2, 3, 5, 8, 13, 21, 34, 55, 89]*

As with any data type in Pascal, we will want to do more complex operations than simply assigning a value to a variable. We will also want the ability to construct expressions using set variables. In Pascal there are seven operators that work on set variables; they are listed in Figure 9-9. These operators fall into three categories.

1. The operators that operate on two sets to produce a new set (union, difference, intersection).
2. The operators that operate on two sets to produce a boolean value ($=$, $<>$, $<=$).
3. The operator that operates on one set and one ordinal variable to produce a boolean value (membership).

If we assume that we have executed the previously shown assignments, then the following are examples of the use of set operators.

> *c := a + b* { *c is ['a', 'b', 'c', 'd', 'e', 'f', 'i', 'o', 'u']* }
>
> *c := a − b* { *c is ['e', 'i', 'o', 'u']* }
>
> *c := a * b* { *c is ['a']* }
>
> *y := y + [red, blue]* { *y is now [white, red, blue]* }
>
> *y := (y − x) − [white]* { *y is now [ ]* }

+	Set union	An element is contained in the *union* of two sets, denoted a + b, if and only if it is an element of set a or set b or both.
−	Set difference	An element is contained in the *difference* of two sets, denoted a − b, if and only if it is an element of set a but not an element of set b.
*	Set intersection	An element is contained in the *intersection* of two sets, denoted a*b, if and only if it is an element of both set a and set b.
=	Set equality	The relation a = b is true if and only if every member of set a is a member of set b and every member of set b is a member of set a.
<>	Set inequality	The relation a<>b is true if and only if the relation a = b is false.
< =	Set inclusion	The relation a< = b is true if and only if every member of set a is also a member of set b. In effect, the relationship a< = b says that the set a is a subset of set b.
in	Set membership	If a is an element of type t, and b is a set defined on the base type t, the relation a **in** b is true if and only if the element a is contained in set b.

Figure 9-9. The operators that apply to set variables.

The following four examples assume that n has been declared to be a boolean variable and that the set variable z is as previously defined.

```
n := ([1,2,3] = z);        { n is false }
n := ([1,2,3] <= z);       { n is true }
n := 1 in z;               { n is true }
n := ([1,2,3] = [3,2,1])   { n is true—notice that the order
                             of the members in a set is immaterial }
```

The set data type is useful in many situations, and the following examples illustrate two of the most important.

One of the more cumbersome programming operations is checking a scalar variable to see if it is equal to one specific scalar constant out of many. (In some, but not all, situations this can be handled using the **case** statement.) The resulting programs frequently contain large, awkward constructions of either boolean expressions or **if** statements. For example, Figure 9-10a shows a procedure that is supposed to count the number of non-blank characters on a line. However, it must exclude from that count the following 11 punctuation marks:

'.' ',' ';' ':' '(' ')' '[' ']' '?' '"' '-'

Notice the somewhat long and awkward formulation of the boolean expression in the **if** statement. This type of construction can be greatly simplified through the use of a set and the set membership operation. Using a set, we can perform the entire compare operation with a single set membership test. This procedure is shown in Figure 9-10*b*. Comparing the previous two programs makes the advantage of a set quite obvious.

Sets are also very useful in the situation where there are n possible events and we wish to maintain a record of exactly which events do and do not occur. For example, during data validation, a number of different error types can be encountered. If we simply use a boolean variable 'correct' to indicate the presence or absence of

```
procedure countchar (line:linetype; maxlen:integer;
                     length:integer; var count:integer);

{ entry conditions:
  line − an array of characters of length <= maxlen
  length − the actual size of the array line.
           length must be <= maxlen
  exit conditions:
  count − the number of non-blank characters in line
           excluding the following 11 punctuation symbols
           . , ; : ( ) [ ] ? ' -
           count is set to −1 if there is an error in length }

var
      i : integer; { loop index }

begin
      count := 0;
      if length <= maxlen then
      begin
          for i := 1 to length do
              if (line [i] <> '.') and (line [i] <> ',') and
                 (line [i] <> ';') and (line [i] <> ':') and
                 (line [i] <> '(') and (line [i] <> ')') and
                 (line [i] <> '[') and (line [i] <> ']') and
                 (line [i] <> '?') and (line [i] <> '-') and
                 (line [i] <> ' ') and (line [i] <> '''') then
                  count := count + 1
      end
      else { illegal size of line length }
          count := − 1
end; { procedure countchar }
```

Figure 9-10. (*a*) Counting characters without sets.

type *charset* = **set of** *char;* { *these declarations and assignments will be in the calling program* }

   .

   .

   .

var *punctuation : charset;*

   .

   .

   .

punctuation := [':', ',', ';', ':', '(', ')', '[', ']',
                 '?', '"', '-', ' '];

   .

   .

   .

countchar(inputline, maxsize, size, punctuation, count)

   .

   .

   .

procedure *countchar (line : linetype; maxlen : integer; length :*
                integer; omit : charset; **var** *count :*
                integer);
{ *entry conditions*
        line — an array of characters of length <= maxlen
       length — the actual size of the array line. length must be <= maxlen
        omit — a set of characters that contains all characters to be excluded from
              the count, including the blank

exit conditions
        count — the number of non-blank characters in line, not counting any
                excluded characters in the set omit. Count is set to −1 if there is
                an error in the length field. }

var *i : integer;* { *loop index* }

begin
      count := 0;
      if *length <= maxlen* **then**
           for *i := 1* **to** *length* **do**
                 if not *(line [i]* **in** *omit)* **then**
                       count := count + 1
      else
           count := −1
end; { *procedure countchar* }

Figure 9-10. (*b*) Counting characters with sets.

an error, we will lose the information about exactly *which* errors occurred. This would be important information to provide to the user who wants to know exactly what went wrong so that he or she can correct the mistake.

A set is a simple way to keep a record of both the presence of errors and the exact type of error that occurred. If we have a set defined over a base type of all possible errors, the empty set would represent the absence of errors, while the presence of any specific element in the set would represent the presence of that specific error type. Figure 9-11 shows a data validation procedure for checking payroll data. The specifications are as follows.

> *2.30 <= payrate <= 15.00*
> *0 <= hours worked <= 54*
> *0 <= social security no. <= 999999999*

The techniques of Figure 9-11 can be generalized to any programming problem in which we need to keep a record of exactly which m of n possible events actually did occur.

One final word about sets. Because of the way sets are generally implemented, some versions of Pascal severely limit the maximum number of elements allowed in the base type. This limit may be fairly small, and it could possibly prohibit you from performing some meaningful and useful set operations. For example, in this section

```
type errortypes = (minpayraterror, maxpayraterror, hourserror, numbererror);
     errorset   = set of errortypes;
var      errors: errorset;
           .

           .

           .

procedure validate(pay : real; hours, number : integer; var result : errorset);
{ entry conditions
     pay — payrate
     hours — hours worked
     number — social security number

exit conditions
     result — a set of the following error conditions:
          minpayraterror   — included if pay < $2.30
          maxpayraterror   — included if pay > $15.00
          hourserror       — included if hours < 0 or > 54
          numbererror      — included if social security number < 0 or > 999-99-
                               9999 }
```

```
begin
    result := [ ];
    if pay < 2.30 then
        result := result + [minpayraterror];
    if pay > 15.0 then
        result := result + [maxpayraterror];
    if (hours < 0) or (hours > 54) then
        result := result + [hourserror];
    if (number < 0) or (number > 999999999) then
        result := result + [numbererror]
end; { procedure validate }
            .
            .
            .
begin { main program }
            .
            .
            .
    validate (pay, hours, socsec, errors);
    if minpayraterror in errors then
        { procedure to handle minimum pay rate error }
    if maxpayraterror in errors then
        { procedure to handle maximum payrate error }
    if hourserror in errors then
        { procedure to handle error in hours worked field }
    if numbererror in errors then
        { procedure to handle error in social security field }
    if errors = [ ] then
            .
            · { here is where we would process completely correct data }
            .
end. { main program }
```

Figure 9-11. Data validation using sets.

we made the following declarations.

```
type letterset = set of 'a'..'z';
     charset  = set of char;
```

In the first case the basetype 'a'..'z' probably contains 26 elements. In the second case the number of elements depends on the size of the character set for your machine and would typically be 64, 128, or 256. Whether either of the declarations just shown would actually be valid depends on the limitation on the size of set basetypes at a particular installation. This information must be provided by your instructor. As a specific example of these limits, one current implementation of Pascal on a Control Data Cyber series computer accepts basetypes with no more than 59 elements. However, the Cyber series has a 64 element character set. So while the first of the previously shown declarations is acceptable, the second one is not, and we would get an error message—even though the statement is, at least syntactically, perfectly correct. This is an unfortunate situation that makes our programs highly machine-dependent. However, it is something that you must be aware of when using the **set** data type.

9.4 CASE STUDY—THE GAME OF LIFE

The Game of Life is a fascinating simulation game developed by the mathematician John Horton Conway of Cambridge University.[1] It is intended both as a diversion and as a model for the life cycle of societies of living organisms. Conway's game is played on a very large (assumed infinite) checkerboard. Each square, or cell, on the board represents the possible location of a living organism. Each cell has eight adjacent cells that may be either occupied or empty.

1	2	3
8	✳	4
7	6	5

When an adjacent cell is occupied by a living organism, we say that it is our *neighbor*. Conway's three basic rules, or "genetic laws" as he calls them, are quite simple.

1. *Birth*. Each empty cell adjacent to exactly three neighbors will have a birth in the next generation. Otherwise, the cell remains empty.

2. *Death*. Each occupied cell with exactly 0 or 1 neighbors dies of isolation and loneliness. Each occupied cell with 4 or more neighbors dies of overpopulation.

3. *Survival*. Each occupied cell with exactly 2 or 3 neighbors survives to the next generation.

All births and deaths occur simultaneously, and the application of these three genetic laws to an entire board position to produce a new board position is called a *generation*. The game is typically played until one of three things happens: the society dies out

[1]See "Mathematical Games," *Scientific American, 223* (4), October 1970, pp. 120–123 for complete details.

Read the initial board position
Repeat the following forever
        Compute births, deaths, survivors
        Produce the new board
        Write the new board
End of the repeat loop

Figure 9-12. Initial Game of Life representation.

completely, it reaches some "steady-state" pattern that either does not change or oscillates forever, or play is halted when time and interest wane. Depending on the initial configuration, the population growth may undergo startling, unexpected, and fascinating changes and will form interesting configurations that move, mutate, grow, or disappear entirely. Some examples of the patterns that can result from the Game of Life are shown on page 353.

The game is ideally suited to being programmed on a computer. In fact, Conway himself used a computer in his early studies of the game to study very complex patterns. The basic outline of the algorithm is quite simple (Figure 9-12).

However, this "solution" is much too simplistic because it does not take into account the pragmatic limitation of finite time and space. This solution is not even an algorithm, since it violates the criterion of termination in finite time. We need a way to halt the program. Our earlier discussion listed three criteria for termination.

1. Population dies out (that is, an empty board).
2. Steady state (i.e., generation [n + 1] = generation [n]; we will ignore the problem of oscillations over more than one generation).
3. Reaching a user-specified upper bound on the number of generations.

All three of these stopping criteria should be included in the algorithm.

Another question is how to represent the playing surface. Theoretically, it is viewed as an infinite two-dimensional checkerboard. Obviously, we cannot make that assumption when writing the program. We will be limited to a finite-sized n × n structure. This essentially puts a "fence" around the area where our organisms are allowed to grow. With these two refinements our algorithm might now look something like Figure 9-13 on the following page.

Before we translate this into Pascal we have quite a few more decisions to make. For example, how shall we input the initial board positions? Instead of forcing the user to specify the initial state of every cell on the board, it would be much more convenient to specify only the cells that are initially occupied. These cells typically represent only a small fraction of the overall board and will greatly reduce the amount of input data required. We can do this by specifying the exact (x, y) coordinates on

START
    Set the generation counter to 0
    Read n, the size of the board
    Read the upper limit on new generations
    Read the initial n × n board position
    Repeat the following until the new generation is empty, the new
        generation is the same as the old generation, or generation
        counter > upper limit
            Compute births in this generation
            Compute deaths in this generation
            Compute survivals in this generation
            Produce the new generation
            Write out the new generation
            Increment generation counter by 1
    End of the repeat loop
    Stop
END OF THE ALGORITHM

Figure 9-13. Game of Life algorithm—first refinement.

the board of the cells that initially contain organisms. To describe the following initial board position for a 5 × 5 game of life:

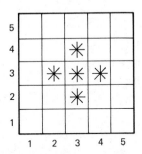

we would say

    2   3
    3   2
    3   3
    3   4
    4   3

To indicate the end of a set of data, we could use the end-of-file condition described earlier. However, that would limit our program to processing a single set of data per run. A more generalized approach would be to use a signal card, for example, 0 0 (again assuming we index our board beginning at 1), to indicate the end of each data set and the end-of-file to indicate the end of all data. This allows us to handle numerous data sets per run. Now the input phase of our algorithm, which was simply "Read the initial n × n board position," can be expanded and refined (Figure 9-14).

Another important question concerns how many distinct boards we will need. It would be difficult to use only a single board for this problem because all births and deaths occur simultaneously. We cannot change the contents of a cell until its effect on all its neighbors has been determined. Then, at the end of a generation, we must change all cells. If we assume that space is not critical, the most straightforward way to approach the problem is to have two boards called old-board and new-board. The births, deaths, and survivals from old-board will be recorded in new-board. When that generation is finished, what was the new-board will now become the old-board and the process will continue. This refinement is shown in Figure 9-15.

When producing the organisms of a new generation we must be very careful about how we handle boundary conditions. In the Game of Life, the board is viewed as an infinite space. In our version of the game, the organisms, of necessity, must be "caged" and strictly limited to the n × n bounds of the board. An attempt to wander

```
While we have not reached end-of-file do
        Initialize all board positions to "empty"
        Read the first board coordinate (x,y)
        While x and y are both not 0 do
                If x, y is a legal board position, then mark that position
                        as "occupied"
                Read the next board coordinate (x,y)
        End of the while loop
            .
            .
            .

            { process this data set }
            .
            .
            .

End of the while loop
```

Figure 9-14. Refinement of the input phase.

Change the current new-board to the old-board
Repeat for every cell in the old-board
    Determine if there has been a birth in this cell of
        old-board and store that fact in the corresponding
        cell of new-board
    Determine if there has been a death in this cell of
        old-board and store that fact in the corresponding
        cell of new-board
    Determine if the organism in this cell of old-board has survived and
        store that fact in the corresponding cell of new-board
End of the repeat loop
Write the new-board
Increment the generation-counter

Figure 9-15. Refinement of the processing loop.

outside this environment is strictly prohibited. So while a center cell (*a*) has 8 adjacent cells, an edge cell (*b*) has 5, and a corner cell (*c*) has only 3.

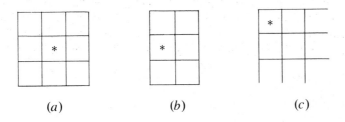

(*a*)   (*b*)   (*c*)

We must be very careful to avoid generating subscript expressions that are invalid and that would terminate the program abnormally. There are several approaches we can take in handling this boundary. For this case study we will assume that the spaces immediately beyond the edge of our board are always empty. Thus, in the previous diagram, the organism in (*b*) could never have more than 5 neighbors, while the organism in (*c*) will never have more than 3.

At this point, we ought to consolidate the pieces of our developing algorithm. If we combine Figures 9-13, 9-14, and 9-15, we have Figure 9-16. This is a fairly detailed algorithmic structure, but we will probably want to perform still another level of refinement before we begin to code in Pascal.

The last algorithmic development has to do with the application of the three genetic rules to a current board position. We will illustrate the refinement for determining whether a birth has occurred; the refinements for death and survival will be analogous (Figure 9-17).

START
    While we have not reached end-of-file do
        { Start a new game }
        Read in the upper limit on new generations
        Read in n, the size of the board
        Set the generation counter to 0
        Initialize all board positions to "empty"
        Read the first board coordinate (x,y)
        While x and y are both not 0 do
            { Read an initial board position }
            If (x,y) is a legal board position then mark it as
                "occupied" in that position of new-board
            Read the next board coordinate (x,y)
        End of the while loop { For initializing the board }
            { Now process that new starting position }
        Repeat until (the new generation is empty) or (the
        new generation is the same as the old generation)
        or (generation counter > upper limit)
            Change the current new-board to the old-board
            Repeat for every cell in old-board
                If there is a birth in this cell, store that
                    fact in the corresponding new-board cell
                If there is a death in this cell, store that
                    fact in the corresponding new-board cell
                If the organism in this cell has survived, store that fact
                    in the corresponding new-board cell
            End of the repeat loop { for one generation }
            Write the new-board
            Increment the generation counter
        End of the repeat loop { One game is now complete }
    End of the while loop { All games are completed }
    Stop
END OF THE ALGORITHM

Figure 9-16. The Game of Life algorithm (consolidated).

When we perform similar refinements to check for death and survival and incorporate these refinements into Figure 9-16, we will probably be in a position where it is worthwhile to begin coding. Now we must begin to choose specific Pascal data structures. The most important choice will have to do with the method for representing our two n × n boards—old-board and new-board. Since the contents of a cell will only be the values "occupied" or "empty," a reasonable structure might be

---

Check all neighbors of this cell (with proper care if the
   cell is on a boundary)
Tally the number of occupied cells
If (tally = 3) and the cell is currently empty then there
   is a birth

Figure 9-17. Checking for a birth.

type *cellstate = (empty, occupied);*
   boardtype = **array** *[1. .2, 1. .maxsize, 1. .maxsize]* **of** *cellstate;*

where maxsize is a symbolic constant that sets an upper limit on the size of our board.
   Another useful data type will be

neighborcount = **set of** *0. .8;*

which defines a set type with members that represent all the possible number of
neighbors of a single cell. We can use this type to define the conditions for birth,
death, and survival.

   var *survival, death, birth : neighborcount;*

   .
   .
   .

survival   : = [2,3];
death   : = [0,1,4,5,6,7,8];
birth   : = [3];

Finally, we will collect all the information related to the Game of Life board and
place it in a single **record** structure. This will facilitate passing the board information
around to the various procedures; that is, instead of passing many, many parameters,
we merely pass one record variable.

type *boardrecord =* **record**
   board   : boardtype;   *{ the actual board }*
   size   : 1. .maxsize;   *{ actual dimensions of the board }*
   old, new   : 1. .2;   *{ used for pointing to which elements of*
                                       board are now old-board and which are
                                       new-board }
      state   : (dead, stable, growing); { the state of the current generation }
      generation : integer   *{ generation # of the current board }*
   end; *{ boardrecord }*

We have now developed a reasonable algorithm, refined it a number of times so that the basic operations are fairly well understood, chosen the necessary data structures and, finally, made certain necessary assumptions where alternatives were available. It is important to realize that the coding phase should begin only now, after we have completed all of these operations to our complete satisfaction. Figure 9-18 shows a complete Pascal program to implement the Game of Life algorithm developed in this case study. The program uses three procedures.

Readboard. Reads in a new board position and validates that the input data are correct.

Writeboard. Writes out a board position on the output file using the character '*' to represent an occupied cell.

Countneighbors. Determines the number of neighbors of any cell on the board.

```
program gameoflife (input, output);

{ program to play the game of life as developed by H. L. Conway at the
  University of Cambridge }

const
    maxsize = 50; { maximum board size }

type
    cellstate   = (empty, occupied);
    boardtype   = array[1. .2, 1. .maxsize, 1. .maxsize] of cellstate;
    neighbour   = set of 0. .8;
    boardrecord = record
                    board      : boardtype; { actual board }
                    generation : integer;
                    new        : 1. .2; { pointer to new-board }
                    old        : 1. .2; { pointer to old-board }
                    size       : 1. .maxsize; { actual dimensions of the
                                                board }
                    state      : (dead, stable, growing) { state of the current
                                                generation }
                  end;

var
    alivecount    : integer; { number of living organisms }
    birth         : neighbour; { number of neighbours needed to cause a birth }
    boardinfo     : boardrecord; { all of the board information }
    change        : boolean; { record the change in new generations }
    death         : neighbour; { number of neighbours needed to cause a death }
    i, j          : 0. .maxsize; { array subscripts }
    maxgeneration : integer; { maximum number of generations }
    number        : integer; { number of neighbours for a specific cell }
    survival      : neighbour; { number of neighbours needed to survive }
    temp          : 1. .2; { used when interchanging old and new board pointers }
```

```
procedure readboard (var boardinfo:boardrecord; maxsize:integer);

{ procedure to read in the initial location of all organisms on the board. An
  attempt to place an organism in an illegal location will be detected and
  rejected. }

var
      i, j : integer; { for loop indices }
      x, y : integer; { location of an organism on the board }

begin
      with boardinfo do
      begin
            writeln ('the board is too big. it will be reset to',
            read (maxgeneration);
            writeln('please enter the board size');
            read (size);
            if size > maxsize then
            begin
                  writeln ('the board is too big. it will be reset to',
                              maxsize:2, 'x', maxsize:2);
                  size := maxsize
            end; { if }
            old := 1;
            new := 2;

            { initially set all elements in old board to empty }
            for i := 1 to size do
                  for j := 1 to size do
                        board [old, i, j] := empty;

            { now place organisms on the board }
            writeln('please enter coordinates of the initial organisms');
            writeln('enter 0 0 to terminate');
            read (x, y); { read the location of the first organism }
            while (x <> 0) and (y <> 0) do { any of the values equal to 0 indicates
                                                end of data }
            begin
                  if (x < 1) or (x > size) or
                     (y < 1) or (y > size) then
                  begin
                        write ('attempt to insert an organism in a nonexistent');
                        writeln ('cell location (', x:3, y:3, ').');
                        writeln ('the value will be disregarded.')
                  end
                  else
                        board [old, x, y] := occupied;
                        read (x, y) { the location of the next organism }
            end { while loop }
      end { with }
end; { procedure readboard }
```

procedure *countneighbour (boardinfo:boardrecord; x, y:integer;* **var**
                              count:integer);

*{ this procedure counts the number of neighbours of cell [x, y] in the old board
  and returns this value in the variable count. the procedure will correctly handle
  the problem of a cell on the boundary of the array   }*

var

down	: 0. .1;	*{ whether or not we have a bottom neighbour }*
i, j	: integer;	*{ for loop indices }*
left	: − 1. .0;	*{ whether or not we have a left neighbour }*
right	: 0. .1;	*{ whether or not we have a right neighbour }*
up	: − 1. .0;	*{ whether or not we have a top neighbour }*

begin
    with *boardinfo* **do**
    begin
        { first check the boundary conditions of cell[x, y] }
        if *x > 1* **then**
            left := − 1
        else
            left := 0;
        if *x < size* **then**
            right := 1
        else
            right := 0;
        if *y > 1* **then**
            up := − 1
        else
            up := 0;
        if *y < size* **then**
            down := 1
        else
            down := 0;
            { now count the number of neighbours of cell[x, y] }
        count := 0;
        for *i := left* **to** *right* **do**
            for *j := up* **to** *down* **do**
                if *(board [old, x + i, y + j] = occupied)* **and**
                    not *((i = 0) and (j = 0))* **then**
                    count := count + 1
                    *{ that last test is to ensure that we don't count the cell
                      itself as one of its neighbours }*
    end *{ with }*
end; *{ procedure countneighbours }*

```pascal
procedure writeboard (boardinfo : boardrecord);
{ this procedure writes out the current state of the new board. it prints an '*' if a
  cell is occupied }

const
     printchar = '*';

var
     i, j : integer; { for loop indices }

begin
     with boardinfo do
     begin
          writeln;
          writeln ('generation number', generation);
          writeln;
          for i := 1 to size do
          begin
               for j := 1 to size do
                    if board [new, i, j] = occupied then
                         write(printchar:1)
                    else
                         write(' ':1);
               writeln;
          end
     end { with }
end; { procedure writeboard }




begin { the main program }
     survival := [2, 3];
     death := [0, 1, 4, 5, 6, 7, 8];
     birth := [3];
     with boardinfo do
     begin
          while not eof do
          begin
               readboard (boardinfo, maxsize);
               generation := 1;

               { now process this new board until the population is dead, stable,
                 or we reach the maximum generation count }
               repeat
                    alivecount := 0; { number of living organisms on the current
                                       new board }
                    change := false; { records any changes in new generations }
```

```
for i := 1 to size do
    for j := 1 to size do
    begin
            { process cell[i, j] in the old board }
            countneighbours (boardinfo, i, j, number);
            { apply the three genetic rules }
            board[new, i, j] := empty;
            if (board[old, i, j] = empty) and
                (number in birth) then
            begin
                board[new, i, j] := occupied;
                change := true;
                alivecount := alivecount + 1
            end;
            if (board[old, i, j] = occupied) and
                (number in death) then
            begin
                board[new, i, j] := empty;
                change := true
            end;
            if (board[old, i, j] = occupied) and
                (number in survival) then
            begin
                board[new, i, j] := occupied;
                alivecount := alivecount + 1
            end
    end; { processing of each individual cell }

{ we have now completed a new generation.
  print it out.                                                   }
writeboard(boardinfo);
{ and set up for next generation }
generation := generation + 1;
temp := old; { switch the old and new board pointers }
old := new;
new := temp;
{ now set the state of the new board }
state := growing;
if alivecount = 0 then
    state := dead;
if not change then
    state := stable                          Continued on next page
```

Continued on next page

```
            until (state = dead) or (state = stable) or
                (generation > maxgeneration);
            { end of one data set. print out how it ended }

        case state of
            dead     : writeln('colony died.');
            stable   : writeln('colony is in a stable state.');
            growing : begin
                        write('maximum number of generations');
                        writeln('has been produced.')
                      end

        end { case }
      end { of while loop for all data sets }
    end { of with statement }
  end. { of main program }
```

Figure 9-18. The Game of Life program.

As an example of the output from this program, assume that we provided the following input data.

5	(the maximum number of generations)
6	(the board will be 6 × 6)

```
3    4
4    3
4    4
4    5
5    4
0    0  (end of the data set)
```

This would be equivalent to an initial board position as follows.

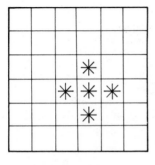

The output of the program would be as follows.

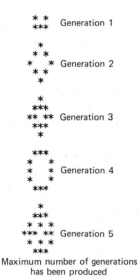

```
* *
***     Generation 1


   *
 * *
*     *  Generation 2
 * *
   *


   *
  ***
 ** **   Generation 3
  ***
   *


  ***
 *     *
 *     *  Generation 4
 *     *
  ***
```

```
     *
    ***
   * * *
  *** **   Generation 5
   * * *
    ***
```

Maximum number of generations
    has been produced

This case study was significantly more complex than any of the programs we have done so far. The development of such a large program was aided significantly by our use of algorithmic notation and the step-by-step refinement of each piece of the algorithm. All of these operations preceded the coding phase and greatly simplified that step, essentially making it not much more than a mechanical translation. In Chapter 11 we will have much more to say about the development of large, complex programs.

EXERCISES FOR CHAPTER 9

*1. Develop a record structure for the following data.

> *textbook information*
>> Author's name (last, first, middle).
>> Title.
>> Publisher (name, city, state).
>> Edition.
>> ISBN number.

2. Modify the textbook record from Exercise 1 to allow a book to have up to four co-authors.

*3. Create a data structure to store the information on 10,000 textbooks, each of which has the record structure shown in Exercise 1.

4. Using the date record definition shown in Section 9.2.1 (page 323), write a Pascal procedure that takes as input the record variable 'today' that has been set to today's date and returns as output parameters the record variables 'yesterday' and 'tomorrow,' which are set to yesterday's and tomorrow's dates, respectively. (Be careful of the end of month and end of year!)

*5. Write the **type** declaration for a record with the following structure.

> Employee name (last, first).
> Social security number.
> Department number.
> Dependents (integer).
> Base pay rate (real).

*6. Write a table look-up procedure that takes a record variable of the structure shown in Exercise 5 and looks up the social security number of that variable in a 2*n array with the following structure.

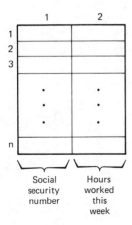

When the social security number is found, compute the total weekly pay from the following formula:

weekly pay = (base pay rate * hours worked)

If the social security number is not found in the table, set weekly pay to 0.

7. Using the definition of the array called dailymail on page 329, write a Pascal procedure that takes as input the variable dailymail and determines the following:

(a) How many packages require more than $10.00 in postage?
(b) Is there a package addressed to Schneider, Ruthann L.?
(c) How many packages are going to the University of Minnesota (zip code = 55455)?

8. Write a "teacher record" with the following variant structure.

(a) Name (last, first, middle initial).
(b) Date of appointment.
(c) Full time or part time appointment.
(d) Rank (professor, associate, assistant).
(e) If professor or associate professor, then
      date when tenure was granted and
      department in which tenure was granted.
   If assistant professor, then
      years of probationary service at the university.

9. Using the definition of maritalrec in Section 9.2.3 (page 332), write a Pascal procedure that takes a variable of this type and changes the status from married to divorced. The procedure must also set the components of the new variant.

10. Assume that:

    a := [1,2,3]
    b := [3,4,5,6]
    c := [2,4,6,8,10]
    d := [5]
    e := []

    What is the value of each of the following set operations?

    *(a) b + c
    *(b) b − c
    *(c) (a + b) − c
    *(d) (a * b) + (c * d)
     (e) a <= b
     (f) (a * b) = e
    *(g) 1 **in** a
     (h) **not** (6 **in** (c − b))

11. Assume that we have defined the following set variables.

    letters := ['a'..'z'];
    digits   := ['0'..'9'];
    special := ['.', '+', '−']

    Write the assignment operations to define new set variables, created from these three, that are as follows.

    *(a) A set called a, whose members are only those characters that can appear in a Pascal name.
    *(b) A set called b, whose members are only those characters that can appear in a real number in Pascal (scientific or decimal notation).
     (c) A set called c, comprising all of the characters just listed except the letter 'o'.

12. Write a Pascal **procedure** called validate that accepts three input parameters:

    lastname. A 20 element array of characters.

    len. The length of the last name.

    idnumber. A 6 digit identification number.

and returns as a result a set variable that indicates the presence or absence of each of the following error conditions.

(a) missing—len $<=$ 0. No last name was specified.

(b) sizerror—len $>$ 20. The name was too large to fit in the array and one or more characters was omitted.

(c) spellingerror—One of the characters in lastname is not an alphabetic character.

(d) iderror—The idnumber is not in the range 0 $<$ idnumber $<=$ 999999.

13. Modify the Game of Life program in Figure 9-18 so that it detects two stage oscillations. What this means is that the board position continuously flip-flops between only two states:

$$\ldots \to state\ 1 \to state\ 2 \to state\ 1 \to state\ 2 \to \ldots$$

Our existing program, which only keeps information on two generations (old and new) would not be able to detect this condition and would continue to produce new generations—even though nothing of interest is happening. The modified program should check for these oscillations and, if located, mark the board state as stable and terminate the data case. Discuss how you might generalize this modification so that it detects oscillations over k generations where k $>=$ 2.

14. Modify the Game of Life program so that the application of the three genetic rules is contained in a separate procedure rather than in the body of the main program:

procedure geneticrules (. . .);

The procedure should apply the three genetic rules to the current old-board and store that information in the new-board.

15. Write a Pascal **procedure** called 'dealer' that accepts as input a "deck of cards" in the following representation

```
type deck = array [1. .52] of cards;
     cards = record
                  rank : 1. .13; { j = 11, q = 12, k = 13 }
                  suit : (spades, hearts, diamonds, clubs)
             end; { of cards record }
```

and then "shuffles" the cards by putting them in some random sequence. (When doing this you may assume the existence of a **procedure** random(a,b,i) that produces random integer values i in the range a$<=$i$<=$b.)

Your procedure should then "deal out" four hands of 13 cards each into the following structure:

type *hands* = **array** [*1. .4, 1. .13*] **of** *cards;*

The procedure should return the four newly dealt hands as its result.

16. Write a Pascal **procedure** called 'bridgecount' that will count the number of points in the bridge hands just dealt in Exercise 15. The rules for determining points in bridge are as follows.

ace	= 4 pts	2 of a suit	= 1 pt
king	= 3 pts	1 of a suit	= 2 pts
queen	= 2 pts	0 of a suit	= 3 pts
jack	= 1 pt		

The procedure should count the points in all four hands and return the point count in a four-element array, one for each hand.

Chapter 10

MORE STRUCTURED DATA TYPES—FILES AND POINTERS

10.1 FILES

10.1.1 Introduction

In Pascal a *file* is a structured data type containing a sequence of elements of identical type. Although this definition may sound exactly like the definition of the array data structure given in Chapter 7, there are some significant conceptual differences.

An array is a data structure that is presumed to fit entirely within the available memory of a computer. Therefore, every element of an array is immediately available, and we simply index the desired element—A[1] or A[5000]. However, with the file data type, only a single element, called the *window*, is immediately available, as shown in Figure 10-1 on the following page. All other elements in the file, occurring either before or after the window, are not immediately accessible. They are presumed to exist on some external storage device such as a magnetic tape or disk drive. (However, the details of the specific storage device are transparent to the language, and we do not have to worry about them.) In order to access a file element not currently in the window we must read sequentially through the entire file until we come to the desired element. Only when that element comes into the window can we access and process it. (However, see Style Clinic 10-1 for a discussion of other possible file organizations.)

A second major difference between a file and an array is that the length of an array must be known at the time it is declared. However, a file can be of arbitrary and unlimited size, since we never look at more than a single item of the file at any one time. Referring again to Figure 10-1, the number of elements that may come before or after the current window can be as large as desired. It is not uncommon for a single file on a magnetic tape to contain 10,000,000 pieces of information!

A file can be viewed conceptually as a way for a program to communicate with

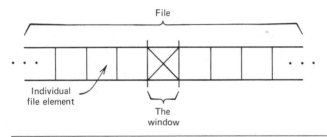

Figure 10-1. General structure of a file.

the "outside world." Information can be presented to a program by placing it in a file on some external storage device and having the program read it in. Likewise, a file can be viewed as a method for saving information and giving it a lifetime that extends beyond the execution lifetime of the program. When information is written out to a file it can be preserved on some external storage medium and made available for future processing. We have utilized these features already with the standard Pascal files input and output. We will now generalize this to arbitrary files with arbitrary elements.

Style Clinic 10-1

Direct Access Files

The file type described in Section 10.1.1 and diagrammed in Figure 10-1 is actually a specialized file type called a *sequential file* in which you must look sequentially through every element searching for what you want. (It is analogous to an audio cassette tape in which you must play or skip over every song to hear the one you want.) Since this is the only type of file supported by Pascal, it is the only type that we will describe in this chapter, and our use of the word "file" should be considered synonymous with the phrase "sequential file."

However, there are situations in which sequential files are horribly inefficient. It would be nice to have a file in which we could go directly to any file element without worrying about skipping over any other information. (This type might be considered roughly analogous to an LP record in which we can lift up the arm and place it down on any desired song.) These are called *direct access files* and are extremely important in many applications.

Standard Pascal does not have a direct access file capability and many people feel this is a shortcoming of the language. It has been included as a "nonstandard extension" in a number of compilers.

10.1.2 Creating and Using Files

To declare a file data type, we use the **type** declaration shown in Figure 10-2. The ''base type'' specifies the data type of each individual element of the file. This base type can be any Pascal data type, except another file. For example,

```
type
        datafile = file of integer;
       colorfile = file of (red, white, blue);
        charfile = file of char;
       arrayfile = file of array [1..10] of real;
     payrollfile = file of
                     record
                   name : array [1..20] of char;
                   dependents : integer;
                   jobclass : (salaried, hourly, piecework)
                     end; { of record }
```

Now, as with all other data types in Pascal, we may create variables using these new data types.

```
var
    x       : datafile;
    y       : colorfile;
    z       : arrayfile;
    master  : payrollfile;
```

The creation of a file variable will automatically create the one-element window into that file shown in Figure 10-1. The file window is more frequently referred to as the *buffer variable*. The contents of the buffer variable are indicated in Pascal by following the file variable name with the special character ' ↑ '. For example, the **var** declarations just given would automatically create the following four buffer variables.

x ↑   which is an integer value.

y ↑   which is one of the following three user-defined scalar constants—
             red, white, or blue.

z ↑   which is a 10 element array of reals. The individual elements would
             be referenced as z ↑ [1], z ↑ [2], . . . , z ↑ [10].

Figure 10-2. Syntax of the **file** declaration.

master ↑   which is a record with three fields. These fields would be referenced as:

master ↑ *.name[1]*. . .*master* ↑ *.name[20]*
master ↑ *.dependents*
master ↑ *.jobclass*

A buffer variable can be thought of as the contents of the location in the file where we are currently reading or writing, and it is the one element of the file that we can immediately access and process. If an element of the file is not currently the buffer variable, then we must move the buffer variable forward to that element before it is accessible. We cannot move the buffer variable backward, except to reset it back to the beginning of the file.

A file and its buffer variable are controlled and tested using five standard Pascal functions and procedures. (File refers to any variable that has been declared to be of type **file.**)

1. *eof(file)*. If the window has moved beyond the end of a file, eof(file) is true; otherwise it is false. We have already used eof extensively with the standard file input. Now we will use it with arbitrary files.

2. *reset(file)*. Initializes a file for reading by setting the buffer variable file ↑ to the first element and setting eof(file) to false if the file is not empty. If the file is initially empty, eof(file) is true and file ↑ is undefined. All files (except ''input'') must be reset before being read.

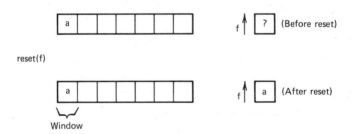

3. *rewrite(file)*. Initializes a file for writing by clearing it completely and setting eof(file) to true. All files (except ''output'') must be cleared before being written to.

4. *get(file)*. This operation is used to move the window ahead one step and read the next sequential element of the file into file ↑. It leaves eof(file) false unless there are no more elements, in which case eof(file) is set to true. If we are at the end of file to begin with, and eof(file) is currently true, then the get operation is undefined.

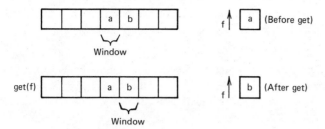

5. *put(file)*. This operation is used to write the current contents of file ↑ onto the end of the file; eof(file) remains true.

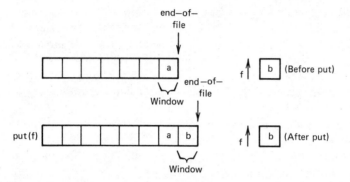

To illustrate the use of these functions, we will write a sample program to "launder" a data file. This is a common operation in which we take one data file, remove all invalid, improper, or unwanted values, and create a second data file containing only the desired information. Assume that we have a data file, called "sensorinput," that contains readings from a physical monitoring device. The information it contains is time and voltage levels in the following format:

type
        sensorinput = **file of** *sensorrecord;*

            sensorrecord = **record**
                time : real; { *from 0.0 to 24.00 in hours and*
                                        hundredths of an hour }

              voltage : real
                  end; { *sensorrecord* }

Assume that we want to process sensorinput and build a new file based on the following two criteria.

1. We only want those sensor readings from 8:30 A.M. to 5:00 P.M.

2. We do not want to keep any information on the new file when the sensor is turned off (i.e., when the voltage levels are approximately 0).

The new "laundered" data should be placed in a file called outdata. Finally, our program should write out a special signal marker to indicate the end of the outdata file. The signal marker has the values: time = 0.0, voltage = −1.0. These special values will be used by the programs that will ultimately read and manipulate the outdata file.

The complete program is shown in Figure 10-3. It illustrates some fundamental points about file processing. Any file that is either created outside the program and passed into it (e.g., the file sensorinput) or is created by the program and passed to the outside world (e.g., the file outdata) is called an *external file*. All external file names must be included in the program heading, as shown on line 1 of Figure 10-3. The standard files input and output (if needed), along with the other external files, are listed immediately after the program name. In addition to this requirement, it is frequently the case that special system commands will be needed to allow the use of external files (see Section 4.8). However, since this information is not part of the Pascal language, but is specific to each computer installation, the necessary details will have to be provided locally.

A file that is not communicated to or from the outside world is called a *local file* and does not have to be included in the program heading. Local files are temporary in nature and exist only for the duration of the program. Figure 10-4 on page 366 shows an example of the use of a local file.

Assume that we have a file containing the names of all students taking a mathematics course which has two separate sections, numbered one and two. We wish to print a list of just those students enrolled in Section 1 in the following format.

Section 1   'nnn' number of students enrolled
    xxxx   (names of all students in Section 1)
      .
      .
      .

    xxxx

The first line of the report requires that we know exactly how many students are in Section 1, but we will not have that value until after we have processed the entire file, at which time it will be too late to write out the names. We could reset the file back to the beginning by saying

reset(studentfile)

or, alternatively, we could create a local file that contains just the names of the Section 1 students. The advantage of the latter approach is that we do not have to perform

```
program launder (sensorinput, outdata, output);
{
        program to build a new output file called outdata from
        those elements of sensorinput which
                1) occur between 8:30 am and 5:00 pm
                2) have voltage levels of 0.0
                                                                    }
const
        minvoltage = 0.1; { any voltage level below this is considered 0.0 }
type
        sensorrecord = record
                        time : real;
                      voltage : real
                                end; { sensorrecord }
var
        sensorinput    : file of sensorrecord; { input data }
        outdata        : file of sensorrecord; { cleaned up output file }
        size           : integer; { count of number of elements in outdata }
begin
        size := 0;
        reset(sensorinput); { prepare sensorinput for reading }
        rewrite(outdata); { prepare outdata for writing }
        while not eof(sensorinput) do
        begin
            if (sensorinput ↑ .time >= 8.50) and { 8.50 = 8:30 am }
                (sensorinput ↑ .time <= 17.00) and { 17.00 = 5:00 pm }
                (sensorinput ↑ .voltage >= minvoltage) then
            begin
                outdata ↑ := sensorinput ↑ ;
                put(outdata); { write out this record to the outdata file }
                size := size + 1
            end; { if statement }
            get(sensorinput) { read the next record from the sensor input file }
        end; { of while loop }
        {
            all of sensorinput has been read. All that remains is to
            attach the special marker record to the end of the outdata file
                                                                    }
        outdata ↑ .time := 0.0;
        outdata ↑ .voltage := − 1.0;
        put (outdata);
        size := size + 1;
        { let's tell the user how big the result file was }
        writeln ('the outdata file is completed. It contains a total of', size:5,
                'elements')
end. { of program launder }
```

Figure 10-3. Sample program using files.

```
program localfile (std, output);

type
      studentrecord = record
            name         : array[1. .20] of char;
            section     : 1. .2
      end; { studentrecord }

var
      count        : integer; { number of students in section 1 }
      i            : integer; { loop index }
      section1     : file of array [1. .20] of char; { temporary file
                                 to hold the names of students in section 1 }
      std          : file of studentrecord;

begin
      count := 0;
      reset(std); { prepare it for reading }
      rewrite(section1); { prepare it for writing }
      while not eof(std) do
      begin
            if std ↑ .section = 1 then
            begin
                  for i := 1 to 20 do
                        section1 ↑ [i] := std ↑ .name[i];
                  put(section1);
                  count := count + 1
            end; { if }
            get(std)
      end; { while loop }

      { we have now built the file of section 1 names. let's print it out on the
        standard output device }

      writeln('section 1', count:5, 'number of students enrolled');
      writeln;
      reset(section1); { rewind it back to the beginning }
      while not eof(section1) do
      begin
            for i := 1 to 20 do
                  write(section1 ↑ [i]);
            writeln;
            get(section1)
      end { of while loop }
end. { of program }
```

Figure 10-4. Sample program using a local file.

any further tests to determine a student's section. We merely print out the complete contents of this local file. A program to implement this technique is shown in Figure 10-4.

Together, Figures 10-3 and 10-4 illustrate the typical sequential nature of file processing in Pascal. A conceptually good way to view a file is by an analogy to another common sequential storage medium we are all familiar with, an audio tape. A reset operation can be viewed as the rewinding of a recorded tape to the beginning of the first song, while rewrite mounts a new "blank" tape and prepares it for recording. (Although it obviously need not be blank; we could be overwriting.) A get operation simply moves us ahead sequentially to the next song and makes it available for "processing" (i.e., playing). Finally, a put operation records a new song on the end of the current tape. However, it is important to remember that the Pascal concept of a file is independent of the particular storage device used. It may or may not be a tape-oriented medium. We have used the idea of tape strictly for analogy.

10.1.3   Textfiles

There is one particular file type that is so important that it deserves special mention. A *textfile* is a file of characters. Pascal contains a standard file type, called text, which is predefined as follows:

type *text* = **file of** *char;*

A textfile can be thought of as a file containing variable-length units, called lines, composed of just the printable characters. Each line in the file is separated from the next by a special *line separator* character as we discussed in Section 4.5.2 and diagrammed on page 114. If "c" represents any printable character, "ls" represents the line separator, and eof the end-of-file, then a textfile can be represented as in Figure 10-5.

We can read and write from textfiles using the regular get and put operations that were discussed in the previous section. However, there are four special and simplified procedures for handling input and output to or from a textfile. They are none other than our "regular" input/output operations that were introduced in Chapter 4 and which have been used throughout this text—read, readln, write, and writeln. The reason we have been able to use these procedures is quite simple—the standard files input and output are textfiles. Our keyboard, punched card input, and printer output are viewed by the system as simply streams of characters and lines, exactly as shown in Figure 10-5.

We can now describe exactly how these four standard procedures, and eoln, operate on textfiles, something that was not possible in Chapter 4. Assume we have

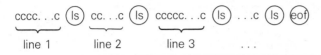

line 1   line 2   line 3   . . .

Figure 10-5. Organization of a textfile.

the declarations

var
  f : text;
  ch : char;

then the standard Pascal textfile operations can be described as follows.

1.	*eoln(f)*	*eoln(f) is true if f ↑ currently points at a line separator character and is false otherwise.*
2.	*read(f, ch)*	*ch: = f ↑ ; get(f)*
3.	*readln(f, ch)*	*ch: = f ↑ ;*

          while not *eoln(f)* **do**
            get(f);
          get(f)

4.	*write(f, ch)*	*f ↑ : = ch; put(f)*
5.	*writeln(f, ch)*	*f ↑ : = ch; put(f)*

          f ↑ : = "ls"; put(f) { "ls" is the line separator character }

Notice that when these procedures are applied to files other than the standard textfiles input and output, the file name must be the first parameter. If the file name is omitted, the default name input is assumed for reading and the default name output is assumed for writing.

As an example of the use of textfiles, consider the problem of creating a textfile of fixed length 80 character lines from a file containing variable-sized lines 1 to 80 characters in length. We will pad the lines with blanks as necessary to fill them out to the full 80 character length. A program to accomplish this is shown in Figure 10-6.

There is one final comment to make concerning textfiles. While it is true that a textfile is a sequence of characters, we frequently wish to consider those characters as collectively forming a data object of a different type, e.g., an integer or a real. We have already done this with the standard files input and output so that when we read (or readln) an integer from input, we get the decimal value 123 instead of the character string '1' '2' '3'. These automatic conversion services also apply to any arbitrary textfile. If f is any textfile (including input or output), then the following operations are valid if the sequence of characters in the textfile corresponds to the proper syntax of an integer or real constant in Pascal.

```
program fixedlength (textin, textout, output);
{
     this is a program that reads lines from a textfile of length
     1-80 characters and produces a second textfile containing
     fixed length 80 character lines
                                                              }

const
     maxline   = 80;    { fixed length line size }
     blank     = ' ';   { the padding character }

var
     textin    : text;      { the input file with variable length lines }
     textout   : text;      { the output file with fixed size lines }
     size      : integer;   { the current line size }
     i         : integer;   { for loop index }
     ch        : char;      { current character being read }

begin
     reset (textin);
     rewrite (textout);
     while not eof (textin) do
     begin
          size := 0;
          while (not eoln(textin)) and (size < maxline) do
          begin
               read(textin, ch);
               size := size + 1;
               write (textout, ch)
          end; { while loop }
          for i := (size + 1) to maxline do
               write (textout, blank);
          readln (textin); { skip to new line in the input file }
          writeln (textout) { put a line separator in the output file }
     end; { of the while loop }
     writeln ('copy operation has been completed')
end. { of program fixedlength }
```

Figure 10-6. Sample program to illustrate the use of textfiles.

```
var
    i : integer;
    r : real;
    f : text;
    .
    .
    .

read(f,i) ; readln(f,i);
read(f,r) ; readln(f,r)

write(f,i) ; writeln(f,i);
write(f,r) ; writeln(f,r)
```

The procedures will either assemble the required number of characters from the textfile into an integer or real value, or disassemble the integer or real value into the appropriate sequence of characters (see Exercise 7). The procedures read and readln will automatically skip leading blanks and line separators when looking for integers and reals. The procedures write and writeln will also allow strings (packed arrays of characters) and booleans to be written. Some installations may extend the read and write procedures even further to include the input and output of data types such as user-defined scalars, arrays, records, and sets. These operations are nonstandard and thus availability will have to be determined locally.

Style Clinic 10-2 _____

Interactive versus Batch I/O

Interactive and batch processing are two fundamentally different techniques for executing programs (see Style Clinic 4-6). They are most different in their views of the standard file "input." With batch, the entire input file must be initially present along with the program, while in an interactive environment, the data are "in our head." Unfortunately, there is only one set of input primitives—read and readln—and they operate in the identical way for both. What seems to be correct behavior for one access technique may appear quite strange when used with the other.

For example, Pascal automatically generates a

```
reset(input)
```

before executing your program. In a batch environment, there will be no problem since the system already has all the data. With an interactive program, though, this reset will require a prompt for input. This initial request for input may seem strange if the very first line of the program is something like

writeln('welcome to the program')

You will get a prompt for input prior to this line of output as Pascal tries to open the standard file input.

Likewise, a readln used in an interactive environment will accept its input and then try to move to column 1 of the next line. But to do that requires a second prompt for input! Thus, your input sequence might look like this.

? data set 1
? data set 2 { this second prompt is caused by the readln }
results for data set 1
? data set 3
results for data set 2
.
.
.

Some installations have attempted to solve this problem by modifying the behavior of the read and readln based on which access technique is being used—batch or interactive.

It would be best to check on the specific behavior of the standard read and readln procedures at your installation.

10.2 POINTERS

All the variables discussed so far, whether simple or structured, share a common characteristic—they are *static*. This means that all necessary memory is allocated for that variable at the time the program containing the variable declaration is about to begin execution. It remains in existence as long as the program is executing.[1] This approach contrasts sharply with the class of variables we will look at next—the dynamic variables.

A *dynamic variable* is created and destroyed dynamically during the execution

[1]The variant record type may superficially seem to be a contradiction, but actually is not. Enough memory is initially allocated for the largest variant form regardless of how much memory is eventually required or which variant is actually used.

of a program. Unlike static variables, dynamic variables are not referenced by a user-specified name. Instead, they are referenced indirectly by *pointers* to the newly created variable. For example,

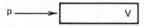

The dynamic variable "V" would be referenced not by name, but by its associated pointer variable p, which "points to" V.

Pascal provides dynamic variables through the **type** declaration shown in Figure 10-7. The type-name just defined is a dynamic data type whose pointers will point to objects of the indicated base type. We say that the type-name is *bound* to the base type. For example,

> **type**
>   *intpointer = ↑ integer;*
>
> **var**
>   *ip : intpointer;*

ip is now a *reference variable* or a *pointer variable* that is bound to (i.e., points to) an integer value, while ip ↑ is the actual integer value being pointed at. For example,

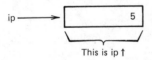

where ip is the pointer value, while ip ↑ is the contents of the thing that is being pointed at, namely the integer 5.[2] As a second example:

> **type**
>   *recordptr = ↑ calendar;*
>
>   *calendar =* **record**
>   *month*   : *(jan,feb,mar,apr,may,jun,jul,aug,sep,oct,nov,dec);*
>   *day*   : *1. .31*
>   **end;** *{ calendar record structure }*
> **var**
>   *r : recordptr;*

---

[2]Inside the computer, pointer values correspond to memory addresses. So the value of ip would be the *address* of the cell containing the constant 5. However, this fact is not crucial to understanding the concept of pointer variables. It will even suffice for now to simply think of the pointer value as an "arrow" pointing to some object.

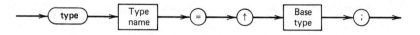

Figure 10-7. Syntax of the **pointer** declaration.

Now r is a pointer variable that can point to a record data structure (called calendar) with two scalar fields. For example,

The two subfields of the record would be accessed by referring to r ↑ .month (dec in the previous example) and r ↑ .day (which is 25).

There are two standard Pascal procedures that create and destroy dynamic variables.

new(p)　　　　New will create a dynamic variable of the base type specified in the declaration of p. A pointer to this new variable is assigned to the variable p.

dispose(p)　　Dispose will destroy the variable pointed at by p and return the space just released to some "available space list" for future use; p is then undefined.

As an example, referring to our earlier declaration of the variable ip, the statement

　　new(ip)

will create an unnamed integer variable and store the pointer to it in ip. To use this newly created variable, we reference it as ip ↑ . Either of the following statements would assign the new reference variable an integer value.

　　ip ↑ := 1;
　　read(ip ↑)

The statement

　　dispose(ip)

will destroy the variable. Any future reference to ip ↑ will result in a run-time error.
　　Likewise, referring to the earlier declaration of the variable r, the statement

　　new(r)

will create a new record variable of type calendar and put the pointer to it in r.

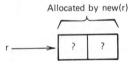

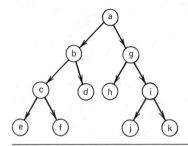

As a more meaningful example, let us consider the case of a very interesting (and important) data structure called a *binary tree*. It is shown in Figure 10-8.

Figure 10-8. A binary tree.

A binary tree is a collection of nodes. Each node contains three values: a left pointer, a right pointer, and a name. This structure can be created in Pascal through the following declarations.

type
    pointer = ↑*node;*

    node = **record**
               leftpointer : pointer;
                  name : char;
             rightpointer : pointer
        end; { *of node record* }

var
    p,root : pointer; { *pointers to nodes in the tree* }

Each node now contains three fields—a one-character name and two pointer variables. Each pointer points to another object of type node. The nodes themselves are never referred to directly by name (notice there is no variable declared of type node). Instead, we make indirect references to the nodes through the pointers called p and root.

For example, to create this one-node tree

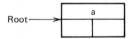

we would write the following.

> new(root);   { This allocates the space for a new node }
> root ↑ .name := 'a'   { Defines the name field of the new node }

However, what should we do with the left and right pointer fields of this new node? As the previous diagram shows, they are not being used. So what should we put there? In Pascal, there is a special *pointer constant* that is used to indicate that a pointer variable is not pointing to anything. This special constant is called **nil** and is sometimes indicated on diagrams by the symbol ⋏. Thus, completion of the creation of the one-node tree just mentioned would require the two commands

> root ↑ .leftpointer: = **nil;**
> root ↑ .rightpointer: = **nil**

and we have now built the following binary tree.

If we wished to build on the existing tree to create the following

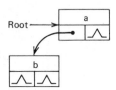

we would require these five statements (notice that p is also a pointer type bound to type node).

> new(p);   { create the space for the second node }
> root ↑ .leftpointer: = p;   { set the left pointer of a to point
>   to this new node }
>
> p ↑ .name: = 'b';
> p ↑ .leftpointer: = **nil;**
> p ↑ .rightpointer: = **nil**

If we wished to remove the node just added, we would write

root ↑ .leftpointer: = **nil;**
dispose(p) { remove the node just added }

As a second example, consider the data structure called a *linked list*.

A linked list is a sequence of nodes in which each node points to the next node in the sequence. It can sometimes be a very efficient way to represent a sorted list, especially if we frequently need to insert or delete elements from the list. If the list were stored as an array, then the addition of one new element would require us to resort the entire array, or at least do a lot of reshuffling. If, however, the information were stored as a linked list, an insertion could be handled by simply changing two pointers.

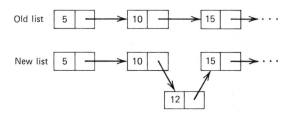

Let us assume that we wished to maintain a linked list of records giving the details of every appointment that we have scheduled for today. We will keep the time of each appointment and the name of the person it is with. Naturally, we will want the list sorted by increasing time so that it will function much like a schedule book, telling us what appointment is next. We can write this data structure as shown in Figure 10-9.

To keep the list in time-ordered sequence, we must search through the list and insert a new appointment in its correct place. A procedure to do this is shown in Figure 10-11 on page 378. (Note that this procedure will allow you to schedule two appointments at the same time! A more intelligent program would not allow you to schedule appointments closer than, say, 10 minutes apart and would not schedule appointments before 8:00 A.M. or after 5:00 P.M. You may wish to modify the procedure to implement this.)

Figure 10-10 depicts the operation of that procedure after (1) finding where the appointment belongs, and (2) adding it to the list.

type

> ptr = ↑ appointment;
>
> appointment = **record**
> > data : **record**
> > > name : **array**[1. .20] **of** char;
> > > hour : 0. .23; { we will use military time }
> > > min : 0. .59
> > > > **end;** { of the data record }
> >
> > next : ptr { pointer to the next appointment }
> > **end;** { of the appointment record }

var

> head : ptr;

Figure 10-9. The appointment data structure.

You should make sure that you understand the operation of the procedure in Figure 10-11 by working through it using the following data set. Assume our linked list currently contains the following appointments.

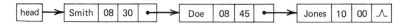

See how the procedure operates when we try to insert each of the new appointments shown on the top of page 379.

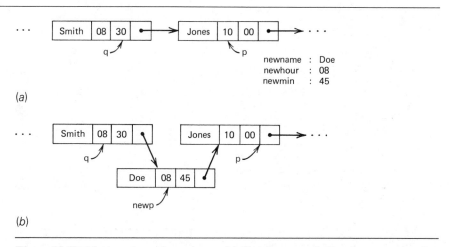

(a)

(b)

Figure 10-10. List insertion using pointers. (*a*) Situation upon finding the correct location to insert the appointment. (*b*) Situation after inserting the new appointment into the linked list.

procedure insert (**var** head:ptr;newname:nametype;newhour,newmin:integer);

{ this procedure will insert a new appointment into the
  schedule at the correct place in the linked list   }

var
        p, q: ptr; { temporary variables used to search the linked list }
        newp : ptr; { new node inserted in the list }
        found : boolean;

begin
        found := false;
        p := head; { start searching at the head of the list }
        q := head;
        while (p <> **nil**) **and** (**not** found) **do**
        begin
            if (p ↑ .data.hour < newhour) **or** ((p ↑ .data.hour = newhour) **and**
                                                (p ↑ .data.min <= newmin)) **then**
            begin
                q := p; { save a pointer to this element }
                p := p ↑ .next { move to the next }
            end
            else
                    found := true { we found where it belongs }
        end; { of while loop }

        { when we arrive here we know where the element properly goes—
          between the node pointed to by q and p. This is the situation depicted in
          Figure 10-10. }
        new(newp);
        newp ↑ .data.hour := newhour;
        newp ↑ .data.min := newmin;
        newp ↑ .data.name := newname;

        { now let's insert the new node into the list by adjusting the pointers }

        newp ↑ .next := p;
        if q <> p **then**
                q ↑ .next := newp
        else
                head := newp
        { this last test was needed for the case where we are inserting the head of
          the list }
end;

Figure 10-11. Program to insert elements into a linked list.

	newname	newhour	newmin
(a)	Falkauff	09	30
(b)	Falkauff	10	30
(c)	Falkauff	08	00

We began our original discussion of structured data types by saying that they are built up from simple scalar types. Likewise, the examples in this section should indicate that the best way to view the pointer data type is as a building block for creating complex linked data structures.

Figure 10-12 shows a number of different linked structures. They all occur quite frequently in computer applications and can all be created and manipulated using the Pascal pointer type. The meaning and purpose of these complex structures is beyond the scope of this text. Our purpose here is merely to show the wide range of structures that can be created from the elementary pointer building block. This dynamic data

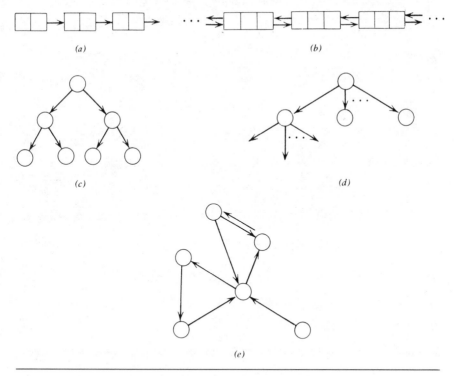

Figure 10-12. Some common linked data structures. (*a*) Singly linked list. (*b*) Doubly linked list. (*c*) Binary tree. (*d*) General tree. (*e*) Directed graph.

structuring ability gives a programmer great flexibility in choosing the most appropriate data structure for the problem being solved.

Style Clinic 10-3 _____

A Comment on Selecting Data Representations

The last few sections have introduced many data structures. The last type discussed, the pointer, is actually just a building block for other interesting structures—lists, queues, trees, and graphs, to name a few. It is the job of the programmer to wade through this maze of potential data structures and select the one most appropriate and most efficient for the problem being solved. Choosing the right one can greatly simplify and expedite the task.

For example, if we wished to store a list of values but were totally unsure about how long the list would be, an array would be a risky structure. If we declared it 500 elements long but the list grew to 501 elements, then we would have a fatal run-time error. However, a linked list does not have this problem. Whenever we wished to append a new item to the list, we would simply say

new(pointer)

and add the value referenced by the variable pointer to the end of the list. The list could grow forever (or at least until the entire memory space of the computer was exhausted).

Just as a programmer must be able to work with and evaluate alternate algorithms, so must he or she be able to work with and evaluate alternate data structures. The two are inextricably related.

10.3   CASE STUDY—MATRIX REPRESENTATIONS

In this case study, we will not be concerned with the development of an algorithm, as we have in all the other case studies. Instead, we will focus on those decisions that concern the selection of an appropriate data representation. As we have stressed throughout this chapter, these decisions are as important to the final result as our choice of algorithm.

A very common data structure that occurs quite frequently in mathematics is the *square matrix*. A square matrix is an n × n grid of elements.

n columns

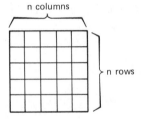

n rows

A matrix can be represented quite easily in Pascal by using a two-dimensional array data structure:

type
  matrix = **array** [*1. .n, 1. .n*] **of** *elements;*

where "n" is either a constant or a symbolic constant and "elements" is a type name. This structure will require n^2 memory locations inside the computer (assuming one location per matrix element). This data representation is probably acceptable under most conditions, but there are situations where this simple approach will either not work or will be horribly inefficient.

For example, what if the dimensions of the matrix were:

const
  n = *5000; { the matrix is 5000 × 5000 }*

This representation would require 25,000,000 storage locations, which is probably unrealistic on most current computers. In this case, we might wish to consider the following alternative representation:

type
  rows   = **array** [*1. .n*] **of** *elements;*
  matrix = **file of** *rows;*

These declarations create a file type in which each element of the file is one row of our original matrix. Since a file keeps only a single element in memory at any one time (see Section 10.1.1), the previous declaration will only require 5,000 memory locations—a reduction of 24,995,000! However, we have now lost the flexibility of processing the matrix in any arbitrary order. We must certainly process it sequentially, one row at a time. Any other type of processing (e.g., accessing the matrix by *columns*) will involve an enormous amount of file manipulation. However, if this loss of flexibility is acceptable, then we have gained quite a bit in terms of reducing our storage demands.

Another special case is the *triangular matrix*. In a triangular matrix the elements above (or below) the diagonal are all zeroes, while the other half of the matrix will contain the desired information. The following is an example of a (lower) triangular matrix.

$$
\begin{array}{rrrr}
1 & 0 & 0 & 0 \\
7 & 8 & 0 & 0 \\
-9 & 1 & -6 & 0 \\
2 & 6 & 4 & 5
\end{array}
$$

If space is no problem, then a two-dimensional array is a reasonable data structure. However, if space is tight, we may not want to waste it by explicitly storing a large number of zero elements. The number of nonzero elements in an $n \times n$ triangular matrix is

$$
1 + 2 + 3 + \cdots + n = \frac{n*(n+1)}{2} = \frac{1}{2} * n^2 + \frac{1}{2} * n
$$

which, for large n, is about one half of the n^2 elements we need to store our triangular matrix using the regular two-dimensional array representation.

An alternative way to represent a triangular matrix is by storing it as a one-dimensional structure. We would just store the nonzero elements of each row consecutively in the elements of the one-dimensional array. For example, given the following declarations:

type
    triangular = **array**[1 . .k] **of** *integer; { k is a symbolic constant }*

var
    matrix : triangular;

Our previous matrix would be stored as

1	7	8	−9	1	−6	2	6	4	5

and we would reduce the storage demands from 16 to 10 locations. However, notice that we have again lost something: we can no longer directly reference an element of the matrix in the straightforward manner, namely matrix [i, j]. Rather, we must compute the location of the [i, j]th element in the sequential one-dimensional representation we have selected. To do this computation, we must notice that the first element of row i has all the nonzero elements of rows 1,2, . . . , i−1 placed ahead of it. The total number of these elements is

$$1 + 2 + \cdots + (i - 1) = \frac{i(i - 1)}{2} = \frac{1}{2} i^2 - \frac{1}{2} i$$

The element in column j of row i will also have the (j − 1) elements of row i stored ahead of it. Thus, the number of elements in front of the [i, j]th one is

$$\frac{1}{2} i^2 - \frac{1}{2} i + (j - 1)$$

and the desired element will be at position

$$\left[\frac{1}{2} i^2 - \frac{1}{2} i + j \right]$$

in our one-dimensional array. Now we must write our programs in such a way that we compute these subscripts every time they are needed. For example, instead of saying

result := matrix [i,j]

we might write

result := extract (matrix, i, j)

where extract is the function shown in Figure 10-13 on page 384.

The function in Figure 10-13 can, with a trivial modification, also be used to handle another special case, *symmetric matrices*. A symmetric matrix is one in which matrix[i,j] = matrix[j,i] for all i,j. For example,

$$\begin{array}{rrrr} 1 & 3 & -8 & 7 \\ 3 & 5 & 6 & 12 \\ -8 & 6 & 2 & 15 \\ 7 & 12 & 15 & 9 \end{array}$$

As with the triangular matrix, if space is at a premium, it is foolish to store all the elements of a symmetric matrix. If we have stored matrix[i,j], then we automatically know the value of matrix[j,i]. If we use the same storage technique that we did

```
function extract (matrix:triangular; row, col:integer):integer;
{
        function to extract the [i,j]th element from a
        one-dimensional representation of a lower triangular matrix
                                                                        }

var
        location : integer;
begin
        if col > row then
            extract := 0
        else
      · begin
            location := round((0.5*row*row) − (0.5*row) + col);
            extract := matrix[location]
        end { else clause }
end; { function extract }
```

Figure 10-13. Function to access triangular matrices stored in one-dimensional format.

before—mapping the values onto a one-dimensional array—then we would store only the following elements:

1	3	5	-8	6	2	7	12	15	9

and our function extract would look like Figure 10-14.

As our final example we will look at potential representations for *sparse matrices*. (We first introduced this concept in Exercise 10, Chapter 7.) A sparse matrix is one in which a great majority of the matrix elements are zero.

```
   0     0  0   2.1   0
   0     0  0    0    0
   0.8   0  0    0    4.5
  38.0   0  0  −6.0   0
   0     0  0    0    0
```

If we use our ''old-fashioned'' two-dimensional array representation, we will need 25 storage locations to store the matrix just shown, even though there are only 5 useful pieces of data. It is not unusual in certain areas of science to have enormously large matrices (e.g., 10,000 × 10,000) that have only 0.01% to 0.1% nonzero elements. It will obviously be to our advantage to think up an alternate representation.

One possibility is to realize that all we really need to remember is the row and

```
function extract (matrix:triangular; row, col:integer):integer;
{
        function to extract the [i,j]th element from a
        one-dimensional representation of a symmetric matrix
                                                                    }

var
        location : integer;
        temp : real;
begin
        if col > row then { switch the row and column indices }
        begin
                row : = temp;
              temp : = col;
                col : = row
        end;
        location := round ((0.5*row*row) − (0.5*row) + col);
        extract := matrix[location]
end; { function extract }
```

Figure 10-14. Function to access symmetric matrices stored in one-dimensional format.

```
for i := 1 to n do
begin
        for j := 1 to n do write (matrix [i,j]);
        writeln
end
```

```
type
        nonzero = record
                                row : integer;
                                col : integer;
                                value : real
                        end; { nonzero record }

        sparse = array[1..k] of nonzero;
var
        matrix : sparse;
```

Figure 10-15. Declarations to create a sparse matrix.

column subscripts of the nonzero elements. If we can assume that there will be no more than k nonzero values, then Figure 10-15 shows a possible alternative data structure. Our earlier sparse matrix example would now be stored as follows:

1	4	2.1
3	1	0.8
3	5	4.5
4	1	38.0
4	4	−6.0

We have reduced our space needs from 25 locations to 15. Of course, we have also complicated the programs that manipulate these data. The programs that operate on this data structure will be longer and more complex than if we had used the simple two-dimensional array. Even the virtually trivial operation of printing out the matrix— which, using two-dimensional arrays, is done as follows—

```
procedure print(matrix : sparse; n, k: integer);
{ procedure to print out, row by row, an n × n matrix with
  k nonzero elements stored in the representation of Fig. 10-15 }

var
      colnum  : integer; { column number subscript }
      i       : integer;
      rownum : integer; { row subscript }
begin
      i := 1; { the next nonzero element to look for }
      for rownum := 1 to n do
      begin
          for colnum := 1 to n do
          begin
              if i <= k then { there are still nonzero elements to place }
                  if (rownum = matrix[i].row) and
                     (colnum = matrix[i].col) then
                  begin
                      write (matrix[i].value:10);
                      i := i + 1
                  end { then }
                  else
                      write('0.0':10)
              else
                  write('0.0':10)
          end; { inner loop }
          writeln
      end { outer loop }
end; { procedure print }
```

Figure 10-16. Procedure to print sparse matrices.

becomes a significant task. A procedure to accomplish the identical output operation is shown in Figure 10-16. Procedures for such things as matrix addition, multiplication, and inversion are also more complex than their two-dimensional array counterparts (see Exercises 12 and 13).

The preceding representation of a sparse matrix has one drawback. It is difficult to insert a new element and still keep the list sorted by rows and, within rows, sorted by column. If we wished to set matrix [1,5] to 28.3 and still keep the list in order, we would have to write a procedure which first determined the proper location in the representation for this new item. Then the procedure would need to make room for the new item by moving all other entries down one row, thus freeing up the available space. Likewise, to delete an entry will leave a "hole" in the representation that will need to be removed by moving all other entries up one row. In general, the sparse matrix representation in Figure 10-15 is not very flexible with regard to changes in the data. Additions and deletions require a major effort in moving and reshuffling.

If we anticipate that our sparse matrix will be very dynamic—with many insertions and deletions of elements—a better structure than that of Figure 10-15 might be a *doubly linked list*. With this structure, we link each nonzero element to the next nonzero element in the same row and the next nonzero element in the same column. Thus our original sparse matrix might now look something like this.

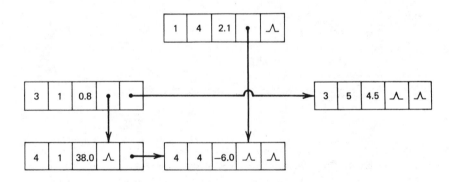

The insertion of a new element is now quite easy. It is simply the adjustment of some pointers, much as we described in Figure 10-10 and discussed in Section 10.2. For example, to set matrix[1,5] to 28.3 would result in the following structure.

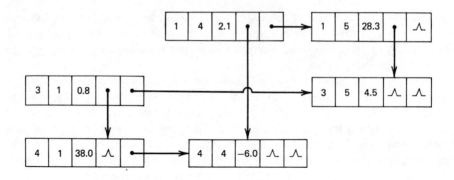

To create this doubly linked data structure, we must make the following declarations.

```
type
    ptr =  ↑ node;

    node = record
               row : integer;
               col : integer;
               value : real;
               colptr : ptr;
               rowptr : ptr
           end;   { node record }
```

Figure 10-17. Declarations for doubly linked list representation of a sparse matrix.

The programs to create the doubly linked list structure and to insert and delete elements are left to the reader as exercises at the end of the chapter (Exercise 14).

In conclusion, we have taken what appeared to be a fairly simple and straightforward data structure—a matrix—and shown that there are many alternative representations possible:

1. A two-dimensional array.
2. A file of one-dimensional arrays.
3. A one-dimensional array.
4. An array of records.
5. A doubly linked list.

Depending on the circumstances and our particular needs, one of these representations may be superior to the original array declaration with which we began our discussion. Too often we think of computer programs only in terms of the design and implementation of algorithms; we forget that the design and selection of an appropriate data representation is also an integral part of the programming process. The concepts of algorithms and data structures are intimately related and must both be satisfactorily addressed before we will have a correct, reliable, and efficient computer program.

*Style Clinic 10-4*_____

The Space-Time Trade-Off

If you look back over the case study of Section 10.3, you will notice that, in all cases, the selection of a data representation involved trade-offs between reducing space and reducing time. When we tried to reduce the amount of space that was needed to represent the matrix (e.g., the one-dimensional array, the sparse representation, or the doubly linked list), we increased the time that it took to extract information from that structure (e.g., Figures 10-13, 10-14) or the time it took to manipulate the structure (e.g., Figure 10-16). Conversely, if we can afford to use extra space (e.g., the original two-dimensional array representation), then the accessing of information will be extremely quick. We can also see this trade-off at work in Pascal where we are allowed to store information in a compressed, minimal space format with slower access (called a *packed* representation) or in the regular format that uses more space but accesses the structure quickly. (You can convert between these two forms by using the standard procedures pack and unpack described in Appendix B.)

Thus there is usually no "ideal" or "best" data representation. It is a question of what objective we are trying to achieve and what our critical resources are.

EXERCISES FOR CHAPTER 10

1. Show the **type** and **var** declarations to create files with the following structures.

   *(a) A file of lines of text. Each line is 136 characters long.

   *(b) A file containing inventory information. For each item in the inventory, we have the following information.

> Part name: 30 characters
> Part number: 6 digit integer
> Unit price: ($x.xx)
> Location: (30 characters)

(c) A file containing a table of geographic feature locations in the form: latitude (xx.xx°), longitude (xx.xx°), feature name (30 characters).

2. Assume that we have two files f1 and f2. We are currently reading from f1 and writing out to f2.

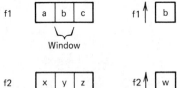

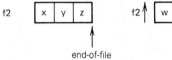

For each of the following groups of operations, show what the affected file contains after all operations have been completed. In addition, give the contents of the buffer variable and the current value of the function eof following all operations. (Assume each group of operations is independent and begins from the conditions just listed.)

*(a) *reset (f1)*
*(b) *f1 ↑ := d; get(f1)*
*(c) *get(f1); f1 ↑ := d*
 (d) *get(f1); get (f1)*
*(e) *rewrite(f2)*
*(f) *put(f2)*
 (g) *f2 ↑ := f1 ↑ ; put(f2)*
 (h) *rewrite(f2); put(f2)*

3. Modify the data laundering program of Figure 10-3 so it does the following:

(a) It transfers a maximum of 100 sensor records to the outdata file. If there were more than 100 valid readings, we would keep only the first 100.

(b) All invalid (or unused) records from the file sensorinput are copied to yet a third file, called discard, and saved for future use.

4. Assume that we have two tapes, called master and update, which both contain employee information in the following format.

Social security number:	9 digit integer.	
Last name:	20 characters.	
First name:	20 characters.	
Department code:	2 digit integer.	
Dependents:	integer.	
Base pay rate:	real.	

Master contains the names of all employees currently working for our company. Update contains the names of all new employees hired this week. Write a program that merges these two files and produces a single "new master" file containing all the names on both files. Each file is sorted in order of ascending social security number. The new master should also be sorted in ascending order of social security number.

Your program should check for the error condition of the same social security number occurring in both master and update. (How can we hire someone who already works for us?!) If this condition is detected, then discard the update copy and write out an appropriate error message on the standard output device.

5. Using the outdata file produced by the program in Figure 10-3, write a program that computes the following values from outdata.

   (a) The average sensor readings between 8:30 A.M. and 12:00 noon, and the average sensor readings from 12:00 noon to 5:00 P.M.

   *(b) The number of sensor readings that exceeded 125 volts.

   (c) Whether or not there was a sequence of three or more *consecutive* sensor readings that exceeded 118 volts. If there was, print out the times of the first and last sensor reading in the sequence.

6. Read in a file of characters from an input file called book, and develop a frequency count of all alphabetic characters contained in the file. The output of the program should be a report in the following format.

letter	frequency count	percent
A	XXX	XX.X
B	XXX	XX.X
.		
.		
.		
Z	XXX	XX.X
Total	XXXX	100.0

Treat uppercase and lowercase as the same character.

7. As we mentioned in Section 10.1.3, the standard procedures read and readln will automatically convert character strings into either integer or reals. However, assume this feature did not exist and we had to perform this conversion ourselves. Write the following functions that will accept a string of characters from the file input and perform the indicated conversion.

   (a) *Function booleanconvert.* Will convert any string of characters beginning with the letter 't' into the boolean constant true, and any string of characters beginning with the character 'f' into the boolean constant false. Any initial non-blank character other than 't' or 'f' is an input error, and the function should halt. If the function encounters an eof it should return and leave booleanconvert undefined. The input pointer should be left at the first non-alphabetic character following the character string.

   (b) *Function integerconvert.* Will convert a string of characters in the following syntax

   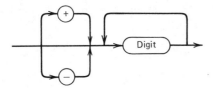

   into a signed decimal integer. The integer terminates upon the appearance of the first nondigit character. The handling of errors, eof, and the final position of the input pointer are the same as in part a.

8. *(a) Write the declarations needed to create a linked list of real values with pointers to the first and last elements of the list.

   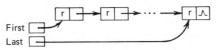

   *(b) Write a Pascal fragment that initializes the list to the following state.

   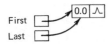

   *(c) Write a Pascal fragment that adds the value 1.0 to the end of the list produced by step b.

9. Write a procedure that takes a binary tree (of the type shown in Figure 10-8) and determines the total number of nodes that exist in the tree. For example, given the following tree

the procedure should return a 5—the number of distinct nodes.

10. Write a procedure called emergency that takes the appointment linked list data structure in Figure 10-9 and adds 30 minutes to the scheduled appointment time of everyone on the list whose appointment time is greater than nowhr:nowmin where nowhr and nowmin are parameters passed into the procedure. (Our golf game is running late!)

11. Write a procedure that reads in a name from the standard input file and searches through the linked list of appointments (Figure 10-9) and prints out either

    ccccccc has an appointment at xx:xx am (or pm)

or

    cccccc is not scheduled today

The time printed should be in the normal 12 hour, 60 minute format, not the 24-hour format currently stored in the data structure.

12. Write a boolean function to determine whether two sparse matrices stored in the representation of Figure 10-15 are identical. The function should return the value true if they are identical and false if they are not.

13. Write a program to *transpose* a matrix stored in the sparse representation of Figure 10-15. Matrix transposition interchanges column and row indices. The final transposed matrix should still be sorted by rows and, within row, by column.

14. (a) Write a procedure to insert a new item into a sparse matrix that is represented by the doubly linked list declarations of Figure 10-17. The parameters of the procedure will be

    head: an array of pointers to the first item in each row.

    row,col: the row and column indices of the new item to insert.

    value: the value of that new item.

    (b) Write a procedure that prints out on the standard output device a sparse matrix stored in the doubly linked list representation of Figure 10-17. The printout should be in the regular n × n notation with all 0 elements included.

15. Assume that we have an n × 2 table set up in the following format.

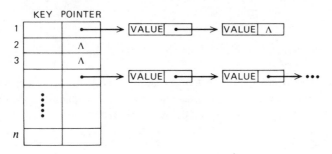

The table contains a key field and a pointer field. The pointer field is either **nil** or the head of a linked list of all the values associated with that key. For example, the key could be a student ID number and the values could represent all the classes taken by that student.

Write a complete Pascal program that reads data cards and builds a table in the format just described. Assume that the data cards all contain two integer values—the key and the value to enter in the table. There may be any number of cards containing the same key, and they do not have to be in sequence in the data. Assume that there is a standard function (which you do not need to write) called place(key) that returns a value in the range [1. .n]. This represents the location in the table to enter both the key and the value. Enter the key in the key field if it is not already there and add the value to the end of the chain pointed to by the pointer field. This method of table management is called *hashing* and is a very efficient technique.

Chapter 11

PROGRAM DESIGN METHODS

11.1 INTRODUCTION

One of the most important characteristics shared by the programs presented in this book is that they are *short*. The great majority contain about 15 to 50 Pascal statements, while the very largest (the Game of Life program in Chapter 9) is still only 175 lines. This contrasts quite sharply with the characteristics of production programs developed in the "real world." Most of these programs contain hundreds, thousands, or even tens of thousands of lines of code. Figure 11-1, for example, gives the length of some of the Control Data Cyber/74 programs frequently used by introductory computer science students at the University of Minnesota. Typical program sizes for other computers or other types of installations (e.g., business, government, aerospace) would yield values of comparable, or even greater, magnitude.

One of the most fundamental ideas in computer programming, and a point that we cannot stress too emphatically, is that length is *not* the only difference between short and long programs. Large programming projects, containing many thousands of lines of code, are intellectually different beasts from the little 50 to 150 line "toy" programs you have designed and programmed as homework assignments. You cannot predict your performance on developing a large program from your performance on a small one; that is, if it took you x units of time to complete a 50 line homework project, you cannot then conclude that it would take you about 100x units of time to complete a 5000 line project. In fact, the unfortunate reality is that when a beginning student attempts his or her first large program (> 1000 lines), it is rarely ever completed successfully.

Big programs are intellectually different from small ones because of the amount of information that must be managed (remembered, scheduled, organized) to complete the task. The human mind has only a finite capacity for remembering details. Small

395

Program	Length (in Source Statements)
1. Pascal compiler	9,000
2. FORTRAN compiler	15,000
3. Text editor	5,000
4. NOS operating system	45,000

Note. Most of these programs are *not* written in Pascal but in a wide range of other high- and low-level languages.

Figure 11-1. Some typical program sizes.

programs do not, in general, tax that capacity. With a short, simple program it is easy to remember everything that needs to be done. When one section of code is finished, we simply "know" what comes next. We can handle in our heads the details of planning, designing, coding, debugging, and testing without the need for any formal management scheme. (At most, we may jot down some rough notes on pieces of scratch paper.) However, as the programs get larger and larger, the amount of detail gets greater and greater and, at some point, it simply cannot all be stored mentally. We begin to forget critical decisions that were made earlier, omit key operations, or forget really important information while remembering insignificant details. (Have you ever noticed how you can forget the details of a meeting held yesterday, but still remember the phone number of a friend you knew 10 years ago?) The program begins to get sloppy and disorganized and, worst of all, errors creep in that may never be removed.

There is another critical difference between long and short programs: the problem of debugging (see Chapter 6). As programs get bigger, the time spent in locating and correcting errors increases at a rate faster than the growth rate of the program itself. Thus a single 5000 line program will take much more time to debug than a hundred 50 line programs, even though the total number of statements is the same. This is because errors can arise either within individual statements or in the interrelationships *between* statements (e.g., the statement sum : = 0 itself is correct, but it may have to appear before the first **for** loop, not after). As programs grow extremely long, the number of possible interrelationships grows as the *square* of the number of statements, and the difficulty of the debugging task becomes overwhelming. It is almost always the case with a student's first attempt at a very large project that he or she totally underestimates the complexity of the debugging phase and gives up in complete frustration. The project is left, only partially correct, fraught with errors, never even coming close to meeting the problem specifications.

The situation of increased size causing a fundamental change in our view of a problem is certainly not unique to computer programming. This phenomenon can be seen in almost any system. For example, to open a one-person street corner lemonade stand, we may be able to get away with keeping all business details (inventory, accounts payable, payroll, etc.) in our head. But if we tried the same approach with a nationwide chain of 1000 franchised "Fruit Juice Bars," the business would collapse immediately into chaos.

What we need to handle these large computer programs is the same thing needed by any large business—a *management technique*. We need a way to manage, plan, organize, and schedule the orderly and correct implementation of our computer programs. The next section will introduce just such a method, called *top-down modular programming*. However, we must state that a thorough treatment of this complex topic is well beyond the scope of this book and is a subject deserving of its own text. We will merely highlight some of the fundamental concerns of this program management technique and let the interested reader refer to any of the appropriate books listed in the Bibliography for additional information.[1]

11.2 TOP-DOWN MODULAR PROGRAMMING

The principles of top-down modular programming are based on decomposing a problem into a *hierarchy* of tasks, and then developing the solution from the highest level down to the lowest. The higher levels are concerned with the broad problems to be solved (*what* must be done), while the lower levels become more and more concerned with the details of *how* we can actually achieve it. The solution develops in a downward growing "development tree" of the type shown in Figure 11-2.

This management technique is not new at all. Figure 11-2 is virtually identical to the management hierarchy of any large business—a president (t_1), vice presidents (t_{11}, t_{12}, t_{13}), directors (t_{111}, t_{112}, . . .), and so forth.

[1]The topic of program design is one of the major concepts addressed in the sequel to this text, G. M. Schneider and S. C. Bruell, *Advanced Programming and Problem Solving with Pascal,* John Wiley & Sons, New York, 1981.

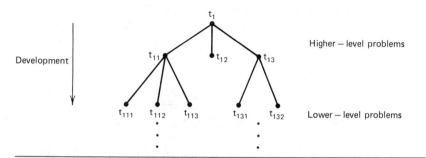

Figure 11-2. A typical program development tree.

Likewise, before we began any large written paper, we were taught how to *outline* the subject in order to manage and organize our thoughts. For example, if we wished to write a survey paper on the syntax of the Pascal language, we might start out with the following outline.

I.   The program heading.

II. The declaration section.

III. The statement section.

Then, if we were satisfied with this structure, we might expand each of the subheadings just listed into a more detailed description.

II. The declaration section.
(A) The **const** declaration.
(B) The **type** declaration.
(C) The **var** declaration.
(D) The **procedure** and **function** declarations.
(E) Examples.

It should be clear from these examples that top-down design is not new, or unique to computer programming.

In a top-down programming environment, the original problem (e.g., t_1 of Figure 11-2) is described in terms of a reasonably small number of subtasks (t_{11}, t_{12}, t_{13}), which, if they existed and were performed in the correct order, would solve the original problem. We now code task t_1 as if procedures to do those subtasks actually existed. We have simplified the problem from solving it in its original form to solving a small number of more elementary procedures. However, we will eventually have to define and code each of these currently nonexistent subtasks. For each subtask (e.g., t_{11}) we again decompose and define it in terms of even more basic and elementary subtasks (t_{111}, t_{112}, t_{113}) and write t_{11} as if procedures for these subtasks existed. The operation of taking a problem step and defining it in terms of more elementary subproblems is called *stepwise refinement*. The stepwise refinement process terminates when a subtask is so simple it need not be expressed in terms of any new subtasks but can be coded directly in the primitives of our programming language.

This relatively simple program management scheme has some important implications for the development of large programs. Probably the most important is the idea of *intellectual manageability*. The problem solution is developing from the highest levels downward, so that we are always "on top of" the problem. We always know where we are heading and what needs to be done. We will never have to make a decision without knowing how we arrived at this decision point. Even when we must begin worrying about the less important details of lower-level modules, we will always know how each detail relates to the other pieces of the growing solution. This is obviously important when we are working on a program that may be composed of 100 or more separate procedures. If we had no overall idea of how these procedures relate to each other and in what order they will be developed, it would be like trying to assemble a jigsaw puzzle with no completed picture to guide us. All that we would have is a jumble of 100 or so unrelated, unconnected pieces.

The top-down development approach is also a way to manage the welter of detail that occurs in any large project. Each layer in the solution is totally independent of the particular algorithmic or programming techniques used to solve a lower-level task. Another way of phrasing this is to say that the implementation details of a lower-level procedure are *transparent* to all higher levels. All that a program unit should concern itself with are the input/output characteristics of its lower-level subtasks: What must I give it and what does it give back to me? It should not care *how* we solve that task. For example, if we have written the following sequence:

```
        .
        .
        .
        .

while not eof do
begin
        for i := 1 to size do readln (list[i]);
        sort (list,size); { sort the list into ascending sequence }
        .
        .
        .
```

for now, we will only care that there is a procedure, called sort, that takes a 'list' of some specified 'size' and returns it sorted into ascending order. We will not worry (yet!) about whether we should use one of the straightforward $O(n^2)$ sorting algorithms—exchange sort, selection sort—or one of the more clever $O(n \log_2 n)$ techniques, such as Quicksort, that were discussed in Chapter 2. Likewise, we won't worry now about the many other vexing problems that may occur during a sort operation—empty lists, duplicate values, missing data, or invalid items. We will postpone all of these details until we actually start to code the routine called sort.

Top-down design can be viewed as a way to temporarily *abstract away* unimportant details until they are actually needed. We can delay a decision about some algorithmic detail until we reach the stage of designing and coding the procedure that implements that algorithm. It will always be to our advantage to delay decisions for as long as possible, because we will always have more information available to us and a better idea of the proper action to take.

Delayed decision making also applies to data structures. For example, during the early stages of the development of a payroll system, we might know that we will be keeping a sequential file of payroll data on each employee.

```
    type paymaster = file of payrecords;
```

But we may not as yet know what the specific data on each employee will be. In a top-down design environment, we can postpone the exact specification of the 'payrecords' data structure until we eventually code the procedures that must go into that record structure and manipulate the individual fields.

Finally, as we mentioned earlier, since debugging time grows so quickly, it will be to our advantage to debug a large program as a number of smaller units instead of as one big chunk. The top-down development process specifies a solution in terms of a group of smaller, individual subtasks. These subtasks thus become the ideal unit of program testing and debugging. When we describe a task in terms of its component subtasks

we will thoroughly test and debug the higher-level task t_1 *before* we begin the stepwise refinement process of lower-level tasks t_2, t_3, t_4, or t_5. By testing our program in small pieces, we greatly simplify the debugging process. In addition, we will have the satisfaction of knowing that everything we have coded so far is correct. When we add a new piece of code, p, to the overall program P, and an error condition occurs, we can definitely state that the error must either be in p itself or in the interface between p and P, because P has been previously checked and certified.

Style Clinic 11-1

How Big Is the Ideal Program Unit?

Figure 11-2 and the discussion in Section 11.2 clearly indicate that a program will be composed of many separate pieces instead of one big monolithic chunk. But the question remains: How many little chunks should we have? Should a 1,000 line program be decomposed into two 500 line pieces, ten 100 line pieces, or 100 10 line pieces? The answer is that there is no answer! There are no fixed rules on the optimal module size. Most people would say that you should decompose a problem into whatever number of logically separate pieces it takes to properly describe the solution.

However, there is a rule of thumb that is followed by many programmers: no program unit (main program, procedure, function) should exceed 60 lines. This limit was chosen for a decidedly nontechnical reason: it is the approximate number of lines that fit on a single page of line printer output. So if our modules are all 60 lines or less, each one can be examined in its entirety without flipping any pages.

The value 60 is obviously just a guideline, but if you find yourself writing program units of 200 or more lines, re-examine them closely. You may be doing too much in a single program unit. If you must err, err on the side of using smaller units. They will be much easier to work with and debug.

In summary, top-down programming is a program design technique that describes a high-level problem in terms of more elementary subtasks. Through the technique of stepwise refinement we then expand and define each of these separate subtasks until the problem is solved. Each subtask is tested and verified before it is expanded further. The advantages of this method are, among others:

1. Increased intellectual manageability and comprehension.
2. Abstraction of unnecessary lower-level detail.
3. Delayed decisions on algorithms and data structures until they are actually needed.
4. Reduced debugging time.

In the following section we try to clarify these concepts and give a better feeling for these ideas by working through a moderately large case study, using the top-down programming design technique.

Style Clinic 11-2 _____

Programming Teams

Another advantage of the top-down development process shown in Figure 11-2 is that it becomes an ideal structure for managing the implementation of a computer program using *teams* of programmers. A senior programmer can be responsible for the design of a high-level task and its decomposition into subtasks. Each of those subtasks can then be "farmed out" to a more junior programmer who works under the direction of the senior staff. We are taking advantage of the fact that the development tree of Figure 11-2 is identical to the management structure chart of any large business.

Since almost all projects of the size of those quoted in Figure 11-1 are done by teams of two or more programmers, this characteristic is very important.

11.3 CASE STUDY

As an example of the technique we have been discussing, let us end by solving a problem that was raised at the very beginning of this text: the rank correlation coefficient problem presented in both Section 1.4.2 and Exercise 15 of Chapter 2. (You may wish to go back and reread Section 1.4.2 before continuing.)

The specifications of the problem are as shown in Figure 1-3 with the following four modifications.

1. There may be more than one data set, each of which will be preceded by a card containing two integer values, m and n, with the following meaning.

    m—the number of students in this data set m$> = 1$
    n—the number of examination scores per student in this data set n>1

    The end of all data is indicated by a signal card with m$=$n$=0$.

2. You are to perform a correlation between *every* pair of examinations in the data set. That is, if there are n exams, we must separately rank and correlate the following exam pairs: (1,2), (1,3), . . ., (1,n), (2,3), (2,4), . . ., (2,n), . . ., (n-1,n). Note that we do *not* need to perform a correlation between examinations j and i if we have already correlated examinations i and j. They will have the same value. Likewise, we do not have to correlate an examination with itself. That value would always be $+1.0$.

3. When performing the ranking operation, you must only rank those scores being used in the current computation. That is, if we are correlating exams X and Y, we should not attempt to assign a rank to an individual score x_i if either x_i or y_i is missing since, in either case, we will not use this pair of scores in our computations. This point can be illustrated by the following table.

X	Ranking of X	Y	Ranking of Y
13	3	66	2
-1	—	90	— (not ranked)
80	1	102	1
72	2	65	3
96	— (not ranked)	-1	—
12	4	40	4

    This implies that we will have to rerank the scores for every new correlation, since different students may have missed different examinations. This approach is taken to ensure the most accurate results.

4. Finally, for each data set the program should identify in the output report the two sets of examinations that correlated most closely (i.e., had the highest value of ρ). The program should print out the following line:

    exams # 'xx' and 'xx' correlated most
    closely with a value of ρ = 'x.xxx'

The problem specifications as previously stated and in Figure 1-3 result in a not inconsequential task. A well-programmed solution to this problem might involve 150 to 300 lines of code and 5 to 10 separate program units. While these values are small (actually, miniscule) compared to the programs listed in Figure 11-1, it is still a large enough project to benefit from a systematic top-down approach to its implementation.

To hold our m × n collection of student examination scores, we will use a simple two-dimensional array structure, in which each row corresponds to the scores of one student.

type
  rawdata = **array** [*1. .maxstudent, 1. .maxexams*] **of** *scores;*

Right now, we won't worry about the exact nature of the data type 'scores.' It may ultimately be integer, real, char ('A' 'B' 'C' . . .), or a subrange of one of them, but we can decide on that detail later.

To hold our rank correlation coefficients, we can use the following structure.

type
  correlation = **array** [*1. .maxexams, 1. .maxexams*] **of** *real;*

The (i, j)th element of this array will contain the rank correlation coefficient between examinations i and j.

Finally, we can use a one-dimensional array to hold the ordinal rankings of the examination to which we are currently assigning ranks.

type
  ranks = **array** [*1. .maxscore*] **of** *rankvalue;*

Again, we will postpone a decision on the exact nature of rankvalue (i.e., integer or real) until we decide on the algorithm for assigning ranks and breaking ties (see Chapter 1, page 14).

With these decisions in place, we can begin to design and code the top-level structure of our rank correlation coefficient program. The code is shown in Figure 11-3 on pages 404-405.

The top-level solution of Figure 11-3 has generated six second-level procedures.

getdata. Input procedure that reads in one complete m × n data set and sets a boolean error flag to false if the input operation was successful. The flag is set to true if the input operation failed for any reason whatever.

errorhandler. Procedure that is invoked when an invalid data set is encountered. It will include recovery operations and error messages.

rank. Procedure to rank a pair of examination scores and place the results in two one-dimensional arrays. This procedure must handle both the problems of missing data and tied scores.

correlate. Function to correlate two rank vectors.

printreport. Output procedure to produce the two reports shown in Figure 1-3.

findlargest. Procedure to find and print the largest correlation coefficient.

As you read over the code of Figure 11-3, you will probably find it not too difficult to follow. Likewise, the overall "intent" and "purpose" of the program is relatively easy to discover. The reason for this is that we have taken a reasonably large (200 to 300 lines) problem and abstracted away, into those six lower-level program units just listed, many of the details of the solution. For example, the program as it stands in Figure 11-3 does not address any of the following issues.

1. The format of the input (type, range, input device, . . .).
2. The validation procedures for the input.
3. The method of assigning ranks to tied scores.
4. The problems of handling missing data (i.e., raw data values of -1).
5. Algorithms to find the largest value in a two-dimensional array.
6. The details of producing the desired output from our internal data structures and representations.

```
program rankcorrelate(input, output);

{ a program to compute and print our rank correlation coefficients between
  examinations given to a class of students }

const
    maxstudent  = ; { the maximum number of students per data set }
    maxexams    = ; { the maximum number of exams per data set }

type
    correlation = array[1. .maxexams, 1. .maxexams] of real;
    rankings    = array[1. .maxexams] of rankvalue;
    rawdata     = array[1. .maxstudent, 1. .maxexams] of scores;

var
    failed      : boolean; { if true, signals an error in the input data }
    i, j        : integer; { for loop indices }
    m           : 0. .maxstudent; { number of students in the current data set }
    n           : 0. .maxexams; { number of exams in the current data set }
    rankone,
    ranktwo     : rankings; { the rankings of the two exams currently being
                              ranked and correlated }
    rho         : correlation; { the matrix of rank correlation coefficients }
    table       : rawdata; { contains a single m × n data set }
```

```
begin
      read (m, n);
      while not ((m = 0) and (n = 0) do
      begin
            { input an m × n data set. set failed to true if we
              encounter an error during the input operation }
            getdata(table, m, n, failed);
            if failed then
                  errorhandler
            else
            begin { process this data set }
                  for i := 1 to n do
                  begin
                        rho[i, i] := 1.0; { an exam correlates perfectly with itself }
                        { now let's correlate exam i against all others, one by one }
                        for j := 1 to (i − 1) do
                        begin
                              { rank examinations i and j and place the ranks in the
                                vectors called rankone and ranktwo          }
                              rank(table, i, j, rankone, ranktwo);
                              rho[i, j] := correlate(rankone, ranktwo, m);

                              { the correlation between exams i and j is the same as the
                                correlation between j and i          }
                              rho[j, i] := rho[i, j]
                        end { inner for loop }
                  end; { outer for loop }
                  printreport(rho, m, n);
                  findlargest(rho, m, n)
            end; { of processing a single data set }
            read(m, n) { read in the first data card of the next data set }
      end; { of all data sets }
      writeln('end-of-file encountered; normal program termination')
end. { of program }
```

Figure 11-3. Top-level code for the rank correlation program.

We will eventually have to address all of these concerns, but we can certainly postpone them for now.

Before we proceed with writing any of these six newly defined routines, we should test our design as it has progressed up to this point. However, an interesting situation now arises: How do we test a program when the procedures that it requires to operate properly do not yet exist? The answer is that we will include temporary code for the as yet unwritten data definitions and lower-level program units.

The inclusion of such "do-nothing" modules is very common and, indeed, quite necessary in top-down program design. Each high-level routine will typically activate a number of lower-level routines for handling some details of the computation. However, in a well-organized top-down design, most of these lower-level routines do not yet exist. In order to test the correctness of the high-level procedures, we must include declarations for all routines invoked by the subprogram being tested. Even if the body of these lower-level routines does nothing useful, it will allow program testing to proceed. These dummy program units are usually called *stubs*. They will eventually be replaced by meaningful code. Typically, these stubs will do as little as possible, sometimes nothing more than writing a message to state that we have reached a particular procedure. Their major purpose is simply to allow compilation and execution to proceed without run-time failure.

As examples of stubs for testing the program in Figure 11-3, we might use the following declarations.

```
const
      maxstudent = 3;
      maxexams = 3;

type scores = integer; { for now, the scores and ranks will be integers }
     rankvalue = integer;

procedure getdata(var table:rawdata; m,n:integer;
                          var failed:boolean);
begin
      writeln('in the procedure getdata. I would now input an',
            m, 'x', n, 'data set');
      failed := false { this is necessary to prevent an error in
                          the main program }
end; { getdata }

procedure errorhandler;
begin
end; { we don't need it yet }

procedure rank(table:rawdata; i,j:integer; var rankone,
                          ranktwo:rankings);
begin
      writeln('we would now rank columns', i, 'and', j)
end; { rank }

function correlate (rankone, ranktwo:rankings; m:integer):real;
begin
      writeln('in function correlate. We are correlating columns',
            i,j);
      correlate := 0.5 { All functions must return a value }
end; { correlate }
```

```
procedure printreport (rho : correlation; m,n : integer);
var i,j : integer; { for loop indices }
begin
      writeln('correlation matrix :');
      for i := 1 to n do
      begin
          for j: = 1 to n do write (rho(i,j):5:1);
          writeln
      end
end; { printreport }

procedure findlargest (rho:correlation; m,n:integer);
begin
      writeln ('now in procedure to find the largest correlation value')
end; { findlargest }
```

With all these stubs properly placed (in the declaration section of Figure 11-3), we can test the general structure of the program. While we will not, of course, get correct answers, we can see whether or not the procedures are being activated in the correct order and whether or not the information being passed into the procedures appears correct. If we were to compile and execute the program in Figure 11-3 with the previously given stubs and the two data cards:

```
3      3
0      0
```

the output produced would be:

   in the procedure getdata. I would now input a 3 × 3 data set

   we would now rank columns 2 and 1

   in function correlate. We are correlating columns 2 and 1

   we would now rank columns 3 and 1

   in function correlate. We are correlating columns 3 and 1

   we would now rank columns 3 and 2

   in function correlate. We are correlating columns 3 and 2

   correlation matrix:

1.0	0.5	0.5
0.5	1.0	0.5
0.5	0.5	1.0

   now in procedure to find the largest correlation value

   end-of-file encountered; normal program termination

And, to this point, everything appears to be working properly.

We will now proceed to replace, one by one, the stubs used for testing purposes with the actual code necessary to solve the problem. As we do this, we will have to begin addressing some of the lower-level details that we postponed earlier.

For example, let us decide that our raw examination scores will be integers and

```
procedure getdata (var scores:rawdata; m,n:integer;
                     var bad:boolean);

const
      missingdata = - 1; { the missing data indicator }

var
      i, j     : integer; { for loop indices }
      value    : integer; { holds a score while we check its validity }
      good     : boolean; { flag to tell if the value is correct }
begin
      statcheck(m, n, bad);
      if bad then
          { something was wrong with the data set parameters m, n.
            we must discard all the scores from this data set so
            that we may begin to process the next set }
          for i := 1 to m do
              readln { discard the next m cards }
      else
      begin
          { the data set parameters m, n were okay. read in
            the m student cards }
          for i := 1 to m do
          begin
              for j := 1 to n do
              begin
                  read(value);
                  validate(value, j, good); { this procedure validates a single score
                                               on exam #j }
                  if not good then { treat that score as missing }
                      scores[i, j] := missingdata
                  else
                      scores[i, j] := value
              end; { inner for loop }
              readln
          end { outer for loop }
      end { else clause for valid data set }
end; { procedure getdata }
```

Figure 11-4. Refinement of the getdata procedure.

entered with the n scores of a single student on one line. Also, let us assume that, if an examination score is invalid, we will treat it as simply "missing" rather than throwing away all of the scores for that student. Now we can begin to write out in more detail the getdata procedure that is referenced by the program in Figure 11-3. One possible refinement is shown in Figure 11-4.

The newly coded procedure getdata itself uses two lower-level procedures:

1. *statcheck(m, n, bad).* This procedure verifies two conditions: (1) that the data set parameters m and n fall within the allowable bounds set by the program (maxstudent, maxexams); and (2) that they will provide statistically accurate results. Correlations are not considered very reliable if we have a very small number of observations, say, less than 5. Statcheck will ensure, among other things, that the value of m will allow us to produce reasonable results. The exact criteria for carrying out this check will have to be determined in consultation with a statistician, but we can postpone that worry for now. It will suffice to know that statcheck will set the boolean flag 'bad' to true if m and n are not acceptable, and false otherwise.

2. *validate (value, j, good).* The procedure validate determines whether an individual score on examination j is acceptable; that is, within the permissible range for that examination. If so, then good is set to true; otherwise, it is false.

These two new procedures must be added to the tree of program units that will be coded and tested. The tree, as it now stands, is shown in Figure 11-5. In addition, the new refinement of getdata in Figure 11-4 must be thoroughly tested before we proceed to code any of the other routines. To do this we will employ stubs for statcheck and validate, in exactly the same way we did earlier. (We will omit the details of this validation step in our discussion.)

Not all refinements will generate new lower-level routines. (Otherwise, we would never finish coding!) For example, a possible refinement of the function correlate is shown in Figure 11-6. It uses the rank correlation formula given in Exercise 15 of Chapter 2. This program unit defines no new procedures, so after testing that routine, we can move on and begin the design of the next procedure.

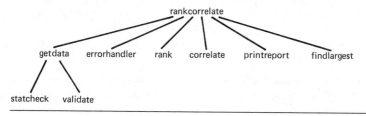

Figure 11-5. Development tree for the rank correlation problem.

```
function correlate (rankone, ranktwo: rankings; m: integer) : real;

{ this function correlates two sets of rankings stored in rankone and ranktwo. a
  value of − 1 means no rank was assigned and this pair is to be disregarded }

const
    missing = − 1;

var
    count  : integer;    { number of pairs discarded because one or both
                           exams were missing }
    i      : integer;    { for loop index }
    sum    : real;       { temporary used in the computation }
    total  : integer;    { number of pairs with two valid scores }

begin
    sum := 0.0;
    count := 0;
    for i := 1 to m do
    begin
        if(rankone[i] = missing) or (ranktwo[i] = missing) then
            count := count + 1
        else
            sum := sum + sqr(rankone[i] − ranktwo[i])
    end;
    total := m − count; { actual number of rankings included }
    if total > 1 then
        correlate := 1.0 − (6.0 * sum) / ((total) * (sqr(total) − 1.0))
    else
        correlate := 0.0
end; { of function correlate }
```

Figure 11-6. Refinement of the function correlate.

If we look back on what we have accomplished so far, we will see that we have written about 110 lines of code (Figures 11-3, 11-4, and 11-6) and defined a total of 9 separate program units (Figure 11-5). However, in spite of the fact that this is rapidly becoming a good-sized project, we are not lost or confused by the amount of detail we must cope with. We have a very good idea of what has been done and what still needs to be done. We are quite clear on what procedures still need to be written, in what order they should be written, and what they must do. And, even though we are well into the design of our program, we have still postponed a number of key decisions. For example,

1. We have not yet decided upon the exact criteria for determining whether a data item is valid. (That is hidden in the procedures statcheck and validate.)

2. We have not decided how to handle ties. (This is hidden in the procedure rank.)

3. We have not decided upon the exact format of the output. (This is hidden in the procedure printreport.)

Finally, it should now be clear how top-down modular programming facilitates the partitioning of work among teams of programmers. For example, if two people were assigned the task of completing the rank correlation problem we have begun, then it might be quite natural to assign, for example, one to code errorhandler and rank while the other codes printreport and findlargest. While each programmer is waiting for the other to complete the assigned units, he or she can use stubs to complete the debugging and testing of his or her own code segments. It will then be the responsibility of the team manager to integrate these newly developed pieces into the overall program and to ensure that they work correctly as a complete unit. (This last point is quite important. It is possible for two procedures to be tested alone and work quite well, but fail miserably when executed together. This is usually due to an error in the *interface* between the two units, as in:

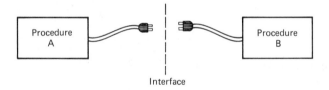

Interface

Each one may be correct, but together they are useless!)

The remainder of the coding of the rank correlation coefficient problem is left as an exercise at the end of the chapter (Exercise 1a).

In summary, we hope that the case study we have begun here has demonstrated the advantages to be gained from using a top-down program design approach. They are:

1. The intellectual manageability of large programming projects.

2. The ability to temporarily abstract away currently unimportant details.

3. The ability to postpone lower-level decisions until the latest possible moment.

4. Easier debugging and testing.

5. A natural way to allocate portions of the overall task to teams of programmers.

Style Clinic 11-3 _____

> ### Beware of Degradation Caused by Change
>
> Working programs need to be changed from time to time in order to correct minor errors or adapt to changing circumstances. While making such changes, one must be very careful. If a program was not well designed, it is possible to introduce major problems while fixing small ones.
>
> This is especially true of programs that have not been properly modularized. One of the keys to writing adaptable and maintainable programs is to ensure that local changes have only local consequences. In other words, to achieve an alteration in program behavior, it should always be possible to isolate a module in which a coding change has become necessary and to change only the contents of that module.

As we mentioned at the beginning of this chapter, we can give only the briefest introduction to the topic of program design techniques. However, we hope that this discussion has made the reader aware of the critical importance of planning and organization during the development of computer software. Without such a structure, frustration and chaos will reign.

11.4   THE ULTIMATE MEASURE OF COMPUTER PROGRAMS

The main purpose of this chapter has been to present a method for developing well-structured and modular computer programs. Likewise, we have spent a great deal of space throughout the text, especially in the style clinics, presenting guidelines for making programs more readable and "elegant." Yet in the final analysis, we must remember that technical characteristics such as coding style, modularity, and computational efficiency are not ends in themselves, but only a means to an end. Our real concern should be with asking the question: What ultimately constitutes a good program?

The answer to that is easy if we simply remember that programs are not written for their own sake (except homework projects!). They are written for *end-users,* and the ultimate criteria for program "goodness" must be those characteristics that make the program easier to use for those people who will work with and use it. These criteria would include things like correctness, a friendly user interface, and cost effectiveness over the life of the program. No matter how efficient and well-structured your program may be, if it isn't what the user wants, it will disappear into the wastebasket! However, most of the attributes of a program that contribute to these user-oriented goals are themselves directly related to such technical concerns as coding style, program structure, and modularity.

Obviously, the end-users want the program to produce *correct results*. But even more, they want correct results or meaningful behavior under all circumstances. Users make mistakes (as all of us do) and a program that would accept incorrect input and produce wrong answers with no warnings that they are wrong is a very dangerous beast, especially in such applications as financial systems, security systems, or real-time control programs, to name just a few. Programs should be able to react in a meaningful way to input mistakes made by users, and should not mislead or misinform. They should tell the user of the existence of the error, how to correct it, and continue on, if possible. When mistakes are encountered, the program should present users with information in a form that they can quickly understand and use. Avoid writing programs with error messages like this.

*** *Error, address trap at octal address 017743*
Interrupt processing suspended, post-mortem dump
to follow ***
pc = 0001734004 st = 1777777777

The user will simply throw up his or her hands in disgust and begin looking for a new programmer!

This program characteristic is called *robustness* and was first introduced and discussed in Style Clinic 6-3. To ensure robustness, we must anticipate possible errors and program defensively to prevent them from affecting our program. Likewise, we must thoroughly validate all input provided by the user. Finally, we must adequately test and verify our code using test data chosen according to the guidelines in Chapter 6. Our programs should be correct, accurate, and reliable under *all* circumstances.

Another important measure of a program is the quality of its *user interface*. Most users will treat your program as a "black box" that accepts some input and produces some output. They could not care less about what goes on inside and how we determine the results.

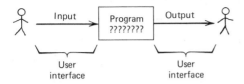

Their evaluation of the program will be based strictly on the interface between the program and the user, and how "friendly" it is.

Input.   Is it easy to prepare and submit?
Is it easy to proofread and verify?
Will the machine accept it in the existing form or do I have to change it manually (e.g., units)?
Are there defaults for things I choose to omit?
Does the program tell you what input it is waiting for?
Does the program have a "help mode" if the user is confused and does not know what to do?

Output.   Is it readable?
Does it give me everything I want?
Is it in the right format (accuracy, units)?

For example, a program that prompts a user for input but does not tell what is being requested:

> ?

or that prints cryptic and confusing information:

> *? input trap address vector followed by cr/lf*

will quickly irritate and anger the typical user. Likewise, an elegantly written program with sloppy output will quickly end up in the garbage!

Taken together, the two points just discussed (robustness, well-designed interface) are directed at producing what could be called "user-friendly" programs. They are characterized by natural input styles and elegant, highly readable output. They are tolerant of errors and help users to correct them. In summary, we would say that such programs are "easy to use." From the end-user's point of view, ease of use is one of the most important measures of program quality.

Users' needs are not static. They change frequently in response to such things as new laws, new ideas, new products, or new computer facilities. The ease with which such changes can be made is a measure of the program's *adaptability*. This aspect of program quality depends not only on program clarity, but also on modularity and program structure. Adaptability comes naturally from a well-structured, modular design because changes are localized to one or a few specific modules. The effects of the changes will not propagate to other program units. An adaptable program is also an easily *maintainable* program. This is because the modification being made may not be in response to changes in user needs but to correct an error that was not discovered during the testing phase. Overall, characteristics like adaptability, maintainability, and portability—which relate to the ability of programs to move, change, and grow—are critically important measures of program quality. They will allow a program to meet a wide range of user needs, run on a wide range of different computers, and remain a useful tool for many years.

Finally, we must come to that most universal of all criteria—money! One of the key measures of program quality is its *cost effectiveness,* that is, the ability to produce correct answers for the lowest possible cost. However, we must remember that costs must be measured over the life of the program and must include both the machine costs and the people costs of producing these programs.

During the 1970s and 1980s, hardware costs have been coming down much more rapidly than costs associated with people—salaries and benefits. Today it is estimated that over 70% of the costs of software development are for programmer salaries. Therefore, to build cost-effective programs, we cannot worry simply about the computer costs of running a program. We must also construct software that is easy for *people* to read, understand, and maintain. This will involve writing well-structured, modular, and "elegant" code. Then, as changes are made to the problem specification, as new errors are discovered, or when new computer hardware is purchased, the maintenance programmers who must read and modify the code will be able to do their job quickly, correctly, and for less money. Programmers must remember that cost-effective software is developed by programming for people, not just for machines.

To summarize, the best measures of a program's quality are not its technical characteristics, that is, the number of procedures used, the proper use of call-by-value parameters, the absence of **goto**s, or some clever indentation scheme. Rather, it is the characteristics and behavior that will make the program easiest to use by those people who will be working with and running that program during its lifetime. These characteristics include (but are not limited to):

1. Correctness.
2. Robustness.
3. Friendly user interface.
4. Ease of use.
5. Adaptability.
6. Maintainability.
7. Portability.
8. Cost effectiveness.

The programming style guidelines and development techniques discussed throughout this text should greatly facilitate writing programs that have these characteristics.

11.5   CONCLUSION

This chapter completes our discussion of programming and problem solving. We have accomplished our original goals as stated in the Preface and Chapter 1: to introduce and motivate all aspects of the programming process, to develop guidelines for producing good, reliable programs, and to teach Pascal. However, as we mentioned earlier, programming, in its fullest sense, must be actively learned and experienced. We hope that you will apply the principles presented here to every programming task, regardless of whether it is in a classroom or industrial environment, or whether it is for practice or profit. This experience is the only real way to gain insight into the programming process and to develop true programming ability.

*Style Clinic 11-4*_____

Beware the Lone Wolf!

The days of the "lone wolf" programmer are over. The person who disappeared into a corner for 6 months and reappeared with a working program is no longer admired, or even tolerated. Too often, their programs were so complex, so intricate, and so poorly documented that nobody else could understand or maintain them. Since there was only one person in the world who knew how it worked, if that person left, no one would be able to fix it if it failed or needed a change.

Because of the enormous increase in software development costs, we cannot tolerate a situation in which we have invested huge sums of money in developing a computer program that only one person understands. This is one of the major reasons for the existence of programming teams and co-operative development efforts. With a team effort, there should always be someone available to pick up the work of someone who has left. Because of the growth of team programming efforts, new programmers must realize that technical abilities alone are not enough. They must also develop their abilities to work *with* and *for* other people. They will need to concern themselves with such matters as clear, concise, unambiguous verbal and written communication, the art of cooperation and compromise, and the ability to suppress one's own ego for the good of the project. In today's programming world, a programmer must be good at communicating with people as well as with computers!

EXERCISES FOR CHAPTER 11

1. (a) Complete the development of the rank correlation coefficient problem described in Section 11.3. Using the existing programs listed in Figures 11-3, 11-4, and 11-6, finish coding all modules included in the development tree of Figure 11-5. You may add additional routines that you feel are necessary

or helpful. Do not code all of the additional routines at once, but try to test one or two at a time using the concept of a program stub introduced in this chapter.

For raw data, have your instructor provide you with the following values from a previous section of your course: homework scores, midquarter examination scores, and final examination scores. (Anonymously, of course!) Then answer the following question: Which is a better predictor of how a student will do on the final exam: performance on the homework exercises, or score on the midquarter examination?

(b) Modify the rank correlation program (described in Section 11.3 and in Exercise 1a) to meet the following new specification.

The users of the program decided that they not only wanted the correlations between each exam, but they also wanted, for each individual exam, the following two additional values.

The *mean*, M, of the scores of all students who took the exam:

$$M = \frac{\Sigma x_i}{N}, \qquad \text{where, } x_i = \text{the individual scores } i = 1, \ldots, N$$
$$N = \text{the number of scores}$$

The *standard deviation*, σ, of all the scores:

$$\sigma = \sqrt{\frac{\Sigma (x_i - M)^2}{N - 1}}$$

Modify the program from Exercise 1a so that, in addition to what it currently performs, it also computes and prints both M and σ for each examination.

Discuss how you feel the modularization of the program facilitated making this change. How many modules were affected by this change? How many were unaffected?

The following three programs are large programming projects that should be attempted with teams of about 2 to 4 people.

2. Design a *document processor* (also called a *text formatter*) that accepts character strings and formatting commands as input and produces a properly formatted document as output. All input commands begin with a period in column 1. No text (except the command itself) can appear on such a line. Commands consist of the following:

.left n	Set left margin to column n.
.right n	Set right margin to column n.
.indent n	Terminate the current line of text and begin a new line after indenting n spaces.
.center	Center the next line of text between the left and right margins.
.spacing n	Set the line spacing to n. (1 = single spacing, 2 = double spacing, etc.).
.blank n	Terminate the current line and leave n blank lines before starting the next line.

Any line that does not begin with a period is to be considered a line of text. Text should be filled with an appropriate number of spaces between words so that the resulting text is flush with the left and right margins. If the current line of text does not contain enough characters, continue accumulating input text until the line is full (subject to any formatting commands that might be encountered). In general, there will not be a one-to-one relationship between lines of input and output text. For example,

Input data

```
.left 20
.right 50
.center
an example
.spacing 1
.indent 3
this is an example of text that will be filled and
justified.
.blank 1
end of example
```

Output text

```
            an example
        this is an example of
        text that will be filled and
        justified.

        end of example
```

In your design of the program, specify the modules you will use, the function of each module, and the interfaces between modules. Design your program in such a way that you can easily add new formatting commands without affecting what has been done so far.

3.   Write a program to develop a *concordance* of some text. This is an alphabetical list of every word that appears in the text and the location (line number) of every occurrence. For example, if our text was

> To be or
> not to be.
> That is the question.

our concordance would look like this:

Word	*References (Line Number)*
be	1, 2
is	3
not	2
or	1
question	3
that	3
the	3
to	1, 2

Your concordance should adhere to the following specifications.

(a)   The input text will be in a Pascal text file called intext. The output should be to the standard output file and should include a complete copy of the input text followed by the concordance itself.

(b)   Make a decision on both the maximum number of unique words and the maximum number of references per word. If either of these values is exceeded, do *not* terminate the program but inform the user that he or she may be losing some information and the concordance may not be complete. However, you are to keep building the concordance and produce the desired output.

(c)   Do not include two references to the same line number for one word. That is, the following line:

> To be or not to be

should have only a single reference for both ''to'' and ''be'' to this line number.

(d) You may limit the length of a single word to 12 letters and consider all words that start with the same 12 characters as identical. Discard the additional characters. Thus,

    characterization

and

    characterizations

are (to the concordance) the same word, namely "characteriza."

4. You are to design and implement a *picture drawing system*. Basically, this is a set of programs that allows you to input picture drawing commands that create points, lines, circles, triangles, and other geometric shapes. These pictures may then be displayed on a computer terminal or line printer.

The programs will be creating the picture by inserting characters within a data structure to approximate the shapes you request. For example,

Line   Triangle   Circle

There are four basic classes of commands that can be provided to your system. The following are intended only as examples of these classes. The decisions on exactly which commands to implement will be part of the system design process.

  I. Basic routines.
    A. initialize m, n
        Clear a picture of size 1. .m by 1. .n. The value of m, n will depend on the output device being used.
    B. displaychar c
        Use the character 'c' for printing pictures.
    C. print x_1, y_1, x_2, y_2
        Print that portion of the picture lying within the rectangle $[x_1, y_1]$, $[x_1, y_2]$, $[x_2, y_1]$, $[x_2, y_2]$.
    D. save name
        Save this picture under the designated name. Naturally we will need some command that retrieves it later.
 II. Simple drawing commands.
    A. point x_1, y_1
        Place a character at location $[x_1, y_1]$
    B. line x_1, y_1, x_2, y_2
        Draw a line connecting point $[x_1, y_1]$ and point $[x_2, y_2]$.

        C. circle x_1, y_1, r
            Draw a circle with center at $[x_1, y_1]$ and radius r.

  III. More complex drawing commands.
        A. dottedline x_1, y_1, x_2, y_2, s
            Draw a line connecting point $[x_1, y_1]$ and point $[x_2, y_2]$
            alternately using line segments and spaces of length s.
        B. triangle $(x_1, y_1, x_2, y_2, x_3, y_3)$
            Draw a triangle between the three points given as parameters.
            However, first make sure that the three points are not all in line, in
            which case we cannot form a triangle.
        C. face
            Draw the following figure.

  IV. Manipulation routines.
        A. move direction, units
            Move the entire picture (up, down, left, right) the indicated number
            of units.
        B. rotate
        C. enlarge
        D. erase

Set up your picture drawing system so that it will be easy to add new commands
to the system at a later time.

5. Using any large programming system available on your local computer, such as:

    The operating system.

    The Pascal compiler.

    A text editor/word processor.

    A data base management system.

    A mathematical subroutine package.

write a report evaluating the quality of the *user interface*. Discuss its clarity, ease
of learning, ease of use, error messages, on-line assistance, and tolerance of user
mistakes. Describe how you might redesign and improve this interface.

6. One of the problems with using a read or readln command to input an integer or
    real variable is that it is very unforgiving. If an incorrect type of character is

entered accidentally, your program will "bomb out" with a not-too-useful error message.

For example, in the Game of Life program in Section 9.4 we read in the board size using the following.

```
writeln('please enter the size of the board');
read(boardsize)
```

If a user was confused about how to enter the board size value and incorrectly typed:

```
? the board size is 6 by 6
```

(instead of simply a 6), the Cyber/74 at the University of Minnesota would print out:

```
** program terminated at line xxx in procedure readboard
      non-digit encountered in digit field
            — readboard —
            .

            .
      .           a post-mortem
      .           dump followed by termination
```

Other systems would produce similar messages. This is certainly not a "friendly" or "forgiving" program.

Modify the Game of Life program so that it will accept *any* input entered by a user, without abnormal termination. If the input is erroneous, print out a useful error message about what was wrong and how to correct it. Your goal should be to produce a program that cannot generate a run-time error and that helps the user recover easily from input mistakes.

SYNTAX OF THE
Pascal LANGUAGE*

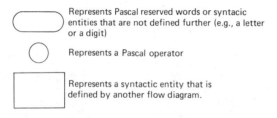

Represents Pascal reserved words or syntacic entities that are not defined further (e.g., a letter or a digit)

Represents a Pascal operator

Represents a syntactic entity that is defined by another flow diagram.

Program

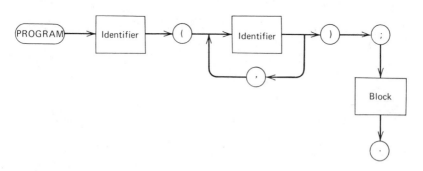

*This appendix is taken from Appendix D, p. 116–118 of Jensen and Wirth, *PASCAL Users Manual and Report*, Springer-Verlag, 1974, with their permission.

Block

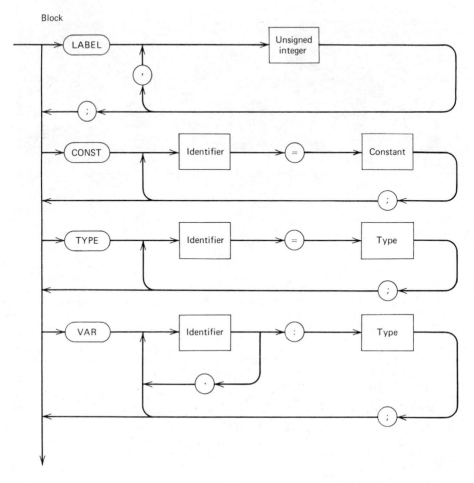

Continued on next page

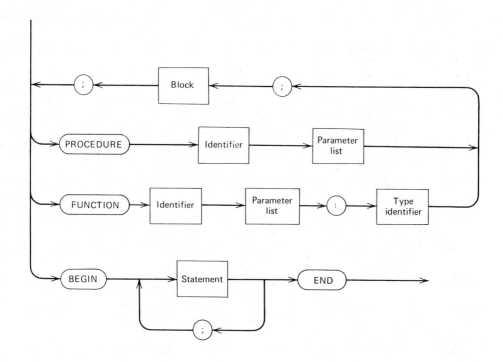

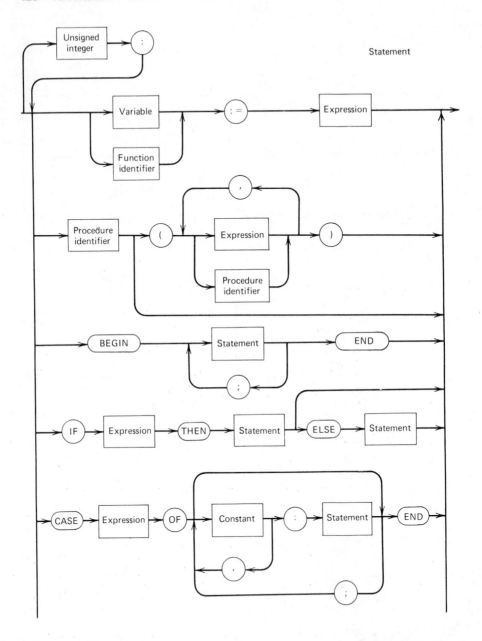

Statement

Continued on next page

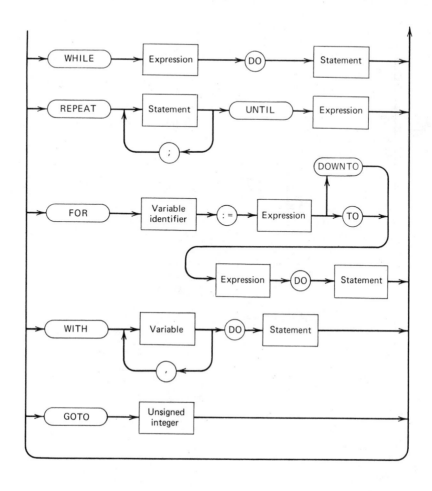

Type

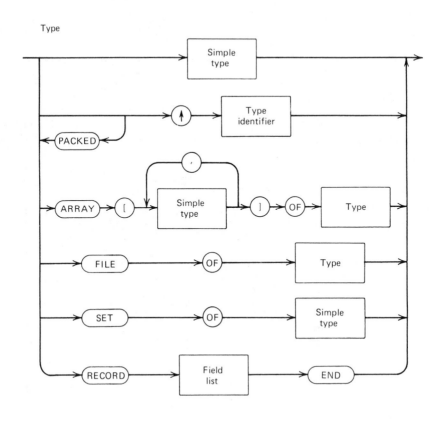

Simple type

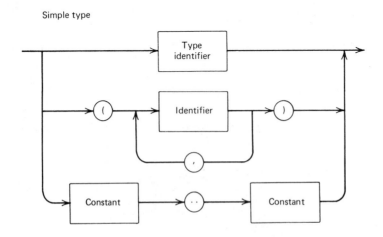

Parameter list

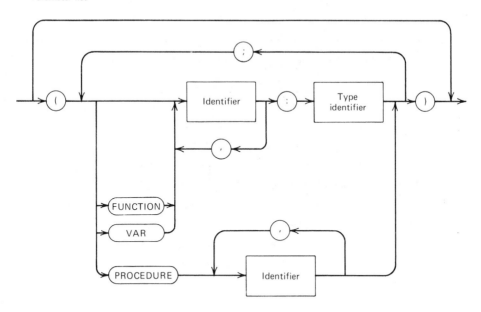

Field list

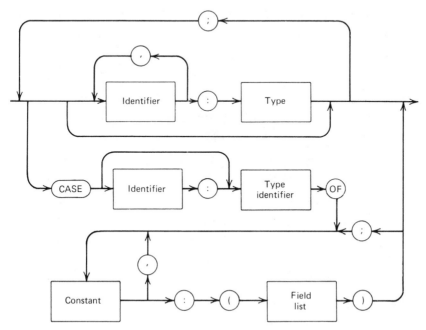

Expression

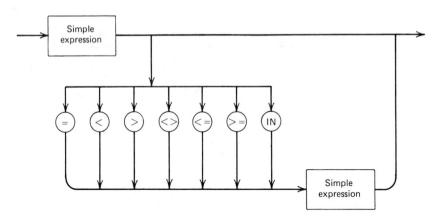

Simple expression

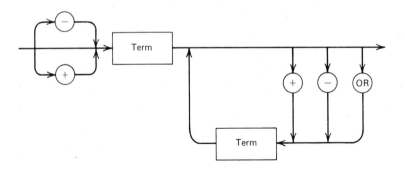

Term

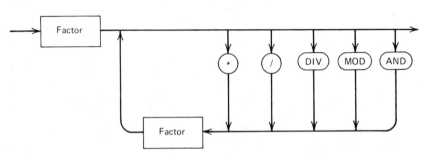

Factor

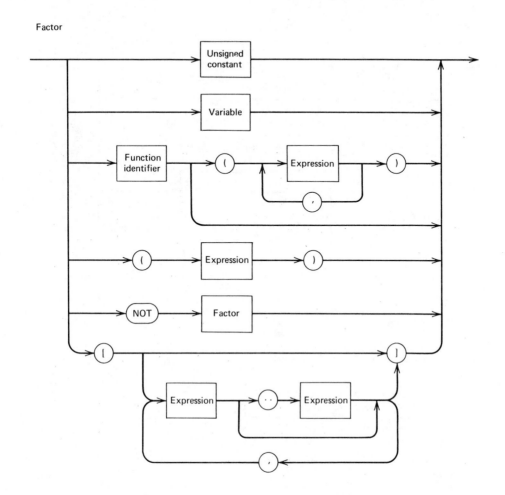

Variable

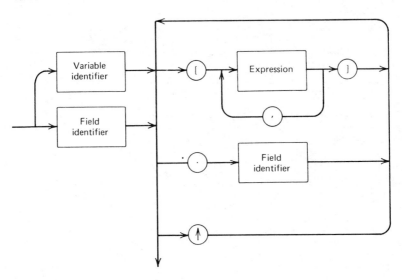

Unsigned constant

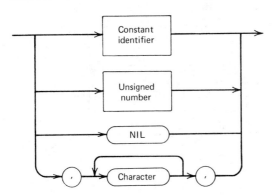

Constant

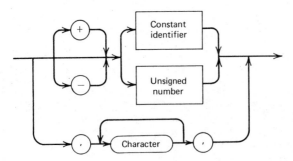

Identifier

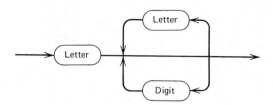

Unsigned integer

Unsigned number

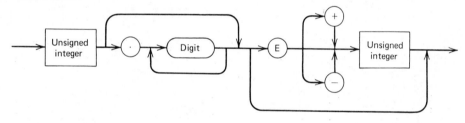

STANDARDIZED
Pascal IDENTIFIERS

B.1 RESERVED WORDS

and	end	nil	set
array	file	not	then
begin	for	of	to
case	function	or	type
const	goto	packed	until
div	if	procedure	var
do	in	program	while
downto	label	record	with
else	mod	repeat	

B.2 STANDARD IDENTIFIERS

Constants

false	*true*	*maxint*

Types

integer	*boolean*	*real*	*char*	*text*

Files

input	*output*

Functions

	Types		
Name	*Parameter*	*Result*	*Description*
abs(x)	integer or real	Same as parameter	Absolute value
arctan(x)	integer or real	real	Inverse tangent

chr(x)	integer	char	Character whose ordinal number is x
cos(x)	integer or real	real	Cosine
eof(f)	file	boolean	End-of-file indicator
eoln(f)	file	boolean	End-of-line indicator
exp(x)	real or integer	real	e^x
ln(x)	real or integer	real	Natural logarithm
odd(x)	integer	boolean	True if x is odd False otherwise
ord(x)	User-defined scalar, char, boolean	integer	Ordinal number of x in the scalar data type of which x is a member
pred(x)	Scalar, but not real	Same as parameter	Predecessor of x
round(x)	real	integer	x rounded
sin(x)	real or integer	real	Sine
sqr(x)	real or integer	Same as parameter	Square of x
sqrt(x)	real or integer	real	Square root
succ(x)	Scalar, but not real	Same as parameter	Successor of x
trunc(x)	real	integer	x truncated

Procedures

Name (parameters)	Description
dispose(p)	Returns the dynamic variable referenced by pointer p to the available space list
get(f)	Advances file f to the next component and places the value of the component in f↑
new(p)	Allocates a new variable that is accessed through pointer p
pack(a,i,z)	Takes the elements beginning at subscript position i of array a and copies them into packed array z beginning at the first subscript position
page(f)	Causes the printer to skip to the top of a new page before printing the next line of text file f
read(. . .) readln(. . .)	Reads information from text files.
reset(f)	Positions file f at its beginning for reading
rewrite(f)	Empties file f and allows it to be written into

unpack(z,a,i)   Takes the elements beginning at the first subscript position of packed array z and copies them into array a beginning at subscript position i

write(. . .)
writeln(. . .) }   Writes information to text files.

B.3 SUMMARY OF OPERATORS

		Types	
Operator	*Description*	*Operand(s)*	*Result*
: =	Assignment	Any, except file	—
+	Addition	integer or real	integer or real
	Set union	Any set type	Same as operand
−	Subtraction	integer or real	integer or real
	Set difference	Any set type	Same as operand
*	Multiplication	integer or real	integer or real
	Set intersection	Any set type	Same as operand
div	Integer division	integer	integer
/	Real division	integer or real	real
mod	Modulus	integer	integer
not	Logical negation	boolean	boolean
or	Disjunction	boolean	boolean
and	Conjunction	boolean	boolean
< =	Implication	boolean	boolean
	Set inclusion	Any set type	boolean
	Less than or equal	Any scalar type	boolean
=	Equivalence	boolean	boolean
	Equality	Scalar, set, or pointer	boolean
< >	exclusive **or**	boolean	boolean
	Inequality	Scalar, set, or pointer	boolean
> =	Set inclusion	Any set type	boolean
	Greater than or equal	Any scalar type	boolean
<	Less than	Any scalar type	boolean
>	Greater than	Any scalar type	boolean
in	Set membership	Left operand: scalar Right operand: set with base type the type of the left operand	boolean

CHARACTER SETS

The charts in this appendix depict the ordering for several commonly used character sets. Numbers are base 10 and only printable characters are shown.

Many other character sets and collating sequences not included here are in current use.

C.1 CDC SCIENTIFIC, WITH 64 CHARACTERS

Left Digit	Right Digit	*0*	*1*	*2*	*3*	*4*	*5*	*6*	*7*	*8*	*9*
0		:	A	B	C	D	E	F	G	H	I
1		J	K	L	M	N	O	P	Q	R	S
2		T	U	V	W	X	Y	Z	0	1	2
3		3	4	5	6	7	8	9	+	−	*
4		/	(	)	$	=	ƀ	,	.	≡	[
5		]	%	≠	↱	∨	∧	↑	↓	<	>
6		≤	≥	¬	;						

Code 45 is the blank (ƀ = blank)

C.2 ASCII (AMERICAN STANDARD CODE FOR INFORMATION INTERCHANGE)

Left Digit(s)	Right Digit 0	1	2	3	4	5	6	7	8	9
3			ƀ	!	''	#	$	%	&	'
4	(	)	*	+	,	—	.	/	0	1
5	2	3	4	5	6	7	8	9	:	;
6	<	=	>	?	@	A	B	C	D	E
7	F	G	H	I	J	K	L	M	N	O
8	P	Q	R	S	T	U	V	W	X	Y
9	Z	[	\	]	∧	—	`	a	b	c
10	d	e	f	g	h	i	j	k	l	m
11	n	o	p	q	r	s	t	u	v	w
12	x	y	z	{	|	}	‾			

Codes 00 to 31 and 127 (decimal) represent special control characters that are not printable. Code 32 is the blank (ƀ = blank)

C.3 EBCDIC (EXTENDED BINARY CODED DECIMAL INTERCHANGE CODE)

Left (Digit(s))	Right Digit 0	1	2	3	4	5	6	7	8	9
6					ƀ					
7					¢	.	<	(	+	|
8	&									
9	!	$	*	)	;	¬	—	/		
10							—	,	%	—
11	>	?								
12		`	:	#	@	'	=	''		a
13	b	c	d	e	f	g	h	i		
14						j	k	l	m	n
15	o	p	q	r						
16		~	s	t	u	v	w	x	y	z
17				[						]
18										
19			{	A	B	C	D	E	F	G
20	H	I							}	J
21	K	L	M	N	O	P	Q	R		
22							S	T	U	V
23	W	X	Y	Z	\					
24	0	1	2	3	4	5	6	7	8	9

Codes 00 to 63 and 250 to 255 represent nonprintable control characters.
Code 64 is the blank (ƀ = blank)

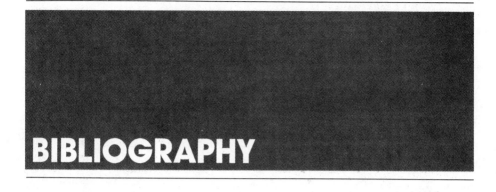

BIBLIOGRAPHY

I. GENERAL SURVEYS

Dijkstra, E. W., *A Discipline of Programming*, Prentice-Hall, 1976.

Weinberg, G. M., *The Psychology of Computer Programming*, Van Nostrand, 1971.

Wirth, N., *Systematic Programming*, Prentice-Hall, 1973.

Yohe, J. M., "An Overview of Programming Practices," *ACM Computing Surveys*, December 1974.

II. ALGORITHMS AND PROBLEM SOLVING

Aho, A. V., J. E. Hopcroft, and J. D. Ullman, *The Design and Analysis of Computer Algorithms*, Addison-Wesley, 1974.

Calter, P., *Problem Solving with Computers*, McGraw-Hill, 1973.

Goodman, S., and S. Hedetniemi, *Introduction to the Design and Analysis of Algorithms*, McGraw-Hill, 1977.

Horowitz, E., and S. Sahni, *Fundamentals of Computer Algorithms*, Computer Science Press, 1978.

Knuth, D., *The Art of Computer Programming*, Vol. 1, "Fundamental Algorithms," Addison-Wesley, 1968.

Pattis, R., *Karel the Robot*, Wiley, 1981.

Polya, G., *How to Solve It*, Princeton University Press, 1971.

Tremblay, J., R. Bunt, *An Introduction to Computer Science: The Algorithmic Approach*, McGraw-Hill, 1979.

Watkins, R. P., *Computer Problem Solving*, McGraw-Hill, 1973.

Wirth, N., *Algorithms + Data Structures = Programs*, Prentice-Hall, 1976.

III. THE PASCAL LANGUAGE

Conway, R., D. Gries, and E. Zimmerman, *A Primer on Pascal,* Second Edition, Winthrop, 1981.

Findlay, W., and D. Watt, *Pascal—An Introduction to Methodical Programming,* Computer Science Press, 1978.

Grogono, P., *Programming in Pascal,* Second Edition, Addison-Wesley, 1981.

Hoare, C. A. R., and N. Wirth, "An Axiomatic Definition of the Programming Language Pascal," *Acta Informatica,* Vol. 2, 1973.

Holt, R., and J. Hume, *Programming in Standard Pascal,* Reston, 1980.

Jensen, K., and N. Wirth, *Pascal—User Manual and Report,* Springer-Verlag, 1974.

Kieburtz, R., *Structured Programming and Problem Solving with Pascal,* Prentice-Hall, 1979.

Webster, C. A. G., *Introduction to Pascal,* Hayden, 1976.

Wirth, N., "The Programming Language Pascal," *Acta Informatica,* Vol. 1, 1971. (The original description of the language.)

IV. PROGRAMMING STYLE

Kernighan, B. W., and P. J. Plauger, *The Elements of Programming Style,* Second Edition, McGraw-Hill, 1978.

Ledgard, H., J. Hueras, and P. Nagen, *Pascal with Style—Programming Proverbs,* Hayden, 1979.

Ledgard, H., *Programming Proverbs,* Hayden, 1975.

Shneiderman, B., *Software Psychology,* Winthrop, 1980.

Van Tassel, D., *Programming Style, Design, Efficiency, Debugging, and Testing,* Second Edition, Prentice-Hall, 1978.

Wetherell, C., *Etudes for Programmers,* Prentice-Hall, 1978.

V. STRUCTURED PROGRAMMING

Basili, V., and T. Baker, *Structured Programming: A Tutorial,* IEEE Publications, Catalog No. 75CH1049-6, 1975.

Dahl, O. J., E. W. Dijkstra, and C. A. R. Hoare, *Structured Programming,* Academic Press, 1972.

Hughes, J. K., and J. Michtom, *A Structured Approach to Programming,* Prentice-Hall, 1977.

Knuth, D., "Structured Programming with GOTO Statements," *ACM Computing Surveys,* December 1974.

McGowan, C. L., and J. R. Kelly, *Top-Down Structured Programming Techniques*, Petrocelli-Charter, 1975.

Schneider, G. M., and S. Bruell, *Advanced Programming and Problem Solving with Pascal*, Wiley, 1981.

Weinberg, V., *Structured Program Analysis*, Prentice-Hall, 1979.

Wirth, N., "On the Composition of Well Structured Programs," *ACM Computing Surveys*, December 1974.

Yourdon, E., *Techniques of Program Structure and Design*, Prentice-Hall, 1977.

SELECTED ANSWERS TO EXERCISES

Chapter 1

1. (a) You will be given a sequence of real numbers entered at a terminal, with one real value per line. The end of the input sequence will be signaled by an end-of-file condition. Your program should accept this input and then compute and print out the following four values.

    (i) Arithmetic mean, M, of all values that were entered. M is defined as

    $$M = \frac{\Sigma X_i}{N}, \qquad i = 1, \ldots, N$$

    where X_i are the input values, and N is the total number of values that were read in.

    (ii) The standard deviation, J, of all values, where standard deviation is defined as

    $$J = \sqrt{\frac{\Sigma(X_i - M)^2}{N - 1}}, \qquad i = 1, \ldots, N, N > 1$$

    (iii) The highest and lowest scores that were input to the program.

    In the event that no values are provided as input (i.e., N = 0), then your program should produce the following error message.

    *** *Error on Input, No input data provided* ***

2. (a) Prime numbers are only defined for integers, k, such that k >= 1. Therefore we may want to include the following three special conditions in our specification document.

    (i) k = 0 If k is 0, we could print out an appropriate error message.
    (ii) k < 0 If k is negative, we could either print an error message or we could determine whether the absolute value of k is a prime number.

(iii) k is not an integer   We could either print an error message or truncate the fractional part of k and then determine whether the remaining integer portion is a prime number.

3. Some of the ambiguities that are present in the current problem statement include the following.

(a) What is the format for the time field on the input cards (e.g., 5:30 P.M., 1730)?

(b) What if an employee missed a day of work? Will there be a blank card, no card?

(c) What is the exact format of the employee master card?

(d) What is the "normal" work week, and exactly when does overtime pay begin?

(e) Is there any limit on the amount of overtime we can accept in our program?

(f) What about deductions from gross pay?

(g) Exactly what format do you want for the final paystub?

(h) How will you know when you have finished processing all the employees?

These are only some of the possible ambiguities. You may add others where you feel the original problem statement was incomplete.

Chapter 2

1.
```
                    START
                       wet hair
                       repeat 2 times
                          lather
                          rinse
                       end of the repeat loop
                       stop
                    END OF THE ALGORITHM
```

2. (a) The algorithm is correct, but poor. It is not using the idea of iteration. This approach would be totally unworkable for any values much larger than 10.

(c) The algorithm is not properly incrementing the value of i. Therefore, the algorithm will incorrectly compute the value $1+1+1+1+1+1+1+1+1+1$.

3.   START
                read k
                if k <= 0 then
                    write "illegal value for k"
                else
                    set i to 1
                    set sum to 0
                    repeat k times
                        add i to sum
                        increment i by 1
                    end of the repeat loop
                    write "the sum of the first", k, "integers is", sum
                stop
            END OF THE ALGORITHM

6.   START
                read a,b,c
                if a = 0 and b = 0 then
                    write "illegal equation, cannot solve"
                else
                    if a = 0 then
                        set root to $-c/b$
                        write "linear equation, the one root is", root
                    else
                        set discriminant to $b^2 - 4ac$
                        if discriminant $<$ 0 then
                            write "roots are complex, cannot solve"
                        else
                            set root-1 to $\dfrac{-b + \sqrt{discriminant}}{2a}$

                            set root-2 to $\dfrac{-b - \sqrt{discriminant}}{2a}$

                        write "answers are", root-1, root-2
                            stop
                        END OF THE ALGORITHM

9. (a) START

　　　　{ assume lists A and B of lengths m and n are already defined }
　　　　set i to 1 { pointer into list A }
　　　　set j to 1 { pointer into list B }
　　　　set k to 1 { pointer into list C }
　　　　while (i <= m) and (j <= n) do
　　　　　　if $A_i < B_j$ then
　　　　　　　　set C_k to A_i
　　　　　　　　increment i by 1
　　　　　　　　increment k by 1
　　　　　　else
　　　　　　　　set C_k to B_j
　　　　　　　　increment j by 1
　　　　　　　　increment k by 1
　　　　end of the while loop
　　　　{ we will get here when we have exhausted one of the two lists. We will then
　　　　　simply copy the remaining items over to the list C }
　　　　if i > m then { we emptied list A }
　　　　　　repeat (n − j + 1) times
　　　　　　　　set C_k to B_j
　　　　　　　　increment j by 1
　　　　　　　　increment k by 1
　　　　　　end of the repeat loop
　　　　else　　　　{ we emptied list B }
　　　　　　repeat (m − i + 1) times
　　　　　　　　set C_k to A_i
　　　　　　　　increment i by 1
　　　　　　　　increment k by 1
　　　　　　end of the repeat loop
　　　　stop
　　　END OF THE ALGORITHM

12.   START
    read N
    if N < 1 then
        write "illegal input, the input value must be greater than or equal to 1"
    else
        set upperlimit to $\sqrt{N}$ truncated to an integer quantity
        set factor to 2
        set found to false
        while factor <= upperlimit and found is false do
            divide N by factor and save the remainder
            if the remainder = 0 then
                set found to true
            else
                increment factor by 1
        end of the while loop
        if found = false then
            write N, "is prime"
        else
            write N, "is not prime," factor, "is a factor"
    stop
  END OF THE ALGORITHM

Chapter 3

1. (a) 3.14159, 0.314159e + 1
   (c) 0.5, 1.0/2.0 (although this is an expression, not a constant)
   (d) 6.02e23
   (f) '7'
   (h) 18.0E9

2. (a) Valid.
   (b) Invalid. You cannot use boolean operators in a **const** declaration.
   (c) Invalid. The ':' is improper syntax.
   (d) Valid.
   (e) Invalid. You cannot use a subrange as a constant.

3. **const**

```
terminator  = '.';
maxlength   = 80;
low         = 0.0;
high        = 100.0;
```

5. (a) Valid, although unnecessary. This is exactly equivalent to the predefined standard meaning of integer.

   (b) Invalid. You cannot apply subrange to the real data type.

   (c) Invalid. The constants 1, 2, 3, 4 would be in two different data types, integer and yearinschool.

   type
   ```
   yearinschool = (freshman, sophomore, junior, senior);
   ```

7. **var**

```
a, b, c        : real;
root1, root2   : real;
answer         : boolean;
index          : integer;
colors         : (red, yellow, blue);
```

10. (a) Reserved word.

   (c) User identifier.

   (e) Standard identifier.

   (g) User identifier.

   (i) Invalid. (If it is a real number, it must have a digit following the letter e. If it is an identifier, it cannot begin with a digit.)

   (k) User identifier.

   (m) Invalid. (No digit before the decimal point.)

12. (a) Equivalence is the same as the relational operator =

   $$p = q$$

   (b) Exclusive-or is the same as the relational operator <>

   $$p <> q$$

Chapter 4

1. (a) 29
   (b) 21

2. (a) -5
   (b) $-4.9277\text{E}3$ (to 5 places)

3. (a) True.
   (b) False.

4. The formula is an incorrect translation. As it stands, the expression computes the value

$$k \sqrt{\sin\theta - \frac{1}{\cos\theta} + 1}$$

To make it a translation of the desired formula, we must write it in the following way.

   k * sqrt((sin(theta) − 1.0) / (cos(theta) + 1.0))

5. (a) **var**

taxable	*: real;*	*{ taxable pay in dollars and cents }*
gross	*: real;*	*{ gross pay in dollars and cents }*
dependents	*: integer;*	*{ number of dependents claimed for tax purposes }*

   .
   .
   .

   taxable := gross − (11.0 * dependents) − 14.0

   (f) **var**

valid	*: boolean;*
score	*: real;*

   .
   .
   .

   valid := (score >= 200.0) **and** *(score <= 800.0)*

6. (a) a = 53   b = 81   c = 102   pointer at column 1, line 2
   (b) a = 53   b = 81   c = 102   pointer just past the 2 in 102 on line 1
   (c) a = 53   b = −601   c = 15   pointer at column 1, line 4

8. (a) The integer value for x must be the first value encountered (excluding leading blanks), and the character ch1 must follow immediately after the last character of x. The integer value for y must be next (without concern for intervening blanks) and the character ch2 must follow immediately after the last character of y. It does not matter how many cards these four values are placed on. A valid set of cards might be

> card 1: ──── 15*   (──── = blank)
> card 2: ──── 35$

Given these two cards, the values assigned will be

> x = 15   ch1 = '*'
> y = 35   ch2 = '$'

9. (a) w = 13
   x = 80
   y = 21
   z = 9

and end-of-file is false. The input pointer will be pointing at the blank character immediately following the digit 9 on the second card.

11. (a) $1.234560000E + 00$ $5.6789000000E + 02$ 10
         $

   (b)   1.2 567.890   10

12. (c) *writeln('   total number   average   range');*
    writeln(' ----------- ------- ------- ');
    writeln(count:14, average:15:1, low:6:1, '–', high:4:1)

Chapter 5

1. (a) **repeat**
         read(ch);
         write(ch)
      until *(ch = '*') or eoln;*
      writeln

3. **for** *currentvalue* : = *150* **downto** *15* **do**
   S

   currentvalue : = *150;*
   while *currentvalue* >= *15* **do**
   begin
       S;
       currentvalue : = *currentvalue* − *1*
   end

5. **if** *v1* **then**
       if *v2* **then** S_1
       else S_2
   else
       S_3

6. **program** *examscores (input, output);*
   { program to compute exam averages in
   the range low to high   }

   const
       low = *0; { lowest legal score }*
       high = *150; { highest legal score }*

   var
score	: *low. .high;*	*{ an exam score }*
total	: *integer;*	*{ total of all valid scores }*
good	: *integer;*	*{ number of valid scores }*
bad	: *integer;*	*{ number of bad scores }*
average	: *real;*	*{ average of all valid scores }*

   begin
       total : = *0;*
       good : = *0;*
       bad : = *0;*
       writeln ('input data');

       while not *eof* **do**
       begin
           readln (score);
           writeln (score);
           if *(score < low)* **or** *(score > high)* **then**
               bad : = *bad + 1*
           else

(continued on next page)

```
        begin
            total := total + score;
            good := good + 1
        end { else clause }
    end; { while not eof loop }

    if good = 0 then
        writeln ('sorry, no valid scores to average')
    else
    begin
        average := total/good;
        writeln ('there were', good, 'valid scores');
        writeln ('there were', bad, 'illegal scores');
        writeln ('average of the valid scores =', average:10:2)
    end { else clause }
end. { of program examscores }
```

8. **program** *celsius (input, output);*

    *{ program to print a table of fahrenheit to centigrade temperature equivalences.
    The range of the table and the increment size are input to the program   }*

    var
low	*: real;*	*{ low end of the conversion table }*
high	*: real;*	*{ high end of the conversion table }*
increment	*: real;*	*{ the increment size }*
centigrade	*: real;*	*{ temperature in °C }*
fahrenheit	*: real;*	*{ temperature in °F }*
temp	*: real;*	*{ temporary variable }*

    begin
    ```
        writeln ('please input the low. .high conversion range');
        writeln ('and the increment size');
        readln (low, high, increment);
    ```

    ```
        { validate the data }
        if low > high then
        begin
            writeln ('your ranges are out of order');
            writeln ('the program will assume you meant,' high, 'to', low);
            temp := low; { interchange }
            low := high;
            high := temp
        end;
    ```

(continued on next page)

```
if increment < 0.0 then
begin
    writeln ('the increment must be positive. The program will
        assume you meant ', abs(increment));
    increment : = abs(increment)
end;
writeln ('fahrenheit centigrade');
fahrenheit : = low;
while fahrenheit <= high do
begin
    centigrade : = (5.0/9.0) * (fahrenheit - 32.0);
    writeln ('fahrenheit:10:2, centigrade:13:2);
    fahrenheit : = fahrenheit + increment
end
end. { of program }
```

Chapter 6

1. (a) Invalid. Parentheses will be required around both boolean conditions.

    (b) Valid.

    (c) Valid. The **then** clause contains only the empty statement. Syntactically that is perfectly acceptable.

    (d) Invalid. Pascal has no operator notation for exponentiation. ** is used in other computer languages. Note the 10 character name circlearea is perfectly acceptable.

    (e) Valid. There are numerous redundancies, but no actual syntactic errors. The **begin-end** pair is not needed, but will not cause problems. The semicolons after z : = x + y and **end** are also unnecessary, but the "empty statement" will allow the statements to be translated correctly.

    (f) Invalid. There can be no implied multiplication in Pascal. We must say 2*a or 2.0*a.

    (g) Invalid. : = is the assignment operator
        = is the comparison operator

    (h) Valid. The writeln command does not require parameters.

    (i) Invalid. The **var** declaration uses the colon to separate the name field from the type field.

    (j) Invalid. The **case** statement allows only a single statement following each case label. If we wish to perform more than one operation we must enclose it in a compound statement. Also, the **begin** is not used in a **case** statement.

    (k) Invalid. Illegal semicolon before the **else.**

2. *Line Number*   *Error*

1	**program** is misspelled (syntax error).
4	The variable ''i'' used by the **for** loop is not declared as an integer (syntax error).
4–5	The reserved word **begin** should appear after the **var** declaration (syntax error).
6	a. Initializing sum to 1 will produce the wrong answer (1 will be counted twice) (logic error).
	b. Semicolon is missing after the assignment statement (syntax error).
7	= should be : = (syntax error). Also, the variable i was not declared.
8	a. = should be : = (syntax error).
	b. The assignment statement should be sum : = sum + k (logic error).
	c. Semicolon is missing after the assignment statement (syntax error).
9	The text printed will be:
	The sum from 1 to k is. 'k' should not appear as a character in the string; rather its value should be printed. writeln ('the sum from 1 to', k, 'is', sum) (logic error).

3. Line 150.   The variable limit is misspelled.

Line 180.   There is an unmatched quote mark in the writeln statement.

Line 205.   A **begin** is needed.

Line 210.   There is a missing ';' after the assignment statement.

Line 290.   Same error as in line 180.

Chapter 7

1. (a) **type**

```
pricearray = array[1. .300] of real;
```

var

```
price : pricearray;
          .

          .

          .
```

```
for i : = 1 to 300 do price[i] : = 0.0
```

(b) **type**
```
      twod = array[1..10, 1..10] of integer;
```

   var
```
      matrix : twod;
```
         .

         .

         .

```
   for i := 1 to 10 do
       for j := 1 to 10 do
           if (i=j) then
               matrix[i,j] := 1
           else
               matrix[i,j] := 0
```

(d) **type**
```
      months = (jan,feb,mar,apr,may,jun,jul,aug,sep,oct,nov,dec);
```

   var
```
      list : array[months, 1..31] of real;
```

3. { *note that this fragment does not check for a value larger than maxint or check for illegal syntax* }

```
number := 0;
sign := none;
i := 1;
while (i <= 10) and (string[i] <> ' ') do
begin
    if (string[i] = '+') then
        sign := pos
    else
        if (string[i] = '-') then
            sign := neg
        else
            number := (number * 10) + (string[i] - ord('0'));
    i := i + 1
end; { while loop }
if sign = neg then
    number := -(number)
```

9. **program** *statistic (input,output);*

   { program to compute means and standard deviations }

   const
     maximum = 10;

   var
exam	: **array**[1. .*maximum*] **of** *real;*	
i	: *integer;*	*{ loop index }*
length	: *integer;*	*{ number of examinations }*
sum	: *real;*	
mean	: *real;*	*{ the arithmetic mean }*
deviation	: *real;*	*{ the standard deviation }*

   begin
     i := 1;
     while not *eof* **and** *(i <= maximum)* **do**
     begin
       readln(exam[i]);
       i := i + 1
     end;
     length := i−1;

     { compute the mean }
     sum := 0.0;
     for *i := 1* **to** *length* **do** *sum := sum + exam[i];*
     mean := sum/length; { assume length <> 0)
     writeln ('mean of all scores = ', mean:10:2);

     { compute standard deviation }
     sum := 0.0;
     for *i := 1* **to** *length* **do**
       sum := sum + sqr(exam[i] − mean);
     deviation := sqrt(sum/length);
     writeln ('standard deviation = ', deviation:10:2)
   end.

Chapter 8

1. Variable a is global to the entire program.
   The variable b declared in outer is available to outer, p2, and p3.
   The variables b and c declared in p1 are available only in p1.
   The variables c and d declared in p2 are available in p2 and p3.
   The variable e declared in p3 is local to p3.

3. x = 6, y = 2, z = 3

4. inside proc1, values for a, b, c are currently   *** 2 6
   inside proc2, values for a, b, c are currently   4 5 6
   still inside proc1, values for a, b, c are currently   4 2 6
   inside main program, values for a, b, c are   1 2 3

6. a   —value
   asize —value
   b   —value, or variable if memory space is at a premium and we cannot
            afford 2,000 extra memory locations
   bsize —value
   c   —variable
   csize —variable
   switch —variable

7. Current values of m and value are 0   3
   Current values of m and value are 1   8
   Current values of m and value are 2 13
   Current values of m and value are 3 18
   18

9. The subprogram should probably be a function since it returns a single scalar
result that will be used within an arithmetic expression. Parameters should be
passed by value.

```
function invest(p:real; n:integer; r:real):real;
const
     freq = 4; { compound quarterly }
var
     value, rate : real;
     year,i : integer;
begin
     value := p;
     rate := r/freq; { interest rates per compounding period }
     for year := 1 to n do
        for i := 1 to freq do
           value := value * (1.0+rate);
     invest := value;
     writeln(p:10:2, 'will grow to', value:14:2, 'in', n:3,
        'years at', 100.0*r, '% interest')
end; { of invest }
```

Possible function invocation:
    result := invest(1000.0, 4, 0.06) { $1000 for 4 years at 6% }

15. (a) The procedure uses global variables for passing all information. However, global variables are not an acceptable way of passing information to an external procedure. We would need to make the following values parameters to the procedure.

list	(value parameter)
number	(value parameter)
average	(variable parameter)
bad	(variable parameter)

(b) The constant values for the legal range of scores (0–150) and the upper bound for the number of scores (200) should be variables passed in as call by value parameters. Or, alternatively, the range checking should be eliminated from the procedure altogether and placed in the read routine. As it now stands, the procedure is too specific for general use.

(c) The i and total should be local variables.

(d) If range checking is left in the procedure, it should return a signal flag indicating that illegal values were encountered.

(e) The procedure should not write out the result, but should return the result to the calling program. Note that this could mean that avg might be better written as a function.

(f) The indentation is not very good and leaves the scope of some of the loops in doubt.

Chapter 9

1. **type** *string* = **array**[*1* . .*25*] **of** *char;*

```
book = record
    author:         record
        last    :       string;
        first   :       string;
        middle  :       char
                    end; { author record }
    title:          string;
    publisher:      record
        name    :       string;
        city    :       string;
        state   :       string
                    end; { publisher record }
    edition:        integer;
    isbn:           integer
end; { book record }
```

3. **const**
   ```
   max = 10000;
   ```

   var
   ```
   textarray : array [1. .max] of book;
   ```

5. **type** *employeerec* = **record**
   ```
         name = record
               last: array [1. .20] of char;
               first: array [1. .20] of char
                     end; { name record }
         socsecurity      : integer;
         deptno           : integer;
         dependents       : integer;
         payrate          : real
   end; { employeerec }
   ```

6. **procedure** *pay (person : employeerec; table : arraytype;*
   n : integer; **var** *weeklypay : real);*
   ```
       {
       person — a record variable with the structure shown in Exercise 5
       table — an n × 2 table containing social security numbers in column 1 and
                   hours worked in column 2
       n — the number of rows in table
       weeklypay — the weekly pay computed by the procedure and returned }
   ```

   var
   ```
       i          : integer; { for loop index }
       found      : boolean; { used to search the table }
   ```
   begin
   ```
       with person do
       begin
           found : = false;
           i := 0;
           while i < n do
           begin
               i := i + 1;
               if socsecurity = table [i, 1] then
                       found : = true
           end;
           if found then
               weeklypay : = payrate * table[i,2]
           else
               weeklypay : = 0.0
       end { with }
   end; { procedure pay }
   ```

10. (a) [2, 3, 4, 5, 6, 8, 10]

  (b) [3, 5]

  (c) [1, 3, 5]

  (d) [3]

  (g) True.

11. (a) $a := letters + digits$

  (b) $b := digits + special + ['E']$

Chapter 10

1. (a) **type**

```
          line = packed array [1..132] of char; { assume 132 chars/line }
          linefile = file of line;
```

  var

```
          thefile : linefile;
```

  (b) **type**

```
          partsfile = file of record
                name : array [1..30] of char;
                number : integer;
                price : real;
                location : array [1..30] of char
          end; { partsfile }
```

  var

```
          part : partsfile;
```

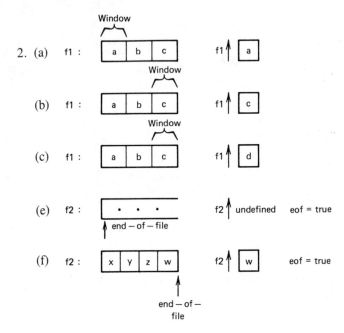

5. (b) **program** *extreme (outdata, output);*
{ *program to read outdata and count how many readings exceed 125 volts* }

const
   max = 125.0; { maximum voltage }

type
   sensorreading = **record**
                    time :   real;
                    voltage :   real
   end; *{ sensorrecord }*

var
   count   : integer; { counter for excessive readings }
   outdata   : **file of** *sensorreading;*
   sensor   : sensorreading;

begin
   count := 0;
   reset(outdata);
   sensor := outdata↑ ;
   while *sensor.voltage <> − 1.0* **do**

(continued on next page)

```
    begin
        if sensor.voltage > max then
            count := count + 1;
        get (outdata);
        sensor := outdata ↑
    end; { while loop }
    writeln ('total number of readings exceeding'
            max, 'volts is', count)
end. { program extreme }
```

8. (a) **type**
```
        node = record
            first : real;
            second : ↑ node
                end;
```
      var
```
        head, tail : ↑ node;
```
  (b) { Assume temp is declared a pointer
     variable bound to type node   }
```
    new(temp);
    temp ↑ .first := 0.0;
    temp ↑ .second := nil;
    head := temp;
    tail := temp
```
  (c)
```
    new(temp);
    temp ↑ .first := 1.0;
    temp ↑ .second := nil;
    tail := temp;
    head ↑ .second := tail
```

INDEX